exclusive access. Here, these never-before-seen texts are the riveting, terrifying testaments to the deterioration of a brilliant but increasingly ill and paranoid Jim Jones. A rich, unforgettable, and *authentic* portrait emerges of the charismatic preacher whose success was deeply rooted in the failure of the 1970s to fulfill the golden promise of the '60s; a man who brought his mammoth flock (he built the largest single Protestant movement in California's history) from the reality of the world into the jungle, and there descended into cruelty, madness, and finally murder. Startling new conclusions come forth from this material . . . including *Jones's premeditation of his apocalypse three years before the event* . . . and some provocative information about Mark Lane's role in Jonestown.

Of Jones's surviving followers, Reston says: "They are far from the robots they are portrayed to be. In their grief they are angry, some at Jones, most at the U.S. government. Jones touched their core of belief in an age of cynicism, and thereby made them vulnerable. . . ."

As seductively beautiful and haunting as a Joseph Conrad novel, James Reston's watershed "novel in reality" makes understandable one of the most horrifying and bizarre events in American history. It should not be missed.

JAMES RESTON, JR., lectures at the University of North Carolina and is the author of several books, including *To Defend, To Destroy*; *The Knock at Midnight*; and most recently *The Innocence of Joan Little*; and co-author of the best-selling book on Watergate, *Perfectly Clear*. He lives in rural Orange County, North Carolina, with his wife and two children.

OUR
FATHER
WHO ART IN
HELL

ALSO BY JAMES RESTON, JR.

To Defend, To Destroy, a novel, 1971
The Amnesty of John David Herndon, 1973
The Knock at Midnight, a novel, 1975
The Innocence of Joan Little, 1977
Sherman, the Peacemaker, a play, 1979

OUR FATHER WHO ART IN HELL

by

James Reston, Jr.

Excerpt from *Kangaroo*, by D. H. Lawrence, copyright © 1923 by Thomas
Seltzer, reprinted by permission of Penguin Books; excerpt from
Wilderness and Paradise in Christian Thought,
by George H. Williams, copyright © 1952 by George H. Williams,
reprinted by permission of Harper & Row Publishers, Inc.;
song "Brother Jonesie," by the Tradewinds,
reprinted by permission of Dave Martins.

Special thanks to:
Alan J. Pakula, Jane Fonda, David Fishlow,
and Louis Gurvich.

Published by TIMES BOOKS, a division of
Quadrangle/The New York Times Book Co., Inc.
Three Park Avenue, New York, N.Y. 10016

Published simultaneously in Canada
by Fitzhenry & Whiteside, Ltd., Toronto.

Copyright © 1981 by James Reston, Jr.

Library of Congress Cataloging in Publication Data

Reston, James, 1941–
Our father who art in hell.

1. Jones, Jim, 1931–1978.
2. People's Temple—Biography.
I. Title.
BP605.P46R47 1981   289.9 [B]   80–25510
ISBN 0–8129–0963–1

Designed by Sam Gantt

Second impression, May 1981

MANUFACTURED IN THE UNITED STATES OF AMERICA

Somers sat rather stupefied than convinced. But he found himself *wanting* to be convinced, wanting to be carried away. The desire hankered in his heart. Kangaroo had become again beautiful: huge and beautiful like some god that sways and seems clumsy, then suddenly flashes with all the agility of thunder and lightning. Huge and beautiful as he sat hulked in his chair. Somers *did* wish he would get up again and carry him quite away.

But where to? Where to? Where is one carried to when one is carried away? He had a bitter mistrust of seventh heavens and all heavens in general. But then the experience. If Kangaroo had got up at that moment Somers would have given him heart and soul and body, for the asking, and damn all consequences. He longed to do it. He knew that by just going over and laying a hand on the great figure of the sullen god he could achieve it. Kangaroo would leap like a thunder-cloud and catch him up—catch him up and away into a transport. A transport that should last for life. He knew it.

—D.H. Lawrence, *Kangaroo*

Contents

Prologue

ON NOVEMBER 18, 1978, an event unique in human history took place. In a remote region of Guyana, an elemental, disintegrating country just above the equator in South America, 913 followers of a captivating American preacher named Reverend Jim Jones joined in a mass suicide, drinking poison (or having it injected into them) and lying down quietly to die together. Their ritual followed the assassination of Congressman Leo Ryan, a flashy, iconoclastic California Democrat from the suburbs of San Francisco, where Jim Jones had built his church called the People's Temple ("the Temple") into a large and powerful force in the mid-1970s. Congressman Ryan is the only congressman in American history to be assassinated.

In this shocking and seemingly incomprehensible event, I saw the glimmering of a profound story, not just of America in the post-Vietnam period, but of human nature itself. Questions of loyalty and obedience, of belief and resistance, of totalitarianism and survival, of ends and means, of charisma, of the power of the word and religious abuse abounded—themes which transcend an age and a country and move to the plane of the universal. The story brought to mind work of writers I admired, Joseph Conrad and Evelyn Waugh, D. H. Lawrence and Graham Greene. It was a novel in reality, a story so incredible, so horrifying, so fascinating that no one would ever believe it, if it were related in a vacuum. And yet, it had happened. That it was authentic heightened the horror and also the importance. It was uniquely an American story, but had lessons for the world. It was a Christian story, but was relevant to all faiths.

I wanted to tell it. I became obsessed to tell it completely, to explain how this event could have happened. Because of its universality, its glimpse into America after Vietnam, its view into the dark side of human nature I wanted to tell it. But there was another reason I leapt to the subject: in the past decade, in my occasional teaching at a Southern university, I have been fortunate in my association with many lively and talented young men and women. I sensed their floundering, their quest for belief and identity, their yearning for the creative and the generous life, their desire for ideals that would satisfy them, and love that would sustain them. Their age never quite provided these things. In many of these students, I saw possible recruits for this man named Jim Jones. Jones had filled a void, and the manner in which he accomplished his place in history bespoke a diabolical genius. In the reaction of the young to the reports from Guyana—never quite expressed in words so much as in the cast of their faces—I saw the metaphorical power of Jonestown.

The news accounts of Jonestown overwhelmed American and international readers for a month after the event. It became one of the most saturated news stories of our time. But virtually all the news coverage of this event focused on the revolting spectacle of nearly a thousand human bodies decomposing in the tropical heat. (The reader will find no description of that spectacle in this book.) How this could have happened and why, who was Jim Jones and what were his techniques, and what was the shape of his descent into barbarism in the jungle, who were his followers and what was the nature of their choice, if any, when Jones proposed that they all die together—these were questions which could be answered only with patient study. It has taken me two years of constant work, a legal suit against the U.S. government, two trips to Guyana, one month in San Francisco, three months in Washington, D.C., and a fair share of emotional strain to accomplish.

From the moment I concluded that this was the story I wanted to tell—some three days after the reports hit the newspapers—I knew that the demise of Jim Jones in the jungle would be my focus. Only detached from the reality of the world could he execute his apocalypse. (Only a year into my work would I discover that his vision of the end had come to him, not in the spontaneous events of November 18, 1978, like some uncontrollable chemical explosion, but three years before. Long before he took his community to the South American wilderness, he had spoken of "that one glorious moment of triumph" when he would bring his movement to a crashing end.) So I went to Guyana twice. The first time was immediately after Jonestown entered world consciousness, when I spent eight days close to madness in Georgetown, Guyana's capital, as the awful details unfolded. The second time was for the month of February 1979, during which the first court proceedings opened against Larry Layton, the only Temple gunman to survive the shootings at the Port Kaituma airstrip where Congressman Ryan and three newsmen were murdered.

I spent the month of May 1979 in San Francisco talking with scores of People's Temple survivors and studying hundreds of documents provided me by the Temple's attorney, Charles Garry. I would spend two days in New Orleans with Louis Gurvich, the father of Jann Gurvich, an attractive, highly intelligent, and sensitive follower who had died in Jonestown. And in the first half of 1980, I spent three months in Washington, D.C., poring through thousands of documents provided by the Federal Bureau of Investigation and listening to well over a hundred hours of nightly sessions in Jonestown, presided over by an increasingly sick Jim Jones. For Jones had taped all his nightly sessions because of his vaulted sense of his own historical destiny.

The research in Washington made it possible to write the book I first envisaged, but the path was not easy. After the Jonestown disaster, it was well known that the FBI had collected some nine hundred tape recordings and boxes of documents in the immediate aftermath. But during 1979 the FBI routinely rejected any request for access to these valuable materials. Also it was known that the Federal Communications Commission had monitored over eighty hours of People's Temple communications over a period of a year and a half. The FCC also denied access.

So during 1979 and 1980, I pursued a parallel strategy. Having exhausted my administrative remedies against the FCC—twice the full commission debated my request and denied it—I filed suit pursuant to the Freedom of Information Act in U.S. district court. Simultaneously, after two FBI rejections of my requests for access, I appealed my case to the Justice Department. In filing that appeal, I enlisted the support of Congressmen Pete McCloskey of California, and L. H. Fountain and Richardson Preyer of North Carolina, as well as legal counsels to President Jimmy Carter, Robert Lipshutz and Lloyd Cutler. The advocacy of my case by these congressmen and the White House became critical in getting the attention of Attorney General Benjamin Civiletti.

In January 1980, with my appeal before the Freedom of Information Committee at the Department of Justice, a draft letter of denial was put before the Attorney General. The timid Justice Department bureaucracy once again recommended I be denied access to FBI tapes and documents on the rationale that the Temple assassin Larry Layton still faced charges in Guyana. If Layton were released in Guyana, then the Justice Department might want to prosecute him in this country, and so, argued the bureaucracy, the overall ·excuse of an "ongoing investigation" could easily be employed. Civiletti refused to sign the letter and directed the Freedom of Information Committee to work out a solution with me. For this decision, thoroughly consistent with the Freedom of Information Act and a notable example of the open administration which President Carter promised, Attorney General Civiletti has my profound gratitude. I must also thank Quinlan J. Shea, Jr., director of the Office of Privacy and Information Appeals at the Department of Justice, who was a faithful advocate for release in this case. Once the decision to release had been made, members of the FBI's Freedom of Information/Privacy Acts Branch, particularly Richard Davis, were both cordial and helpful in responding to my every request during the months that followed.

With the FBI's Jonestown tapes and documents, along with many other documents and tapes I gathered in Guyana and San Francisco, I have tried to narrate the last part of Jim Jones's life using primary materials and not the stories of Jonestown survivors. (For many reasons, I considered the stories of survivors suspect.) When dialogue is reproduced, it comes chiefly from FBI tapes or from the narrative of people like Louis Gurvich from New Orleans who I felt were telling the truth. Many lies and distortions have been handed me in the past two years, and I have done my best to identify them as such and to discard them. What is related here is as close to the truth of Jonestown at the end as I know how to come.

Many people have helped in this long and difficult process. Denise Leary, my wife and an attorney, has always complained that I was an impossible, stormy client. Despite that, she undertook all the legal work of this book, performing superbly, without pay, when other responsibilities pressed hard upon her. The file on *Reston* v. *the Federal Communications Commission* eventually grew to several inches in thickness. Her legal arguments in my appeal were the ones which persuaded Attorney General Civiletti to be cooperative. Without her love and encouragement, but also without her work, I could not have prevailed with this work. In New Orleans, Louis Gurvich laid bare his soul about his daughter, Jann, and I can only thank him and wish him and his family a measure of happiness in the future that may begin to counterbalance the cosmic sadness, almost beyond human endurance or even comprehension, of the past. I wish this same measure to all the families who suffered from Jonestown. Charles Garry, the attorney for the People's Temple, opened his files to me, with the certain knowledge that some materials therein would not be complimentary to him personally. I consider that a gallant act. Dr. Hardat Sukhdeo, a fine psychiatrist and gentleman, was also generous in his help, not only in his research, but also in his consultations with me personally, as was later Dr. Morris Lipton. Galen W. Holsinger, Congressman Ryan's administrative aide, spent many hours responding to my questions about the Congressman's public and private life. Ruell Tyson, William Peck, and Charles Long, members of the Religion faculty at the University of North Carolina, were crucially important in guiding me during the conceptual stage of this book toward the important theological questions which Jonestown raised. Also philosopher Maurice Natanson at Yale was insightful as always, this time about the nature of choice and responsibility. I thank Laurie Efrein, Sandra Bradshaw, Bea Orsot, Kathy Tropp, and Tom Adams, devoted People's Temple survivors, for their time. I listened to their desolate stories of fear and suspicion, of hate and lost idealism for hours, and tried to understand. Several news reporters were most generous in turning over to me tapes of their interviews with survivors and other documents: Peter Arnett of the Associated Press; Carey Winfrey, Joseph Traester, and Jon Nordheimer of *The New York Times;* Robert Geline of *Time* magazine; Timothy Nater of *Newsweek;* Bob Flick of NBC News; David Blundy of *The Times* (London); and Robert Bazemore of the *Modesto Bee.*

Finally, I thank John Simon of Times Books and William Shawn of *The New Yorker,* who saw at the outset that this was the right project for me and provided the support to get me going. I thank also the writers of Chapel Hill and William Styron, who buoyed me in this enterprise when so many saw it as perverse masochism, and Ned Chase, Susan Kane, and Hugh Howard, who took such care in the final editing process.

J.R.
Fiery Run, Virginia

OUR
FATHER
WHO ART IN
HELL

O N E

The Bishop's
Sanctuary

[1]

IARRIVED ON THE DOCK a half hour before the *M. V. Pomeroon* was scheduled to depart. On Mondays, when she left for Morawhanna in the North West District, laden with spare parts and tires and other manufactured items you could get only in town, her schedule was fairly reliable—by Guyanese standards. It was on the return journey, when her decks were covered with heaps of bananas and cages of parrots and macaws and the half-drums filled with tropical fish bound for the aquariums of America, that you could never quite count on a departure time.

My instructions were to board the vessel and get settled, and the comrade who made the trip up and back every week in the company of fellow traders and did his political organizing for the party at night would contact me. I would be easily identifiable now. It had been some weeks since any Americans had been seen on board.

The *Pomeroon* was a 110-ton steamer, over 130 feet long, with her boom and hold in the bow and her "passenger section" to the stern. Six months before she had been painted, so they said, but you would never have guessed it. If they had painted her, they had done it in two colors, green in the rear below the single smokestack, a rusty cream to the front, as if to accentuate the two functions of the ship, one of those whims of authority that seem to abound in Guyana. The problem was, the crusty engineer told me later, the *Pomeroon* was never maintained. It was the problem of the whole country.

At the reasonable rate of $13 Guyanese, or a little over U.S. $5, I bought my first-class ticket. All four cabins, staterooms they were called, had been booked, but once I saw them I was not disappointed. The ticket would entitle me to a canvas deck chair and a little space on the upper deck, but it turned out not to mean much. I made my way through the chattering crowd of blacks and East Indians on the dock,

3

avoiding the determined, fast-moving, sweating porters loading bags of pig feed, still bound for Jonestown, and settled in for the siege. A lawyer in Georgetown had told me to expect a long and tedious journey. It was not only that it would take twenty-four hours to travel from that dock on the Demerara River the hundred miles up the coast, up the river to the terminus at Kumaka, but it would be very rough as well. The *Pomeroon* looked small enough as she swayed gently by the dock there in the chocolate river, but she would seem much smaller still when she got out into the ocean. Most of the journey would be made far out to sea, where land was barely distinguishable in the haze of the horizon. These jungle rivers—the Demerara, the Essequibo, the Berbice, the Barima—were bracketed by the awesome giants, the Orinoco just across the Guyana border in Venezuela and the Amazon far to the south. The silt deposited by these great life forces flung itself far off the coast, so far that as we would make this trip up the coast some fourteen miles out, the boatswain constantly took depth soundings. Sometimes he found himself in only two fathoms of water, and while this posed no danger of running aground, the propellers churned up the silt, making the engine run less efficiently. I was all for the *Pomeroon* running as efficiently as possible.

I settled my backpack on the river side of the ship and waited for my contact. From the bridge above, two East Indian deckhands were sprawled out lazily on benches, and they found this Caucasian traveler, in a baseball cap, short pants, and sunglasses, tethering his backpack to the railing, a figure of mild curiosity.

"Hey, Jim Jones," one of them called down to me with a smile. I nodded back hesitantly. It was a joke that time, but two days later, as I boarded the *Pomeroon* again for the return, the same thing happened, but with an edge to it. "You Jim Jones?" a muscular, unsmiling Oriental shouted over to me, and before I could answer he said, "If you Jim Jones, you a skunk. Jump overboard, I say," and he turned away angrily. The report had just been published in the *Guyana Chronicle*, the government newspaper, that seventeen of the children at Jonestown had been adopted Guyanese. Many still believed that Jim Jones had a double in Jonestown, that he was still alive.

Not long after one o'clock the *Pomeroon* shoved off with a ceremonial blast of the horn, and we soon headed out to the viscous sea. Not long after, a short, stocky, round-faced black, with a curly chin goatee, approached me.

"Hello," he said, looking me deep in the eyes, as if hello was a bona fide of some sort.

"Mr. Neblett?"

"Yes, Comrade," he said with a broad smile, and we shook hands heartily. "I thought Comrade Harry was coming with you to the dock, but I see you came alone."

"Yes," I replied. "I had to pick up a few things at the hotel at the last minute. . . . "

"He said you would have a letter for Comrade Mendonza."

I nodded.

So, I was safely in the hands of these jungle Communists, the organizers for the People's Progressive Party (PPP) headed by Cheddi Jagan and his American-born wife, Janet Jagan, once so feared by American authorities. They had been helpful from the beginning, but it was an equal trade. American writers had access to information in this socialist country that the opposition could not hope to get on its own, and information was coinage of some value in early 1979. I had explained to Janet Jagan that I wanted to find an Amerindian who lived on the Amakura River, and while the request was not the normal sort of thing other Americans were asking at the time, she put me in touch with Comrade Harry Nokta, the party's chief organizer for the North West District. More than once, Janet urged me to fly up. When I insisted on the journey by sea, she lent me her hammock and her comrades as guides, warned me about the mosquitoes, and with half-amused good wishes sent me on my way.

"Our comrades Harry and Winston make that journey often," she said, "but they're tough." I let the comment pass.

Winston and I leaned against the railing and talked, as the *Pomeroon* began its northwest passage. He had been a farmer on the coast near Morawhanna before he moved to Georgetown, bringing his children to town, where there were better schools. The soil in the North West was more fertile along the sandy coastline but easily depleted; so if you were going to farm for a long time it was better to go farther inland. It was another of those contradictory signs that Jones had made a long-term commitment to the country. But as I got to know Winston better—I was never too sure if addressing him as Winston instead of Comrade Neblett was being too familiar—I suspected that another reason than the depletion of the coastal soil or the better education of his children had brought him into the trading business. In 1973–74 he had spent fourteen months in Moscow, training as a party organizer, and his job now, taking him away from his family for four days of every week, was one of those sacrifices that the dedicated made in the Struggle, in which "Victory is Inevitable."

In the next twenty-four hours, Comrade Winston did his best to make me comfortable. Below deck, amid the military gear of the soldiers of the Guyanese Defense Force (GDF) who traveled with us, he expertly strung my hammock next to his between the exposed pipes. When the sea got very rough in the night and the water crashed over the side, tossing the empty, snaggle-edged half-drums for the aquarium fish noisily about below me, Winston kept a constant eye out, and that gave me considerable comfort. Never far from my mind was a recent report in the *Chronicle* of a ship that had broken in two off Georgetown in a high sea. The captain had said that several minutes before the disaster he felt a shudder pass over the vessel. The cause, he said, was simple "steel fatigue." I kept listening for a similar spasm.

The other travelers on board formed a fair sample of the country's population. They were nearly half and half, black and East Indian, with a few sullen Amerindians sprinkled in. After the ordeal of the night, as the sun began to rise and the soldiers resumed their exuberant game of dominoes on the nicked round table of the cabin, one Amerindian woman caught my attention. She had the flat, round saffron face, the high curved cheekbones, the shiny long black hair that would have made her a fine model for one of those etchings that hang in the London Museum. When she smiled she revealed a few solitary teeth on the right side of her jaw. From time to time she would bare her breast to suckle her baby, as he would cry out with teething pain. The contentment on the mother's face was evident, and it brought me back to something Janet Jagan had said several times. How could it be that, at the moment of decision, the mothers of Jonestown could transgress the most basic instinct of survival. It was a simple question, transcending ideology or mind control or the phenomenon of American cults or civil disobedience—all the seemingly endless words that had already been written about this awful event. How could this be?

At length, the *Pomeroon* turned toward the shore and was soon in the wide mouth of the Waini River. With my binoculars I scanned the shore, searching the grand manicol palms, placed at intervals as if by the hand of a landscaper, or the other foliage on the bank, for those salty oysters that Sir Walter Raleigh claimed grew in the trees here. It was a claim, I was sure, that he had contrived for a gullible English audience in his narrative on the "Large, Rich, and Bewtiful Empire of Guiana," but this was an environment that lent itself so well to hyperbole.

Not long after, the river forked, and the ship turned right into the narrow Mora Passage that would take us eighteen miles up to the Barima River and the village of Morawhanna. As we entered the passageway, two scarlet ibises exploded from the bank and flew across our bow, a fluttery warning shot. Had I been one of Jones's faithful, some months before making this journey for the first time to my Utopia from the "asphalt jungles of America," as Jones often referred to our cities, I would have looked with some trepidation into that forest that pressed close onto the steamer on either side. With every mile that the boat moved deeper into the forest, its passage foretold the final commitment.

The character of the forest is described as "three-canopied," with the palm and banana trees forming an intermediate level between the ground cover and the massive trees, some eighty feet tall, and who dared to deny the dangers that surely lurked just beyond the shore? For the urban American, no exercise of imagination is needed to feel the dangers. The worst of them is the camouflaged bushmaster snake, with its frightful double whammy: this snake can kill you in minutes with either its bite or the poisonous lash of its tail. Or the boa constrictor, or *camoudi* as it is called in Guyana or *matatora* in Venezuela, meaning "bull killer," which roots its tail on a branch and slowly wraps its massive length around your chest, waiting for you to exhale. (In the early 1800s a Dutchman came upon one of these frightful creatures which had swallowed a stag, but could not get the antlers down. The snake's plan evidently was to wait until its stomach digested the body of the deer, and then hope that the horns would drop out, but the Dutchman cut the process short.) Or the labaria, common as a copperhead (Dr. Larry Schacht, the unlicensed doctor at Jonestown, the part-time Hippocrates, once touted as a modern-day, youthful Albert Schweitzer, had been particularly proud of saving the life of a Port Kaituma schoolboy who had been bitten by this pit viper three days before the boy reached the clinic run by the People's Temple.) Or the "tigers," really ocelots or jaguars—or the red ranger ants—or the malaria-bearing mosquitoes—or the vampire bats, whose sucking action on a human toe, according to one eminent naturalist of the nineteenth century, made the person sleep *more* soundly rather than less—or, perhaps worst of all, the danger of walking deep into the forest and losing one's way.

The arrival of the steamer was the event of the week in Morawhanna, as well as in Kumaka, the terminus farther up the river where the Temple had its store. Predictably, the horn blast brought the whole village to the dock. Here we were only five miles from the Venezuelan border, and Morawhanna did a brisk business in contraband goods. To the outsider, the trafficking in goods forbidden by the Guyanese government appeared pathetically nickel and dime. Two days later, I would watch loads and loads of plastic buckets and tubs go on board the *Pomeroon*—the kind one might buy for a dollar or two at the local drugstore. The contraband plastic goods of foreign manufacture were loaded openly, as a Guyanese policeman in livery watched solicitously from the pier. The banned items—cosmetics, drugs, sardines, Irish potatoes, and even onions—went on more furtively. In an area speckled with gold mines and diamond workings, onions were fast becoming the jewels of the realm. Before I left Georgetown, there was a report of an onion smuggler who was surprised by the police. Acting on a tip from an informer, the cops burst into the suspect's apartment and found thirty pounds of onions in her kitchen. She was charged on the spot with dealing in goods to defraud revenue and released on G$5000 bail. The American practice of interesting sentences, like forcing the marijuana smoker to cut the courthouse lawn for a week, had not yet reached Guyana, but I could imagine some room for such an action for these onion and garlic profiteers. Guyanese, I found, have little sense of humor about such a suggestion.

Winston and I were soon bouncing along a dirt road in a Land Rover toward Kumaka, ten miles away. My plan was to see if the local PPP man, Mendonza, knew the Amerindian I sought, and, if so, whether he could arrange transportation to him. If I could not locate the Amerindian, I would then catch the riverboat from Kumaka for the six-hour trip upstream for Port Kaituma. The riverboat's name was the *Damon*, and her dependability was also an iffy proposition. During the latter part of 1978, she had been laid up for repairs for over six weeks, and the Temple boat, the *Cudjoe* (or the *Marceline*, as she was in the process of being renamed), had substituted for her. The *Cudjoe* was a classic shrimp boat, and in the Temple literature her functions were described as "hauling, transportation, and deep sea fishing," but the natives knew that the trips she made in recent times into the deep sea were primarily for rendezvous with the Temple's new oceangoing freighter, the *Albatross*, which brought supplies from Trinidad and other islands. The *Albatross* was about 300 tons, twice the size of the *Pomeroon*, and between the *Albatross* on the sea and the *Cudjoe* on the river, the Temple could circumvent any official customs control, such as it was.

On the dock at Kumaka, Winston soon produced his Comrade Mendonza, a diminutive Spanish-Indian, who peered at me suspiciously through yellowish eyes and communicated with nods and short bursts of soft language I could not make out. I gave him my letter of introduction from party headquarters, and he leaned against a sack of buck yams, scanning its lines for an embarrassingly long time. Finally he handed the letter to Winston, and Winston read it to him.

Comrade: This is to introduce James Reston, Jr., an American writer, who wishes to find one Cecil Thomas, said to live near Hauling Over on the Amakura River. All assistance provided to him will be much appreciated by the Party.

The note was based largely on surmise. The name of Cecil Thomas had been given to me by Jim Bogue, one of the survivors of Jonestown, during the ghastly days immediately after the event, when Bogue was reeling from the horror he had just endured. This Amerindian, Cecil Thomas, he said, had taught his son, Tommy Bogue, how to survive in the tropical jungle, as Tommy had planned to escape from Jonestown. Later, after Congressman Leo Ryan and four others were shot dead at the Port Kaituma airstrip, Tommy Bogue, although wounded, had survived for three days in the jungle, eluding the Guyanese and

American soldiers who were searching for him—all the time afraid that his pursuers were really Jonestown guards on a manhunt. But whatever information Jim Bogue had given me in those first days was suspect, for he was the first man I ever dealt with personally who was beside himself with fear and paranoia. So I was guessing from my notes that Cecil Thomas lived near Hauling Over, but Mendonza would know. Hauling Over, a collection of shacks a mile from the border, got its name from the spit of land, about a mile long, where the smugglers from Venezuela had to haul their boats on rollers to get from one river to another.

Mendonza gazed out across the river and shook his head.

"Gone to Venezuela two months ago," he said, but he still looked confused. "Richard Thomas?"

"No, no, Cecil Thomas," I replied, with a trace of irritation. "Cecil Thomas, and his wife, Bernice."

Mendonza shook his head. "Cecil Thomas. Cecil Thomas. Cecil Thomas." He kept shaking his head.

That my Amerindian had left for Venezuela was always a possibility. The stream of people departing Guyana forever, particularly the skilled, was making the government frantic. In a country of three-quarters of a million people, well over one hundred thousand Guyanese had emigrated, primarily to the United States and Canada, in the past twenty years, and the flow increased dramatically in the past few years with shortages of essential items. In Brooklyn alone, there was said to be a Guyanese population of some forty thousand, most of whom held dual citizenship and were entitled to vote in Guyanese elections. Ministers of the Guyanese government regularly campaigned for votes in New York. In the fall of 1978, for the first time, the government floated the idea of curbing the flight by requiring a seven-year tenure in Guyana after the completion of a citizen's education. The reaction to the proposal was swift and negative. Most of the professional class were leaving legally from the international airport, taking with them their paltry allowance under the law of G$15 (U.S.$6), but many of the working class were slipping across the border into Venezuela, among them, perhaps, my Cecil Thomas.

On the dock came another piece of disappointing news. The *Damon*'s propeller shaft was bent up in Port Kaituma, and the word was that she might be repaired "by nightfall." *Which* nightfall was not specified. I was learning fast that travel in the interior requires patience. One of Winston's other local men, a scowling young Indian named Showkat Alli, who also had spent nearly a year in the Soviet Union for political training, put me on the back of his motorcycle, and we bounced along a dusty, red-dirt road to the nearby village of Mabaruma.

Mabaruma was situated on a high ridge above the jungle and

commanded a magnificent vista across the vast, flat Orinoco Delta to the north. In colonial days, the village had been a rubber plantation, but all that remained now was a corridor of towering rubber trees that canopied the road through the village. A favorite pastime of the local boys was to cut a gash in one of the trees and make a ball from the putty that oozed out.

In the village I met Claude Broomes, an American-Guyanese, lounging loosely at his store on the edge of town. I had heard of Broomes in Georgetown, where he had been described as a young black American businessman and the owner of the only guesthouse and eating establishment in Mabaruma. His father was a Chicago physician and the Guyanese Honorary Consul for the Middle West, who had departed his native shores for America many years before, leaving an estate of over a thousand acres. His land encompassed all of Mabaruma and the river port of Kumaka below, and so the Broomes were the new landlords of the new society. Two years before, after the Honorary Consul became anxious about the decline of his Kumaka estate in his absence, he asked his only son, Claude, to consider returning to the homeland. Then in his early thirties, having bounced around in several jobs as an industrial chemist, Claude was glad to return, pleased with the change from the streets of East Chicago. He had been in Guyana for fourteen months when I saw him.

Gazing out across his spread from the ridge of Mabaruma, Claude Broomes served up the beers and spoke of the group of American missionaries who had run a store on his property in Kumaka for the past two years until, seven days before the Event, they had packed up and left. Claude had never liked them. He despised their secretiveness, hated their begging, and thought they were openly cheating the local people. The Temple business in Kumaka had started modestly. At first, the four Americans sold old clothes with American labels in the covered passageway at the Kumaka dock, until the rivermen and porters complained that the concession was blocking their loading and off-loading of the *Pomeroon*. So the business moved to a house on the dirt road a few hundred feet away. Slowly, the Americans began to introduce electronic items into their line: new and used tape decks and stereos. Nothing of the sort could be purchased anywhere else in Guyana, and the concessionaires put outrageous prices on them, as high as G$2000, or a month's pay, for even the best heeled of the local people. Drugstore watches went for G$250 and tube socks for G$20. On the average, the store grossed G$3500 a week, and in one of the Temple documents the claim was made that the store could take in between G$8000 and $10,000 a week if it could only get more items. When the items arrived, the *Cudjoe* brought them in in the dead of night and was gone by morning.

Claude Broomes had no use for all this, and he particularly had no use for one of these profiteers, Charles Beikman. In his mid-forties, Beikman was a stocky white ex-Marine who carried himself in a tough-guy military fashion. The natives considered him to be an enforcer in the Temple outpost, a Lenny type, for he could neither read nor write. Neither could he believe in the Divine. "I was never a believer in Jesus Christ or God, 'cause I never saw nothin' he's done," Beikman said as he hunched on his bunk in a Georgetown prison in the winter of 1979. "You can crawl on your hands and knees, cry your eyes out all day long, but no burden's lifted. How can they prove to me there's a God?" But Jim Jones could prove his unnatural power. Once in Jonestown, Beikman was working with heavy machinery when a bar snapped and hit him across the forehead. Dazed, he was taken to his cabin, and he thought he would die. "But I had a picture of Jim Jones on me, and as I gazed at it, it kept fading. I just lay on the bed and held the picture. The more it would fade, the better I would feel."

One day in 1978, Beikman came begging to Broomes, speaking of the good church work the Temple was doing and asking for a donation of a mere five thousand grapefruit and five thousand oranges from the Kumaka estate. Claude cussed Beikman out and sent him packing.

In April 1980, Charles Beikman pleaded guilty in Georgetown to the murder of a Temple organizer in Georgetown, Sharon Amos, and her three children on the night of November 18, 1978. In his seventeen-month wait for his trial, one thought haunted Beikman. Why, he said to a member of his defense, had someone not had the presence of mind (or was it simply courage?) to kick over that bucket with the potion? "Poison was hard to get, and that would have been the end of it."

Why, indeed? That moment when Jim Jones put forward his prodigious proposal that they all die in a heroic gesture of revolutionary defiance, when the tub of potassium cyanide was mixed by the doctor and hauled before the assemblage, that moment presented the existential choice of our time. Had they all, all 913, believed Jones when he told them that their suicide was a noble act that would be admired by the outcasts of the world, touted by revolutionaries, feared by the oppressors and the enemies? Or did some see the proposal as a contemptible, squalid notion in which acquiescence was moral cowardice, the supreme act of giving up? How many knew Jim Jones was dying of natural causes anyway and would likely be dead in another two weeks? What would it have taken for one individual to approach that dented tub of poison and kick it over?

--------◄ ►--------

The sun was getting low, and it was time to get settled. The government guesthouse in Mabaruma was full—the Regional Minister was in the village with an entourage—so Claude took me down to his family home that he was in the process of converting into a private guesthouse. On a second-story balcony, overlooking bougainvillea and coffee trees, I strung my hammock and then walked down to a grove of cocoa trees in the dwindling light to watch the hummingbirds, big as robins, dart about the succulent foliage. The next morning I awoke, relieved to find no blood on the hammock. Despite a glimmering memory of flapping furry wings above me, the "surgeon," as the vampire bat is called, had stayed away. Across the expanse of the Orinoco Delta, the jungle floor had a Jupiter-look, covered with a steamy cauldron's mist in the dawn light.

The Mabaruma ridge was the strategic hill in the area, and no doubt the local Guyana Defense Force commander had often gazed through binoculars far off into the hostile land of Venezuela. For this was a border in dispute. Indeed, Venezuela claimed all of the North West District of Guyana. More in fact. It claimed five-eighths of Guyana. On Venezuelan maps, the claimed area was marked *Venezuela Esperia*. The eastern border of Guyana with Suriname was also disputed, with Suriname claiming some six thousand miles of that boundary, so if Guyana were ever to lose all its disputed territory, it might someday consist only of Georgetown and a finger of desolate savannah land to the south.

The dispute with Venezuela was grounded in sheer greed. The contested 58,000 square miles of Guyana west of the Essequibo River was rich in resources: gold and diamonds, manganese and bauxite, uranium and iron ore. Along the rapids of the Upper Mazaruni, a magnificent tableland that looked like northern Arizona transported to the tropics, there was the potential for a vast hydroelectric project matching any body of fast water in the world. If Guyana would ever tap that potential it could produce not only finished aluminum from its raw bauxite, but also provide, as the CIA-installed Prime Minister Forbes Burnham had said, "a reliable source of energy for the entire country." In view of the constant blackouts in Georgetown and elsewhere in the country, that was a highly desirable goal. The Guyanese dreamt of a two-hundred-square-mile lake behind a massive dam that might one day be a jungle Lake Meade full of pleasure boats.

But so long as the border remained in dispute, it was only a dream. For the vast Upper Mazaruni project needed foreign underwriting, and what country in the world would underwrite a multimillion-dollar project in disputed territory? Certainly not the Soviet Union. In the spring of 1978, on Burnham's visit to Moscow, en route to Pyongyang and East Berlin, the USSR finally told him that there would be no Soviet support for the Upper Mazaruni. For one thing, the Soviets were doing business with Venezuela that amounted to more than $600 million a year.

Venezuela seemed to be waiting for Guyana's independence from Great Britain to stake its border claim. Internal self-government in Guyana began in 1961, with independence from Britain coming five years later. In 1962, Venezuela reopened its demand to the North West, a claim which was thought to have been settled in 1899 through international arbitration in Paris. But in 1949 newly discovered documents suggested collusion between the British member of the arbitral commission and a supposedly neutral member of a five-member panel. Venezuela did not press the issue as long as Britain remained firmly in control. From 1962, however, Venezuelan-Guyanese relations deteriorated. The dispute had the feel of a conflict between Europe and South America. From its colonialist tradition, Guyana had always looked toward the English-speaking Caribbean and Europe, particularly the United Kingdom, since the sugar pipeline to Britain was the basis of the Guyana economy. In 1966, in one of the more esoteric international outrages of our time, Venezuela heightened the tension along the border by occupying and fortifying the entirety of Ankoko Island, a piece of real estate in the middle of the remote Cuyani River, which forms part of the border between the two countries. Guyana, quite properly, cried out that its neighbor was entitled to only half of Ankoko. It was a point of pride only (unless one cares that a 166-ounce gold nugget was found in Ankoko in 1957), because very few people live in this vast hinterland on either side of the border.

Still, the tension over the years has run to negotiation rather than armed clash, despite the bellicose rhetoric from Venezuela. In 1970 the two countries signed the Protocol of Port-of-Spain. In this agreement, the dispute was shelved for twelve years, during which time, it was agreed, Guyana would do its best to develop the border region. Part of Venezuela's position was that Guyana was doing nothing to develop its North West, and the mood from the Port-of-Spain Protocol was: "Let's see what Guyana can do in the 1970s." An uneasy calm prevailed in the intervening years, with even a touch of reconciliation in recent times. In October 1978, a month before the Jonestown cataclysm, the President of Venezuela, Carlos Andrés Pérez, made a state visit to Guyana. In his parting press conference Pérez spoke of good neighborliness, even suggesting that Venezuela might contribute financially to the development of the Upper Mazaruni and then buy electricity from the completed project. But Pérez was already a lame duck president. He had been defeated by the opposition party, whose rhetoric on the Venezuelan claim had been the most vociferous in the 1960s and 1970s. Never far from the minds of Guyanese politicians was the thought that someday an armed clash would take place.

Thus, when the curious Bishop from San Francisco came to the government and offered to settle some one thousand Americans only a few miles from the Venezuelan border, the Guyanese government saw a foreign policy advantage, among other pluses. In September 1977, when the Temple's bad publicity in the United States was rebounding on Guyana, the Ambassador to Washington, Lawrence Mann, wrote to his Foreign Minister about "L'Affaire Jones."

> We have not, of course, told the press that the peopling of the North West region of the country near the Venezuelan front by American citizens is a consideration not to be dismissed lightly, since the death of American citizens in a border war cannot be a matter of indifference to the Department of State. Nor have we told the press that Bishop Jones's endorsement of the Party, the Government, and its philosophical objectives is not a matter of regret to us.

On that brilliant morning, walking up the hill to Claude Broomes's house in Mabaruma, all of this seemed a game of toy soldiers. The only true soldier I could ever picture here was Sir Walter Raleigh, searching for the city of El Dorado, or the Spaniard de Berrio before him, the real explorer of the area, who wrote in 1593: "If God aids me to settle Guiana, Trinidad will be the richest trade center in the Indies, for if Guiana was one-twentieth of what it was supposed to be, it would be richer than Peru." To Raleigh and de Berrio, Guiana encompassed Venezuela as well.

———————=► ◄=———————

The word from Claude was what I expected.

The *Damon* was broken down for good, and I would not go to Port Kaituma that day, unless I wanted to hire a speedboat for G$200. Even then, there was a question about the availability of gasoline. The shortages had hit the hinterland first. The price seemed high, and the reliability of the local men chancy.

On the dock at Morawhanna, amid a chattering, teeming throng, as Winston Neblett watched over his newly acquired sacks of cassava, he agreed to make inquiries about a boat for me. At one point he drew me aside and whispered that I should take note of a stocky, swarthy man sitting on a pile of cassava meal sacks behind me. He, too, was trying to hire a boat to Port Kaituma, Winston said, but his reason for the trip was to contact some Amerindians along the river who had some of Jim Jones's greenbacks.

This was the first I had heard of a third stash of money. There had been U.S.$600,000 found buried in Jonestown, and the U.S.$35,000 turned over to the Soviet Embassy in Georgetown. But several days after the suicides, a group of Amerindian railway workers found two suitcases along the railway tracks between Port Kaituma and Matthews Ridge, brimming with packets of cash. In what must have been a cackling, rapturous banquet, they split the money between them. But in the days that followed, the police got wind of the discovery and "terrorized" the workers, as one official put it. To flush out the cash, the police spread the word that it was all counterfeit, hence spawning another of the maddening rumors in Georgetown that this diabolical genius was even printing money in Jonestown. Between December 1 and 3, to their great surprise, the police recovered U.S.$296,000 and G$11,898. There was no telling how much money the suitcases had originally contained. Up the streams around Port Kaituma, a brisk business was being done at the exchange rate of U.S.$1 to G$1, one-third the official exchange rate, and one-fifth the black market rate. In relating this tale, Winston shrugged his shoulders.

"The money doesn't belong to anyone," he said.

I decided it probably was not a good idea to travel up the river with these riverside bankers, and not long after I had given up on the idea of reaching Port Kaituma and was back at sea on the *Pomeroon*, heading for Georgetown, Winston told me another story that removed all doubt about the wisdom of my decision. For some years the captain of the *Damon* had been William Duke, a popular man in the North West, and the government's party representative in Port Kaituma. A man quite friendly with Temple members over the last two years of the Temple's existence, Duke had captained the *Cudjoe* between Morawhanna and Port Kaituma when the *Damon* was laid up for six weeks in the late fall. On December 29, 1978, more than a month after the Event, the *Damon* was still under repair, and William Duke hired a boat at Morawhanna from a "wayside preacher," one William Andrews, and they headed down the Barima River the five miles to the Venezuelan border. Duke never returned. In mid-January, Amerindians noticed carrion crows, as vultures are called, circling, and later, across the Venezuelan border, they discovered Duke's remains, identifying him later by a watch and a shirt.

On the dock at Morawhanna, the explanation was clear: Duke had been persuaded that exchanging Jones's dollars in Venezuela constituted a better gamble than exchanging them in the North West, now crawling with suspicious (and greedy) police and soldiers. Later, from the reports of various local people who had given the captain their money to exchange, an official estimated that Duke headed for Venezuela with U.S.$58,000 and a quantity of raw gold. Once in Venezuela, beyond the jurisdiction of the Guyanese police, he had been killed.

So the victims of Jim Jones—this American El Dorado gilded with fool's gold—continued to mount, and I had no intention of joining them.

[2]

Several weeks later, I tried the other route Jonestown survivor Jim Bogue had suggested to find Cecil Thomas. I flew to Matthews Ridge and took the train the distance of thirty-six miles to Port Kaituma. There I was to search for another Amerindian, John Thomas (no relation to Cecil), who could take me by canoe to Cecil Thomas in a day, Jim Bogue had said.

Matthews Ridge had been the site of the first public government proceeding in the aftermath of Jonestown. In mid-December 1978, in the T-shaped building on a hill overlooking the village, a coroner's inquest had taken place, and it had been a curious affair.

The evidence was relatively straightforward. Twelve witnesses testified, including a number of survivors who had told often-differing stories to the press and the police in the previous weeks (this time under oath). The Crime Chief of Guyana, C. A. ("Skip") Roberts, an American-trained, efficient policeman, presented five letters carried out of Jonestown by members of Jones's inner circle, which bequeathed the Temple fortune of U.S.$7.3 million to the Communist Party of the Soviet Union. All but one of the letters was dated November 18, 1978. But Chief Roberts felt from the manner in which the typing of the words was arranged on the page that they were all prepared well in advance. The notion that Jones premeditated the suicides before Leo Ryan ever entered Guyana was strengthened by the fact that one of the bequeathing letters was dated November 6, 1978. Dr. Leslie Mootoo, the government's pathologist, also testified. He had performed autopsies on Jim Jones and the nurse, Anne Elizabeth Moore, who, along with an unidentified male, were the only victims to die by gunshot wounds at Jonestown. Mootoo had observed needle marks on eighty-three of the hundred victims he examined, suggesting they had been injected with the poison rather than drinking it. The question, of course, was whether their submission was voluntary or coerced. Regrettably, Dr. Mootoo failed in his autopsy to take a nitrate test or neutron activation test of Jones's hands. As a matter of procedure, American forensic pathologists take the nitrate test on victims, where suicide or murder is at issue, for the test's purpose is to determine if a trace of gunpowder is present on the victim's triggerhand. The bullet wound in Jones's head was behind his left ear, consistent (in theory) with suicide by a left-handed man. But Jones was right-handed. In February 1979 a reggae tune was released in Guyana with the title "Who Killed Jimmy Jones?"

Establishing the cause of the Jonestown deaths might have been made a lot easier for the coroner's jury at Matthews Ridge had the jurors been permitted to listen to the forty-five-minute tape which recorded part of the death ritual. But for unexplained reasons, the coroner's jury was not allowed to hear the tape. It was "classified," along with some nine hundred other tapes found in Jonestown. So the decision about the cause of death in Jonestown was left to the jury as a matter of interpretation. No expert testimony about subtle methods of "coercive persuasion" was presented to the jury.

The foreman of the panel was an elderly, respected pillar of Matthews Ridge, Albert ("Uncle Albert") Graham, who was the Commissioner of Oaths and Affidavits (notary public) in the village and who for eleven years had overseen the manganese operation at Port Kaituma. Graham began to announce the verdict: 912 suicides, including that of Jim Jones (even though the pistol which killed him was found thirty yards from his body), and one murder: Anne Elizabeth Moore.

The magistrate in charge of the hearing, Haroon Bacchus, exploded angrily as Uncle Albert announced the verdict in relation to Jones: "James Warren Jones committed suicide? Suicide is when a person intentionally kills himself while of sound mind. The fact of suicide has to be proved by evidence. What evidence have you that he died of suicide?" he screamed at the jury foreman.

"We understood that Jim Jones was suicidal," Graham replied softly.

"We never said suicide, said he died from a near discharge . . . ," Bacchus bellowed. "The gun was found thirty yards away [from Jones's body]. How can it be suicide?"

The high-pitched monologue from the magistrate continued intensely for some time, punctuated once by his pounding of the table in front of him with his fist. Finally, Bacchus guided the foreman toward the verdict he wanted.

Jim Jones was murdered by some person or persons unknown, but the Bishop was "criminally responsible" for the death of his nine hundred followers.

———————————— >◁ ▷◁ ————————————

In mid-February I tossed my rucksack on one of the converted gondolas that served as the passenger car for the ride between Matthews Ridge and Port Kaituma. In my pocket was the brochure of Guyana Overland Tours. "Port Kaituma, a 36-mile trip through dense forest, farms and savannah is a popular excursion," it read. Not that day. The yellow, twenty-year-old diesel pulled the toy train out of the village into the wilderness and soon reached its top speed of eighteen miles per hour. Another reggae tune, cut after the disaster, occurred to me: "Jonestown Express" it was called, and it was a rather poor parody of Jones and several other major figures of the story, including the rattled Minister of Information, Shirley Field-Ridley. That tune, along with "Who

Killed Jimmy Jones?" and a Trinidadian tune called "Brother Jonesie," was banned on the government-controlled radio.

The tiny train had in fact been an express out of Jonestown for ten refugees who had fled from the armed camp on the Saturday morning of Congressman Ryan's visit. The group, led by a thirty-three-year-old oil rig operator from New Orleans, felt that the best chance for a successful escape would be at a time when a dignitary was in the settlement. To another of this bedraggled band, who had come to Jonestown only for a visit and then was held captive, Jim Jones had said that the only way he would ever leave Jonestown was "in a box." Following a path they had planned for weeks, the group had made it onto the tracks, and on Sunday, November 19, when the train came along, the engineer informed them of what had happened the night before.

In Port Kaituma, I went directly to the police outpost and stated my business. The men on duty knew the Amerindian John Thomas, and they agreed to send word down the river the half mile to his hut. After a time, Thomas appeared around the bend of the river in his low-riding dugout scooped from a Kabacally wood. He was a short man, less than five feet tall, with a scraggly goatee and dull, distrusting eyes. He wore a battered felt hat, with its brim turned up in the front, and grease smudged cut-off trousers above his bare feet. He nodded silently as I talked of Jim Bogue. In due course, he became more communicative, and we were soon heading down to his hut on the bank of the Kaituma, where he lived with his ten children on the bare wood floor, protected from the elements only by a thatched *trouly* roof. (A trouly roof is made of palm fronds spliced and stitched tightly.)

He had worked for the Temple during its first two years in Guyana, when the "pathfinders"—Jim Bogue, Charles Beikman (whom Thomas knew as a shoemaker), and several others—lived in Port Kaituma and commuted to Jonestown. In those days, when the jungle was cleared, the road built, and banana trees planted, Jim Bogue was the foreman for a team of sixty local workers, and Thomas and Bogue had become good friends. The Indian returned to work for the Temple in 1976, when they built the piggery and the cassava mill, but he had not been to Jonestown for over a year and had not seen Jim Bogue for some time, until on the night of November 18 he heard of the killings at the airstrip and went to visit his friend, the survivor, at Jeff Semple's rum shop down on "the floor." Bogue told Thomas then that he tried to get a message to the Indian a week before, asking help for an escape by canoe down through Hauling Over, but no way to get the message out of Jonestown had presented itself.

Thomas knew a great deal about Jonestown, but when he did not know something he responded with mixed pronouns. "Me can't say."

Did he know Cecil Thomas. "I don't know he." Or his wife, Bernice? "I don't know she." But soon his diminutive, sagging wife suggested that perhaps I meant Cecil Thomson and his wife, Bernadette, who had indeed worked for the Temple and lived not in Hauling Over but several rivers over, on the Aruka. To reach Thomson from Port Kaituma would take seven hours by canoe. With that disappointing news, I gave up my search for them for the time being. I would have to make do with the information that John Thomas could provide on the difficulties of surviving in this forest if you were trying to escape a madman and his guards.

Of the creatures that moved in the wilderness, Thomas had little fear. He rarely saw a bushmaster, and if one were struck by the more common labaria or fer-de-lance there was the bush medicine, the root of the kunami plant which the natives boiled and then applied until you could rush to the local nurse. Although "tigers" filled the night with their piercing cries, Thomas knew of only one man killed by a cat, and that had happened some twelve years before.

But getting lost was a different matter. It had happened to him once, and it had terrified him. Still, "if you got sense," if you can read the clouds and the stars and the sun, you can come out. Without food, you can last three days, the length of time that young Tommy Bogue had survived. In the jungle there was little to forage. But if you knew your "seeds" or knew how to extract the "cabbage" from the fruit of the manicol palm, you could prolong your stay. Some people ate the jungle turtles, but it was said that if its meat did not agree with you, it gave you leprosy. And there was always the three-toed sloth, but you had to cook its meat for a very long time before it was edible.

In my mind floated a passage from Evelyn Waugh's *Handful of Dust:*

> There is medicine for everything in the forest: to make you well and to make you ill. My mother was an Indian, and she taught me many of them. I have learned others from time to time from my wives. There are plants to cure you, and to give you fever, to kill you and send you mad; to keep away snakes, to intoxicate fish, so that you can pick them out of the water with your hands like fruit from a tree. There are medicines even I do not know. They say it is possible to bring dead people to life after they have begun to stink, but I have not seen it done.*

The following day I walked the mile down "the floor" from the village to Port Kaituma to the airstrip. The floor was the name for the flat tableland that separated the warehouses and government buildings of the village from its suburb, called, Florida-like, Citrus Grove, where most of the residents lived. I needed a better sense of how the dirt

---

*From *A Handful of Dust*, © 1934 by Evelyn Waugh (Boston: Little Brown), p. 289.

airstrip was laid out, the site where Congressman Ryan was slain, particularly since in February the government of Guyana had sued the People's Temple for its remaining assets in Guyana banks, demanding recompense for damage to an airplane of Guyana Airways Corporation and damage to the Port Kaituma airstrip. The idea of suing the Temple was obviously inspired by the action of the U.S. government, which sought to reclaim the cost of the military airlift in the aftermath by a civil suit in the amount of $4.2 million. As I expected, there was not much damage that bullets could do to a dirt airstrip, but under the circumstances the court in Georgetown might not require an expert analysis.

On this walk down the floor, a policeman named Hays accompanied me. Hays was never really convinced that my mission in the area was to gather information. He peppered me with cryptic questions, particularly about my visit with John Thomas. "He's playing it smart," Hays said, with a constable's sense of the depravity of man. At length, he asked me forthrightly what was really on his mind: "You really came to buy some dollars, eh?" To Hays, undoubtedly, the big-time American dealers had finally arrived to capture Jones's buried treasure.

Actually, I had asked John Thomas if any of Jones's money had come his way, and he replied in disgust that the soldiers and police had blocked his entry into Jonestown recently, and "they're the ones who stole most of the stuff." (In fact, an Indian was stopped by the police, trying to carry a refrigerator out of Jonestown on his back.) On the night they reunited in Jeff Semple's rum house, Jim Bogue told John Thomas that he buried $14,000 a quarter of a mile from the piggery, and that Thomas could have it—if he could find it. But Bogue failed to tell Thomas which direction from the piggery the stash was buried.

There are two "discos" in Port Kaituma: Jeff Semple's on the floor, where the survivors of the airstrip shooting were kept for four days, and another establishment up in the village. At the latter, called The Weekend Disco, Don Harris, the NBC newsman, had bought a few drinks on the night of Friday, November 17, and heard a report that Jones had recently received an automatic rifle. If the American authorities were in doubt about atrocities in Jonestown, the residents of Port Kaituma certainly were not.

Semple's establishment was a modest low-slung building with a cement floor, walls glowing with primitive arrow and sunburst designs in fluorescent paint, and a jukebox near the wire-caged kitchen. Semple had been in the village on the afternoon of November 18, and his Amerindian wife was minding the store. When she heard the crackle of gunfire not two hundred yards away, she feared for her tiny daughter. Whenever a plane landed, the children of Citrus Grove turned out for the show. Quickly, Mrs. Semple closed up the rum shop and hurried up the road. At the end of the airstrip, a thin, vacant-faced American stood alone. Mrs. Semple rushed up to him, exclaiming her concern for her daughter. The American said flatly for her not to worry, but that she should not go any closer.

"Are you from Jonestown?" she asked.

"Yes."

"Did anybody get killed?"

"Yes."

"Why?" Mrs. Semple asked.

"I don't know," the American replied in a daze.

Mrs. Semple thought his advice not to proceed any closer was probably wise, and she returned to her establishment. After a time the same American wandered up the road and sat down on a log outside her door, gazing vacantly at her little garden patch for a while. At length he got up and drifted off in the direction of Port Kaituma.

Sometime later, Elaine Semple learned that the American was Larry Layton, and that later in the day, at the police outposts, he announced that he was one of the Jonestown killers. As such, he demanded his rights *as an American citizen*. Three days after that, Larry Layton signed the following confession:

> I, Larry Layton, take full responsibility for all the deaths and injuries that took place at the Port Kaituma airstrip. I had begged Bishop Jim Jones that I be allowed to bring down the plane, but he disapproved. . . . I felt these people were working in conjunction with the U.S.A. to smear the People's Temple and to smear Guyana. I got a gun from a friend of mine and went to the airport, intending to bring down the plane. But when the shooting started, I also started shooting, as I thought it was all too late. I don't know why I did it.

[3]

Georgetown, a city of 200,000 laid out by the Dutch with canals dividing the major thoroughfares that in modern times have been converted to grand promenades, shaded with gnarled flamboyance trees, lies eight feet below sea level. If one sits atop a Chinese restaurant gazing across the roof lines of the city, it would be hard to know what to make of the hodgepodge: the Disneyland, blue minarets of the city hall; the gray, solid mass of the Catholic cathedral on Brickdam; the Tuscan dome of the pastel pink Parliament house; the clock steeple of the teeming downtown market; or the trouly cone of the Amerindian Umana Yana. But the eye fixes on the massive red gables of the Victorian Law Courts.

The sprawling cream citadel with its red roof seemed built for medieval defense. A grand balcony surrounded its second story, and on business days a sizable collection of jury members and court functionaries take the air outside, enduring the inevitable long wait. The British built this fortress of justice in the 1880s, and until 1953 a statue of a dumpy Queen Victoria stood in the garden in front. But during the turbulence of that year, when Cheddi Jagan came to power and held on for four months (before the British sent troops and suspended the Constitution), the statue was pulled over on its side and beheaded. With independence in 1966, the Queen was carried to an obscure plot in the Botanical Garden, but her head at least stands firmly once again upon her shoulders. The Victorian Law Courts, the Victoria statue, and the pizza-sized Victoria Regina lily, the national flower—these were the last tributes to Her Majesty in Guyana.

On February 19, 1979, the case of *State* v. *Larry Layton* was finally called. The three American networks were present, their correspondents ready to rush to their Lear jets waiting at Timehri Airport for the flight to Trinidad or Barbados, where they would beam their transmissions to America by satellite. There was no television in Guyana: its introduction had a low priority in the state's socialist objectives. The networks brought their sketch artists along, even though the Guyanese officials had said no filming or sketching would be permitted in the courtroom. The artists were forced to make mental notes about the vaulted ceilings and European styling and peaked windows and then rush to their vans to render their thoughts into visual art.

The courtroom was jammed with lawyers, spectators, and prospective jurors as I took my seat at a table below the judge's bench. Without my noticing it, the defendant slipped in and took his place in the elevated railed wooden dock behind the press and the defense tables. He sat quietly, a diminutive figure in khaki pants, a pale, pinkish short-sleeved shirt, sneakers without socks, legs crossed, arms folded, seeming to crouch as if to appear even more insignificant than he really was. His features were sharp and rather attractive in a fastidious sort of way. He exuded cleanliness. His sideburns were long and razored square (Jim Jones had penciled his sideburns to give them sharper definition). Layton's pale-blue cat eyes darted around the room and finally rested on the NBC artist who had been staring and smiling happily at him, to extract some flash of emotion. Layton managed a weak smile. The artist was a veteran of the Son of Sam trial, and she whispered a comparison to me and then smiled back at Layton.

We were all sure that the proceeding would be over in two hours. Layton was charged with five counts of murder, three counts of attempted murder, a count of possessing an illegal firearm, and a count of possessing illegal ammunition. The prosecution and defense both had told the press in advance that a deal had been consummated.

Layton would plead guilty to one count of attempted murder, and the testimony would proceed to the question of mitigating sentence. But on a conviction of one count of attempted murder the defendant could receive probation or life imprisonment. The prosecutor, a cheery young Indian named Namdram Kissoon, told me that this was a "fit case for life," although he was quick to point out that no official plea bargaining is permitted under Guyanese law and that he took no part in sentencing. That was the sole province of the presiding judge. If Layton were convicted, he would literally be sent up the river, to a prison deep in the jungle, where access was possible only by boat. At the defense table, Layton's four lawyers huddled in whispered consultation. There was a trace of irony in the presence of Rex McKay, the chief defense lawyer. His reputation rested on his role as a prosecutor for the state in politically sensitive cases, and he often negotiated commercial deals abroad for the government of Guyana. Later, he would bask in his new reputation as the F. Lee Bailey of Guyana. Irony or intention? For McKay, the government's man, to spring this American nebbish would remove the embarrassment for the Prime Minister.

After some wait, the Chief Justice of Guyana, Harold Bollers, entered the court. Silver-haired, wearing half glasses lodged in full frames, clothed in a green, time-worn justice's robe, tattered and frayed at both shoulders, Bollers bowed deeply to the assemblage. His place was high above us, so that only his head was visible, silhouetted against the seal of Guyana. Its motto, scrolled beneath two jaguars, one holding a pickax, the other holding stacks of sugar and rice, is, "One people, one nation, one destiny." The "prisoner at the bar" was addressed by the clerk and asked after each count was read, "How say you?" To the surprise of all, Layton answered "not guilty" to each count in a firm alto. To the further astonishment of the crowd, the chief defense counsel, Rex McKay, requested a delay of ten days. One of his witnesses, whom he identified only as an eminent American psychiatrist, had been unable to secure transportation between New York and Georgetown because of the Trinidad carnival. (All flights between the United States and Guyana pass through Trinidad.)

"Unfortunately, Guyana Airways does not fly as far as New York," McKay chortled amiably.

After several interchanges in which Bollers gratuitously lamented that the defense did not have all its witnesses ready, the trial was adjourned for nine days. There was an audible groan from the few members of the American press, particularly the four-person television crews. The taste of collusion was in everyone's palate. The eminent psychiatrist was Dr. Hardat Sukhdeo, and he could testify only on the psychology of mind control, not on the guilt or innocence of Layton. Sukhdeo's role, then, could apply only to mitigation of sentence *after* conviction, and the prosecution had said that it had about ten days' worth of prosecution witnesses. The strategy of delaying to frustrate American coverage of the proceeding (again, to avoid bad press for Guyana) was clear.

On February 28, the trial reconvened and the strategy began to work. This time, only two of the three networks were present. Defense counsel McKay led off with another surprise. He asked Chief Justice Bollers to excuse himself from the case because of his "friendship" with People's Temple staff member Sharon Amos. McKay presented the particulars of his motion slowly, monotonally, avoiding the Chief Justice's steady glare. Sharon Amos, he said, had been a frequent visitor at the home of the Chief Justice, and vice versa. Specifically, the Chief Justice had visited Sharon Amos's home on the night of November 17–18, 1978 (the night before Amos and her three children were found with their throats slit in the Temple's Georgetown headquarters). McKay offered to provide evidence of the "close friendship." Right-minded people might conclude that, regardless of how impartial the Chief Justice might be, his sitting at the trial favored or prejudiced the accused.

Bollers waved the motion aside. Even if the charges were true, he said, they contained nothing that should compel him to disqualify himself either from the Layton trial or the trial of Charles Beikman, accused of murdering Sharon Amos. But the Chief Justice was shaken by the personal attack on him. To a Guyanese journalist some days before, he had stated that in the midst of all these stories of collaboration, sexual and otherwise, between Temple members and high government officials, the judicial system must appear beyond reproach. After all, the whole world was watching.

But with the Amos relationship in the open, the best recourse was to ensure that the world watched as little as possible. After McKay presented another motion, arguing that the change of venue from the Magisterial District of the North West to the Magisterial District of Georgetown was improperly handled, court adjourned. On March 1, the technical arguments over criminal procedure filled most of the day. Finally, Bollers recessed the trial for a week to write a legal opinion on the motion. The remaining two American television crews groaned again and repaired empty-handed once more to their Lear jets.

A week later, with no major American media present, Bollers granted the defense motion for a mistrial. Consequently, the legal process against Larry Layton had to start all over again, with a new preliminary hearing. It would be another fourteen months before Layton would again assume the dock in a Guyanese court.

In the weeks when this scenario unfolded, Larry Layton told his story to the defense team, and its pathetic quality led them to conclude that the defendant needed considerable schooling before he ever took the stand. Jim Jones possessed him as totally as ever. Neither the killings at the airstrip nor the deaths in Jonestown caused Layton the least remorse. Twelve weeks after the disaster his chief concern was that he not "betray" Jim Jones. To this devotee, Jones was still "the most highly evolved person in the universe." Not that Jones was God: "He didn't create this mess called the universe," but he was "the only metaphysical power there was," and only through him had there been any hope that the world could be saved. The sentiment was echoed by another faithful:

"He [Jones] was the God I could touch."

Loyalty to his leader was Layton's highest value, the only virtue that really mattered. Didn't it bother him that Jim Jones had caused the death of so many people? On the contrary. "He [Jim Jones] figured death would be better for them than to go back under the corrupting influences [of American society]. Maybe he felt they had evolved as much as they ever would." What Layton "dearly regretted," however, was that he had been left alive, and everyone else was dead. It was not supposed to work out that way. Was he then suicidal? He *was* terrified of what the future would hold, he admitted, "but if I could work somewhere with people, *helping them*, I wouldn't commit suicide. . . . Anyway, I wouldn't want to hurt those who are concerned about me."

Had he ever disagreed with Jones about *anything?* Oh, yes, he disagreed with Jones that Jonestown had to move through a Stalinist phase before it reached its millennium. In February, his defense asked him to read aloud his self-analysis letter to the Bishop, dated July 11–12, 1978. Layton began in a firm voice:

"Basically, I could be termed a revisionist of the anti-Stalin faction. I always blamed him for current Zionist conspiracies. . . . The great purge which led to the liquidation of Poland's leadership. . . ." At that point, Layton broke down in sobs.

Altruism and self-pity were the poles of his mind. Almost any action, including murder, was justified as long as it was helping people. Help was the code, the trigger word, the queen of hearts. His failure was that "I never could be the sensitive person I wanted to be." Life was suffering. One tries to be responsible and sensitive, but the world laughs and there is not much joy in it.

Within this mental midden, the ability to think was all but lost. Layton looked at pictures of himself taken near the carnage of the airstrip, and to him it appeared as if he was floating "somewhere between a dream and a nightmare." Dr. Sukhdeo, the defense psychiatrist, ran several concentration tests on him. Starting at one hundred, Layton was asked to subtract by sevens. Each subtraction took him about ten seconds, until he arrived at seventy-nine. Seven from seventy-nine was . . . sixty-two! Sukhdeo asked him to name the past presidents, starting with Carter and moving backward. Twice Layton answered, "Carter, Johnson, Kennedy, Eisenhower." He had forgotten the two presidents whose terms spanned most of his stay in the Temple. When this was pointed out to him, he said with self-satisfaction, "Oh, yes, I *would* forget Nixon, wouldn't I?"

The irony of Layton's behavior on November 18 was that this vacuous loyalist was faced, even within the construction of his loyalty, with a judgment which required him to think, and to make distinctions—the very process Jones had destroyed. That Saturday morning he watched with growing anger as Temple members announced their desire to leave. It was not so much that the members were "defecting," but that they were doing so on national television. People who used to be satisfied were coming up before "all those cameras" and saying that Jonestown was a terrible community. It meant that the organization would be destroyed, and "it was common knowledge that I would do anything to protect the organization."

A separation then took place in Layton's brain. Reflecting later on those who were leaving, Layton said, "I was quite fond of Patricia Parks. I couldn't imagine her doing something wicked. . . ." "I always liked Vern Gosney. I felt a little sorry for him, because people picked on him. . . ." "I always thought Tina Bogue was kind of cute. . . ." But before the cameras these people lost individual identity and transmogrified. Two in particular were marked: Monica Bagby and Vern Gosney. At the very end of NBC's interview with Jim Jones, the reporter, Don Harris, had handed Jones a crumpled note signed by Bagby and Gosney, pleading for help to escape. Jones took account of the names and passed the note to an aide.

"People play games, friend," he said. "They lie. What can I do with liars? Are you people going to leave us? I just beg of you, please leave us. Anybody that wants to can get out of here. . . . They come and go all the time."

By Layton's narrative, he approached the leader and pleaded with Jones to let him take care of the whole crowd. "I volunteered of my own free will," he insisted, without the least appreciation of the irony of his phrase. First, the loyalist suggested dynamite, but Jones replied that the Temple did not have any. Then he suggested shooting the pilot and bringing the plane down in the jungle. No, Jones answered (so Layton said), the people have a right to leave. Nowhere in his account did Layton express any anger against Congressman Ryan or the television crew. They were irrelevant, almost unnoticed.

As the minutes passed and the truck was being loaded for the Port Kaituma airstrip, Maria Katsaris, one of Jones's mistresses, whose orders were to be followed as if they were the leader's, came to Layton and approved his sabotage plan. Remember, she said, you (posing as a defector) are to board the *first* plane that comes, and once it is airborne, you will bring it down. Layton got a pistol, a Saturday Night Special, *the* Saturday Night Special of all time, and in his state somewhere between dream and nightmare, boarded the truck for the airstrip.

At the airstrip he sat down in the open metal shack, apart from the others, draped in a poncho, and waited for the first plane. To his horror, not the expected nineteen-seat, twin-engine Otter of Guyana Airways, but a six-seat, single-engined Cessna approached the runway. Layton had expected only one large plane. As the small plane touched down, Layton recalled, "I was terrified, because I knew that whatever I did would be a waste, but I had to go on." He barged forward to make sure he was at the head of the line to board the first plane. He slipped onto the Cessna and placed his pistol under the seat. Ten minutes later, the Otter landed.

A fugitive from Jonestown, Dale Parks, had been particularly nervous about Layton's presence in the party all along. He insisted to both Congressman Ryan and the American diplomat Richard Dwyer that everyone be searched before the planes took off. After some discussion (with Layton back out on the cinder airstrip) a cursory search was conducted, first of the five passengers on the small plane—Layton, Monica Bagby, Vern Gosney, Dale Parks, and ten-year-old Tracy Parks. Once this group boarded, the pilot started the propeller. "When I was on the plane, I didn't know if I was Jim Jones or myself," Layton declared, speaking proudly, almost angelically. But out of the corner of his eye he saw the tractor trailer moving alongside the Otter. "Hurry up and take off!" he shouted at the pilot. "There's going to be trouble!" Then the shooting outside began, and Layton realized that it was "too late." He turned to his left and shot Vern Gosney, then Monica Bagby in front, stuck the pistol in Dale Parks's chest behind him, and pulled the trigger. The pistol misfired, but Parks fell back in his seat, thinking he had been struck. Layton turned again to the signatories of the defection letter and shot Gosney and Bagby a second time. As he did so, he shouted to ten-year-old Tracy Parks to throw herself on the floor. "I was afraid that she might be hurt," he recalled. Realizing that he was not shot, Dale Parks recovered and began wrestling with Layton for the pistol. In the course of the struggle Parks shouted, "Larry, you fool, *I'm here to help.*"

With that, Layton went limp. Moments later, Layton could not understand why the child Tracy Parks was so terrified of him.

———————————⇒—◄—◁—————————

In the days following the Jonestown holocaust, authorities in Guyana questioned the survivors who had escaped from the settlement and the

Temple members, some forty-two of them, who had been in the Temple's Georgetown headquarters on November 18. As the Guyanese authorities determined that individual members were in no way involved in the Port Kaituma killings or the Jonestown suicides or the killing of Sharon Amos and her children in the headquarters, they were released. In the last two weeks of December, they began to trickle back into the United States. How they returned became a matter of considerable concern to some of them. When at one point the American Embassy proposed that all the survivors fly back together on a U.S. military plane, Jim Bogue and his family were hysterical with fear. Somehow, Jones or his "hit squad" might still have the power to make a plane fall from the sky.

Once on American soil, they were received by the FBI and Secret Service for questioning. The chief concern of these agencies was to explore a rumor, emanating from several survivors, that Jones had devised a grotesque grand design, called Operation Four Prong, of which the mass suicides were only the first prong. Prong Two consisted, supposedly, of a well-publicized renunciation of Jones by his nineteen-year-old son, Stephan, who had been in Georgetown on November 18 and had survived. Jones had told the group often that if anything ever happened to him, his own son Stephan would take over. Whether or not a renunciation was part of a premeditated strategy, the disavowal happened on November 22, 1978, four days after the Event. Stephan Jones called his father a fascist and a sick man. He hated his father because Jones had destroyed everything for which the boy had worked. Of Jones's talk before the group that he was the reincarnation of Christ and Lenin, Stephan Jones said the claim had become a private joke between him and his mother, Marceline. Only he, Stephan, had had the courage to speak out against Jim Jones. *He* would never have sat idle at his father's invitation to death. "If it had come down to it, I'd have had to denounce him." Although American officials made attempts to prevent his return, and after he had been refused entry into several other countries, Stephan Jones eventually left Guyana in early March 1979 for San Francisco.

The third prong was supposed to go into effect some six months after the first prong. "Angels" of the Temple would seek out the "defectors" and visit vengeance upon them. And the fourth prong would direct the same treatment against hostile politicians and writers. In mid-March 1978, the ex-wife of a California newsman who had written many stories on Jonestown received two early morning calls. The voice on the other end said, "My family died in Jonestown. Now your family is going to die." In February 1980, two of the Temple's "class enemies," Al and Jeannie Mills, were murdered in Berkeley, California.

During the first months of 1979, the FBI made little headway in establishing the existence of Operation Four Prong, and by late March was coming to the conclusion that it was just another wild rumor. But the FBI and Secret Service interrogators were clearly confused by their subjects. The survivors did not react to lengthy, hostile questioning in customary ways. They were mannerly and gentle, and seemingly responsive throughout. They did not tire from a four-hour interrogation, nor did they appear resentful of tough questions, nor did they show any particular emotion or sadness. None, apart from Stephan Jones, were quite sure what they would have done had they been in Jonestown on November 18. The question perplexed them in an abstract way, a kind of insignificant quandary like the brand of tomato catsup one might choose.

In the reggae contest in Guyana in early 1979, a Trinidadian group called the Tradewinds was competing with a number they called "Brother Jonesie." The lyrics, set to a foot-tapping, steel beat, ran like this:

Brother Jonesie come to town and preachin' brudderhood
No more fear and sorrow
Open up a Temple in da jungle far away
All the people follow
When he tell them, jump, they're jumpin'
When he tell them, bump, they're bumpin'
When he tell them, dance, they're dancin'
When he tell them, scratch, they're scratchin'.

Brother Jonesie livin' like a king in olden days
Rulin' men and women
And the Yankee money comin' in by aeroplane
Brother Jonesie countin'
When he tell them, dig, they're diggin'
When he tell them, shake, they're shakin'
When he tell them, rise, they're risin'
When he tell them, sleep, they're sleepin'.

But the vibration turn bad, and the people want to leave
Brother Jones's bawlin',
Let me tell you people when I rise, you rise with me.
When I fall, you're fallin'
When he tell them, move, they're movin'
When he tell them, groove, they're groovin'
When he tell them, blink, they're blinkin'
When he tell them, drink, they're drinkin',
When he tell them, drink, they're drinkin' . . .

T W O

The Power
of the
Profane Word

[1]

To ARRIVE AT Timehri Airport from the cold of a North American winter well after midnight, as most international flights do, conveys the first honest taste of displacement. The field is dark, with an infinite, incomprehensible vastness beneath the firmament, that suggests the very curvature of the earth, as the tropical breeze sweeps across the face. Perhaps because my first landing there was on such a bizarre and frightening occasion, I felt this must be some military base, perhaps Saigon (if anyone remembered that name), and, indeed, if I could have seen through the night across the runway, the American military transport with its lugubrious cargo might have confirmed the impression. My corduroys stuck limply to my legs, giving that prickly sensation one always gets when overdressed, but as I waited to clear immigration in the flat, flesh-colored terminal building, watching the opaque salamander run in fits and starts across the soundproof ceiling above the black immigration officer, the prickliness in my legs became quite uncomfortable.

Patiently, I endured the fisheye of the customs official, who seemed to ask with his expression, why, or how, I had so much money to declare. Once past these formalities, a horde of spirited taxi drivers on the outside greeted me with shouted salutations about taking me the twenty-six miles to town. How was one to make a choice? That first time, the choice was made for me as I surrendered my bag of toiletries to the first hand that reached for it, and I simply followed it through the crowd and the chatter to a broken-down Toyota, with graceful, pink plastic swan's wings adorning its hood. In due course, I learned not to look askance at these Japanese jalopies that passed for taxicabs. A new car had not been bought or sold in Guyana for two years, and one reason their drivers were so anxious to be paid in American dollars was that the spare parts dealers in Trinidad or Suriname would not honor Guyanese dollars.

The person on the other end of my bag turned out to be a pleasant, middle-aged East Indian. We were soon bumping out of the airport and climbing to an alarming rate of speed toward Georgetown, twenty-six miles away. The speedometer read only fifty-five miles per hour, but the road was so narrow, uneven, cracked, and heaved to one side that it seemed twice that. Under socialism the British custom of driving on the left side of the road survived—not that politics has anything to do with the side of the road one drives on—but in this case my driver zoomed along on the right. "The surface is better on the right, sir," he explained politely, in his singsong, deferential tone. He slowed for a sharp curve, and out of the darkness loomed a huge billboard: WELCOME TO THE COOPERATIVE REPUBLIC OF GUYANA.

Houses, raised on stilts, began to dot the side of the highway as we sped along toward the capital. The coastal plain of Guyana, where 80 percent of the people live, is some feet below sea level, and the elevation of the houses on pilings has its origin in the fear of flooding. But there is an added advantage. A little height catches the pleasant breezes that blow most of the time, and the air is often in need of freshening. It was late on a Saturday night, November 25, 1978, but a number of people still walked along the side of the road. They neither turned nor stepped off the road as we bore down on them, despite the blaring of our high-pitched horn and the flicking of our lights, strobe-like, at them. Such trust! Halfway to Georgetown, as we talked casually about the reason for my visit, the car swerved sharply. I hesitated to ask the reason, but did.

"Oh, there was a man lying on the road, sir," the driver said nonchalantly, and we returned to the previous topic of conversation. I would become accustomed to missing people by millimeters, whether they were standing or lying.

Our interchange ranged broadly from politics to colonialism to the dismal state of breakdown in the country. I asked him whom he supported, Burnham or Jagan, and he said neither. In the last election he voted for some third party I had never heard of, but he did not pay much attention to politics, he said. It was an answer I would hear often. Who managed the country had lost interest for all but the ruling few. Several times the driver came back to words of caution. Be very careful. Always walk with another man. Don't walk at night.

I would come to do so anyway. Four or five days later, in Georgetown, I would see this same liveryman waiting for a fare outside the Tower Hotel, and he hailed me with an agitated look.

"Yesterday, sir, I saw you walking along Robb Street, wearing your watch in full view, and I almost called out to you, but you wouldn't have known me. You mustn't do that, sir. Very dangerous."

It was only an inexpensive drugstore watch, I replied. "It only cost me seventeen dollars."

"It doesn't matter, sir. *They* don't care whether it's expensive or not. Please, sir, don't be walking alone anymore."

I thanked him again for his concern, feeling rather touched, not realizing it was his way of bidding for my constant attention, but it was not until the end of my first week in the country, when a man staggered back to the Tower in his undershorts with a knife wound on his belly, that I began to curtail my nighttime perambulations.

"Did the police come?" I asked another cab driver who had seen the man return to the hotel an hour earlier.

"Oh, yes, they came," he said with a smile. But the victim had been caught around the neck and dragged into Tiger Bay, the oldest slum in the country, a sprawling wooden rats' nest next door to the American Embassy on Main Street. "The police never go in there at night," he declared. "In the morning, they will come again. They will take a statement, and make inquiries, but it's not like America. The police don't shoot people here." The comment seemed to shift the point rather deftly.

On the outskirts of Georgetown we passed the factory Thirst Park, the pride of the country, where the delicious Banks Beer is made along with other assorted beverages, like Maubi, the bitter nonalcoholic concoction of the common man brewed from bark. It was run by Peter d'Aguiar, the last capitalist in Guyana, who was once the powerful political figure. His party, the United Force, in coalition with the ruling party, the People's National Congress (PNC), enabled Forbes Burnham to wrest the prime ministership from the more leftist Cheddi Jagan in the mid-sixties (with the help of the Central Intelligence Agency). In the early sixties, there was such concern that Guyana not become the second Latin American country to turn Communist that President John F. Kennedy became the veritable chief of the Guyana desk at the State Department. But once Burnham consolidated his power, he broke up the coalition with d'Aguiar, and the capitalist withdrew from politics altogether to Thirst Park. Well, not altogether. D'Aguiar did sell his large estate with three houses and considerable land to the Soviets for a sprawling diplomatic and intelligence complex. Of such contradictions is the political atmosphere in Guyana replete.

Georgetown is a Dutch city in its layout. Once canals graced its major thoroughfares, but these have been largely filled in and made into broad promenades. The massive banyan and flamboyance trees shade these walkways and accentuate how long it has been since the Dutch were here. Many of the streets still have Dutch names, and the best address in town is Brickdam Street, where lovely three-story colonial houses remind one of the past elegance a few Europeans knew. Perhaps the most distinctive feature of these old colonial mansions is their jalousied "Demerara shutters," an ingenious device of fixed slates which angle out from the top of the window, allowing one to keep the window open and catch the breeze in the heaviest tropical downpour.

In all the commotion over the past three decades concerning the radical politics of Guyana, it was not easy to imagine the wealthy planters behind those shutters in Brickdam, but in the 1850s Anthony Trollope was there and described the mood:

> "Sugar!" said an enterprising Demerara planter to me. "Are you talking of sugar? Give me my heart's desire in Coolies, and I will make you a million of hogsheads of sugar without stirring from the colony! Now, the world's supply some twelve years ago was about a million hogsheads. It has since increased maybe by a tenth. What a land, then, is this British Guiana, flowing with milk and honey—with sugar and rum! A million hogsheads can be made there, if we only had the Coolies. I state this on the credit of my excellent enterprising friend. But then the Coolies!"

He never got his heart's desire in coolies, only a trickle, and had to make do with slaves and East Indian indentured servants.

And yet the colonial exploitation of Guyana is often overblown. In fact, the British approached this jungle timidly. They concentrated their efforts on the coastal plain and never made any substantial efforts to settle—or exploit—the hinterland. They were interlopers in South America, where the Portuguese and the Spanish were the real powers, and seen in Continental terms, the British huddled along the coast, uncertain of when they might be kicked out. "We were not exploited," one Guyanese official would say. "We were just used a little, and then abandoned."

As I entered Georgetown for the first time in November 1978, late on a Saturday night, the downtown streets were largely deserted. We passed by Guyana Stores, once called Bookers. We passed by the Toyota dealer, once Bookers, and the Rice Company, Bookers Rice, and the Bookers hardware store. Only the ice factory on River Road had not been nationalized. Above, low-wattage, naked bulbs lit the empty streets.

"The lights used to be brighter, when the British were here," my Indian driver said disdainfully, ". . . and there was no crime. That's what happens when you turn things over to the politicians." (Colonialists were not politicians, obviously.) "Too much fighting among ourselves, and everything goes on the decline."

Along Brickdam, the gray imposing Catholic cathedral lent an air of immemorial solidity to the street. The Catholics have been ministering in Guyana since the 1880s, and their priests fanned out in the interior to spread the word to the heathen with that grand missionary spirit. Converting the ignorant and the barbarian was a special challenge. V. S. Naipaul wrote of the process:

> The missionary must first teach self-contempt. It is the basis of the faith of the heathen converts. And in these West Indian territories, where the spiritual problem is largely that of self-contempt, Christianity must be regarded as part of the colonial conditioning. It was the religion of the slave owners and at first an exclusive racial faith. It bestowed righteousness on its possessors. It enabled the Dutch in Guiana to divide their population into Christians and Negroes: the Berbice slave rebellion of 1762 was a war between Christians and rebels. The captured rebels were tried for "Christian murder."*

Self-contempt would be central to the conversions of Jim Jones as well.

Across the street from the Brickdam Cathedral, in the Catholic presbytery, Father Andrew Morrison presided over a community of Jesuits. He was a tall, angular Englishman, with a benign, cheery, blanched vicar's face. His gray hair was sparse on top, but rather longer on the sides, and when he put his straw hat on to protect him from the high sun, his hair curled up on the sides under the brim, and he was not hard to find in a crowd.

In late 1974, Father Morrison had a visit from a group of young Americans representing a new group in the country, calling itself the People's Temple Christian Church. By the time of the visit, the organization, whose stated purpose was "to further the Kingdom of God by spreading the Word," had applied for a lease of 25,000 acres in the North West District of Guyana, for a period of twenty-five years, and promised to invest G$1 million over the first two years of development. An agricultural community in the hinterland was the goal of the group, initially to involve five hundred persons, and since the Guyanese government wished to encourage hinterland development any way it could, toward the middle of 1974 it granted permission to settle. Father Morrison had heard of the arrangement and was under the impression that this energetic American group was doing the Lord's good work. He greeted the visitors warmly.

Two women in the group, identifying themselves as Sharon Amos and Paula Adams, did most of the talking. They had come to ask for the use of the Sacred Heart Church, a large, alabaster edifice on Main Street up from the Tower Hotel, for a service by their pastor, the Reverend Jim Jones, who would soon be in the country for a short visit. Christians should show their love for other Christians in the spirit of ecumenism, they argued, and their philosophy was to carry out the teachings of Christ by building a cooperative multiracial society, where the scourges of racism, sexism, agism, and avarice might be

---

*From *The Middle Passage*, © 1962 by V. S. Naipaul (London: Andre Deutsch), p. 172.

expunged. The Sacred Heart Church, they added, would be used simply to promote their agricultural project in the North West.

Father Morrison found the argument persuasive and the women's charm disarming. After he put the matter to his parish council an arrangement for the use of the church was agreed to. Within days, posters and banners began to appear all over Georgetown, announcing a healing service by the great Jim Jones, the greatest humanitarian in the world, the wonder-worker from California.

> This Modern-Day Prophet Manifests All 9 Gifts of the Holy Spirit: Wisdom, World of Knowledge, Faith, Gifts of Healing, Discerning of Spirits, Prophecy, Working of Miracles, Tongues, Interpretation of Tongues.

I Cor. 12:8–10

> The Blind See! The Deaf Hear! Cripples Walk! See the SIGNS, MIRACLES and WONDERS that God Is MANIFESTING through PASTOR JONES!

The high-powered advertising campaign was something new in the lazy, tropical capital, and it engendered intense interest. But Father Morrison became very worried. This was not what he had acceded to at all, and so he sought out the two women and asked them how they could do this. They had asked for the church to talk about their agricultural project and, instead, a healing service with this great Jim Jones was being semaphored about town.

"Oh, Father, I just don't know how it could have happened," Paula Adams replied with an expression of hurt and injured innocence. "Our advertising man must have gotten out of hand." She promised to see if the mistake could be rectified.

Predictably, the advertising campaign continued unabated in the days that followed, and Father Morrison weighed the cost of canceling the service. But the matter had gone too far. Hundreds were planning to attend. Cancellation would cause an even worse flap, and the members of the Charismatic Movement within the Catholic Church were particularly interested. The Charismatics believed, as did Father Morrison, that the power of prayer can heal physical ailments, that the Holy Spirit can enter the bodies of the intensely devout and cure sickness that is beyond the pale of worldly medicine.

On the morning of the appointed day, January 5, 1975, an advertisement on the front page of the government paper, the *Guyana Chronicle*, read:

> Pastor Jim W. Jones, the greatest healing ministry through Christ on Earth today!

Pastor Jones is the dynamic leader of the People's Temple Christian Church, an interracial church family of all religions now beginning an agricultural mission here in Guyana.

This full Gospel deliverance ministry has been widely acclaimed for its humanitarian works. God has blessed Pastor Jones with all nine gifts of the Holy Spirit and thousands have been healed of every kind of affliction.

That afternoon Father Morrison took a place in the choir loft to the rear of the Sacred Heart Church, with a collection of priests, nuns, and Charismatics. The church was packed, spilling over into the church-yard, as Father Morrison had never seen it. In the sanctuary, movie cameras were stationed at important angles and kleig lights glared at a chorus of singers dressed in blue robes who burst exuberantly into swelling spirituals. Cheerleaders below the holy rood clapped their hands to the beat and exhorted the crowd in the nave to do likewise. The joy and energy of the faithful were infectious, and the singing was excellent. Especially moving were the gospel songs, rendered in the manner of Aretha Franklin by a young woman in her early twenties with visible scars on her cheek and neck. Later she would be identified as Deanna Wilkinson, a former prostitute who had been on her way to a career as a Las Vegas singer until someone threw acid in her face.

Between songs, one witness after another took the pulpit to testify about the changes in their lives that the great Jim Jones had produced. Drug addicts, convicts, and prostitutes, in procession, told their stories of life in the gutter before their Savior had appeared to lift them out. One witness, from the straight side of life, poured forth his faith: "He told me things that no human being in an ordinary state of conscious-ness could possibly know. Even though I am a lawyer and a skeptic, I had to be convinced, because what's real is real, what I could see, I could see. He told me about my back, told me about the treatments I've had and how they hadn't worked. . . . And then he reached out his hand and said, 'In the name of Christ, you're healed,' and my pain was gone. Now, a year and a half later, the pain is still gone, and I thank God for that."

To a crescendo of song and chanting, Jim Jones finally emerged from the sacristy into the chancel. In the tropics, he had dispensed with his customary red canonicals. His vestments were secular: a white, well-tailored suit, red shirt, angle-striped tie against a cream back-ground, knotted with an oversized Windsor bulge. With his shiny black hair, his long thick sideburns, razored and penciled to give them sharper definition, his sensuous amber Indian skin, and his dark glasses, he was a commanding presence. The voice was soft, washing consoling words over the standing, cramped, fascinated social body. His pace was unhurried. He paused deliberately between his sentences, his voice climbing in pitch at the beginning and falling off gently at the period. Behind him, his wife, Marceline, stood rigidly, a small, devoted, pious smile plastered on her flaccid face, attentive to his every cue. In the stiffness of her posture, her doting, the forced martyr's joy, she evoked Patricia Nixon.

To Father Morrison, far in the back of the church by the organ pipes, Jones possessed the familiar voice of the evangelical preacher, with the intensity and grandiosity of the Sunday morning radio program—with one difference. The references to the Almighty were occasional and offhand. Humility was not the pastor's message. Jim Jones spoke eloquently about Jim Jones's special gifts and his many powerful works done for the outcasts and the oppressed of the world. It was as if this Jim Jones who stood before them was the mere human vessel of some grander creation. Father Morrison soon found himself uncomfortable with this palavering, riding the line of blasphemy, but he told himself that he must, in the name of ecumenism, make allowances.

Soon enough, the pastor was onto the theme of healing. Yes, his spiritual healing ministry had cured many diseases, but, as inspiring as that was, this healing of individuals was secondary to the healing of the social body, of which all men and women were a part.

"All good things come down from the Father of Light, in whom there is no shadow," he said softly, "so God is in medical science, and we should utilize that to the nth degree. We are not the panacea for all ills here, for as God is in medical science, it is important for all of us to get regular checkups, where faith has not touched the need.

"We're not here to say what the causality of human disease is. I don't know what ailed one member of our congregation who came before me five years ago in a wheelchair. All I know is that for the five years since, she's been free. We're not minimizing healing, but it's a murky field. Many in the healing field cause me great consternation, because of their presumptuousness. They tell people, don't go to doctors. . . ."

He put his fingers to his forehead and, closing his eyes tightly, he became a model of concentration.

"Now, let us meditate. God is love, and love *is* a healing remedy. We're going to reach out to areas where man is seen to have difficulty. We must concentrate on the gifts of the Holy Spirit, so that that Spirit may function on what the secularists might speak of as the paranormal. . . . Let us believe. . . . Let us believe. . . ."

His eyes still closed, he passed his outstretched arm across the fold.

"Sister—," he said abruptly, his arm stopping at the right section of the church. "Sister—," he repeated the name more forcefully. In the midst of the tumult, a hesitant voice acknowledged the call. A disciple with a microphone rushed to the side of a bespectacled, middle-aged black woman.

The pastor's eyes opened. "Sister—, you're concerned about losing your sight. You're not able to see me clearly. Things are blurred for you. You have to stumble around, and you're not able to see faces that are even close to you." His voice carried the tone of genuine concern.

"That's true," the supplicant replied.

"You've told me nothing about your condition. . . ."

"No, Pastor, I haven't."

A baby cried out on the opposite side of the church, and a frightened gasp went through the gathering, as if the bond between the sister and the healer would be broken by the child's wail. He did not move his eyes from the sightless woman. "Give that little sweetheart a little love over there," he said with a glimmer of a smile, waving his hand in the direction of the child.

"Now, sister—, one of our sisters was blind or sightless, whatever you call it, and now she sees. You cannot see these fingers in front of my face from where you are?"

She shook her head.

"Now concentrate hard," he commanded, and then softened. "I love you. The people love you. Jehovah in all the goodness of all the world's great religions loves you. Most importantly, Christ loves you." Again his eyes closed for a long moment, then opened suddenly.

"Now, in the name and in the goodness and all of the mercy of Jesus, wherein I stand, what do you see?" he said with a piercing sharpness, holding three fingers up before his face. "How many fingers?"

"Three."

The choir burst into claps and shouts, and one deep male voice filled the church with the melodious bars of a spiritual about the power of the Almighty.

"How many now?" he said, even sharper.

"One."

"Take off those glasses, darlin'," he said. She obeyed. "Now how many fingers do you see?"

"Five."

"You don't even need your glasses, child," he said, smiling now. The woman began to cry. The exclamations of joy and awe grew louder.

"Let us all be thankful that she cries. Let's all cry and rejoice with her."

He saw in his mind a man who had been troubled with arthritis in his knees for many years, a father of three, somewhere at the back of the church—a man who had bicycled all the way from Queenstown, who had a prescription for Darvon in his medicine cabinet ("Who can know such things?" he asked. "Only God can know, father," came the answer), and such a man went forward and knelt several times upon command before him. He called forward an elderly woman from a wheelchair, and before long she was prancing before the congregation, first slowly, painfully, then briskly. He divined that a woman in the midst of the congregation had a dull pain in her stomach, which he diagnosed as cancer, and sent her away to the church bathroom in the crypt for the growth to be passed to his expert helper and wife, Marceline. When the woman returned, the offensive piece of bloody intestine, liberated from some body, was displayed with triumph and disgust, and the pastor assured the patient that through his psychic surgery the cancer would never again appear. "Praise God," he said. More cures followed, mainly with the elderly, and as the hysteria of the church rose, swelled by the music, Jones waded into the throng, encouraging the ailing to touch him, as if merely touching the hem of his garment would work his wonders. "Peace, Peace," he repeated, as they pressed forward to him, pressing so hard that some felt he was in danger of being crushed.

From his perch in the choir loft, Father Morrison was becoming more and more uncomfortable. Apart from his concern for the dignity of his holy church, he felt a growing contempt for the amateurishness of this transparent magic show. He fancied himself "a bit of a conjurer," often using sleight-of-hand tricks to please children when he traveled to unfamiliar parts of the interior, and thus to reach their parents. Angrily, he began to make plans for the following day. In the front of the church, a white girl with her head tied in a cloth, so that only part of her face showed, was waving her arms furiously for recognition. Finally, Jones rested his eyes on her.

"Yes, sister."

"I have a breast tumor," she blurted out.

"And you are ashamed to go to the doctor about it."

"Yes, father."

"Come forward, child."

She struggled across people hurriedly to reach the healer. Jones looked at her deeply for a long moment and then moved toward her. Slowly, to the hushed crowd, he raised his hand to her breast, and then his eyes to the ceiling, and after a long, riveting silence, pronounced her cured. Above, Father Morrison felt his embarrassment well from his depths, and he had a desperate urge to escape.

The following morning, very much heated, the Jesuit drove to the Georgetown headquarters of the organization. Before he left the presbytery, he received information that the white woman with the breast tumor had in fact been a member of the Temple all along. At the modest headquarters on a back street, he indignantly demanded to see this Reverend Jim Jones. They were sorry, but the pastor had left for Jonestown in the middle of the night. Well, then, the priest demanded to meet one of those whom Jones had cured, anyone. Surely, if Jones had cured so many, he should be able to meet just one, he insisted.

"Oh, Father, how can you treat us like this?" Paula Adams said. "How can you accuse and blame us? We do such good work, and we're so harassed. People are constantly attacking us. We try to do good, and this is what we get," and then she burst into tears.

Father Morrison would have none of it. In the *Catholic Standard*, the weekly newspaper of the Guyana Diocese, he wrote his somewhat restrained apology to his flock.

> The Sacred Heart Church wishes to dissociate itself entirely from what took place at the alleged healing service in its Church last Sunday and regrets any embarrassment that its loan of the building for this service may have caused its members and the Christian Community in Guyana. . . . The Sacred Heart Church acted in good faith in the interests of ecumenism and it would seem that their faith has been abused.

He did more. He went to see Kit Nascimento, the oily Minister of State in the office of the Prime Minister, to ask how the government could be supporting a group that was so obviously fraudulent. Nascimento was conciliatory.

"They shouldn't have been performing in Georgetown," the minister said. "All they're authorized to do is develop land near Port Kaituma."

The Temple quickly sensed its mistake, and its public relations team was prompt in redressing any possible damage. On January 12, 1975, they issued a statement that was printed in the Guyana papers. Once again, the theme of injury and innocence, intended to evoke sympathy, was central. The statement declared:

> The People's Temple in Guyana intends to be an agricultural mission. Our only interest is to produce food to help feed our hungry world in whatever way best suits the people of Guyana. It is the desire of our Pastor, Jim Jones, that all of the members of our agricultural mission join with others in an ecumenical spirit to glorify Christ by faith through works. . . .
>
> We love the U.S. Good changes towards a more perfect democracy are being made there. If we cannot serve Guyana, then we will have no reason to remain. Certainly, we are not interested in your land. We just want to utilize it to help serve the people and have no other interest in it.
>
> We will gladly prove that to you by withdrawing and letting good Guyanese people carry on with or without connection with our denomination of 2,000,000 members in the U.S., including Congressmen, members of all political parties, and Governors. We can easily live in North America. We will leave on a good note. If you don't feel we can serve well, just write to us and let us know or write to the Government. We have no desire to leave this wonderful country, but we have no desire to impose on your people.

In the four years that followed, Father Morrison became accustomed to the saccharine apologies, the show of injured innocence, the secretiveness, and the tears of Paula Adams and her colleague, Sharon Amos. For a time, they courted him, paying visits always in twos and threes, and never staying long. There was always someone waiting in the car, and appointments elsewhere were always pressing them. After the Sacred Heart service, when the Temple applied for membership on the Guyana Council of Churches, Father Morrison felt that he must forgive the fraud of 1975, for he could not prove that the ample and impressive representations the Temple made about itself were false. The group got its seat on the council. Still, Father Morrison kept his suspicions. Whenever political issues came to a vote, the Temple members always voted the government line, and once, when it came the Temple's turn to deliver the invocation and the benediction at a meeting of the council, Father Morrison had to instruct the Temple representative beforehand on how to do it.

In mid-November 1978, when U.S. Congressman Leo Ryan arrived in Guyana, Father Morrison followed him around, taking notes on the visit for a report in the *Catholic Standard*. The Jesuit was anxious to accompany the Ryan party to Jonestown when it went up to the North West, for he had received numerous invitations to visit the settlement, but somehow things had never quite worked out. Again, on November 17, it did not work out. Ryan had room for only a few press members, and the *Catholic Standard* was low in the Congressman's priorities. On the night of November 18, when a few scattered rumors began to sweep through Georgetown about bizarre happenings in the North West, Morrison called the Temple's headquarters and asked for Sharon Amos.

"She can't talk right now," Paula Adams replied, sweetly but firmly. The reason, Father Morrison was to understand the following morning, was that Amos lay dead on the floor of the bathroom upstairs, her throat and that of her three children slit from ear to ear. On Monday morning, as the reports of hundreds dead in Jonestown were confirmed, Father Morrison again called the Temple headquarters and again spoke with Adams. She was very glad to hear from him, she said, her voice as soft and sugary as ever.

"Paula, what happened?" an astonished Father Morrison asked.

"We have a lot of police here," she replied. "They think we're going to do some craziness, but you know me, Father. Do you think I'd do that? Do you think I'd do that? Do you think we'd do the sort of craziness they did up there? I just can't understand it. We're not that sort of people."

"Well, what happened to Sharon?" Morrison asked.

"She slit her children's throats and then her own," Adams replied.

"But, Paula, I've talked to a doctor, and he said it's very difficult for someone to cut her own throat." He did not add that Sharon Amos was four feet eleven inches tall, weighed perhaps 105 pounds, and that her twenty-one-year-old daughter was a hefty 120 pounds.

"Father, if you killed your three children, it wouldn't be difficult to cut your own throat."

Father Morrison hung up the phone with profound anguish. Finally, he was beginning to believe that this woman, with all her sweetness and loveliness and charm over the years, all her protests about the Christlike good works of Jim Jones and the Georgetown efforts of her church to serve the needs of humankind, could be a cold-blooded killer.

[2]

The healing service in the Sacred Heart Church in Georgetown in early 1975 was actually a rather mild, uncomfortable affair for Jim Jones. Its staging in a foreign country made the normal planning for such a production more difficult, and so the display of the pastor's magical powers was less than fantastic. The intense negative reaction of the devout Catholics of Guyana convinced Jones that he should never again hold a service in his adopted sanctuary, for it was harder there for him to appear to be something he was not.

Jones, of course, had been at this healing ministry for many years. He had worked out the procedures for the services with extraordinary attention to detail. Those who had been with him from the early days of his church in Indiana, and later in Ukiah, California, insisted, even after the holocaust, that at the least, the man had a "gift," perhaps not divine power, but a very special talent nonetheless. If the healings were fake, one Temple member who was a graduate of the University of California told me, his simulation was "awfully good."

By the mid-1970s, a considerable body of literature existed on spiritual healing, much of it appearing in American women's magazines like *McCall's* and *Cosmopolitan* and the fast-selling paperback books, and Jim Jones followed it very carefully, searching for confirmation and refinement of his own techniques. As extravagant as his claims in a healing service appeared to the novitiate, they were based on a number of principles, well accepted in both the religious and the medical community. The central belief is that a healing force exists in the world—to the deeply religious, the force of the Holy Spirit; to the physician, the power of the mind over the body—that is superior to the capabilities of human science. Negatively put, medicine is often dispensed to the ill as a placebo: the patient must have a pill to think that he is on the road to recovery, even if the pill is inactive. *Believing* the medicine is working makes it do so.

For the outcasts of American society, primarily the elderly and the black—the recipients of the impersonal, overstrained, and inferior medicine of the welfare clinics—Jones offered the first gesture of love and caring, and this alone was salubrious. He touched them often, the "therapeutic touch" one article in the *American Journal of Nursing* calls it, the touch that improves the enzyme balance in the body and increases the hemoglobin in the blood. He held their hands, stroked their cheeks, called them "darling" and "honey." If in the end they gave him their money and their property, and swelled his membership, soothing his own need for aggrandizement, he spoke to a deep void in their lives. In Jonestown, this letter, written in the feeble and ungrammatical hand of a seventy-three-year-old woman, whose nickname was "Grandma," was found. The date of Grandma's letter was July 12, 1978.

Dad, you are the savior of the world. If other people new about you they would give the world and follow you. I met you at Mesconia. I was called bye my niece. She explain that a man would be at her church. They say he could heal everything, even raise the dead. I was there when you walk in the pulpit. I said to myself that if I ever got well, it would be an Indian who would do it. You started to talking, and called on a Jewish lady and she wouldn't listen. Next was a girl I knew. She had a back operation. You ask her to bend. She replied she had a back operation. You ask her to bend again. She replied I have a steel brace on. You told her you didn't care what she was in, to bend. She tried and did bend. We all jumped up and hollered. When colection was taken up, the preacher was watching the money. You said I don't want money, you wanted people to get well. This touched my heart, by suffering so much myself. Then the preacher said he had gotten a room for you at the Hilston Hotel, a sweep. You stop him and told him you live with your people. I said to my friend, what matter of man is this.

We went to Redwood Valley, and we were treated with Courtesty. You healed many people that day. We was still astonished. I said, I was going to follow you to the end, not just for healing, but the principle we saw you stand for. It was different from what we had been attending and we love it. Then I taken sick and was in the hospital and every day, and sometimes at night you had someone their to see after me. Sometime you called, sometime mother called. What more can one man do? You even knock a nurse down on her big fat bellie about hollerin at me. Finally one day, you called, said, Grandma, I want you up here close to me. Boy oh boy! I went. Dad, you have showed so much love and understanding.

I saw so much honest principle, fairness with us all, I saw God in you. You went up and down the road every week and keep us from all hurt, harm and danger. You carried us on vacation with you. In Mexico, you told the fish and the shock to go back, so we could swim. You played ball with us, made the rain stop so we could have a good time. You turned water into wine. Dad has keep me alive more times than I have fingers and toes. You saw that the U.S.A. was falling, hating black, middle class whites, Mexicans, Indians. Many years ago, you decided that we should leave that mean U.S.A. You was going to find a place for us, and you saw Guyana was that place. You made a trip over to talk to the high men. You wanted to see that we had a health place. . . .

Dad, you are our God. I will never turn back. No matter what the cost, I am going all the way with you. . . .

To Grandma, feeling good was a factor of community spirit and concern, of mission and interracial contact she had never shared previously, not of pills and potions. In his lectures on *Varieties of Religious Experience*, William James seemed to speak of Grandma:

The God of many men is little more than their court of appeal against the damnatory judgment passed on their failures by the opinion of the world. To our own consciousness there is usually a residuum of worth left over after our sins and errors have been told off—our capacity of acknowledging and regretting them is the germ of the better self *in posse* at least. But the world deals with us *in actu* and not *in posse:* and of this hidden germ, not to be guessed at from without, it never takes account. Then we turn to the All Knower, who knows our Bad, but knows this good in us also. . . . So the need of a God very definitely emerges from this sort of experience of life.

Jim Jones spoke to the residuum of worth in Grandma. She wanted to believe in the cosmic energy of healing, not only of the individual's body but of the social body, of which Jim Jones spoke, and threw herself open to it. This was the healer's highest goal: to create the atmosphere where all would be open to the healing force, even if the initial "catalyst" for the energy was artificially implanted. Once the right atmosphere was there, a metaphysical bond between the healer and the patient could come into being, and the sick would heal themselves. The pastor then was not a healer but a "motivator."

This notion is hardly unique to Jim Jones. It has given rise in the 1970s to the holistic movement (promoted by Ruth Carter Stapleton, much to Jim Jones's benefit), which views the body, mind, emotions, and spirit as inseparable parts of the total person. In the holistic approach, each organ of the body has an inherent intelligence and is connected to a larger harmonious whole. One English healer, Harry Edwards, whose methods and beliefs were brought to the attention of Jones, believes that breast cancer in women is not viral but psychological. To Edwards, sometimes referred to as the World's Greatest Healer, most breast cancer develops in women who either wanted children and could not have them, or had them and did not want them, or wanted to be married but were not. (Edwards's scientific support for this conclusion is not clear.) So frustration in the mind is the source of breast cancer. Seeing an erotic image activates the mammary cells in a woman's breasts, Edwards theorizes, and when these cells are frustrated they become rebellious and lunatic, reproducing themselves wildly and eventually creating a tumor. Perhaps this is what Jim Jones had in mind when he healed the woman of breast cancer in the 1975 Georgetown service that so embarrassed Father Morrison, but the difference was that the woman "healed" in Georgetown was actually Karen Layton, Larry Layton's second wife and Jones's current or future mistress.

In Ukiah, where the People's Temple moved in 1965, ostensibly to escape the racism of Indiana and to find sanctuary in the event of a nuclear conflagration (he maintained with some pointedness that he could not imagine people to be mad enough to make nuclear weapons and then sane enough not to use them), Jones demonstrated his psychic powers without staff preparation. But so exhausting and consuming were the healings for him that he would often collapse with fatigue, drained of his physical and emotional energy. In late 1970, however, ostensibly to save the leader's strength, a new method began. A group of ten or so from the inner circle were given the task of identifying first visitors to the church and of secretly gathering background information on them. Some of this could be done overtly, by checking court or telephone or insurance sources, but the real payoff came from home visits and from rummaging through the garbage of potential converts. This method soon developed into a fine art, and it was the origin of the People's Temple as a modern intelligence organization in microcosm. A number of ruses were employed to gain access to a visitor's home, such as the broken-down car, use-the-phone routine, or baby-sitting service, but the old standard for the advance team became the pose as polltakers. Since the converts were mainly black, and the inner circle of the Temple mainly white and female, the Temple pollsters often made themselves up as black people with theatrical burnt cork and greasepaint, along with cheap wigs and Goodwill clothes. Black people in the ghettos of San Francisco and Los Angeles, they found, were usually naive and kind, and so were easy marks.

Jones demanded great attention to particulars. Pictures on the wall, names of children, relatives with different names in different cities were all to be noted, but particularly important was a visit to the bathroom, so that the drugs in the medicine cabinet could be scanned. From that, of course, the ailments of the possible adherents could be divined, and Jones would have the stuff of his clairvoyance. From the garbage can, other vital information on diet, financial situation, and personal relationships could be deduced. Between the "direct" sources, the home visit, and the garbage can, the "chart" or "healing notes" were meticulously typed up as memoranda for Pastor Jones. To stay in keeping with the church-like atmosphere of the organization, the memoranda were called "revelations."

An example of a 1972 revelation, which came to Sharon Amos through hard work in a back alley, contained these items on a possible husband-wife recruit. (I will call them John and Mary Doe.)

Revelation to SA, 5/16/72 (direct) (from John's office)

—checks: Saving Bank of Mendocino acct # 0406-553-035
  1. Model Bakery $1.21 4/18/72 (Mary signed)
  2. Farmer's produce $27.84 3/27/72 (Mary)
  3. Mendocino County Recorder $3.00 4/6/72
—bill from City of Paris, S.F. $20 4/2/72
—statement of payment, Bankamericard, #CB26 6556 F3933, of $11/previous balance $68.07, annual percentage rate of 18%

Revelation to SA, 7/18/72 (indirect)

Garb:
  —telephone credit card 1971, John Doe, #483 7192 223 N
  —card to John, on cover a picture called "Stag and Two Does, Early Morning" by East African artist Jesse Allen. Card says: "Dear John, Many thanks for rescuing us. Remember what I said about your first baby. With warmest regards, Sue."

Garb food:
  —Vanilla imitation flavor Lucerne Instant breakfast (includes sucrose, corn syrup solids, carrageenan, starch, pyridoxine & other ingredients).
  —package Tabby Tender dinner seafood flavor, 9, soft-moist cat food.

These revelations, or more accurately spying, continued after a person joined the Temple, as material for Jones to confront members who did not obey Temple orders. Another item of an Amos revelation from the garbage read:

  —Swanson Chicken Pie Discount 28 cents (with monosodium glutamate, chicken fat, lard, lactic acid). We were warned not to eat meat pies.

As thorough as this snooping was, it occasionally produced embarrassments. The information gathered was sometimes inaccurate or led to the wrong conclusions, and the healer had to do some fancy dancing in the pulpit. The best of the Temple advance team was a woman in her mid-forties, Patricia Cartmell. She was a rather large person, with a cheerful and gregarious disposition, and she made a particularly good black person (as well as proving herself adept at the sleight-of-hand tricks with chicken gizzards cum cancer tumors during the cancer cures). But so good did Cartmell become at mining the personal details of potential black recruits that she got a little sloppy once in her makeup and was picked up by the police in a black section of San Francisco, her wig askew and greasepaint smeared. Eventually, she was released without charge, when she told the police that she was researching a book on the plight of black people in America.

But Patty Cartmell had been crucial to Jones's rise, and he paid her tribute in his singular fashion in an interview found in Jonestown.

The first time [I healed] I had people screaming and hollering and the second night you couldn't get in the damn building. I'd just call people out and they'd get healed of everything. Much like I do now, with help, but then, I didn't have no help, really nothing. Just closed my eyes and call. Such a drain. It got so heavy. Jesus Christ! I thought, "I can't stand this." Wasn't long before I started taking little notes. For years and years and years, it was me, my gift, and whatever I could take down. Till Patty came along. That was hell, twelve years ago. From 1954 till Patty came, about eleven years of that shit. I carried it, and I carried it. Packed out the biggest auditoriums in Indiana and Ohio. I should have left it that way. But I'd of been dead.

People pass growths and then by sleight of hand I'd start doing it, and that would trigger others to get healed. But I never had anybody help me, not even Marcie. Marcie never knew there was one thing but reality. Carried the entire operation on myself. I don't know how the hell I got away with it. They never would've caught on if I'd kept it that way. I didn't trust people, and I should've kept it that way.

Well briefed on the background of the selected few that he could "call out" of a meeting, Jones moved to the pulpit confidently. Especially in new cities—Seattle, Chicago, Detroit, Houston, and others, where the Temple held crusades—the "catalysts," or the Temple members secretly posing as bystanders, had to be carefully rehearsed. If Pastor Jones divined that a potential recruit had a relative in another city with a different name, whose telephone number was 942-7583 (area code 213), the information needed to be accurate, as if only God could know such a thing. But many longtime followers swore that even though they knew these catalysts were planted or technical information was gathered beforehand, the happenings thereafter were truly amazing once the "metaphysical bond" was established. Real miracles, they insisted, followed fake ones.

To Jones's court, the fraud of the catalytic healing demonstrations simply did not matter. Healing was only a means to get to a more important end of revolutionary social action. To be powerful, the organization needed members. Calling the institution a church was a "strategic" appellation, a sop to gain black members by the hundreds. Jones carefully studied the speech rhythms of Pentecostal and Free Will Baptist ministers, as well as their lines of reasoning and the quotations in the Bible important to them, so that he could reproduce the sounds and cadences and biblical references that made the newcomers from that background feel more comfortable in his presence. His sermons became a masterful interweaving of ecumenical themes, depending on the audience he believed he had, and he mixed the religious with the political, packing his message with facts and figures from the newspapers that Richard Tropp, his college professor member, gathered for him.

He used the Bible effectively when he needed it, finding passages to justify his activism and his communalism.

And all that believed were together, and had all things in common;
and sold their possessions and goods and parted them to all men,
as every man had need. And they, continuing daily with one accord
in the temple, and breaking bread from house to house, did eat
their meat with gladness and singleness of heart.

> Acts 2:44–46

For I was an hungered and ye gave me meat;
I was thirsty and ye gave me drink;
I was a stranger and ye took me in;
Naked and ye clothed me;
I was in prison and ye came unto me.

Then shall the righteous answer him saying,
When saw we thee an hungered and fed thee?
Or thirsty, and gave thee drink?

When saw we thee a stranger and took thee in?
Or naked and clothed thee or when saw we thee sick?
Or in prison and came unto thee?

Verily I say unto you,
Inasmuch as ye have done it unto one of the least of these,
Ye have done it unto me.

> Matt. 25:35–40

He told his followers that they were returning Christianity to the style of the earliest Christians with their "apostolic ministry," that if

Jesus came back to see his church of empty "prayin', preachin', and singin'" and slapdash community service, he would not know it. Jones's "gospel of liberation," on the other hand, was so abrasive to the establishment, it was bound to elicit fierce opposition and persecution, just as the early Christians had experienced it. If there was not persecution of them, Jones said, he would be nervous. His measure of harassment, real or supposed, was his measure of self-importance.

For the young and the intelligent in the flock, accepting the insignificance of fake healing was a gigantic leap toward moral depravity. After self-surrender, acquiescence in his other authoritarian methods was easy. It amounted to the total acceptance of the "ends justify the means" precept, which Jones promoted unabashedly in his meetings with his staff. Therewith, they accepted the essential duplicity of their leader without qualm. Their acceptance also contained an element of racist condescension implicit in the old saw about the ease of tricking black folk and laughing at them behind their back. The whole recruitment process was a kind of symbolic nigger joke. This acceptance must have instilled in Jim Jones early on a deep contempt for his followers, for they were so easily degraded, so easily fooled, so easily manipulated. He began to refer to them as his "measly people." He took particular notice of a 1974 *Psychology Today* article entitled "The Meek Don't Make It," which argues that a political group made up of the timid and the unskilled could be successful if it operated under the law of the jungle and treated their struggle as "a political combat situation." "They must therefore be organized like a combat group—with willing, committed people who know what to do, and a command structure that can keep its people out of the wrong fight at the wrong time," the article argued. To Jones, the article certified his authoritarianism.

Still, many stayed long after they knew the true nature of these healing services. Those who came only for the magical healings left soon after, when the magician's helper behind the curtain exposed himself. But those who were lured by the healings and stayed, stayed for the political message and the surrender of personal responsibility. He convinced his recruits from the minor colleges of California that their acceptance of any means toward radical ends made them a tight, disciplined band of hardened revolutionaries. In the 1970s, when no real revolutionaries existed anymore in America, they embraced him.

To whom in their experience could they compare Jim Jones?

[3]

The soil that spawned and nurtured Jim Jones toward his much-coveted place in history was uniquely American. His ministry began on a note of pure hypocrisy, but with the genius of a political flimflam man he quickly saw his calling. It seems beyond question that his visceral abhorrence of the failings of American society in the early 1950s was genuine. In Indiana, where historically the power of the Ku Klux Klan accentuated the strong racist currents of the state, Jim Jones, like so many other Americans in the post-World War II era, found in the race question the first impulse toward social action. In the execution of the Rosenbergs in 1953, he found his immediate projection toward a rough Communist orientation. In June 1953, as the Rosenbergs neared execution, Jones had contracted infectious hepatitis, and, by his own testimony, lay near death. During the last days in Guyana, as Jones was preparing for his apocalyptic funeral in the dark jungle by dictating his autobiography, he described his early rise. Not only is the story interesting, but the way in which a delirious Jones told it is important. For ten years his speech had taken a turn toward profanity, inspired, he told his congregation, by the Free Speech Movement at Berkeley, which he felt so pierced the hypocrisy of his homeland.

I kept thinking—they can't kill these people [the Rosenbergs]. I'd march till there were holes in my shoes trying to get petitions. The fucking Pope—their children came up and kissed him through the screen. *I just died a thousand deaths.* I wish I could have died then. Hell, you can only have so many revolutionary deaths. You care for people—you die. You die. So, hell, death isn't any problem for me anymore.

I was in this goddamn miserable coma. I'd drift in and out and look up at the clock as it ticked away. Say, Marcie, are the Rosenbergs dead yet? And she'd say, no dear, not yet, and I'd drift back. I thought it's futile, an inhuman system that kills people based on a bunch of scrap paper, just because they had Communist affiliations. No more had given atomic secrets than I had. I hate that system. I wept when I got out of that coma, wept until the sheets were soaked. I wished I had died. Someplace along the line, I quit crying. Don't cry anymore. It's rough being a Communist.

So this dry-eyed Communist began to hitchhike around his state. Then twenty-two years old, he spread his politics, which were probably more nihilism than Marxism. Along the way he encountered a superintendent in the Methodist Church. Whatever happened between these two men is hardly encompassed by Jones's narrative of it. He claimed that he dressed the Methodist up and down about the hypocrisy of religions, and the result was that the superintendent offered him a church.

I said, you giving me a church? I don't believe in anything. I'm a revolutionary. He said, why don't you take a church, and he appointed *me,* a fucking Communist, to a goddamn church, a Communist who believed in nothing. That's how religious I was, and still am. To Marceline, I said what am I going to do with this goddamn thing? But I took the church. *I remember I thought I was going to die a thousand deaths when I got up in that pulpit.*

In the issue of integration, he found instantly the message to set him apart from the rest of the religious community. To him, the member- ship he inherited was nothing but a "handful of old bigots," until he encouraged blacks to attend. He wanted "an inclusive congregation," for he felt that he could never politicize his following (toward what end is not clear) until blacks and whites sat together. To gain black members, he "toyed" with Pentecostalists because he found them more accepting of blacks than other white denominations of the time.

Soon enough, the Methodist elders saw their mistake, and the pressure they exerted on the young preacher encouraged his second bold act, after accepting the church in the first place. He "conspired" to get his whole church to vote itself out of the Methodist Conference, something that never had been done in that denomination in Indiana. To his healings, his abrasive message, his ascetic lifestyle, he added one further symbolic act of great importance: he adopted a multiracial family which included black, Korean, and Chinese members. This, as much as any other thing, made him a lightning rod for racist scorn and gave him the sense of persecution that would later develop into such cosmic proportions.

Still, it gratified him to see how his ministry was catching on. He watched other healers and thought of them as "assholes" doing no healing, but the fact that they drew great crowds fascinated him. He thought that "there must be some way you can do this for good, that you can get the crowd, get the money, and do some good." In the delirium of the jungle, he saw thousands in the early days, including the crippled, clamoring through the windows to get to him. "But you see, nobody gives a shit as long as you don't become political."

But, to quote from Jones's rambling, vulgar, often inane last self-testimonial can be confusing, for it risks underplaying his frighten- ing appeal, especially during the years of the mid-1970s when his movement took off. For his sermons were forceful and fascinating, as much for his pure embrace of evil and his unashamed projection of himself as the socialist Anti-Christ. His message came wrapped in the cloth of fundamentalist religion and 1960s civil rights politics. The music of his church was a mixture of freewheeling black spirituals, integrationist freedom songs, and structured and often stiff white- church organ numbers. Marceline Jones often sang solo, and one of her favorites was a maudlin number called "My Little Black Baby." The trappings of the place, the music, the handclapping, the spiritualism, were no different from what one might find in many large urban black churches of America. But the genuine interaction of his mixed congregation did create a highly unusual, if not unique, phenomenon in a Sunday morning service, where blacks and whites together worshipped ecstatically and idolatrously before a highly informed, smooth, and devious American atheist.

Jones did indeed have charisma, and *charisma* is one of those words which has crept into American speech without much thought to what it means or who really possesses it. In religious parlance, looked at positively, the quality could mean no more than "the power of the Word." When a leader seems to project a magnetic quality from a podium which attracts many followers who are fascinated by his voice or program or style, he is pronounced charismatic—a quality he never loses, unless he abuses his aura and falls into disgrace, as so often happens with this type. Of the political leaders in modern times, John F. Kennedy and George Wallace represent two poles of this gift of engendering crowd hysteria, just as Billy Graham and Martin Luther King, Jr., might represent different poles in the religious field. But for many Americans there is something suspicious about these figures. Where appeal rests on style and performance, subsuming substance, the line between charisma and demagoguery is vague. But while the charismatic leader makes many uncomfortable, his followers are often more disturbing—robots intoxicated by false ecstasy.

Still, for many other Americans, especially in the late 1970s, when primary skepticism of authority of any kind had been washed away in the plunge back into tranquility, the magnetic personality provides a welcome relief from individual responsibility. The dangers of blind obedience have been largely forgotten, especially among the young and educated.

In his *Sociology of Religion*, Max Weber separates charisma into two categories—primary and acquired—the gift of appeal obtained naturally and that acquired artificially through self-conscious hard work or other extraordinary stimulus. In the acquired variety, charismatic powers can develop only when the germ of magnetism is already there and would have remained dormant but for some unusual circumstances to activate the gift.

Weber also distinguishes between the prophet and the priest. The priest lays his claim to authority on his service in a sacred tradition, dispensing salvation by virtue of his office. But the prophet does not receive his mission from any human agency. He seizes it. The prophet's claim to authority comes from personal revelation, and the personal call to a self-proclaimed mission. His ministry is based solely on his personal gifts. Traditionally, Weber writes, the bearers of the prophetic message needed the authentication and validation of magical powers.

It must not be forgotten for an instant that the entire basis of Jesus' own legitimation, as well as his claim that he and only he knew the Father and that the way to God led through faith in him alone, was the magical charisma he felt within himself. It is doubtless this consciousness of power, more than anything else, that enabled him to traverse the road of prophets. During the apostolic period of early Christianity and thereafter, the figure of the wandering prophet was a constant phenomenon. There was always required of such prophets a proof of their possession of particular gifts of the spirit, of special magical or ecstatic abilities.*

By all standards, Jim Jones was a modern prophet, even if in the end he was Lucifer's handyman and the apotheosis of evil. He was highly critical of American religion and American society in a message which rested upon no established tradition, but solely upon his personal magnetism. He proclaimed a new doctrine of salvation and authenticated it and himself with a display of magic. And he moved people by the thousands. If he invoked a grab bag of religious traditions, he violated many others contemptuously. He made no effort to conceal his atheism and his mission to destroy the conceits of modern Christianity. His theological thrust was a return to the apostolic spirit of service that existed in the time of Christ, a thoroughly solid theological action, and his claim to divine power, or, as he called it, the highly evolved level to which he, a man from the lowest ranks, had attained, rested upon the uniquely Christian doctrine that God had come to the earth once in the shape of man in Christ, and that there would be, someday, a Second Coming. His followers asked, Why not this man? Why not now, in this time? Just as the phenomenon of Jim Jones could spring only from the America of the 1960s and 1970s, it could spring only from a Christian tradition.

During his better days, from his spare dais absent of any trappings of the Christian faith, he did not stand, but sat behind his pulpit in a raised, throne-like swivel chair whose restriction no black evangelist could ever endure, as he delivered his sermons. Dressed in a red clerical robe, his bare arms often shot upright from billowing sleeves in the raised fist of the black revolution, projecting an animal sexuality. Again, no black evangelist would ever preach bare-armed. And he conveyed a preeminent sense of control. This man would never lose himself in irrational ecstasy, blithering in tongues (although he could use tongues when he needed them), or rolling on the floor. To his followers, despite his atrocities, here was a man who could shake this society at its foundation.

We want no condescending saviors to come to us with their pity from some judgment hall [he preached]. That has been pawned off on us too

---

*From Max Weber, *The Sociology of Religion*, © 1963 by Beacon Press (Boston: Beacon Press), p. 47.

long. I'm here as an example to show you that you can bring yourself up by your own bootstraps. You can be your own God, not in condescension but in resurrection, in upliftment from whatever downtrodden condition you've had to endure. Within *you* rests the key of deliverance. We are looking to the key that is in every heart and breast. That I, the God that came from the earth of earth, from the dust of these toilsome fields, from hardship and labor, from the lowest of economic positions, from the poverty near the railroad tracks, *I* came to show you that the only God you need is within you. That's my purpose in being here.

When the transition comes, there shall be no need for Gods, or for any other kind of religion, the opiate of the people or any other ideology. Racist traditions shall be removed from the concepts of mankind. There shall be no need for religions when freedom comes. No need for a concern for tomorrows because everyday will be heaven. We will have built the heaven that man has suppositionally dreamed about. We will have the heaven that the white masters have taught would one day be given us, so that we might shine somebody's shoes in the throne room. . . .

But in the meantime, I come in the phenomenon of religion to get people *out* of religion. Of the very God of heaven in all his might and fullness, all the power you say God has, *I* have come to make one final dissolution, one final elimination of all religious feeling. Until I have eradicated this appeal from the face of the earth, I shall do all those miracles you said your God would do and never did. I shall come and heal you of all the diseases that you prayed for . . . and never happened.

In his doctrine of the immanence of God in him, and in his following, as heretical and idolatrous as it is, Jones made a biblical quotation the core of his blasphemy. Ignoring the first of Moses' Ten Commandments ("Thou shall have no other gods before me"), Jones leapt upon the Gospel of St. John, 10:31–34, which told of the reaction to Jesus' profession of deity before the multitude.

Then the Jews took up stones again to stone him.

Jesus answered them, Many good works have I shewed you from my Father; for which of those works do ye stone me?

The Jews answered him, saying, For a good work we stone thee not; but for blasphemy; and because that thou, being a man, maketh thyself God.

Jesus answered them, Is it not written in your law, I said, Ye are gods?

Over and over, Jones repeated this last phrase. They were gods, or at least they had that glimmering potential within them. In this, he was doing Huey Long one better, everyman not a king but a god. In Jones's early ministry, he could still describe "the beauty of Jesus" as seeing "the form of God in man," and speak of Jesus' perfection as created by suffering; the agony and death on the cross simply the last act of perfection in a long process. If their godliness was embryonic, his was fully realized, and until they walked like Jim Jones, talked like Jim Jones, looked like Jim Jones, acted like Jim Jones, he would be God, Almighty God.

But Jones was also employing a considerable body of theological examination, reaching back into the eighteenth century, and applying it for his own contemporary obsession. Indeed, it could be argued that Jones was the realization of the radical theological doctrine of "Christian atheism" or the Death-of-God theology concerning which there was much writing in the 1960s and 1970s.

In the vision of William Blake, the divine is simply the best that is in all men, particularly imagination and creativity, and that is the only God. Seeing the divine in great men is to see the divine in oneself. Wrote Blake,

> The worship of God is: Honouring his gifts in other men, each according to his genius, and loving the greatest men best: those who envy or calumniate great men hate God; for there is no other God.

In *The Essence of Christianity*, a classic work which Jones would doubtless have studied and which had a great influence on Karl Marx, Ludwig Feuerbach argued that consciousness of God is merely self-consciousness; knowledge of God, self-knowledge; feeling simply the noblest, most excellent, and therefore the divine quality of men. "So far as thy nature reaches, so far reaches thy unlimited self-consciousness, so far are thou God. . . . By his God, thou knowest the man, and by the man his God, the two are identical." And Emile Durkheim, the father of modern sociology along with Max Weber, took this notion further, separating the profane body from the sacred soul, which in Christian thought lives on. The soul is at the very least the "spark of divinity" in all men, and from this sacred particle *in men*, not in God, moral ideas and moral force derive.

From the unique Christian belief that the Word was made Flesh and would be again (the Second Coming), theological room for movement became possible for Jim Jones. In orthodox Christian thought, God was both immanent and transcendent, but the power of the Christ story has diminished the power and the majesty of an incomprehensible God in heaven. From this evolved the concept of "kenosis" in theological circles: Christ's action of emptying or pouring himself out in becoming man, humbling himself even to the point of experiencing a human death. God became so launched into humanity that little was left in the sky. Indeed, say the modern Death-of-God theologists like Thomas J. J. Altizer, nothing is left in the sky, and we can rejoice in that fact. The new Christ will move even more comprehensively in real life and experience. We can now concentrate on immanance of God and forget

about transcendence. "The historical realization of the death of God,"
writes Altizer, "is a full unfolding of the forward movement of the
Incarnation."

Jim Jones executed this doctrine of Christian atheism (to be
distinguished from the scientific atheism of the Marxist), and at times
he sounded as if he was paraphrasing Altizer. To Jones, the divine is not
expressed in the creative or imaginative energies of men, as Blake and
Feuerbach would have it, but in the social goals of justice and equality
and human service.

> When all this is done, when I have eliminated all the condescending
> savior images, removed all the judgment hall concepts, expunged all the
> heavens in the sky and the Sky God concepts, People will know there is no
> God but what is in us. What is God anyway? God is perfect justice,
> freedom, and equality. The only thing that brings perfect justice, freedom
> and quality and love in its beauty and holiness is socialism!
>
> In *me*, the twain have been married. In this dispensation, I have taken
> on the body, the same body that walked in the plains of Palmyra, of whom
> Solomon said his hair is black as a raven, and, who, as Isaiah said, 7:20,
> would shave with a razor. I *do* shave with a razor. My hair *is* black as a
> raven's. I came as the God to eliminate all your false Gods. Men have
> dastardly distorted the spirit that I have, but it was necessary for me to
> come upon the scene and I have. From time to time, I shall show you
> proofs, so that you will have no further need of religion. I have
> accomplished all you imagine your God to do, but has never done. I have
> repeatedly resurrected the dead before your eyes. You have never seen
> anyone shot down before your eyes and heal themselves, yet I, the socialist
> leader, have done it. I am the only God you've ever seen, with blood
> gushing out of his chest, who, after the nurses put their fingers in the
> bullet holes, just wiped his hand across his chest, and closed them. Your
> God is one of the people. He is the instrument of all you've ever desired,
> all that freedom embraces, all that justice embodies, all that sensitivity
> involves. That is what your God is.
>
> I must say that it is a great effort to be God. I would lean upon another,
> but no other in the consciousness we are evolving in has the faculties that
> I possess. When they do, I will be glad to hold his coat. In the meantime, I
> shall be God, and beside me, there shall be no other. If you don't need a
> God, then fine, I'm no problem to you. But if you need a God, I'm going to
> nose out that other God, I'm going to nose out that other God, because it's
> a false God, so you can get the right concept in your mind. If you're
> holding onto that Sky God, I'll nose him out ten lengths every time.
>
> And when all this has been done, I shall go into the obscurity of the
> conscious collective principle of socialism, and I shall have no further
> intrusion into the affairs of man.

With that, he would take the Bible and fling it before him, spit on it,
and stamp on it with his feet. He would raise his bare arm to the roof of
his Temple and shout, "If there is a God in the sky, I say, FUCK YOU,"

and when he was not struck dead on the spot, this was his proof of the silliness of the Sky God and proof of their superstition. They were forever terrified that evil acts would attract a bolt of lightning from the sky, and what happened? They would work hard to perform good deeds, and the next day they might be run down by a truck. That was the problem with the "Unknown God." You did not know the rules of his game. But believe in Jim Jones, "the great motivator, duplicator, reproducer, dynamo, generator," and you would achieve protection and eventually perfection. His rules would be clear. His rewards and his punishments would make sense and be just. His doctrine would not have the contradictions and the stupidity of the Bible.

This is not the cry of the crazy man that Americans so profoundly wanted to see after the Jonestown apocalypse. It is something deeper and far more disturbing. Had this appeal been singular, like the piercing shriek of the leopard in the dense forest, that would have been one thing. To label a man as crazy is to discard him, to dismiss anything he says. But this man attracted thousands of followers and he was giving them a pretext for self-worship—the meek had become the chosen. He exercised fierce political power in San Francisco with that city's establishment eating from his hand. It is not the voice of lunacy. He was too controlled and too devious; his marriage of religiosity and politics was too perfectly worked out. He picked up too cleverly the strands of powerlessness and discarded responsibility, of guru seeking and selfishness, of atheistic liberalism in his age, to be a lunatic. His temptation of his followers to their mission and finally to their deaths sprang from the spiritual floundering of post-Vietnam America. It was, instead, the voice of the modern Anti-Christ or, more precisely, a small-time parody of the Anti-Christ.

> Didst thou forget that man prefers peace and even death to freedom of choice of good and evil? Instead of giving clear-cut rules that would have set man's conscience at rest once for all, thou didst put forward things that are unfamiliar, puzzling, and uncertain. . . . By doing so thou didst act as if thou didst not love mankind.

So said Dostoevski's Grand Inquisitor to Christ. The Anti-Christ argues that those who can cope with freedom of choice are few and, therefore, Christianity is elitist. For the masses, he can find no divine justification which would give meaning to the people's suffering in God's name. The masses look not for God, but for tangible miracles.

> Thou didst not come down [from the cross], because thou wouldst not coerce man by a miracle; thou didst crave for a free faith and not for one born of marvels; thou didst crave for willing love, not the obsequious rapture of slaves before the might that overawed them. But thou didst think too highly of men: they are only slaves, even though rebellious ones.

It is pitiless of thee to value man so highly, for thou didst require too much from him. Hadst thou respected him less thou wouldst have asked less, and that would have been more like love, to have given him a lighter load. He is weak and despicable. . . .

Thou mayest well be proud of these children, of their unconstrained love, of the glorious sacrifice that they have freely made in thy name. But remember, they were only some few thousands of them, and they were Gods—what of the rest? Are all those weak ones to blame that they could not endure what the strong endured? Is a weak soul to blame if it cannot take thy terrible gifts? Is it not true that thou didst come only to the elect and for the elect? Did we not love mankind in that we meekly admitted its weakness and wished lovingly to ease its yoke?

Of course, there was too much hatred and bitterness in Jim Jones for him to be the real Anti-Christ, for the real Anti-Christ would be only one inch shorter than the real Christ. He would come to humankind smoothly, come with a message so logical and so loving that he could destroy the faith of all men, not just a few thousand, and, if need be, lead all humankind to mass suicide, instead of just nine hundred. The real Anti-Christ would never dehumanize, brutalize, or tyrannize his following as Jones, the petty tyrant and false prophet, did, because in the end that posture could never be effective. The real Anti-Christ would be too smart for that.

And yet to Jones's following, separated from the real world in their steamy glade, their leader was the miniature Anti-Christ, and Jones-town the dominion of Christ's competitor. Their community was founded upon the three qualities for which Dostoevski's Anti-Christ said humankind thirsted: *miracle, mystery,* and *authority.* If Christ rejected "the base raptures of the slave," Jim Jones thrived upon the chorus of their idolatry, having to worry only if the chorus was sincere. If Christ wanted love and faith given freely, grounded in choice, Jones would take their devotion any way he could get it. If he could not have faith and love, he demanded at least acquiescence.

"We shall even allow them sin," the Grand Inquisitor declaimed. "They are weak and impotent, and they will love us like children, because we allow them to sin. We shall tell them that every sin will be expiated, if it is done with our permission. We allow them sin, because we love them, and the punishment for these sins we take upon ourselves." The Anti-Christ, writ large or writ small, had "corrected" Christ's work.

To the rest of us, metaphorically, Jones is the portent of what is possible, the sinister caricature anticipating the true apocalypse. To many of the post-Vietnam young, the children of the nuclear age, the expectation is that the earth in forty years will be nothing but sand and cockroaches. The nuclear weapons get more powerful; they proliferate into more hands—Israel, India, South Africa, Pakistan—and yet the bare-breasted talk about safety in armament remains as tired as ever. The leader who could create the wasteland would be so silky smooth, so loving, so reasonable, so melodious, so theatrical, that we would all line up on cue. In this sense, Jones was the real prophet, the man, as he said, born out of season. For what oddsmaker can argue that his vision of the world melting was a fraud and an impossibility?

Behind the howl of the small-time Anti-Christ from the jungle, there was this sentiment: that in the end, he eased the yoke of his weak and miserable following, who symbolically stood for the mass of human-kind. For them, the choice between good and evil was too terrible a burden. Finally, for an instant, they were not outcasts anymore, but the majority; they could live as such only on the level of the symbolic, and it was on the level of the symbolic that Jim Jones deserves to be taken seriously. (On the level of reality, he was merely one of the great political criminals of modern times.) Finally, in their last moment of life, they had achieved their heaven on earth, before they moved into nothingness.

In his last days, Jones was asked about his feelings of responsibility for all his people in the outpost who would never understand the complexity of his views. His reply was loving. Early on, he said, he had made a covenant with himself, never to let anyone down who needed him. From the beginning, people's need for him had been great. The gratitude of his people was not important to him, for the true lover loves beyond reward. "When they get through with you, they throw you aside like an orange with all the juice squeezed out." He had come to expect that. But he had always been loyal to them.

So it was an act of loyalty that he would wish to have none of his disciples alive after the holocaust to bear the terrible burden of explaining his prodigious act and his complicated view which they could never understand, much less expound. In that monumental conceit, presenting himself in the end as their condescending savior, erecting his own secular judgment hall, he was the very soul of evil.

T H R E E

Jann

[1]

IN MARCH 1977, Louis Gurvich, a silver-haired, well-tanned, dapper executive from New Orleans, flew to Pasadena for the national tournament of the American Contract Bridge League. Gurvich was the president of the league in 1977, and he enjoyed these trips to tournaments around the country, especially when they took place in the West, because that gave him a chance to see his daughter, Jann. Even though she was half a continent away, Gurvich had seen his daughter on a regular basis in the past few years. She had traveled from Berkeley to see him at several other national bridge tournaments: Vancouver and Chicago among them, and the relationship between father and daughter was deeply affectionate, if complicated. Gurvich was the head of a three-hundred-man detective and protection agency. In 1977 he had a client in Malibu, so on trips to Los Angeles he often saw his daughter there as well.

Louis Gurvich was profoundly unsettled about what was happening to Jann, who was in her middle twenties. As an ultraconservative, by his own description, he was not happy with his daughter being in Berkeley, that seat of wild politics and uncontrolled experimentation, and he had watched with considerable disquiet the changes that the Coast had produced. By temperament, Louis was an English professor. Had it not been for World War II, he would have completed a Ph.D. in Literature. But the war cut that short, and when he returned from duty overseas afterward, he joined his father's lucrative detective firm, which provided security along the docks and elsewhere in New Orleans, and he settled into the dreamy, social whirl of his town.

In the elegant turn-of-the-century stucco house in the Audubon district—which he bought with the proceeds from the sale of his $160,000 stamp collection—with its French doors and Gothic-style windows and the droopy lush vegetation that obscured from view the

Governor Claiborne mansion across the street, the patriarch impressed upon his son and daughter the importance of language and style. He wanted his son to know discipline, so he sent him off to a strict military academy in Alabama, but he could not come down hard on his daughter. She was his soft spot. Louis took great pride in Jann's blossoming beauty, and when she came home from École Classique, the proper girls' school which served the Audubon district, he often played records of Shakespeare to her to impress upon her the value of a good line, well rendered. Together, they would compare Richard Burton's and Lawrence Olivier's Hamlet. In *Hamlet*, one line particularly caught the young girl's attention, that of the guilty King Claudius:

My words fly up, my thoughts remain below:
Words without thoughts never to heaven go.

This line would later have great relevance to Jann's life, as would another Shakespearean line father and daughter would discuss, that of Wolsey after he had been dismissed by Henry VIII:

Had I but served my God with half the zeal
I served my king, he would not in mine age
Have left me naked to mine enemies.

In her early teens, Jann developed an interest in Oscar Wilde as well, and she became something of an expert. (Did she ever read Wilde's caution that the greatest of all the vices is superficiality?) She was a girl easily impressed with the refined guests who frequented the Gurvich home. Once, with an imploring look, she said to her father, "Sometimes I'm overwhelmed by people, when they talk about a subject I know nothing about."

Louis was the consummate father. "Jann, never fear that someone else knows far more about a subject than you," he counseled. "They're picking their subject, and on another occasion they might go home and say, as you're saying to me, 'I met this lovely, brilliant girl tonight who was talking so eloquently about Shakespeare and Oscar Wilde.'"

At École Classique, the social graces became important to Jann. On outings, she breezed about town in her father's Shelby convertible. With the decision approaching of whether to have a coming out, she urged her father to become more active in the Mardi Gras balls, even though as a second-generation Yugoslav he probably would never have had a shot at being King of Rex. However, even though the balls bored him, and he knew their social importance was fast dissipating as New Orleans became a bustling, industrial city in the 1960s, he became more active for her sake. In the end she decided against a formal introduction to her society, for her tastes were becoming more bohemian. At eighteen, she concluded that her nose was wrong, so she insisted that her father take her to a cosmetic surgeon. She wanted a more classic look, as she was then interested in the stage and wanted to look her best. But the doctor told her that patients often came to him requesting the very nose that Jann wanted altered.

"I can tighten your skin a little, Jann, but you'd be crazy to do it," the doctor remarked. "You're a very pretty girl, and you shouldn't change a thing."

Disappointed, Jann insisted that her father take her to another specialist, but her mother put a stop to the whim.

Jann Gurvich did well at École Classique, and she had no trouble getting into Newcomb College, the sister institution to Tulane. For a time, the Gurviches had considered a college in Switzerland for her as an alternative. She had won a gold medal for her language proficiency, the first prize in the city of New Orleans, and a fourth-place award at a state competition in Baton Rouge, so the plan was to send her to Lausanne in the French-speaking provinces. But because Lausanne had not worked out well for the daughter of a family friend, a girl of nineteen, it was decided that Jann would go to Newcomb for a few years, and perhaps go to Lausanne later as a finishing school.

At Newcomb Jann discovered men, the campus newspaper, and Vietnam. The ferment at Tulane over Vietnam had the mild, genteel veneer of Southern opposition to the war, and the debate in the Gurvich household was animated, but civilized. From his World War II experience, Louis felt that, aside from the merits of this war effort, an American should support his country if the government had committed its forces. He worried that, apart from the wisdom of the policy, the country simply would not get a good fight from an army whose presence in the war zone was challenged at home. Secretly, Louis liked these dinner-table debates, for Jann was developing the skills of language and the agility of thought he cared so much about.

When she came to him midway in her freshman year and said she wanted to transfer from Newcomb to Vassar at the end of the year, he liked that too. Her grades were good, and Vassar would be a step up not only academically, but socially. The teachers would be better, and the girls more challenging, more on Jann's level. So she went, and in 1971, on a visit to her there, it would come as a surprise and something of an amusement for Louis to see a massive campaign poster, at least one hundred feet tall, not of Richard Nixon or even George McGovern, but of Shirley Chisholm.

But the Vassar transfer turned into a mistake. Jann missed the young man with whom she had fallen in love in New Orleans. Her roommate turned out to be a lesbian. She developed a case of hypoglycemia, and her grades plummeted. In early 1972, she called her father from New York to tell him she had dropped out of college and was living with friends in Greenwich Village. He was not to worry. She could return to Vassar in the fall if she wanted to, but she needed a breather. She had secured a job translating French, she told him, but weeks later she admitted to her father that she was waitressing. Louis was horrified.

"You must be out of your mind, Jann," he fumed, long-distance. "What the hell is going on here?"

"Look, Dad, I like it. I want to stay a little while. I don't want to cost you money."

"Jann, you know money is no problem for me. Now, knock this off."

"Let me work a little while longer," she pleaded. "I'm enjoying it. I'm learning a lot."

"Yeah, you're learning that the restaurant owner's going to try to hustle you . . . and the guys. . . . Now, just cut it out."

She promised she would be home in a few months. Before she appeared again in New Orleans, she called again to announce her desire to attend Berkeley, to flee to the San Francisco of S. I. Hayakawa and the Berkeley that Ronald Reagan had invaded with his troops, and Louis was again in a state of high agitation. But he told himself that he always wanted his daughter to be able to handle herself adeptly at any level of conversation, and while Vassar might be better socially than Berkeley, Berkeley was better academically.

"Jann, how do you expect to get into Berkeley with your Vassar grades?"

"Truthfully?"

"Of course."

"I'm going to give them only my Newcomb grades."

"How long can you get away with that?"

"In the red tape of the college offices, forever."

She was right, of course. In the fall of 1972, she was admitted to the University of California. Little known to Louis, the Berkeley where Jann would spend the next three years had taken on a new face from the days of its notoriety. Curbside vendors of leather and homemade jewelry and tie-dyed T-shirts had taken over from the angry orators. Students roller-skated joyfully in tandem, rather than stand hotly in crowds before speakers. The causes for which their political passion could reach a fever pitch were causes such as the plight of whales and trees, rather than people. The jar next to the cash register at the Telegraph Avenue coffee shop, where the cappuccino was just as good as in the 1960s, read "Cynicism Relief Fund" rather than "Tips," and the discussions about graduate school at the tables now related to the best MBA programs in the country. As if to make her father proud of her, and probably to bait him a little as well, Jann took up California residency, so as not to cost him as much money. It became a standard refrain. Once, when Louis was in Malibu, she hitchhiked down from Berkeley with a friend, again stressing the money she was saving him. Characteristically, Louis rose to the bait.

"Don't give me that crap about money," he seethed. "You know money is no problem with me. You cost me ten times the amount of the plane ticket in anxiety, and I'm despairing about your ability to take care of yourself."

But, more disturbing to Louis, Jann began not to care about her appearance. Her normal dress came to be sweat shirts and tattered jeans. She had begun to smoke marijuana regularly, and in the summer of 1973 she dramatically ended the lingering thought that she would ever return to Vassar, when, on an acid trip, she "symbolically" flung her Vassar ring into the Pacific. Often, especially to her father, she began to talk about the chasm between the rich and the poor.

"Is it necessary," Louis asked her, "to live like the poor just because you support their cause? You don't have to be dirty to be concerned about the poor, you know."

"I'm not dirty," she replied indignantly. "I bathe every day."

"It's not that. It's the look of unkemptness. You don't have to have holes in your jeans."

Whenever he saw her, Louis insisted that she go to the beauty parlor and, giving up on dresses, dragged her reluctantly to the local jeans shop. Still, while he saw his daughter's sloppiness as a waste of a beautiful girl, Louis perceived an honest search. Jann's sense of adventure and of romance was strong, and she possessed no fear whatever. But she also had no perseverance at anything she undertook. There was a frantic helter-skelter quality to her interests, but she embraced every new caprice with tremendous joy and spirit. Soon she was into vegetarianism, drinking only herbal teas, swallowing fistfuls of vitamins at the same time she was consuming mountains of junk food. Occasionally she rubbed tea bags and seaweed on her face, supposedly to improve her complexion, and she started brushing her teeth with an orthodontically approved charcoal powder that was big in the natural food store. When she smiled black for them, her roommates thought she was brushing with mud, but she assured them that it was all totally natural. Among her friends, she became known as a delightful nut.

By the fall of 1974, she was into Zen Buddhism, spending hours meticulously studying Sanskrit. The world was a vast cornucopia of ideas, tastes, and experiences. "I had run into the burgeoning West Coast triangle of worshiping the Upanishads, being a hippie, dropping L.S.D.," she wrote about this period. "I ran off with a Canadian hippie who was talking about love and living in weird places. We ultimately settled on a pile-driving barge in Sausalito, built in the shape of a woman—it was called 'The Madonna.' In three weeks we hitched from Berkeley to Toronto and Quebec to New Orleans, just spending enough time to see my parents where I had shown up a year earlier. Interestingly enough, at this stage you could look at the languages I was studying and figure out what I was doing. I had really gotten excited by the Upanishads and started studying Hindi and Sanskrit. Later I was to get enthralled with Maoism and study Mandarin for a year and a half."

One night the phone rang in New Orleans, and Jann asked for money from Louis for a trip to northern India, where she planned to hitchhike with a girl friend. At first, Louis tried persuasion.

"What do you propose to do, wandering through India?" he asked.

"I'm sort of curious about the yogas and their philosophical origins," she replied.

"Jann, here I've sent you to school, and you should have some common sense. At Newcomb you asked me who Leon Trotsky was, and I felt like getting my money back for your education. Now, it's India. They're starving to death over there, and they'll cut your throat before you get fifty miles. What the hell are you looking for?" There was silence on the other end. "Besides," Louis said as an afterthought, "Paramahamsa Yogananda is dead!"

"What?"

"Yes, Paramahamsa Yogananda is *dead.*"

"Well, daddy, you're a little more with it than I thought. . . . But his school is still going."

"Jann, I'll be frank with you. If you go to India with a girl, I'll personally come over and haul you back to the United States. But rather than threaten you, please listen to reason. Please talk to people and ask them what chance would two girls have hitching in India." It was the first, though not the last, time that Louis Gurvich would think about having to kidnap his daughter in a foreign country.

Then, just as abruptly as she had taken up Indian studies, she dropped them. In her customarily theatrical way, she wanted to put an end to that period of her life. Just as earlier she had thrown her Vassar ring into the Pacific, one day she carried bundles and bundles of her meticulously drawn Sanskrit exercises and dropped them ceremoniously into a garbage can. Paralegal work had now caught her fancy, and she began to focus on her own society. The plight of the oppressed and the imprisoned moved her deeply. In her emotional commitment there was a particle of Southern guilt. In her memory of her childhood, she perceived the poison of racism and wondered if she had not partaken of it. "I learned that not all whites join the KKK. The higher their social caste, the less likely they are to be vigilante, cross-burning types. They practice their racism in a much more insidious fashion." She worried that "petty racist thoughts" sometimes popped into her head, and she ascribed the reason to the segregationist context of New Orleans. She began to be ashamed of her whiteness, of her wealthy and genteel roots, and eventually, under Jones's influence, even of her intelligence. She was hurt by the hostility that black and Mexican inmates showed her when she went to interview them as a volunteer for the public defender's office, as if only by living their color, and their torment, could she truly understand. "The fact is that I'm out and the defendant is in—that I'm free to leave when the interview is over, while the defendant is ordered back to his/her cell," she wrote. "To them, I represent the law, the system that brought them to jail. I try to convey a sense that I understand the economic or socio-political contingencies of their case. But hostility hurts. I was really hurt the other day when a woman in custody refused to be interviewed by me. Frankly, I'm still unsure as to how to go about letting someone know that I will do my best to get his case together, that I care, that I will not disappear and stop working on the case when I leave the interviewing room."

Jann Gurvich met Jim Jones in the fall of 1974, when she was studying Hindi and planning to go to India. She remembered it well. "I remember distinctly that I was in search of a teacher—*The Teacher* —and from all I'd read I expected to find him in India. Instead, I found Jim Jones at a school called Benjamin Franklin. Coming from the South, I had never seen blacks and whites doing anything harmoniously together. But here there was no racial animosity—instead there was unswerving loyalty to the principles of love, of harmony between the races, and of commitment to change. I cannot say, though, that I wholeheartedly embraced the Temple when I came. Jim taught about world-wide suffering and of the possibility of change, but the Temple at that time was not able to show itself for what it really was without losing its religious following. For two years I went to the Temple, but I was not really with it. I had this Che Guevara image of change, and I did not understand the importance of the church as an institution for fomenting change in the black community. I would spend my time checking out the Communist Party, going to Panther gatherings, and generally window-shopping the Bay area leftist movements."

In the months of late 1974 and early 1975, as Jann moved away from Zen Buddhism and window-shopped leftist movements in search of her Teacher, she began to think about law school. By that time, she had been to the People's Temple enough to get members to write letters of recommendation. Among her supporters was Timothy O. Stoen, then assistant district attorney in Mendocino County, and Jim Jones's number-one aide. Describing Jann as "brilliant," Stoen wrote of her fine grasp of the English language, as well as her conscientiousness and industriousness. In August 1975, she graduated from Berkeley with honors in English Literature and was nominated by the Dean of Letters for the National Women's Honor Society for demonstrated leadership ability.

In the fall of 1975 she entered Golden State University School of Law—a school with a progressive image, but not progressive enough for Jann Gurvich. On her first day in her property course, the professor began unsuspectingly with his stock question: "What is property?" Jann raised her hand.

"Property is *theft!*" she exclaimed, quoting Pierre Joseph Proudhon.

The comment revealed a degree of confidence in her beliefs now, as well as her spunk, but it did not start her law school career on an auspicious note. It alienated her instantly from many of her classmates, who were more in the 1970s mold of students scrambling for a secure place in the American scheme, in statu quo. In the months ahead, she alienated many still further by the company she kept. She socialized constantly with blacks, usually those who were particularly dark-skinned and hip, and she had taken to wearing bright-colored dashikis and fixing her hair in a halfhearted Afro. Behind her back, many wondered why such a sharp, assertive, attractive girl was hanging around with such jerky guys, the con artists and jailbirds about town, but Jann ignored this talk when she got the drift of it. Fellow students knew of her prosperous New Orleans background and never took her constant talk about being broke seriously. They found her behavior, acting as if she were a poor black, annoying. It was as if she did not know who she was. Still, no one doubted the sincerity of her deeply held beliefs.

Of her classes in law school, only criminal law seemed to hold her interest. She began to attend class less and less, and got behind more and more. Other demands were being made on her time. She was taking bus trips to Los Angeles every weekend to attend Temple services. She was going to San Francisco Housing Authority meetings to observe her Teacher in action. Jones's ability to organize large numbers around an issue particularly impressed her. She bubbled about the Temple's support of the poverty-stricken tenants of the International Hotel when the city threatened to evict them. She loved it when Jones organized a protest in Fresno, California, where four newsmen, dubbed by Jones the "Fresno Four," were jailed for refusing to reveal their sources in a criminal case. At his Fresno rally, with over a thousand followers, Jim Jones, looking very upstanding in a cream-colored leisure suit, carried a sign bearing a quotation from Thomas Jefferson: "If it were for me to choose between the government without the press or the press without government, I should not hesitate to choose the latter." He would not feel so sentimental a year later when he became the target of the press. Still, Jones's triumphs in California were hardly revolutionary—rather an expression of mainstream liberalism.

In her deepening involvement with the People's Temple, and with political causes, Jann Gurvich never lost her poetic sensibility. But the passages that caught her eye in literature were shifting. She seemed to get more distant from her society, as if she was looking in from the outside—just as she was getting more involved with it. The themes of society's demise and of falsehood gnawed at her. During this period she read Shelley's "Ode to Naples," and chose to squirrel away these lines about the dead city.

> I stood within the City disinterred;
> And heard the autumnal leaves like light footfalls
> Of spirits passing through the streets; and heard
> The Mountains slumberous voice at intervals
> Thrill through those ruthless halls.

Her friends ribbed her about Jones's healing powers, but instead of defending the healings, she shrugged them off, saying simply that she was not in the organization for them but for the social message. Alone in her room, she was reading *Troilus and Cressida*, and at least, in the lines of Cressida, the archetypal false woman, that she chose to note down, she seemed to have an element of doubt about her course. She would certainly have appreciated the irony of the character's words. Did she identify with Cressida?

> If I be false, or swerve a hair from truth,
> When time is old and hath forgot itself,
> When waterdrops have worn the stones of Troy,
> And blind oblivion swallow'd cities up,
> And mighty states characterless are grated
> To dusty nothing; yet let memory
> From false to false, among false maids in love,
> Upbraid my falsehood!

In the development of her political view of the world, the trial of the San Quentin Six in March–April 1976 had the most profound impact on her. Mary Sundance, the daughter-in-law of the old Vietnam dissident David Dellinger, had urged her to attend. She passed through the layers of security in the Marin County Court House, the frisks, the metal detectors, the picture-taking devices, the locked courtroom door, the admonitions from the heavy deputies not to talk to the defendants. For the first time, Jann felt truly close to revolution, and it thrilled her.

"When I walked into the courtroom one of the first things that happened was Johnny Spain turning around and looking at me. Finally, he said, 'What's your name?' and I didn't know what to do, since this huge Plexiglas partition separated defendants from spectators and supporters, and I knew I wasn't supposed to speak through it. He sent me a note through Charles Garry [the attorney for the Six and, six months later, for the People's Temple] and we began a correspondence on tiny slips of paper that Charles would take from Johnny to me and then from me to Johnny during recess."

In due course, she was approved on Spain's visiting list, one of the many attractive women so approved—Johnny's harem, as some called it. Many suspected that Charles Garry encouraged the visits to Spain to keep his confidence up during his long ordeal. The excitement for Jann of visiting "a hated and feared Black revolutionary author," as she called him, whom the prison was doing its "utmost to destroy psychologically as well as physically," was evident. Here, incarnate in this bristlingly handsome, defiant figure were the elements for which she had come to yearn: revolutionary fervor, black vibrancy, literary consciousness, a victim of oppression, manacled and separated beyond her reach. After one visit, she wrote:

"When you love someone, you want to touch him. I have never been able to touch Johnny Larry Spain. When I visit him in San Quentin, his arms are chained to his waist and his legs are chained together. We see each other through an uncleaned Plexiglas partition that reaches from wall to wall and ceiling to floor. We are locked in a tiny room divided by this partition. But we are not alone. On his side a guard watches us. There is an unseen electrical device that monitors our conversation, and the real conspiracy to deny the humanity of those who 'live' in San Quentin, goes on."

For two months she observed the trial. At Golden Gate Law School, eschewing schoolwork, she threw herself into organizing a forum of speakers on the San Quentin Six, which, predictably, included a reading of Johnny Spain's poetry. She was irrepressibly amusing and uplifting to be around, an "intensely sexual and vital womanchild," as one fellow organizer called her, but she couldn't be relied upon to undertake the slogging drudgery that makes an effective organizer. Her grades were falling, but her forum was a great success, except for the publicity on it, which had been her responsibility. More ideas sparked from her about how to help. They were always flashy and dramatic. To Charles Garry, she offered to drive all the way to Mississippi to bring Johnny Spain's mother to the trial, a proposal which instantly gained her the reputation within the defense team for having poor judgment.

In the trial nevertheless, she saw the vision of America. She perceived the judges as partisan for conviction, helping the district attorney whenever he needed help, before a predominantly white jury, preventing the "real story of the conspiracy" against the defendants from being told, and, in the end, she was horrified by the conviction of the defendants, including her revolutionary poet. To her, it was a display of "the reality and the utter failure of the American justice system."

"The trial of the Six would ultimately convince me of one thing," she wrote, "that Jim Jones and the People's Temple provide the most effective movement for change in the U.S. and certainly the only viable alternative I could go with. I was to see that 'justice,' even with the best lawyer, was no justice at all." Still, she hung on for a while to the notion that radical lawyering was important. In the summer of 1976, she went to work in the Los Angeles office of Leonard Weinglass, who was then representing Emily Harris against the charge of kidnapping Patty Hearst. With her penchant for hero worship, Jann seems to have had a crush on Weinglass as well. Before she went to Los Angeles, Weinglass asked about her as a law intern and was told that she would keep his office in high spirits but not to count on her to get his briefs written. Before she went, however, she dutifully wrote to Jim Jones asking his permission to work with Weinglass. Jones reluctantly gave it. He seemed not to have approved of Jann's connection with these true activists of the Left. He had particularly criticized her in open meetings for her infatuation with Johnny Spain.

"Can't you see," he challenged, "that he's just using you to get what he wants?"

Given her preoccupation with the San Quentin Six, the weekend trips to services in Los Angeles, and the addition of all-night security vigilance at the Temple after a supposed, but unconfirmed, assassination attempt on Jim Jones, the inevitable happened: she flunked her first year of law school and was forced to repeat it. To make matters worse, her health began to deteriorate rapidly. Her habit of trying to compensate for all the junk food she ate with kelp and seaweed and fistfuls of vitamins had finally caught up with her. By midsemester, she was having medical problems throughout her tortured system: teeth, eyes, kidney, thyroid, and skin. For none of these conditions would she go to a doctor, for she insisted that under no circumstances would she accept "special privileges." Under the influence of Jim Jones, she had to atone for her sin of being born into a wealthy family—*her* sin in particular because she was probably the "best born" of any in the organization. How, then, could she spend money on good food when so many in the world were starving? If people only knew that at Vassar in a month she had spent as much money on cosmetics as a poor family spends altogether! Think of the doctors the oppressed have in America. How could she continue in law school when so many others did not have the chance?

At Christmastime 1976, Jann returned home to New Orleans for the last time. She had never told her family about her involvement with the San Quentin Six. She knew that knowledge would have brought her father to Berkeley in a hurry. Nor had she mentioned her work with Charles Garry or Leonard Weinglass. She always mentioned the names of their less notorious partners to her father. But Christmas was a time for forgiveness, not politics. For once, she took care of her appearance, fixing her hair nicely and donning a fancy dress her mother had sent her, one which had lain crumpled in the floor of her closet for months. Her roommate could remember only one other time when she had dressed up. It had been when vice-presidential candidate Walter Mondale was to meet with Jim Jones. That occasion was one of the few times that Jann was admitted to the inner circle of Temple leadership, for she was not considered disciplined enough for leadership. Late that night, she came back to Berkeley effervescent about the talk between Mondale and Jones. To her roommate she reported that Mondale had asked what Jones wanted in exchange for delivering the considerable votes of his constituency for the Carter-Mondale ticket. "The ambassadorship of Guyana," Jones had replied. "You got it," Mondale said (according to Jann), but later things got a trifle too complicated. (Mondale subsequently wrote me that he had only met Jones in a receiving line at the San Francisco airport and did not "recall any offer of support or any request of favors from Jones.")

The Christmas visit in 1976 was joyful. Through all she experienced in the previous years, including distancing her family from her unorthodox California life, with all the small deceptions that had involved, Jann's love for her family never cracked. Not that Jim Jones had not tried. Before this last New Orleans visit, Jones's "spirit" had divined that Louis Gurvich was a CIA agent. But the news from heaven had not affected Jann's attitude toward her family. She had simply made a clear distinction between love and symbol. She was able to blank out the lies or practices of the Temple of which she did not approve, as if she just blinked her eyes and had not seen or heard them. She loved her father but hated what he represented now, just as she never liked Jim Jones personally, while she loved what he stood for.

At Christmas there were no confrontations, but three months later, when Louis was in Pasadena for a national tournament of the American Contract Bridge League, things were different. For the three-day visit, she arrived in her familiar jeans and sweat shirt, and had with her a Salvadoran boyfriend named Franco. By this time, Louis had gotten wind of the organization called the People's Temple, for unsettling stories had begun to appear in the California press, and he confronted her with it. Her speech, he noted, was more terse and more vulgar.

"I'm not into that shit," Jann said curtly.

"Damn it, Jann, don't be dirty and don't ruin your vocabulary," Louis, the instinctive English professor, replied.

"Daddy, you're still so old-fashioned. But, really, I'm not heavily into it. Don't be worried."

"I think you're more involved than you're admitting."

"Really I'm not that hooked."

To Louis, organizations like the People's Temple, with an 80 percent black membership (which Jann reduced for her father to 60 percent) attracted the outcasts of California: the "cuckoos" from the hills and the blacks from the ghettos. Association with such extremists could hardly be beneficial to her at this stage of her career, Louis felt.

"The People's Temple is *not* an organization of misfits," Jann insisted.

"There are no outcasts in the Temple?"

"Yes, there are some, but I don't want to associate with them."

"What about the violent ones?"

"There aren't many of them. There are some, but I don't have anything to do with them."

"But the majority of your associates are not socially or intellectually up to you, Jann. In all organizations like this, the freak element gets involved because they can't go anywhere else. Invariably, the extremists take over and lead the movement down the drain."

"Listen, daddy, let me get one thing straight with you. Last week Jerry Brown made a speech at the People's Temple with his arm around Jim Jones. On the bulletin board there's a letter from Rosalynn Carter and a letter from one of *your* boys, Senator Jackson. The former mayor, Alioto, has been there, as well as the present mayor, Moscone. Now, *that's* establishment. Tell me what you want. I agree that there are some freaky people involved, whom I'd rather not be with, but that's true of any organization. But we're not disassociated from the establishment."

Louis threw his hands up in exasperation. He was getting nowhere.

"Jann," he said finally, "where did it happen? Where did your society rebuff you? Where did our family fail?"

[2]

The exodus of Jones and his pilgrims from the society whose rules they could not abide had been planned for two years before it actually took place all at once in August 1977. But his vision of a symbolic leave-taking with a kind of rats-leaving-a-sinking-ship flavor, was spawned as early as 1973, when during the Watergate period Jones saw the country moving irreversibly to the right. Indeed, when he shifted the Temple's main activities to San Francisco in 1975, from Redwood

Valley in the north, he considered the Bay Area as merely a staging spot
for the move to Guyana. In San Francisco, the logistics of the exodus
were more easily handled, and while methodical planning for departure proceded, a big push for membership went forward, so that the
final move would have the political impact that Jones envisaged.
Besides, the leader could not control his exploding membership when
it was so large, and when his influence had to contend with the
temptations of the street, drugs in particular. Only when he controlled
the environment totally, when there was no other "reality" to compete
with but *his* reality, could his reeducation program be completely
successful. As early as March 1977, months before he came under real
attack in the press for his practices, he indicated to a New York
audience that he and his whole community would soon be taking off
from America to a place which he coyly refused to identify.

When an article in *New West* magazine got into the works in the
spring of 1977 and it became clear that the writers were focusing on the
charges of Temple "defectors," the plan for an organized egression over
a two-year period suddenly got compressed into six weeks. During
February and March, Jim Jones made several trips to Guyana, and in
July he left the United States permanently. He left the planning of the
secret exodus in the hands of the indefatigable Sharon Amos. She
proceeded on the heroic premise that if the public knew they were
leaving, the emigration would be halted—a unique idea in American
history which turned the Statue of Liberty on her head. In intelligence
terminology, the exodus became a "black operation," with Temple
buses leaving for Miami in the dead of night. It was as if they were off
to burrow underneath the Berlin Wall, except in reverse. No one knew
exactly when they would leave, until Amos whispered the word. It was
all very hush-hush, for, as one devotee would tell me later, the Temple
operated on a "need-to-know basis." Still, to move seven hundred
people in six weeks, all with proper documentation and shots and
tickets, was a considerable undertaking, and its accomplishment, even
chased as they were by the furies of conspiracy, was another example
of the Temple's remarkable organizational acumen.

After Jones left the country in July, Jann Gurvich's passion for the
movement seemed to slacken for a month or two, but in mid-August
she got her orders along with the rest, and without phoning New
Orleans she left the country on August 21. A year after the San
Quentin Six trial, she went to Jonestown with one guiding thought
which she wrote in a document that later came into her father's
possession: "That there should be a place where no murderous
executions of leftists take place. That there should be a society where
people live free of oppression and exploitation. Let there be no more
executions or political frame-ups. Jim Jones is building that society,
and there is victory in that fact alone."

In the basement of the Charles Garry firm in San Francisco, I was later to find her passport picture, taken at this moment in her life. It appeared on a contact sheet, set amid the photographs of five middle-aged, proud and plump black women, all dressed in their finest, with wigs and purses and rings on their fingers. To them, having their picture taken for a U.S. passport was a major event. On the back of the sheet only Jann's name was written to identify her, as if the others were without identity. Often in the months of my concentration on Jonestown, I have gazed upon that photograph. It was a study in dishevelment. Her frizzy hair was untouched; her jeans patched; the white blouse with rolled-up sleeves and the bottom button sloppily undone was too big for her, as if it had been donated by a larger person or had come from the dime store. Yet, with judicious cropping and a little something done to her hair, it was just as easy, perhaps easier, to imagine her in the Court of the King of Rex, rather than in the court of the Jonestown Potentate. Gracing the oval face and cameo skin, her pale-blue Serbian eyes were her best feature. The frozen stillness of the photograph suggested a Noh mask, and I saw her at the last moment performing a stylized ritual in a slow-motion drama, miming silently close to the main character, occasionally uttering spare lines that referred to herself in the third person. The set of her mouth was not generous, hinting irritation, even haughtiness. The occasion was something she was tolerating, as if she wished the photographer would hurry up, so she could rush off to do fifteen other things she had on her mind. Still, in her face and her demeanor I saw a hundred students who had passed by me in my occasional teaching in the last nine years. Had she walked into my class on the first day of a semester, before she had uttered her first word, I would have been glad for her presence. For her look projected a defiance that would let any teacher, much less The Teacher, know that she was there for a purpose beyond grades and future security, and if that purpose was not fulfilled she would not be around for long. It is a posture that I have come to treasure—the sensitivity to it has made me a better teacher—precisely because it has become so rare. Yet if Jonestown was genuinely felt as a tragedy by anyone in America, it was the college generation. Perhaps they did not verbalize or seek to define the nature of their sorrow in the wake of the Event, but their mourning was evident as they moped about the campus, newspapers tucked under their arms. Their identification was clear. As the generation that felt rather than intellectualized, they felt their own susceptibility to the Joneses of their decade. Jonestown was their Kent State.

----◄ ►----

Some days later, Louis Gurvich called Berkeley. He was anxious to have a tender conversation with Jann because their last talk had accentuated the matters that divided them. Before their last conversation, Louis had received a letter, written in red ink, warning him that Jann was heavily involved with Jones. "You don't know how dangerous this organization is," the scrawl read, and the envelope contained a copy of the *New West* article. When Louis challenged her with the letter, Jann's protestations of innocence turned to sharp and angry denials, and once again Louis was at a loss to know what to do. She was, after all, about to have her twenty-fourth birthday. Like many other parents of Temple members, Louis had finally concluded that he could do little to change her connection. He could only express his undying devotion to her.

Now, on the line in Berkeley, a Chilean roommate stammered about Jann's whereabouts and finally admitted that she had left the country. At long last, this shock jolted Louis into the realization that he needed to start thinking like the detective he was. That she should secretly leave for the jungle of South America, where she would be totally under the spell of this dubious evangelist, called for serious thinking and action. For the first time in his life, Louis began to think that he had been too soft on her, that he must bear some of the responsibility for this.

As a matter of principle, he had never used his investigative capabilities to find out about his daughter behind her back, even during his highest state of anxiety about her Berkeley life. But now he realized that she could be in physical danger. His first action was to call the American Embassy in Guyana. He spoke at great length with Richard McCoy, the U.S. Consul in Georgetown, about the Temple's Jonestown experiment and about the press reports on the organization's practices. Not wanting to fuel rumors for which he had no confirmation, McCoy was dutifully diplomatic, stating that the Embassy had no hard evidence of atrocity, and while it would continue to watch the situation, it could do nothing until there was a proven infraction of either American or Guyanese law, if then. Louis asked if there was a fence around Jonestown, not perceiving yet that the eighty-foot forest at the perimeter was the greatest fence of all time. He was relieved to hear there was nothing of the barbed wire or chain-link variety. McCoy's mention of the First Amendment's protection of religious freedom and of the Privacy Act was veiled, and he did not convey the extent of the restraint which the law placed on him. In this first contact with American authorities, the first of a number which together make a sorry record of inaction and insensitivity, Louis was not too disappointed. He was a man who respected professionalism, and while he assumed that a U.S. consul based in an insignificant little country like Guyana was not likely to be the brightest star in the constellation, he was prepared to give the government a chance. After he hung up the phone, he wrote a letter to Cyrus Vance commending

McCoy's responsiveness, thereby hoping that the letter's aura would make McCoy still more responsive to him in the future.

But the U.S. Consul had made enough of the constraint on official options that Louis began to think about his own executive action. He was aware, of course, of that contingent of his own business that sprang from the queer phenomenon of American cults in the 1970s: those swashbuckling detectives, only a few of whom were legitimate, commissioned to kidnap the children of the wealthy from organizations like the Unification Church and to "deprogram" them forcibly and against their will on the spot. Indeed, Louis himself had, upon occasion, located friends' children lost in the mire of some dubious spiritual quest or another. But never had there been quite so formidable a target for a private police action as a remote encampment in a South American jungle. Still, Louis had considerable experience in commando operations in jungle settings. During World War II, as a weapons expert, he had fought in Italy and had been in North Africa, Liberia, and Brazil. Later he would operate in the Indonesian jungle. If ever there was a parent with the background, the wherewithal, and the passion to rescue his daughter from Jonestown, this was the man.

Through the fall of 1977 he investigated what was involved. There were, he concluded, three options, none very attractive: (1) to bribe Guyanese officials and employ Guyanese mercenaries to conduct the operation; (2) to launch his own operation from Georgetown; and (3) to launch an operation through eastern Venezuela across the border the thirteen miles to Jonestown. The first option was instantly rejected as too costly and too public; the second, too susceptible of being blown by Jones's influence on the local constabulary. The third option, staggering as it was to Louis in its danger, cost, and risk of violence, contained the vital element of surprise, and he began to focus on it. He paid a visit to the Venezuelan Consul in New Orleans, and there he studied the maps of eastern Venezuela and *Venezuela Esperia*, holding a discussion with a minor diplomat who knew the terrain. He also spoke at length and often with a Vietnam veteran, a Louisianan living in the San Francisco Bay Area who had known Jann and who promptly volunteered for the raid. The old Vietnam hand offered to recruit ex-green berets and black berets (the Navy counterpart) in California, an idea Louis found unwise, since those types might be too quick on the trigger. He wanted no strong-arm tactics used if they could be avoided, for he knew that he would diminish in the eyes of his daughter if they were employed. In the search for his raid commander, he spoke even more frequently with a professional soldier in Texas, a colonel, who had trained the bodyguard for the Shah of Iran and was a close personal friend who knew and loved Jann, and therefore, was eager to volunteer. From another friend in aviation he received an estimate on the charter cost of a twenty-passenger airplane and a helicopter. In all his research, from the cost of equipment to the payroll for his soldiers of fortune, Louis guessed the bill would be at least $100,000.

With all this planning, one nightmare gnawed at him. What if Jann didn't want to leave? She was no Jesus freak. This was not the classic deprogramming situation. How did one deprogram a person who believed so strongly in racial equality and justice and freedom for all? What if this operation were undertaken, with its cost and danger of people being hurt, only to find that Jann would turn around and slip back into Jonestown at the first opportunity?

In due course, Louis's pressure on the U.S. Embassy engendered a limited response from Jonestown. Several letters arrived from Jann in the fall. They were stiff and squeezed of the spontaneous richness that had always marked Jann's writing. Her notes to her mother were childlike, written as if she were a girl of thirteen at a summer jamboree. To her father, she gushed about her Guyanese paradise and asked for items that would make it even more idyllic—like an electric typewriter and a cassette tape of Tchaikovsky's Sixth Symphony (actually anything of Tchaikovsky's except the "Nutcracker," which she found too "racy").

On January 11, 1978, Louis received a telegram from the U.S. Embassy in Guyana, reporting that the consular officer, Richard McCoy, had met with Jann for several minutes and that she appeared well and happy and enthusiastic about her teaching duties. She would soon be in contact with him by radio phone, the message said. McCoy's visit to Jonestown was his second; the first took place four months earlier, and shortly after his January visit he transmitted a cable to the Department of State, embodying his impressions from the two visits. He found it improbable that Temple members were being held against their will for he had not sensed from his conversations that any were fearful or under duress. He found them adequately fed, satisfied with their lives, and spontaneous in their responses to his questions. The diplomat was "alert" to the possibility that a favorable scenario had been staged for his visit, but did not believe such a thing could have been managed, given the conditions of the community. The categorical clean bill of health to the department did not quite express McCoy's lingering suspicions about Jonestown, however. He had noticed that Jim Jones appeared disconcerted when the Consul talked with Temple members unexpectedly, but, nevertheless, McCoy did not think the answers were rehearsed. Later, in the aftermath, an official State Department report recommended that U.S. consular officers receive training in the techniques of psychological coercion and mind control. (Had Americans in the 1970s become so susceptible to mind control the world over that such a policy was required?) But if

Richard McCoy had been the Viennese doctor himself, it is hard to know what he would have done with the detection of brainwashing. In diplomatic priorities, the constraints on official options, given the First Amendment and the Privacy Act, demanded the utmost caution, and in the entire Jonestown affair the officialdom was the very soul of caution, if not timidity. Mandated inaction, after all, is easier than action in the bureaucratic scheme. This posture would naturally lead a Louis Gurvich to consider taking the matter into his own hands.

Whether or not Jann viewed Jonestown as the symbolic victory against the oppression, exploitation, and racism of the world until the end of her life is impossible to determine. Whether this fine mind and searching, poetic soul and exuberant womanchild underwent a profound change in the isolation of the jungle is hard to say. In Jonestown, at least toward the end, the intelligent operated on the level of secrecy and self-delusion, as they do in any totalitarian situation. The important question is whether, to herself, she became a dissenter, looking for a way either to change the place or to escape it . . . or whether she ceased to be honest with herself, a false Cressida whose initial critical blink led her to close her eyes completely to atrocity toward the end.

Without doubt, Jones used her as a foil. She was the epitome of the wealthy haves in the world—the elitist whose father, unlike anyone else's, was somebody important—and so she could never cease trying to disavow her roots. In a widely distributed narrative by the satrap, Sharon Amos, called "My Experience in Jonestown," Amos mentioned Jann early on in the paper: "I was pleasantly surprised by the changes in many people that I had known. Some of these people I thought would have had great difficulty in adjusting to the so-called simple life of Jonestown. Jann Gurvich was one. She, as many of you know, was an elitist person who had studied law in the United States, and she had fantasies of herself as being a revolutionary in the most romanticized sense. She lived vicariously through other revolutionaries like Johnny Spain, of the San Quentin Six, and in no way had made peace with being a proletarian worker. She was extremely positive about her experiences since she came to Jonestown. Initially, for several weeks, she worked all day in the fields and said that for the first time in her life she had the opportunity to know first-hand what it was to be a worker doing something useful, feeling cooperatively involved in putting food on the table of people."

But soon enough, the management realized she might be better used elsewhere than in the fields, and she was made a teacher of English and history on the high school level, and, later, socialism to both teenagers and adults. She became popular as the teacher everyone wanted, and the adults in particular liked the way she simplified socialism, never talking over their heads. Until the end, she continued to put in her hours in the fields, finding no doubt in the Tolstoy she was reading in the fall of 1978 further confirmation of the virtue of manual labor for the intellectual. At nighttime she took over the excess legal work that the other two lawyers in Jonestown could not handle. Despite the special burden of privilege she bore, she gained a reputation as a hard worker, dedicated to the success of the experiment, and one who understood far better than most what socialism really meant. In her enjoyment of children, she realized that she had missed her real calling by wasting her time in law school.

Home for her was the back row of the pastel-colored cottages in Cabin 48 which she shared with a sixty-two-year-old retired college teacher from Connecticut named Edith Roller. The back row was reserved for the female leaders of the community, including several of Jones's sexual playmates, like Karen Layton, who lived in somewhat better circumstances than others. But Jann's presence there was to enhance her prestige as a teacher rather than to mark her as a leader. She was too outspoken and inquisitive for that—"nosey" some called it—and to be inquisitive in Jonestown was not to be trusted. Within view of her cabin was the ingenious, home-fashioned windmill—two oil cans set in reverse to one another to catch cupfuls of the tropical breeze, placed atop a three-tiered tower. Endlessly, the inhabitants of Jonestown were instructed to call the guard tower a pagoda. On the shiny tin of the windmill was painted a languorous brown smile-face with large sensuous eyes and thick lips, spreading black, yellow, and red rays in a sunburst design. It seemed to suggest, at least in the wake of the Deed, the sunbaked vigilance and arbitrary violence of Graham Greene's Tonton Macoute.

In the fifteen months that Jann spent in Jonestown, there is much that must have jolted her. If she ever had the inclination to escape, her best chance came in May 1978, when Temple member Deborah Blakey slipped away through the auspices of the American Embassy. One of the minor aspects of that crisis for Jones was how to replace Blakey, and Jann was recommended for Georgetown duty. She was brilliant. She had the law training, and with her spirited personality she could undoubtedly handle the public relations side as well. But Maria Katsaris, Jones's first assistant and first mistress at the time, blocked the appointment, probably from jealousy and distrust.

One morning in early July 1978 in New Orleans, Louis Gurvich woke up in the night with a wave of anxiety about his daughter. The situation had been drifting along for many months now, with no word from Jann about when she might come home to resume her schooling. In their telephone conversation in the winter, she had promised him that she was in Guyana only for a breather. The "breather," as far as he was concerned, was over. At his office that morning, Louis dictated a letter to his secretary. He had never been so formal before. The letter blended paternal concern with anxiety, and it showed how much in the dark Louis still was. Given Jann's fate, it was also prophetic. He asked her whether she planned to finish law school and, if so, urged her to return for the fall semester. Whom was she teaching in Guyana? Whites, blacks, Guyanese? Was she afraid to teach at a higher level in another society?

> Is it your intention at this time to leave Guyana and if so when? None of us live forever, and I must confess, I am wondering when and if any of us shall ever see you. . . . I do not attempt to belittle what you're doing. I simply feel that you're settling for an aspect of education not commensurate with what you might do. None of us stay young forever and Fate often slips in, in both fortunate and unfortunate ways. Even in the world of today there are obligations we should not shirk and decencies and civilities that should not be discarded. You must be aware that your future does not lie in Guyana. In fact, it is entirely possible that you are in an area that could well inhibit your future, in that Guyana possesses something of an alien society, the knowledge of which will probably not serve you in the future. I have never felt so futile in trying to communicate with you as I do now. I do not doubt your sincerity nor the accuracy of your feeling more productive than you have ever been before. That does not, however, mean that I have to approve or that you are pursuing the most productive course open to you. Please try to answer my questions and stay in touch with Richard McCoy in the event of an emergency.

He sent the letter, along with the book *Passages*, and naturally, the letter never made it through the inner circle's censors. Louis would receive short letters in August and September which made no references to his questions or to *Passages*. (Her last letter arrived on November 27, 1978, when she had been dead for nine days.) In July, Jones had had other plans for the literary pursuits of his following.

The resident academic in Jonestown was a tall, balding, bespectacled man named Richard Tropp. The product of a Jewish upbringing in the Bedford-Stuyvesant section of Brooklyn, New York, Tropp was the son of a Russian Jew who had lost most of his family in the Nazi holocaust. His academic achievements were impressive: he graduated Phi Beta Kappa from the University of Rochester and had been the valedictorian of his class, had studied abroad for a year on a scholarship, and was a Woodrow Wilson Fellow at Berkeley in 1966–67, when the Vietnam and Black Power protest was at its peak. After he finished his master's degree in English Literature, he taught at Fisk University in a black studies program. But late in the sixties, when the fad in Berkeley was moving from activism to withdrawal from society in a back-to-nature movement, Tropp and his wife moved to Mendocino County to forget the ferment of the sixties and settle down to the simple and somewhat hedonistic life of the country. Tropp spent much of his leisure time playing the cello and the sarod.

But in 1971 the Tropps went to a meeting of the People's Temple in Ukiah. They were greeted openly and cordially, hugged warmly by black members, as they never had been before, and moved when a black girl stood up to sing Buffy Saint Marie's song called "My Country, 'Tis of Thy People: You're Dying." A rush of nostalgic emotion for the sixties revolution passed over them, and they realized that in their country life there was no spiritual element. Jones challenged them on the level where they were vulnerable. What are you doing with your life that contributes to society? he asked them. What are you doing that will make a difference?

In the mid-seventies, Richard Tropp did much of the research for the factual material from the newspapers with which Jones packed his sermons, while he taught at Santa Rosa Junior College. In December 1977, he left for Guyana along with his sister, Harriet, who was a lawyer. Tropp's wife, Kathy, stayed behind in San Francisco to work in the print shop. In the first half of 1978, apart from his duties in the Jonestown school alongside Jann Gurvich, Richard Tropp undertook a number of writing projects. He followed the religious journals of America scrupulously and saw in the publication of articles about the Temple a way to continue to legitimize the organization's work as religious, long after it had ceased to think of itself as such. He submitted several articles to church publications, sprinkling them with biblical references on communalism. The pieces amounted to breezy and overblown prose about the miracle of Jonestown. (Example: "A long time fighter for minority rights and justice, brilliant organizer, social critic, and fiery, dynamic personality, Reverend Jim Jones has come under attack for his socialistic views. The story of Jonestown is *overwhelming*. It will delight and challenge your readers.") In the June–July issue of *Churchman*, an Episcopal journal describing itself as "an independent journal of religious humanism," Tropp published his first piece, and he submitted another article, entitled "Charting a Way Out of 'Mass Society' " to *Christian Century* . Although the *Century's* editors found the piece promotional, they took it seriously, but rejected it in the end. One of the editors commented, "There is something there, but for reasons I cannot explain, I don't quite trust the group or the writer. . . ." But for the inexplicable instinct of that editor, the piece might have been published around November 1978.

Within Jonestown, Tropp's writing bent had more of an edge to it. In early July, he wrote a letter to Jones which became the weighty subject of a nighttime catharsis session. The elitists should be killed off if their contribution to the community was not enough to warrant the good they consumed, Tropp wrote. Jim Jones found the letter and the theory an excellent topic for an educational discussion by the whole community. He ordered everyone to write him a "self-analysis" letter. Members were to state not only what they thought of Tropp's postulate and whether they felt elitist sentiments welling inside them, but also what other negative impulses they felt, such as yearning for the States. They were also to examine their sexual appetites, particularly as they related to him.

"Relate your own faults," he exhorted a People's Rally on July 9, 1978. "Open yourself up like Tropp. He is white! Say that no matter what weakness there is in me, I will stick. I will go through. I will never turn back. It's not enough simply to look into yourself, but you must correct your weakness. You must feel sickened at your elitist attitudes. I want to see that searching inside of you, because I want you to be saved. I love you by asking this. Pour out yourself in the deepest analytical way about the worst things you see in yourself. I love you."

The technique of self-analysis within communalist groups goes back much further than the mass therapy movements like est and Esalen which burgeoned in the mid-sixties and seventies in America, although the modern use of the "catharsis" undoubtedly influenced Jones the most. In the Oneida community in upstate New York, which flourished for over eighty years in the middle nineteenth century, for example, group criticism was standard fare at community meetings. Members' faults were exposed with candor, and the process was thought to enhance the socialistic impulse. Confessions of weakness and selfishness were encouraged. But the July self-analyses in Jonestown were used by Jones strictly as a technique of degradation. Unlike Oneida, no mention of a member's virtue was permitted. It is hard to imagine that Jonestown residents did not realize how low they were being forced to stoop. If Richard Tropp was truly charting a way out of Mass Society, he might have considered what the modern French philosopher Gabriel Marcel said in his work *Man Against Mass Society:* "It is hardly possible that even the most radically degraded being should not sometimes be pierced by flashes of awareness and know the depth to which he has fallen."* Did Jann know?

More than any other evidence, the "Dear Dad" letters found strewn around Jones's house in the jungle compelled the impression that the residents of Jonestown were the dregs of their society. So pathetic were these confessions of sexual aberration, so fawning the expressions of Jones-worship, so horrifying the declarations of readiness to die for the cause of socialism, that these people hardly seemed a part of the American body politic.

---

*From *Man Against Mass Society,* © 1962 by Gabriel Marcel (Chicago: Henry Regnery Co.), p. 45.

- I feall that, I as one person in this work for communism, should do my verry best to offer all I can. I have a alettest atutude twards my work and would destroy someone else coffedence to make my own ass look better. . . .

- I would rather commit suicide and come back for 1000 generations than to do anything that would hurt this cause or you. I agree with Dick Tropp that the best thing to do with an elitist would be to shoot them, myself included.

- Dying doesn't interest me yet. I know its coming any day. I would really like to see this cause grow and see our little babies grow up. I would be mad if I had to die for some stupid thing somebody did while their head was up their ass. I will gladly die to protect this cause, but not gladly for a mistake.

- I think it is your responsibility to eat the foods and drinks and medicines that are needed for your health. You said yourself that this cause could not continue without you at this point in our development. I'm sure there is personal feelings involved, but above that, for the sake of the cause, I think you should drink whatever you need, and if it bothers some people, so what? You shouldn't make your decisions about your health on some self indulgent stupid M-Fs. Perhaps another day we could shoot the folks that are bothered, but in the meantime I would hope you take care of yourself. We hardly are your equal. We need not have equal nutrition and medication.

- [Speaking of a previous suicide drill] If the potion we drank had been the real thing, then it would have been the end of Dad's pain. He would not have to suffer for us anymore. Just like last night, the more he talked, the more pain in his tongue. The rest of the people would be in peace with our loving leader if it was the real thing there would be no more pain and no more suffering. We would be in peace today. That would have been the best way to die. Everyone wouldn't have to go to the pavilion. There would be no more toots of the horn or talking about strategy. If it was real, of course, we would have been free. We would have died the best way. Any other way we wouldn't be sure if it would work or not, and we would have suffered. I know that Dad wouldn't let us suffer like that. Thank you Dad for the test and not letting us suffer.

Taken at face value, these letters were misleading, for they demonstrated none of the baneful intelligence at work there. To talk to Temple members was not to talk to idiots, so much as to secretive and suspicious and terrified drones, humankind downtrodden not by their society but by their savior. They expressed a much greater horror than illiteracy and blind obedience because for the most part the letters were dishonest. Jonestown residents knew full well what the leader required in these situations. There had been many catharses before, so many that they were simply exhausted with all the pressures and had come to wish for the end. Many times before he had demanded demeaning, incriminating documents, simply as a hedge against treason. The letters, in short, were a cosmic example of bad faith.

Of all the self-analyses, that of Jann Gurvich, the community's symbol of elitism, was the most riveting and probably one of the few specimens of honesty. When Jones had assigned the task, he had been at the top of his speaking form, talking mesmerizingly not only of elitism but of a "Jonestown consciousness" which would be higher than black consciousness. He had talked not just of expunging their lust for the *beast* called USA, but of Jonestown standards for beauty and ugliness. In this last, it was as if he were speaking directly to Jann, perhaps implicitly complimenting her on the changes her search had brought.

"You who got to have your hair just right, got to have your little cosmetics just right, you're already stupidly ugly to me," he hissed, falling easily into street rhythms. "I'd like to see you get your head as straight as you've got your damn body. Then you might be beautiful. Some of you men shine like you've been under lava all day, while others are working and sweating. You're uglier than shit. Don't matter how long you work on that body, how much you shine, somebody's always going to come along who's got a little more razzmatazz than you got. So you better have something in your fucking head, 'cause you who are just developing your body, you're going to lose. Everyday you look around, that body's not the same.

"So Miss Body Beautiful, get out of my face.

"Mr. Atlas, get out of my face.

"You don't impress me. If I were a woman, some of these older men with lines in their face, who've fought the system, been out on the streets raising money for these babies, they're the ones who appeal to me. These women with lines and bent backs, they have faces like you'll never have, because you ain't got nothing in your head. Somebody said, I look so young. I wouldn't brag about it, baby. We want to see some boots on your sweet legs, darlin'. See you in overalls with dirt on your knees. We're tired of smelling your sweet ass, when some of us have sold all our perfume and cologne. Oh Glory! Some of you don't work, you must strut around here looking beautiful, and you look like a store-bought dummy. I never did want to go to bed with no dummy, a plastic doll. . . . Jesus Christ!"

As if in response to this, Jann wrote her self analysis to Jones. Dated

July 23, 1978, it was four legal-sized typed pages, and its opening
suggested that this was not to be a perfunctory response.

> I am impelled to preface this self analysis w/ 1 genuinely heartfelt
> statement—I apologize for not having written what I have to say sooner. I
> really want you to know me the good & the bad—but especially the bad.
> It's almost like I'm purposely keeping a secret from u if I don't let u know
> what's happening in my inner thoughts. I've started to write this 3 times
> & never turned it in. I have so many pent-up feelings about different
> things, I'm not surprised that I recently couldn't sleep more than 1–3
> hours at night for thinking all the time about problems. I can only say w/
> the deepest conviction thank u for giving this whole community the
> chance to be straight w/u & let it all out. There's a catharsis in telling
> these things—letting everything surface & then dealing w/ it.

Her confessions fell into six categories: thoughts about going back,
sex, attraction to u, guilt, ambiguities, and suggestions. The "bourgeois life" of the United States held no attraction for her, she wrote, for
she knew how people with "$" lived and what they did with their "$,"
and they made her sick. Jones had told them that if they were to know
themselves, they must know themselves sexually, and so she addressed herself to that. She had had no sex in Jonestown and generally
had no desire for any, but as if she felt the knife of obligatory
self-debasement, she described a sexual exploit or two, even fantasiz-
ing deviation she occasionally felt in her heart, reaching characteristically for a literary allusion, this time to Günter Grass's novel *The Tin
Drum*. She admitted a tinge of attraction for Jones, but then in the
peculiar parlance of the place, she delivered a backhanded slight: "I
thought of the times u said how many white asses u've fucked for this
organization and were disgusted by it. I thought—in hostility—this is
1 white ass u'll never have to fuck and be disgusted w/!"
　But inevitably, the touchstone of guilt received the most extensive
treatment:

> I feel particularly bad about the education I got. For all the educational
> opportunities I had, what I mainly did w/ it is demonstrate my bourgeois
> laziness & assumption that the world owed me something. I feel
> uncomfortable when people say 'Jann, u're so smart, u're exceptionally
> bright.' It's just not so. I'm educated but I'm not gifted w/ any extraordi-
> nary intelligence & there's a big difference. If 1/2 the children here had the
> chances I had, the achievements they would make in the professional field
> would make me look like a fool and a dunce in comparison.
> 　There is 1 more thing I have to say on the topic of my education. There
> are 2 main reasons that I am as articulate as I am. My dad who had a great
> impact on my life was by nature a very gifted orator. He can hold an

audience rapt for hrs. He is so eloquent & convincing that given his politics he is very dangerous. So I learned speaking (& much detrimental ideology) by listening to his very convincing soliloquies. Much of my ability to be articulate can be traced directly back to the twin bourgeois privileges of education & a chance to absorb the dominant culture of the day at a very early age. (Another big factor in learning to express myself was listening to you talk. I listen intently & I pick up a lot.)

The material within parentheses, clearly a strategic aside, seems to have been added as a gesture of self-protection.

I think that a person remedies the guilt over education by sharing as much of one's knowledge as possible & being humble about what u do know. I could spend my whole life remedying the gap that exists between me & others because of the bourgeois privileges I enjoyed.

But there is a problem here. For some reason I don't take on guilt & I don't incorporate it into a plan of action. I don't understand it but a real sense of guilt has not become part of my personality. When it does there will be a more humble, self effacing Jann around here. But I'm not going to lie about it—at this stage of my development guilt ain't got a hold of me like it should have.

This had always been the issue for me. Was she a follower? Or was she a resister, even a secret one? If she had the strength of resistance, perhaps it showed at the end of her July letter, when she put forward her suggestions.

What is treasonous in me? My intellectualism that causes me to trust my own judgment sometimes better than yours. Also I have this fear that unless we take much caution to eliminate racism now, after u are gone, racism & factionalism could break this community apart (unlikely, but a possibility). If I thought this community was falling apart because of that, I would make the strongest efforts to keep it together & resolve the differences. If that failed, I would leave & devote myself to some other revolutionary work. I think that is treasonous in me. The right thing to do would be to stay, to stay no matter what even if it fell apart. To go down w/Jt if we couldn't make it together. I do not want to be a prophet of doom, but I don't think revolutionaries are made by always looking on the brighter side of things.

Thank u Dad, for this community, for trying to help Johnny [Spain], for making racism functionally obsolescent & thank u for seeing us for our potentials and not for the assholes that we are. May I one day live to appreciate the sacrifice u have made.

Jann Gurvich

The critical tone was there but wasn't sufficient. She sometimes trusted her own judgment instead of his, but the impulse was treasonous. The moral act was to stay till the end. Reluctantly, much as I wanted to believe otherwise, I concluded that she was a lamb, caught at the last moment in a slaughter pen too ingeniously devised, a lamb, not a dissenter. As such, the horror for her was even greater. With her ability to step outside herself and outside her society, to look in with unexpressed objectivity, she had a clear awareness of choice, whereas for the others it was only a glimmering. Perhaps she was not muscular enough to knock down a man with a gun, nor could she run fast enough to out-distance a guard, nor even articulate enough in that existential moment of our decade to argue down Jim Jones. Perhaps even at the end she reached for a literary mooring to explain the spectacle that unfolded before her, and to define her own complicity in it romantically—Juliet, perhaps, reaching for the potion when she saw her Romeo, and the highest value of her life, dying before her. But she would have seen a plurality of possibilities, not just the one which the leader demanded.

One of the possibilities that Jann and a number of others saw, I believe, was that this was not a heroic mythic revolutionary death at all, but a squalid, seedy spectacle, whose grand proportions would elicit—and deserve—only grand contempt. For those who recognized choice, their acquiescence was simply the supreme act of giving up, action taken in bad faith, underlining a sense of their own worthlessness . . . a cosmic image, bred in America, of human worthlessness.

To paraphrase Jean-Paul Sartre, I act, and in my action, I reflect my image of mankind.

For Jann, acquiescence seemed genuine and honest. Much as I wanted to find rebellion against Jones, I could not. Toward the end of my work on this book, a letter came into my possession that removed the question from conjecture. Jann's letter was undated, but from its context, it seemed to be written toward the end, for it began "In what are perhaps the last hours of life . . ." The subject was her last feelings about socialism and it had the air of an assignment from the top. Again she returned to her old motif of her privileged upbringing and the racial impulses instilled in her in a literary fashion. Her father, she wrote, had quoted to her from the *Essay on the Inequality of Human Races* by the "Aryan supremacist" Comte de Gobineau. (Actually, this was a harsh distortion. Once when Jann was reading William Shirer's *The Rise and Fall of the Third Reich*, she had asked her father about the reference in the book to de Gobineau, and they had discussed his influence on European thinking and his contribution to the growth of anti-Semitism. To Jones, as Jann wrote it, the reference meant something altogether different.) After a testament to the compassion of Jim Jones, the letter made an announcement:

Instead of taking great leaps forward to overcome the teaching of my parents, I have taken only baby steps. Several days ago, I resolved to finally take Jim's words to heart and marry a black man. Finally I decided that the most important thing was developing a revolutionary consciousness of oppression and putting behind me notions of compatability and individualistic choices based on egotistical need. Why did I wait so late to start a process that might have already borne fruit in terms of my being personally touched by the solidarity of Black and white together that Jim has always taught?

I too have fear. But I go over in my mind how Victor Jara and Salvador Allende died. September 11, 1973. The Chilean coup took 40,000 lives. What is my one life to that?

[3]

There is a footnote to Jann's story, so unspeakably awful that I will be brief. Louis Gurvich caught the first plane to Guyana when he heard the news on New Orleans radio. He arrived on Monday, November 20, 1978, when the news, no doubt bred of rational human optimism, reported hundreds fleeing the death camp and wandering aimlessly about in the jungle. Immediately he went to the American Embassy and was told that Jann was not among the survivors of whom the Embassy then had knowledge. Even this information was reluctantly conveyed, and only after Louis threw a considerable brouhaha. The Privacy Act barred the release of such information, the Embassy functionary kept saying with sublime fidelity to regulations. How could he get to Jonestown? Louis asked. He flatly was told that he should discard that appalling idea and return to New Orleans. Who, then, was in charge? The Police Commissioner of Guyana was the answer.

At police headquarters, Louis was ushered into the office of Lloyd Barker, a heavyset, slow-talking officer who, unknown to Louis, had been receiving a monthly bottle of good American whiskey from the diligent Temple staffers in Georgetown as a token of friendship. Louis stated his business, stressing his war record and his credentials as a detective, masking with a professional's hauteur the brittleness that he felt. The commissioner listened sympathetically.

"Mr. Gurvich, as we talk, I don't know how many People's Temple members are still running around with guns. I don't know if you will go mad. It's very bad up there. There are many risks."

"I will be happy to absolve you of any responsibility in writing," Louis offered.

"You know that would be worthless. If I let you go, there will be others."

"Commissioner, you know my history. You know we are in the same line of work. I want you to look me in the eye and tell me you're not just quoting me what you would tell anybody. All I'm asking is for your instincts to tell you: Am I not the exception?"

Barker looked at him for a long, lingering moment and then reached for a button. His secretary appeared at the door.

"Mr. Gurvich here has just skillfully maneuvered me into giving him a pass," he said with a smile.

"But you haven't given anyone a pass," she murmured.

"I've just given one to Mr. Gurvich. Make sure he gets on the plane with the two going in to quarantine the camp. Otherwise, even *I* can't get him in."

The secretary departed. Barker's eye fell again on Louis.

"I too am a father," he said.

Soon Louis was on his way to Matthews Ridge. He arrived too late in the afternoon to catch a helicopter into Jonestown and so holed up for the night on the dusty main street in the Charlo Hotel, an establishment that will never receive a recommendation from the Women's Rest Tour Association. At dusk, he wandered out onto a promontory to watch the sun set in the harsh, empty, roseate empyrean. At that moment, as much as he wanted to loathe Jonestown and Guyana, pondering the abomination ahead of him, he stood transfixed by the shimmering beauty of the place.

The following day, for over five hours Louis searched the stinking open-air mausoleum for Jann. Before him, the pogrom became a kaleidoscope of Montgomery Ward colors and pottery shapes. It was as if, except for the smell, some gigantic game of "Ring Around the Rosy" had been played, and the maestro had forgotten to tell everyone after the "Ashes, ashes we all fall down" to wake up. In agony, he tried to maintain his composure, struggling to keep his mind on an organized plan for covering each area. He started in the Pavilion around Jones, working from the premise that the people there had surely gone voluntarily, and the ones farther out had been murdered. Under the roof the ink on the tags had not been washed away by the rain, as the ones outside had, and he noticed the name Richard Tropp. But no Jann. He moved out toward the perimeter, toward the ditch below the Pavilion. His eye focused on a large man in a white football jersey bearing the number 15. The man lay on his back, his face frozen in agony, bleeding from the mouth and nose, a slash across his forehead. Elsewhere in his scramble, Louis came upon a black man, bleeding also at the mouth and nose, his female companion and child behind him, his arms crooked with the palms of his hands flat in front of his upturned face, fixed in the attitude of defense. "Christ, tell me that's a suicide," Louis remarked to a TV cameraman who trailed him. In due course, Louis returned to this figure and noted two blood spots on his shirt at the small of his back. The detective lifted the jersey to find not bullet holes, but needle marks. Months later, in the craterous dark of Louis's memory, he would remember that figure and think of the frieze at the Temple of Apollo in Bassae, in which the Greek soldier hovers over the Amazon woman with sword upraised, as she holds her arms and hands in the same position, to protect herself and another woman beside her from the inevitable blow.

His hideous labors were in vain. He never found her. By this time, death in the rain forest had been the monstrous leveler. Louis had had to pull down the socks of the victims to distinguish between the white and the black.

FOUR

The Child
in the
Triangle

[1]

IN JANUARY 1977, there occurred in San Francisco the opening
scene of this generational tragedy that would end twenty-two
months later. Into the office of a young lawyer on Turk Street
named Jeffrey Haas, a tall and terrified twenty-five-year-old woman
named Grace Stoen came for advice and assistance. The progeny of a
Maltese father and Mexican mother, she possessed large, brown
luminous eyes and a radiantly olive complexion. With a certain stagy
manner of using her long-fingered hands to bolster her halting speech,
she projected an alluring Latin sensuality. But on that day, from the
drawn quality of her thin face and the deep circles under her eyes, it
was clear that she had been through a period of great stress. In a
hesitant tone that bespoke insecurity as well as fear, she told Haas an
amazing story. Six years before at the age of nineteen, she and the man
she was dating in Redwood Valley, a white lawyer named Timothy
Stoen, who was thirteen years her senior, had joined an organization
called the People's Temple. The couple were married in the Temple
shortly afterward by its pastor, the Reverend Jim Jones, whom attorney
Haas recognized only as a current political power in San Francisco and
chairman of the San Francisco Housing Authority. In 1972 a child
named John Victor Stoen was born. In July 1976, Grace Stoen left the
church and filed for divorce against her husband, who by then had
become an assistant district attorney. More important, Tim Stoen was
Jim Jones's chief aide. The child, John Victor Stoen, now nearly five
years old, had been taken to the Temple's agricultural mission in
Guyana and was the ward of the church. Grace Stoen had come to Haas
to explore what might be involved in an effort to gain custody of her
child and to secure his return to the United States. After their first
session, with trembling poignancy, Grace Stoen asked Haas to walk
her out the door and down the street. She was afraid that she would be

gunned down as she left. Time and again, she claimed, Pastor Jones had threatened to kill her or John Victor if she ever tried to get the child back.

The story was bizarre and complicated, but from the start Haas felt his client was telling the truth. Through the month of January he met with her three more times, each time building her confidence to go through with an action. By early February she was ready, and the custody papers were filed. In the early stage Haas's legal strategy was low key. By instinct, he felt custody cases, particularly messy ones, were best resolved privately, to minimize the damage to the parents and the child. Since the parents were then hostile to each other, Haas assumed that Timothy Stoen would be adverse to Grace Stoen's petition. At the time the papers were filed, the attorney learned that Timothy Stoen had gone to Guyana as well, and thus was beyond the reach of the court. But Haas learned something else on the day the papers were filed. He saw Charles Garry, soon to be the Temple's attorney, in the hallway outside the judge's chambers.

"You know that that boy is Jim Jones's, don't you?" Garry quipped in his grainy doggerel.

Haas did not know, and does not know to this day. It had been assumed by many that John Victor Stoen's raven hair and the olive cast to his skin came from Jim Jones, but he could have derived them solely from the genes of his Mexican mother. But attorney Haas did know from the legal standpoint that a third party, especially if he were the natural father, could file a counterclaim for custody, and, with great frequency in the California courts, such custody was being granted to the third person.

In the weeks ahead, the case turned more macabre and more frightening. On February 12, 1977, Grace Stoen received a letter through the mails that read as follows:

> I am writing you in care of your mother's address in hopes that you will be seeing her before you leave the Coast. Have you really made the decision to move to Syracuse so soon? Syracuse is a cold, dreary town. I think it is a mistake for you to go there. If that is what you want, it's your future. If you love someone, you respect their decisions. I sure won't try to stop you. . . .

Frantically, Grace Stoen insisted to her attorney that this was a death threat. New York, or any town in that state, with its description as "a cold, dreary place," was the Temple's version of the black spot. But how could she prove it? In the next year she would receive three other such letters, and while she turned them all over to the Treasury Department (which was then looking into, among other things, allegations of the illegal shipment of firearms to Guyana) each letter drove her to the point of distraction.

As the case proceeded, another strange document surfaced as well. Dated February 6, 1972, twelve days after the birth of John Victor Stoen, the affidavit presented a family court judge with a rather unusual problem, especially where a minister of the cloth was concerned (although in the end it was never introduced formally into evidence).

To whom it may concern:

I, Timothy Oliver Stoen, hereby acknowledge that in April, 1971, I entreated my beloved pastor, James W. Jones, to sire a child by my wife, Grace Lucy (Grech) Stoen, who had previously at my insistence, reluctantly but graciously consented thereto. James W. Jones agreed to do so, reluctantly, after I explained that I very much wished to raise a child, but was unable, after extensive attempts, to sire one myself. My reason for requesting James W. Jones to do this is that I wanted my child to be fathered, if not by me, by the most compassionate, honest, and courageous human being the world contains.

The child, John Victor Stoen, was born on January 25, 1972. I am privileged beyond words to have the responsibility for caring for him, and I undertake this task humbly with the steadfast hope that said child will become a devoted follower of Jesus Christ and be instrumental in bringing God's kingdom here on earth, as has been his wonderful natural father.

I declare under penalty of perjury that the foregoing is true and correct.

The document was signed by Timothy Stoen and witnessed by, of all people, that woebegone figure, Marceline Jones. Later, the story circulated that the child had been conceived in the back of a Temple bus which had been specially outfitted as Jones's suite for the long, tedious weekend trek to his Los Angeles Temple.

Who were these people, and what were they doing inside that church? one was certainly compelled to inquire early on, and, indeed, the questioning did begin in earnest in the spring of 1977.

The course of Timothy Stoen into the clutches of Jim Jones was roundabout. He came from a family which took its religion fundamentally and its Bible literally. In the late 1960s, Stoen was a bright young professional in search of some broader meaning to his life. He had a taste for the good things of the world. He drove a Porsche. He appreciated elegant food, fine books, and foot-tapping jazz. In his personal habits he was meticulous to the point of obsession. Self-consciously, he set himself personal goals, as if he were a college basketball player determined to become an All-American by his senior year.

In pinched block letters he wrote memoranda to himself about his demeanor and mannerisms, as if his superego were intent on a never-ending self-improvement program. The superego demanded that he get haircuts every ten days, use cologne, part his hair precisely; that his face should have a comely, tanned, and self-assured cast; and that his body be taut from weight-lifting and diet. On the telephone, he should wait to talk until he had prepared a deep pitch, and when he met a girl, the drift of his conversation should be well thought out in advance, as should his maneuvers at greeting and parting. At all costs, said the superego, his voice should be confident yet seducing, commanding yet nonchalant, urbane yet proper.

He had his "terribly relevant rule," in which he enjoined himself never to discuss his personal life with his paramour, so as to appear mysterious, permitting himself only "innuendos at most." He vowed to write poems to her, using her as inspiration, "but wait for the right groundwork." These exacting notes covered the gamut from soup to nuts: "Play piano well," "Be skillful in one sport," "Do one thing at a time and do it thoroughly." Attention to detail would serve him well as a lawyer and later as a devotee-turned-traitor to Jim Jones, but it may have caused him difficulty with another of his goals: "Have a sense of humor—wit." With his diminutive form and circular horn-rimmed glasses and ivy suits, he possessed the look of a truncated, muscle-toned John Dean.

His political development toward "radicalism" had the twists and bumps of a live oak tree. With the adventurism of Jann Gurvich, he went into East Berlin in the early sixties, when the great powers were eyeball to eyeball, took pictures, and inevitably got detained by the Communist authorities. Later, he described his ordeal to a Rotary Club: "The first thing I noticed was the blank expression on the faces of everyone [in East Berlin]. You could tell they were just waiting for the day they might have freedom." He got his law degree and registered as a Republican, until 1969, when he came to represent a Black Panther. To his pleasure, he was becoming the *Republican* lawyer whom the Panthers trusted, because he represented them so vigorously, and he came to see himself as a bridge between "the outcast community and the establishment." But he felt guilty about driving down to Panther headquarters in his Porsche and sought help in the Bible. He recalled Jesus' admonition to the rich young rulers to sell what they had and give it to the poor, and considered that to be the essence of Christianity. In that guilt corner of his brain, created by the tension between privilege and denial, Jim Jones rushed in like a tumor. Jones's altruism appealed to the young attorney; he could be moved to tears when he saw the pastor holding hands with an old black cripple. Equality was suddenly the highest value in life. Jones used him as a symbol of respectability for the church, and through the early and mid-seventies he served as a rousing, if somewhat overearnest and maudlin, toastmaster for Jim Jones at public occasions. In his adulatory warm-ups for "Father," this pin-striped cheerleader would quote from Scripture: "By their fruits shall you know them." This was "the most principled person you could ever want to meet; the best friend you could ever want to have."

But in his private role within the Temple, Stoen acted the consummate revolutionary. He became articulate about the actions of the true rebel in America, once suggesting poisoning the water supply of Washington, D.C., when the Temple felt under attack by the Washington bureaucracy, and poisoning the water of Lester Kinsolving, the religious columnist, who was first to expose Jones's claim to divinity in 1972. Stoen was even taken with the scene in the movie *The French Connection* in which an enemy was cut down on a department store escalator as he went up and the killer went down. Perhaps this was the way to deal with Kinsolving, Stoen reportedly suggested, and there was talk of poison darts. Through Stoen, any threats against the Temple or incriminating letters by Temple followers were passed for "legal clearance." As a good administrator he made sure that compromising statements by shaky members were current. He "strategized" about keeping members in line, often asking where members' "heads were at" in relation to "Father." In 1974–76, the big growth years for the church, Stoen was the man to pass on doomsday information to the Lilliputians, to keep their loyalty and their anxiety high.

A vintage Stoen message, circa 1974, contained the flash news for Temple eyes only that the Attorney General wanted one million aliens deported by the end of the year, and ten million altogether. "Since there are only 500,000 illegal aliens in the country now," Stoen told a member with the voice of the insider, "you know who they're trying to take. A vast number of blacks can't establish citizenship, and Jim has inside information that the plan is for them to be deported. He's trying to establish the citizenship of all our members, but the situation is getting to be like it was for the Jews in Hitler's time." Stoen spoke of troop-train sightings in Los Angeles as if they were the boxcars to Dachau. Since the economy was collapsing, a race war was coming, and people would be fighting over food. "Walter Cronkite says 800,000 will starve if something isn't done, and Jack Anderson, if you read him, says the Pentagon is laying plans to start a race war in Africa, according to secret documents he has. And Anderson always just deals with the facts." As if this wasn't bad enough, Stoen confided to a member, the United States "planned to attack Libya and to support an invasion of Jews into Kuwait to gain control of the oil there. So the future was not bright in America." Nuclear war was inevitable. Members were to stock food. "Jim says you'll be able to tell when nuclear war is about to happen, because it won't happen quickly. There's to be a lot of tension before the final blow." But not to worry. The people in the Ukiah church were in a position to break through to safety in the north, presumably the icy barrens of Canada.

Still, Timothy Stoen had not forgotten the bridge to the establishment. As chairman of the board of directors of the People's Temple, he wrote a letter of support on Temple stationery to the embattled Richard Nixon on April 7, 1974, stating how horrified the People's Temple was at abuses being hurled at one of the greatest American presidents ever. Jim Jones and his Temple had only one request to make: never resign. Indeed, wrote Stoen, in a curious twist of Jonesian doctrine, it would be preferable to endure a nuclear holocaust than to see Nixon leave office.

The paths of Tim and Grace Stoen crossed at a peace demonstration in 1970. With his maturity, intelligence, education, and prestigious job which held every promise of greater things, even perhaps elective office, he possessed all the things she ever wanted. In his Porsche, he whisked her to his house in Berkeley and sat her in his living room lined with books. He introduced her to guests with impressive credentials from the public defender's office. He wrote and read poetry to her, bought her books, told her how intelligent she was. By her own definition, she felt like Dorothy in the Wizard of Oz with Berkeley her yellow brick road. And he took her to his Temple. When Pastor Jones read from newspapers from his perch on the stage, it fed her appetite for learning and confirmed her instinct that her society was sick.

But after they were married, Oz seemed to be taken over by the wicked witch of the west. Jones classically set out to divide her from her husband. The Pastor told Tim Stoen disgraceful stories of Grace's selfishness and narcissism, and told Grace horrendous stories about Tim's snobbery and elitism. In meetings, Grace was challenged for her clothes that were too nice, her house that was too well appointed, her general bourgeois leanings that proved her to be the quintessential "white bitch" without principle. More than anyone else, at least in her perception, she was challenged on the sexual level, accused of "compensating" with all kinds of men. One way or another, she became pregnant in 1972, and after John Victor was born the charge that she was a poor mother was added to the litany. Even her ethnic background was fair game.

"You Mexicans make me sick," Jones said to her once. "You're weak, and you never have any leaders."

To Jones, family ties were counterproductive to the revolutionary impulse, and to implement the theory, his practice moved from the tawdry to the depraved. Within the church, the story spread that Timothy Stoen was homosexual, and his alleged incapability was the reason why Jones, out of socialistic duty naturally, had "related" to Grace Stoen. Tim Stoen, in turn, wrote letters attesting to a homosexual orientation, and even to episodes that he had had with Jones himself. In one note, Stoen thanked Jones for showing him his "deep-seated repression" on the sexual level and extolled his leader for pure motives. To back this up, Grace Stoen wrote about how her husband had gone out and bought nylons, women's underwear, wigs, slips, and negligees for himself.

Perhaps this display of decadence, fit for the scientist's laboratory, was all a hedge against defection later. Since Tim Stoen was presiding over the compromising letters department, perhaps he was operating as, say, a psychiatrist does: to be a good psychiatrist, medical school demands that the candidate go through psychoanalysis. Whatever the case, all this appealed to one side of Grace Stoen. She bragged to others that John Victor was her child by Jones and traded on the story for special privilege. Soon enough, she moved into a position of trust. She proved to have a head for detail and a talent for organization, and was made head counselor for the membership. For the first time in her life, she felt important and gained the confidence that she was good at what she did.

Over time, despite the front, she began to feel rotten inside. It dawned on her gradually, as it would later on Tim Stoen, that no matter how good the goal of the Temple, it simply did not make people happy. The principles of altruism and service were set against the techniques of degradation, dishonesty, and guilt. At long last, ends and means, first for Grace, later for Tim, moved into perfect counterpoint.

Yet Grace Stoen knew she had been "brainwashed." The world outside the Temple was an unfriendly place, where life was Hobbesian —nasty, brutish, and short—and so ripping away from the Temple and Jones would not be easy. Still, in September 1976 she left. But in leaving she could not slip away without a trace, especially since Jones held John Victor. As a matter of conscious organization, Jones always seemed to have a hostage. From a secret place, Grace phoned Jones several times. It has often been said that Jim Jones was a master manipulator of people, that for each member, depending on his background, he spoke to areas of vulnerability. For Grace, the soft areas were guilt, fear, and insecurity, and in these endlessly long phone conversations, punctuated by Grace's tears and marked by Jones's firm purpose, softly expressed, the master was at his best—but he had to be. The gist of the conversation follows:

"You did not maintain strength, hon, and this is the worst decision you've ever made. You can't imagine the pain you've caused. If it will give you any satisfaction, I've suffered to the point that I felt heart pains, had a mild heart attack. . . . But I've come through it. You just broke my heart. But the point is, I've rescued my senses enough to keep you from having to suffer any pain if you want to return. People here think you're on a mission, and I'll hold it that way as long as I can. This organization is the best in the world, and I don't know how in the hell you can do any better. No individual can give what a group can. . . ."

"It just got to be too heavy," Grace replied softly. "I feel bad, feel bad for a lot of people."

"What a position you put me in! I put so much faith in you, put you on such a very high level with my kids."

"I feel so inadequate. . . ."

"How do you think I feel, the way I recommended you, made you head counselor. Do you have any idea how lonely and inadequate I must feel? What happiness do you think I have?"

"I don't see how you could have any happiness," said Grace, tearfully.

"I don't have. Don't you think I need happiness, . . . peace at least? A little peace. It's hard enough when I've got a few to have faith in. But then, to be jolted like this!"

"I couldn't stand being yelled at by you or anybody," she managed.

"You couldn't. You with your good mind. I thought you'd see the light. How much do you think I go through? The love you get out there will not sustain you, honey, because it isn't love like you know love to be. You'll never be loved again like I love you. You never will. I wish I'd known some love like this; no, I don't wish someone else would love the way I do. It's pain. It's pain. But it's also sensitiveness. . . ."

"I know. You've taught me all that."

"My God, if I'd had someone love me as much as I love some of you, that's all I'd have needed in life. Nobody's ever loved me that much."

"I was just selfish, I guess, but. . . ."

"So you were selfish. But, my God, honey, you know how many times people have done this to me? Haven't you seen me suffer? How much can a human being take?"

"It just started to get heavier and heavier. . . ."

"It's getting heavier and heavier for me too, you know. All the things I've got to go through: getting people out of jail, risking my life every day. Yesterday, for instance. I never saw such a bad jail as I saw yesterday. People don't get any sunlight. Their skin looks bad. Nobody cares. Nobody fights for 'em. Nobody stands up for 'em. I walked in there and the deputies started saying who I was, and I never met them in my life. Kept whispering, 'That's Jim Jones. He's a powerful man.'"

"That's good. That's good."

"What I go through every day, well, you don't know the half of it; and you say people shouted at you all the time. But people don't shout at me. They just pull on me constantly, asking me for a million things.

What a great mission you had, Grace, and you leave to avoid being yelled at. My God!"

"I got weary. I got tired," she groaned.

"You don't know what weariness is. I'm just a human being, with all the same feelings of inadequacy. All my children not minding me. Not cooperating. I'm the pastor, the Shepherd, but I feel like Mother Hubbard, nothing in the cupboard, and don't know what to do. I don't know how to take care of all these people's needs, but I keep on doing it, because there's nobody else.

"I've wanted to die ever since the age your son is. Least, I felt that way. You can't do what you want to do in life. There's a real destiny to perform. We owe something to humanity. We *must* stay alive and try to stay healthy. I do practice that. . . . I'm sure you know where the nicest place I'd like to retire is. It wouldn't be planting potatoes in the mission. . . . Fish need food, throw me there. Take my kidneys. I don't know what more they would want. I've got awfully good eyes. . . . Nobody wants me anymore. . . ." He broke for a moment into a quiet sob, and then mastered himself. "Growing old in America is not pleasant. . . . " and then his voice trailed away.

He sighed, as if to demarcate the bottom of true weariness. "I'll adjust to whatever the hell you do. You know I'll stay alive as long as I can," he muttered.

"You always said you would, no matter what," she said.

"I have to, because I have a duty. I wouldn't hurt anyone, not one child. I wish you'd come home and help me watch these children grow. I love you and I miss you. The only thing that's important is to make a better world for the defenseless ones."

"I know it's selfish," she repeated.

"But, honey, you let me down; you're letting the principles down. You'll see that if you're honest with yourself. I just represent the principles. You see, people can't handle guilt. I handle guilt every day, and I utilize guilt. I take on guilt even for the things I'm not responsible for. But that's a healthy thing. You *produce* with guilt. But most people get out and start criticizing and finding fault, like you did. A good healthy sense of guilt is what made me produce here, and I use it in a constructive way."

"There's no way I will ever fit back into society comfortably the way I was before I came to the church. There's no happiness out here."

"That speaks well for you, Grace. You've built some character out there. And people who have left and have come back can be even more esteemed because of that character. If I thought about what people do to me, all the time, I'd become bitter, but if you take guilt, look at your own faults, you don't feel hostile to others. I think about moments when I could become more giving, less self-centered—I don't know when that would have been, in my childhood perhaps—well, that's what keeps me going. . . . But what are you going to do with your fine mind out there? It worries me, because I know you're a very sensitive person."

"People can be very mean out here," she said hollowly.

"I know. I just can't imagine how you're living out there."

"It's not that great, believe me."

"No, it wouldn't be for me. I think if I were you, I'd want to get home to Principle."

"I was so dissatisfied with everything that was going on."

"So dissatisfied with the number of people we get out of prison, the number of lives we've saved?"

"No, I was never dissatisfied with that."

"The streets are madder, the people are meaner. That's the way the world is. But Inside, there's a sense of togetherness. The higher relationship of the family is preferable to one on one, at least until one gets to the place of peace. If you put too much count on your own life, you'll always be in distress.

"I've been tempted many times, just to be like Thoreau and wander into the woods with these kids. But I couldn't let one of them down. Now I've got to explain to all these children about you. I've got to protect the children and protect the cause too. You know the battle I'm in."

"I need some time. I need some time."

"Well, live in peace, if you *can* live in peace. Don't run from your thoughts. Don't run from your conscience. Don't let the old man down, nor your family back here. You won't feel good if I die while you're gone."

"Well, look, I guess I better go. I'm not feeling too good right now."

"You sick, hon?"

"It's just nerves."

"Do you have someone with you?"

"No, I'm by myself."

"Did you go to Colorado?"

"No, I'm not in Colorado."

"Do you know how it feels when you don't know where someone you love is, especially when they're sick?" A note of irritation crept into his voice. "You know where I'm at, whether you love me or hate me. . . . I'm not going to trace you down. You don't have to worry about that. I'm just worried about you."

"I'll call you again."

"Remember, hon, you'll be much more esteemed if you come back. No harm will come to you. I can hold it off for a while longer. And don't do any foolish things. Take care of yourself. You know what's happening in America. You can see what I've been saying to you; you can read the papers. Look at what the courts have just handed down: no appeal in criminal cases. Straight to the gas chamber with 'em. Basic civil liberties are going down the drain. There's a big article in the newspaper about how everything is taped nowadays in the government offices: every welfare office, the DA's office, even the interdepartmental meetings, even in Ukiah. They push a button and tape everybody's phone. It's horrible. . . ."

He paused, perhaps looking at the tape machine that was recording this conversation with Grace, perhaps exchanging an amused glance with Tim Stoen, who had been by his side through this whole conversation.

"How in the world could you leave me, honey, when I'm fighting this battle, and trying to prepare a place for these kids?"

Always, always, Jim Jones had his hostage. In the case of Grace Stoen it was her child, John Victor. With talk of guilt and principle and his sacrifice, he was failing to bring her back into the family. So it was time for cruelty.

"The one thing I'm grateful for is that your child shows no scars. Something miraculously took that out of his mind. I don't think I could have stood seeing him go through anguish," his calm voice said.

"I miss John terribly."

"I'm sure you do, but evidently you prefer a life without him."

"I just had to leave. Things got too tough."

"Tough! What could be tougher than now? The separation of a mother from her child. Everything pales before that. But I'm glad you don't have guilt as well. You never did a more sensible thing than leave your child here. It was a beautiful sacrifice. You would have destroyed him if you took him outside with you."

"I . . . I never want to hurt him."

"If you had taken him from his daddy, you would have had a very sick child, very, very sick child. If you'd have taken him, he would have been destroyed."

"Yes."

"He's remarkably self-contained. It's a miracle. Of course, I've put you in an exceedingly good light in his mind. He thinks that you're out doing good things for the Cause. That makes separation easier for a child, if he's proud of his Mama. I tell you from the depths of my heart that I'm trying to keep the knowledge that you've left the Cause away from your child. I think that would build an alienation between you two that would never, *never* be breached. He can't understand at all about people who leave the church. Right now I've put you on the highest plane in his mind."

"I appreciate that."

"He's coming now. I'll tell him you're calling from overseas. Just tell him you're out making a better world for him and the other kids. And tell him you love him, but please show no emotion. Don't show this child your weakness."

"I hope I can do it."

"If you can't, we'd better not go through with this. He's working out so well. . . . Here he is."

"Hello," the child's voice murmured sleepily.

"John?"

"What?"

"How are you doing? . . . It's me . . . I miss you terribly."

"No," he said flatly.

Grace caught her breath. "No?"

"Yeah."

Her astonishment caused another pause. She struggled for the upbeat.

"I hope you're working hard. Mama's working hard helping people. Jim likes us to work for the people. Jim loves you very much. Who loves you the best?"

"Jim."

"That's right. He loves everybody."

"Yeah."

"Well, I must not keep you up," she said exasperated, running out of things to ask, feeling his distance, perhaps even the hate that Jones had instilled in him. "I've enjoyed talking with you. Bye-bye, honey."

"Bye."

In the background, like a sound effects man, Jones kissed the child loudly, told him to go to bed, and returned to the conversation.

"I'd like to see John," Grace said.

Jones was silent for a moment, as if he was taken aback. "Honey, how do you want to arrange that?"

"I could come there."

"It's going to be a little hard. He's happy now, with you over there fighting for freedom. How you going to tell him you come and then go away so quickly? I'd much rather you thought about it and came back home."

"I could come to L.A., as if I were coming back on business from the mission."

"It'd be difficult to explain to him. You're playing with a little child's life, his mental health. You have to be extremely careful what you do."

"I wouldn't do anything to upset him."

"You create such a problem, Grace. I don't want him to think of you as typifying the people who are on the Outside. He's proud and he's happy, because you're doing things that are right. He isn't dependent, not on you or his daddy. That's what leaders are made of. I'd never tell him you're around. He'd never understand. He would never, never be told that you've left the organization."

"I appreciate that."

"Well, let me think about how to work this out."

"Whatever would be convenient for you."

"How about in five weeks."

"Five weeks?" she said with a stab of pain.

"If you decide to come home sooner, we'll be grateful and happy. Grace, if you come home where you belong, you'll have security. There are lots of great people here. The best friends you'll ever have are here. And nobody will ever love you as much as I do."

She was reduced to incoherent, unfinished sentences. "Well, I just . . . I never meant . . . it was only . . ." Her humiliation was complete: talking to her child now pitted against her, making her lie to him, toying with the notion of seeing the child in some distant time, but it still was not achieving his purpose.

"By the way," he said, "to offer the people some consolation, will you say something to them? You know we've kept a very positive image of you in case you ever want to get your life straightened around."

She knew this technique, but it was less painful than talking about John Victor. "What do you want me to say?" she said with drooping fatigue.

"Something from the heart. We've said you're at the agricultural mission. Give love to various people."

"Oh, God, I can't. Give love to who?"

"The people you like and care about . . . or just something in general. Send my love; I'm much happier over here, something like that . . . and start with the date."

"The date?"

"Yeah, start with the date . . . in case someone here didn't believe it."

"What do I say? I don't know what to say."

"I don't know how I want . . ." he mumbled, reaching for what would be the most incriminating. "I'd just say it's July 29, I miss all of you, but we're getting a lot of things done in the mission field."

She cleared her voice, and Jones pretended to switch on the tape recorder.

The Bishop tried to prompt her. "I am talking with Grace Stoen on the twenty-ninth of July, 1976, and she was just telling me some of the interesting things that you're doing for the Cause . . . how's it going?"

"Fine . . . everything is going fine. I miss everybody. I hope everybody is well." Her voice trembled.

"People getting the hang of the mechanical end of things, are they?"

"Yeah, sure are. . . . We're very happy. Any place'd be happier than stateside. . . ."

Jones made as if to turn off the recorder. "Honey, it just doesn't sound real," he said with irritation. "Come on more as your buoyant self. Give love to various people. Say the date first, remember."

"I'm too nervous." She cleared her voice. "OK, let's start. . . . 'This is July 29, 1976. I have the privilege of speaking to my friend, Jim, and I'm calling from the mission field. I just want all of you to know I miss you very much, although it's more pleasant here, in the promised land. A lot of things are being accomplished. Although I'd rather be with my family . . . the greater mass of the family . . . I'm over here trying to help all of us.'"

Grace's tone was scarcely better than her first attempt, but Jones was satisfied.

"Good, that's good enough. I don't know that I'll ever play it publicly though. Sometimes when you do anything, it causes more paranoia."

He was masterful. She was weak. He left her without an ounce of self-respect, ridden with fear and longing for her captive child. And yet, she did not come back. Somewhere, in her soul, there was enough strength left to decide against him, to make a choice.

But she was hiding in the *reality* of America.

[2]

In the winter of 1976–77, Jim Jones was at the height of his power in San Francisco. By his appointment to the chairmanship of the San Francisco Housing Authority, he clothed himself in respectability. Sitting under the seal of the city, in his clerical collar and suits of seedy material and flashy cut, he flaunted his identification with "the defenseless ones." Always, he made sure that a large complement of his "seniors" from the Temple attended the housing meetings. Old people had a particular stake in the housing policies of the city. From the outside, he was seen as powerful and hardworking—once collapsing from exhaustion at a public meeting of the Authority after reportedly counseling until dawn a suicidal drug addict going through withdrawal. His power rested, as much as anything, on his ability to organize hundreds, even occasionally thousands, of his followers for demonstrations against social injustice. In September 1976 he had mobilized over a thousand demonstrators against the jailing of four reporters in Fresno, California, for refusing to reveal their sources. In December his followers formed the bulk of three thousand demonstrators in behalf of William Farr, a *Los Angeles Times* reporter who was making a similar stand from a jail cell. And in late December, Temple members joined such friendly fringe groups as the Bay Area Gay Liberation, the Revolutionary Communist Party, the Pickle Family Circus, and the Bay Area Progressive Musicians Association (to name a few) to protest the eviction of Filipino seamen from a decrepit building called the International Hotel. With this support, the seamen had been holding out against a Thai developer since their eviction notice in January 1969. (The basement of the building once housed the nightclub called the *hungri i*, where the Kingston Trio and Barbra Streisand got their start.) Before he lent his support to the mobilization, Jones later told a reporter, he wanted to be sure that the other groups were pacifists, for it was a volatile, dangerous situation, where street violence was always just below the surface.

As much as Jones complained about the hostility of the press toward him and his organization over the years, his press clippings, looked at as a whole, hardly bear out this assessment. His good works were extensively and favorably reported. His share of superlatives from the press, especially when he received yet another award such as the Martin Luther King, Jr. Humanitarian Award in January 1977, should have been enough to satisfy the most spectacular ego among our public figures. To be sure, he occasionally looked ridiculous in the press, especially when his healing services were reported, but for the most part he was portrayed as a unique humanist with a unique ministry, building in microcosm the perfect interracial society.

In March 1977, for example, the *San Francisco Bay Guardian*, a weekly that fancies itself as the West Coast version of *The Village Voice*, printed an extensive article on the Temple under the headline: A CHURCH THAT PUTS ITS FAITH INTO ACTION. The piece called the Temple the biggest religion story in the Bay Area (which would seem like something of an understatement later) and described the Temple as the largest Protestant congregation in California, with more than 20,000 members, and the publisher of the Bay Area's largest circulation newspaper, distributed free to nearly a million households. The article was written by Bob Levering, a bright and sophisticated young journalist who had spent a year in a seminary in the mid-sixties before he moved into the antiwar movement as an organizer, and finally, after exhausting himself as a political organizer, into journalism. With his religious training and an appreciation for how difficult the mobilization of modern protest is, Levering was well suited to notice the strengths of Jones's movement.

The journalist went to the sprawling old church, in the Fillmore ghetto, already impressed with Jones's ability to mobilize his followers into disciplined nonviolent protest. He had followed the International Hotel controversy carefully, and had admired from afar Jones's steady hand in a difficult and potentially violent situation. At the church, Levering was impressed instantly by the furious activity. Every corner of the old building, once a Masonic Temple, pulsed with church business. The scale and intensity of the effort would be the envy of any church in America, Levering thought, with Temple members purveying a dedication and discipline as they went about their work. Levering's guides spoke of their organization in religious terms: the mixed congregation accentuated what was common among men, not what divided them. The central unifying theme was human service. Biblical references fell easily from their tongues. One member quoted Matthew 25: "Verily I say unto you, in as much as ye have done it unto the least of these, my brethren, ye have done it unto me."

In due course, Jones arrived, late for this meeting, and thus, late for the others that were scheduled to follow. He wore the look of unfathomable fatigue. His wrinkled suit was classically Goodwill. Levering might have expected Jones to be somewhat aloof and pressed: he was obviously a very busy man, but the two sat down to talk, and only two hours later did they part. The journalist found the pastor engaging, relaxed, and challenging. Tired as he was, Jones projected tremendous intensity. His delivery was personal, his formulation interesting, and to Levering the notetaker, endlessly quotable. He never rested upon clichés, a considerable attribute to this religiously trained writer, used to the puffed-up piety of ministers—and his preacher-like manner came complete with a touch of the sanctimonious. When a church really does what Jesus Christ said it should, Jones discoursed, people get angry. They want the church to be only "preaching, praying, and singing," but, quoting Jesus, " 'I will make you fishers of men.' " To Levering, here was a man who was truly trying to live the gospel, and he found it vaguely disquieting when Jones challenged him directly with the question: Who are *you*, and what are *you* doing with your life? Is what you are doing today more important than what we're doing here at the People's Temple?

Poor Bob Levering. After the events of November 1978 he went through a profound soul search over the favorable article he had produced in March 1977 for the *Bay Guardian*. How could he have been so taken in? Many people would ask that question. Through it, he emerged with a startling theory. Jim Jones, he insisted, was the most Christ-like figure he had ever met. Here was a pastor who had punctured the hypocrisy of modern Christianity and had truly put faith into practice. But Jones had lived *too long*. If he had died at the age of thirty, as had Christ, he would have made the perfect martyr. But thereafter, with the wearing, relentless demands of his sleeve-tugging flock, he sank first into the self-pity of Mother Hubbard and eventually into the contempt of Satan. The line between the messianic and the demonic was close and dangerous. At root, Levering came to believe, was an essential flaw of Christianity. No man could challenge his society so consistently, devote his life to human service so totally, and remain sane and hopeful forever. Jones's commitment was too thoroughgoing. As a person, he had no way of regenerating himself.

It is a theory worth pondering, but in the end, at least for Jim Jones, it founders on the shoals of method and technique.

———————=◄ ►=———————

In the spring of 1977, two other San Francisco writers had begun to focus on the People's Temple. As time passed, and Grace Stoen's confidence grew, she began telling her story to Marshall Kilduff, a *San Francisco Chronicle* reporter, and Phil Tracy, who together planned an article for *New West* magazine, the West Coast version of *New York* magazine, owned by that Australian interloper in American publishing, Rupert Murdoch. The Jim Jones story was perfect for Rupert Murdoch. The two men deserved each other. From Grace Stoen, Kilduff and Tracy began talking to a handful of Temple apostates. The allegations of violence against recalcitrant members, of Jones posturing as God and Marx and God knows who else, of financial pressures on members to turn over valuable property, began to mount. No doubt the stories were embroidered with each telling. But it is in the nature of apostasy against messianic movements (Brigham Young's problems with Mormon apostates in the mid-nineteenth century are a good parallel) that apostates tend to embellish stories of squalid behavior within their formerly beloved organization. It also seems to be in the nature of West Coast journalism that the aggrandizement of these charges of Temple "defectors" was not closely checked. Perhaps there was no way to get to the truth of the allegations, bizarre as they were, because in this case certainly, both true believers and treacherous apostates had become so used to distorting the truth that nobody knew anymore what reality was. There were no disinterested observers in this weird phenomenon. But Jones should have been smart enough to know that nothing makes investigative reporters salivate quite so profusely as locked doors, behind which, people whispered, the most delicious depravities were taking place.

Soon enough, Jones learned that the writers were talking at length with "defectors." In his scheme of things, this was the challenge of his life, for it soon became clear that Kilduff and Tracy were out to portray a scandal—as indeed many of Jones's practices qualified—and there would be no attempt to depict his good works. In times past, Jones had been effective in intimidating newspapers and magazines that planned negative stories about him. In 1972, when the *San Francisco Examiner* began an eight-part series on "The Prophet Who Raises the Dead," by the bombastic reverend-writer Lester Kinsolving, Jones brought out one hundred fifty pickets to the newspaper's front door to protest the "negative and erroneous inferences" in the first three Kinsolving articles. The result was that the paper canceled the last four articles in the series, and the editors were sensitized to the dangers of taking on this man. In other instances, Jones used the threat of lawsuits against critical writers and their organizations, and these threats were often based on his magical ability to get copies of the offending articles in *draft* form. (A congressional report would later contend that Jones got the drafts through break-ins or by infiltrating newspaper offices.) The technique of extensive letter-writing campaigns to media was also standard, and as Jones's political power grew, letters from such luminaries as San Francisco Mayor George Moscone, Lieutenant Governor Mervyn Dymally, the head of the San Francisco school system, and assorted members of the California State Assembly were sent. These campaigns had been effective with the *San Francisco Chronicle* and even the supermarket rag, the *National Enquirer*, for which in the past no outrageous distortion of truth seemed too dangerous to print. As the *New West* article got closer to completion, Jones even got the northern California affiliate of the American Civil Liberties Union to write a letter of protest to Rupert Murdoch.

June 3, 1977

Dear Mr. Murdoch:

Staff members of the People's Temple, a San Francisco church, have contacted me about an article which they believe is forthcoming in *New West* magazine. Since I have great respect for the work of the People's Temple, and because I have high personal respect and regard for the individuals who contacted me, I thought I would write to express my concern.

The organization I represent, obviously, is the last one in the world which would attempt to tell the publisher of a magazine what ought or ought not to be published from a legal point of view. On the other hand, as members of the community and believers in justice, we are not insensitive to the consequences which may flow from the publication of material which is derogatory or inaccurate.

In my personal experience, the People's Temple has made a solid contribution to social justice in our community, using its voice as one of the largest religious congregations in the City to speak out against injustice and inequities in many areas.

The most moving incident to me, as a professional civil libertarian, was that in which large numbers of poor, black members of the church journeyed to Fresno to picket a jail where journalists were being unconstitutionally (we believe) held because of their exercise of their First Amendment rights. That poor people, confronted with the daily problems of food, shelter, and clothing could be made sufficient[ly] aware of the import of an abstraction like freedom of the press to travel far from home and picket for middle-class, whiter [sic] journalists is an indication of the valuable service which the People's Temple can perform.

I will not presume to make any judgments whatever about an article which I have not read, and of whose contents I am entirely ignorant. I do ask, as an individual member of this community, that you make certain that any article about the People's Temple published here be fair and accurate.

Sincerely yours,
David M. Fishlow
Executive Director

The Temple's technique of intimidation had not always been stick-like. In 1976–77, Jones made contributions totaling $4400 to the *San Francisco Chronicle* , the *San Francisco Examiner* , and ten other newspapers "in defense of a free press." Once when Marshall Kilduff came to a Temple service, Jones made sure that a senior editor of the *Chronicle* was seated next to him (just to make the point that Kilduff's bosses were watching what he did). In the case of the money, only the *Examiner* returned its share, although the *Chronicle* sent its check to the journalism fraternity, Sigma Delta Chi.

But with *New West*, none of this was working, and so Jones turned the ratchet one more notch. Temple organizers began approaching merchants and businesses which advertised in *New West*, in an effort to undermine the magazine economically. But Murdoch, the muckraker, persisted. For Jones it was time to play as meanly as he knew how.

Since 1974 the People's Temple, this organization so often described as "the Church dedicated to the Plight of Condemned Men," had had a Department of Dirty Tricks. The Charles Colson of the piece was a flat-voiced satrap named Terri Buford, and with the sanitized language so symptomatic of the age, the section was called the Department of Diversions. At its inception, Timothy Stoen was involved in its practices, as was the Temple's radio operator, Elton Tom Adams, once the husband of Paula Adams, Jones's "prostitute" in Georgetown. But by far its most creative and enthusiastic participant was Jones himself. The leader had a "natural gift" for diversions, as Tom Adams would later describe it.

In the early days of this activity, a threatening phone call to some target was scripted in advance and then cleared through Timothy Stoen for legal implications. When anonymous letters, containing veiled threats or innuendo were written, great care was used to wipe fingerprints from the sheets and envelope. The practitioners in the department, Buford and Adams, were encouraged to read extensively in the literature of their craft. Their standard manual was a book called *The Big Brother Game* by one Scott French, whose previous work included *A Complete Guide to the Street Drug Game*. On the frontispiece of *Big Brother Game* was a quotation from a legendary private detective in San Francisco, Hal Lipset: "It's too bad when the prosecution can and does utilize these techniques all the time, but the defense is not permitted the same liberties." A few chapter headings of the book were "Electronic Surveillance," "Telephone Surveillance," "Private Espionage," "Locks and the Opening Thereof," and "Files, Files, and Getting to Them." Buford and Adams read deeply about the practices of the FBI and the CIA, especially Philip Agee's *Inside the Company: CIA Diary*, as well as a book or two on the practices of the Mafia. Of Donald Segretti's slapstick diversion in the cause of Richard Nixon, they were not much interested.

"We didn't want to imitate failure," Tom Adams told me smugly.

By April 1977, the Department of Diversions began to operate with an intensity it had never had before. With apostates telling of beatings at Jones's meetings, Tom Adams, posing as a member of some other political organization, began making calls to reporters on all sides of the political spectrum, testifying to beatings within that organization. The rationale, of course, was to establish a pattern of beating in political groups so that the original story of Temple malfeasance was undermined. Anonymous calls were not limited to confusing reporters or threatening apostates. Tom Adams's most enjoyable recollection was the time he set out to get the "appropriate attention" for a march of Nazis in San Francisco. Posing as a Nazi himself, he called radical Jewish organizations in the Bay Area and threatened that Jews had better not come within blocks of the Nazi march or they might "get stomped," but, more cleverly, he also called black karate societies, again announcing his rank as a *Sturmführer*.

"You niggers better not show up within a mile of our march, or you might find a boot up your ass," Adams taunted.

To the Department of Diversions this was simply playing the devil's advocate, and toward June 1977 Adams's advocacy was persistent. Every morning he took a long list of names and began his telephoning. He disguised his voice in a number of traditional ways: raising or lowering its pitch, holding the receiver a good distance from his mouth, even putting a cloth in his mouth. Additionally, when a "defector" needed to be scared, a Temple ruffian or two were dispatched to a nearby corner late at night, an old Black Panther trick, as it was described to me, as if that conferred standing on the tactic.

By Temple lights, these practices of intimidation were "all bluff," for no pattern of actual violence developed from them. But the bluffs were very effective. They kept dissidents in high anxiety and intense fear, and Jones's *potential* for violence, given his supposed supernatural powers, his phantasmagorical creativeness, his well-appreciated vindictive strain, was taken seriously. If Jones could miraculously save the devoted from injury in car wrecks (as members often testified in meetings), how difficult could it be for him to will injury on the defector?

Apostates knew how to operate only as Jones had taught them—in opposition. The world was simply a competition for interlocking conspiracies, each charged with positive and negative elements, each having attracting and repelling forces. So fearful of Jones's influence with legitimate authorities were they that no contact with law enforcement entered their minds. There were enough instances of official collusion with Jones to make these fears justifiable. One apostate settled on Ralph Nader as the only person he could trust with the details of Jones's ministrations and so wrote the consumer advocate a letter. Stating that he feared for his life, the letter closed:

> If you want to help us, please write in the personal column of the *Chronicle* to "Angelo" and sign it Ralph and then we will respond and talk to you.

Instead of doing that, Nader passed the letter on to the district attorney's office in San Francisco, where, of course, Timothy Stoen was in residence, sometimes sleeping on a cot overnight. Soon thereafter the letter writer received a phone call.

"We know all about your letter to Angelo," the muffled voice said.

In another instance, so sure was a group of apostates that some violence would come to them in an arranged meeting with Temple members in a subway station that they hired a private detective to observe the meeting clandestinely, so he could be a witness to violence if it happened. And when Grace Stoen slipped away to Lake Tahoe, fed up finally and determined to leave the Temple, she found it impossible to relax on a beach.

"Every time I turned over, I looked around to see if any of the church members had tracked me down." In her mind was Jones's ominous statement to her on the phone, "Oh, come off it, honey, I'm not going to trace you down." The power of contrary suggestion. Threatening phone calls were extended to reporters perceived as hostile, with the effect that one reporter relocated his children and another obtained a gun for protection.

The intensity of these "diversions" became counterproductive. News travels fast within the newspapering club, and the Temple began to be besieged by reporters, as many as five in one day, inquiring about Temple programs and practices. Richard Tropp, the Temple's professor who was still teaching at Santa Rosa Junior College and editing the *People's Forum*, wrote a letter to Bay Area publications, complaining that so many newsmen were coming to the Temple that it was being turned into a "tourist attraction" and the Temple programs into "objects of curiosity." He pleaded with the reporters to "let up," for the church could not function when "the overworked staff have had to spend many hours a day escorting media representatives."

But the reporters did not let up, especially not the *New West* writers. Already perceiving the shape of the piece and having failed to block it in a number of ways, Jones played his last card, submitting to an interview with one of the *New West* writers, Phil Tracy. Jones was contentious and Tracy defensive, and the interview accomplished little for either side. Jones charged that the article was sensationalism, suggesting characteristically that he did not want to be "legalistic." And Tracy replied that the characterization of his work would be left to individual readers. Jones was not to think that his questions about Temple programs implied "negative inferences" about the Temple. It was a term Jones had used many times before.

"One of the questions that is asked over and over by the editors of *New West* is, why a minister and a congregation that have a respected reputation in the city would be so fearful of press coverage," Tracy forayed.

"Mr. Tracy, it is also difficult for us to communicate this apprehension: we seem to be up against an impenetrable wall. When you get publicity, particularly negative coverage, you get violence associated with it. . . . We had one very bad experience years ago in which a reporter never bothered to go through our children's home, and made up an article that bore no relation to reality. Subsequently, our building burnt down; an attempt was made on our community swimming pool. One of my adopted children had his cat skinned, apparently alive. These painful memories are best forgotten. But those deeds came right on the aftermath of an article, so we have to work hard to undo concern in people's minds, especially the alienated, when we are trying to help, and we have the very real worry about the danger to property. . . ."

By June, Jones had concluded that his San Francisco protectorship was moving inexorably toward an abrupt and ignominious end. Over the years, he had evolved his personal eschatology that entwined his own fate with the future of progressivism in America. He had become the master of Omega, so often foretelling the demise not only of his movement but of the reformist forces in the country that he had obviously come to believe it. In the attacks against him, he found confirmation of his doomsday prophecy. "The use of the media for carrying out the persecution is only the outer shell of the plot," the *People's Forum* editorialized, "and the People's Temple is only one of many targets these days. Ultimately, the entire progressive movement . . . is endangered. It is for this reason that we will continue to urge unity in the face of a growing climate of racism and right-wing reaction that is resurgent today in American life." The grandiosity of his self-pity was not so great, however, that he was prepared to let events overwhelm him. His actions in June through early September 1977 were a rehearsal, in many ways, for what would take place fourteen months later. If things had to come to an end, it was essential to Jones that he appear, at least to his constituency, as the victim, and his followers, the righteous driven to pilgrimage and wandering, persecuted like Moses and his people in Egypt.

On July 16, 1977, two weeks before the *New West* article appeared, he left the country permanently. In Guyana, he drafted his letter of resignation from the San Francisco Housing Authority. Addressed to his political friend, Mayor George Moscone, the draft first contained this paragraph: "I am aware of a forthcoming article in *New West* magazine that will air some vicious allegations in an attempt to smear me and the People's Temple. People evidently do not like to see groups of poor and minority people who are achieving results to succeed. We are in the midst of an obvious effort to undermine our work. I know you have enough problems without being saddled with my own." But at some point Jones was convinced that this was undignified, and the paragraph was deleted from the final version, dictated over shortwave radio, which simply pleaded bad health and the demands of his ministry. But the *People's Forum*, ever reaching for the simulacrum of providential validation, found in Psalm 37:14,15 the just reference for the departure:

> The wicked have drawn their swords
> > And strung their bows
> To bring low the poor and the needy
> > And to slaughter honest people.
> Their swords shall pierce their own hearts
> > And their bows shall be broken.

Toward the end of July, as the ghostly departure of the Temple buses for Miami and points beyond took place in the chiaroscuro of late night Geary Street, the copies of *New West* were delivered to the newsstands. The article *was* sensational, if by *sensational* one means full of wild and unsubstantiated and biased and fascinating charges. The meat of the article was a series of reports by ex-members on Temple atrocities, from beatings to fraud to Jones's pretensions, and a plea at the end that Jones be investigated. While the accounts raised a number of serious questions, it was hardly the definitive exposé it purported to be. It avoided any treatment of the motivation of the ex-communicants, conferring upon them the mantle of heroism for stepping forward and speaking for the record to *New West* . The article put forward no more than the thin explanation of fear as the reason that these apostates had submitted themselves for so long to the very technique of humiliation and degradation they now excoriated so passionately. The writers made no mention of Tracy's two-hour interview with Jones, thus denying the Temple a chance to respond to the charges. The article's plea for an investigation of Jones amounted to a veiled admission of failure. The writers themselves could not prove that the rumors they were putting out were true. The inability to prove Jones's depravity remained a problem until the end, but for many it became an excuse for inaction as well.

Instantly, Jones's friends came to his defense. The *Sun Reporter*, the Bay Area's black newspaper, owned by Jones's friend and later his personal physician, Dr. Carlton Goodlett, referred to the ex-members in the exposé as "malcontents, psychoneurotics, and provocateurs" who were wildly spreading "rumors, half truths, and mental variations." An editorial in the paper stated that Jones and his Temple represented "the most invigorating and challenging" religious movement to appear in California in years. "In attempting to use the moral force of Christianity in dealing with man-made problems that bedevil, haunt, and dehumanize the social order, Jones has created a cyclone where formerly the political leaders, economic scoundrels, and even impotent religious leaders have failed the very foundations of their ethics." And then the editorialist got a little carried away. "Their leadership mantles have been rent, torn asunder, leaving these pompous pseudo-leaders naked and unclothed to be viewed as the hypocrites that they have been for decades."*

Presumably, the *Sun Reporter* did not mean to include Mayor George Moscone in this characterization. For he too was outraged at this example of yellow journalism. In a statement, the Mayor saw no reason to take any action against Jones when there was no hard evidence that the pastor had violated any laws. "I will not comment upon the alleged practices of the Temple, as it is not my habit to be a religious commentator. If anyone in San Francisco or anywhere (and that includes the authors of the article) have any evidence that Rev. Jones has broken the law, then it is his or her absolute obligation and duty to bring that to the attention of the appropriate law enforcement officials." Jones had worked hard as chairman of the Housing Authority, the Mayor said, and a measure of the confidence that the city had in his ability was the unanimous confirmation of him to the chairmanship of the authority by the Board of Supervisors.

———————⊃◄ ►⊂———————

Between his devout supporters in the minority community and his political associates in the city's establishment, who remained unshaken by the *New West* article, Jones could have survived this attack. His departure, then, was not a matter of necessity but of character. It was one thing to spin tales for a flashy magazine which can be dismissed as having its eye on the newsstand and quite another to testify under oath for a court of law, under the threat of perjury. Two legal documents would address themselves to Jones's practices at this time. The first

*The Sun Reporter, July 21, 1977

was an affidavit from Yolanda Crawford, who had been in Jonestown from early April to late June 1977, the period in which Jones decided that he must go into exile. Twice during this period Jones had made trips to Guyana to prepare for the final evacuation, and according to the Crawford affidavit, the leader was already slipping into the barbarism of the jungle potentate. To the early pathfinders, as Crawford described it, Jones announced that the entire church would soon arrive en masse. They were coming permanently, and, once there, nobody would be permitted to leave. He proposed to station guards on the perimeter of the settlement, and anyone who attempted to leave would be "offed," their bodies left to rot in the jungle forest. He boasted that he could get a hit man for fifty dollars and that he had Mafia connections who "will stand by me all the way." Already, he told the congregation, Marshall Kilduff, the *New West* writer, had been killed. "The angels have taken care of him," Jones declared. How would the gathering know any different? "We all knew," the affidavit declared, "that the 'angels' were his people who would do you in, if you crossed Jim Jones."

Meanwhile, Grace Stoen was readying her custody petition, hoping it would secure the return of her son, John Victor Stoen, from Guyana. To leave John in Guyana, the document declared, would be to condemn him to psychological, moral, and possible physical harm. She alleged the following:

- that beatings of the children were commonplace within the church, and that John Victor Stoen had witnessed many, including one of a seven-year-old girl and another of an eleven-year-old "straddled spread eagle and beaten 75–100 times."

- that after a child was beaten, he must say "Thank you, father" to Jones, and that the beating was considered an act of divinity.

- that the possibility of even more frightening torture was often described to children, such as the ministrations of "The Blue Monster," who corrected obstreperous behavior with electric jolts.

- that Jones had indoctrinated children in believing that he was the ultimate moral authority, the reincarnation of a "host of divinities," from other ages including Christ, Buddha, and Lenin (if Lenin a divinity be), and that on several occasions, with John Victor present, "Reverend Jones exhibited bloody hands, which he instructed the congregation were stigmata."

Even given under the penalty of perjury, these allegations sounded too preposterous, too un-American as it were, to gain any wide currency with the general public. Temple members and Temple apostates alike had often put the wildest stories in legal documents before, using a Temple member as notary. So the mere form of the complaint gained it no special acceptance or authenticity. With one difference: in a formal custody battle, the court would have to take formal notice of the allegations, and it would soon do so.

But the departure of Jim Jones on July 16 for his verdurous refuge was more than a departure from America. It was a departure from reality. No longer would the outside influences like the streets of San Francisco or the free press pester him in the pursuit of his messianic vision. He could now do and say what he wanted, and what, in his state of tormented, feverish revelation, came naturally. In the early days of his Ukiah ministry, he had appropriated Isaiah 44:6: "I am the first, and I am the last, and beside me, there is no God." Now, in the remote North West of a corrupt and disintegrating tropical country few Americans had ever heard of, he could live that prideful nonsense. The profane could truly become sacred and the sacred, profane.

A Protestant theologian like Reinhold Niebuhr might say that Jones had finally achieved the true shape of evil. In his *Nature and Destiny of Man*, Niebuhr defined the real evil as man's unwillingness to accept the finiteness and dependence of his situation, and true sin as the vanity and pride by which he imagines himself and his civilization to be divine. "The catastrophes of history, by which God punishes pride," Niebuhr wrote, "are the natural and inevitable consequences of man's effort to transcend his mortal and insecure existence and to establish a security to which man has no right." In Guyana, all checks, all controls of reality dropped away. The safeguards against idolatry disappeared. "For Biblical faith," Niebuhr continued, "God is revealed in the catastrophic events of history as being . . . the structure, the law, the essential character of reality, as the source and center of the created world against which the pride of man destroys itself in vain rebellion."* Whether or not one believes that it was the wrath of God at work, the catastrophe of Jonestown lies partly in Jones's vision of himself, but even more strongly, in his departure from a dependent reality.

On July 31, 1977, the howl from the jungle began. The congregation, or what was left of it, gathered in San Francisco, and the radio patch to Guyana was made ready. On the dais was a gaggle of politicians and activists including the powerful and ambitious Willie Brown, the smooth assemblyman who ruled the seedy Fillmore district and who many felt would soon run for mayor, or even governor. After the usual warm-ups, the switch was thrown, and through the crackle of static, Jones's voice filled the Temple. A great fogbank of rhetoric flowed forth, full of hate and injured pride, ringing condemnations of his detractors and prophecy of the demise of progressivism. No longer was

---

*From Reinhold Niebuhr, *The Nature and Destiny of Men*, © 1941 by Charles Scribners Sons (New York: Scribner), p. 137.

there any pretense to a logical progression of ideas. He floated from idea to idea with the consistency of a wood satyr. It was tiresome, disjointed, endless. A distillation of it went like this:

"We are now being used as a tool to set off a new wave of McCarthyism that could spread from the West Coast to the East. I owe it to my friends to say that these charges against us are totally ludicrous. It would be funny if it wasn't such a cruel hoax that has been put upon this community. Are you copying me? [Applause. Roger.] We do not have to apologize about People's Temple lifestyle. But I owe it to my friends to say. This is ridiculous . . . such charges as I have preached that I am God, when you don't even believe there is a damn God. [Applause. Applause.] We've never put any emphasis on healings, though I can heal, and I am sure there are people listening who can vouch for that. I've said that it's not important whether healing is real or not real. What the hell's the difference? It's not significant, but they *are* real. . . . And all this bullshit about beatings. We never beat anyone in our life . . . or kept people up all night. The only time we've been up all night is trying to counsel hundreds of people off drugs, getting people's lives straightened out or preventing some suicide. The only time we've been up all night is to try to plan how we can get somebody out of jail who had been framed because they were black or gay. . . .

"Friends, they want to charge us with fraud. I notice churches all over America have taken hundreds of properties, and I imagine we could number on our hands whatever has been donated to us. . . . We've got seniors here retired that don't have a penny. I think black seniors are entitled to retire in a black country to a multiracial society where there's a little damn peace, where the Ku Klux Klan isn't forming chapters every other day. Now if this church has ripped off money, how in the hell could it transport over three hundred people across the airways without a cost of a dime to them? How can it build dozens of lovely houses and a great dining room and schools and purchase all this agricultural equipment and road-building equipment? How in the hell could we have doctors here with every precision equipment? You know I have never bought a piece of new clothing. Jim Jones has helped every political prisoner in the entire United States. . . .

"I'm just too damn generous. I know some of you are just sitting on pins and needles, wanting to fight, but that's exactly what the system wants. They want to use us as sacrificial lambs, as scapegoats. Don't yield to violence! No matter what these people do. The major sources of that rag that was thrown out today . . . there's not one of them that's not a criminal. If we go on the offensive, we will have justice. I say challenge these bastards. Show what these characters are: one of them embezzled money from a bank, another molested a child, another involved in making weapons. I'm telling you every damn one of them is a blackmailer, a criminal, or a violent terrorist. . . ." Etcetera. Etcetera.

He shrouded himself in the tradition of civil disobedience, invoking the image of Thoreau in the Concord jail receiving Emerson. What are you doing in jail? Emerson asked. What are you doing *outside* jail? Thoreau replied. Jones called up the image of the German priest who did not object when the Nazis came first for the Communists, then for the Jews, then for the trade unionists, and then for the Catholics, because he was none of these. "When they got around to come after me, there was nobody left to speak out or to defend me. And that's what's going to happen!"

The dismal incantation went on and on. What did Jann Gurvich think of it as she listened in the nave of the Temple? Within it all, his voice told of his sickness and weakness, and, by now, Jann knew that within weeks she would be under his total control.

FIVE

The Greatest Decision in History

[1]

GOOD TITLES often sound contradictory, and no doubt Huey Newton, the Black Panther leader of the late sixties and seventies, was proud of *revolutionary suicide* when he thought it up and made it the title of his autobiography. In that surprisingly interesting work, drawing on the considerable philosophical grounding of the author, Newton distinguishes between reactionary and revolutionary suicide. In his construction, *reactionary suicide*, especially when it applies to black Americans, results when a person is overwhelmed by social conditions, bereft of self-respect, and mired in the helplessness of his condition. This quiet, agonizing desperation, Newton says, defines the spiritual death of the oppressed, and he cites a study by Dr. Herbert Hendin in 1970 which demonstrates an alarming rise in suicides by blacks in recent times.

Revolutionary suicide, on the other hand, rests on the premise that blacks face genocide every day, and to oppose these angry forces at work in the society, the same forces that drive so many to self-murder, is to risk the likelihood of death. Only in resistance is there dignity and hope, and if that resistance results in a probable, or even expected, premature death, that death has not only meaning but heroism. Since the revolutionary lives dangerously, his survival is a miracle. This concept, Newton claims, transforms the word *suicide* into an idea of greater magnitude, applicable to the new complexity of American society.

In January 1977, when Jim Jones was at the peak of his power in San Francisco, this Newtonian axiom received a severe strain. That month Jones traveled to Cuba, and on the face of it the trip seemed consistent with his leftist stance on the political spectrum. He toured the predictable sites—the schools, the factories, the state farms—and praised with predictable superlatives almost everything he saw,

119

including the red snapper for the reasonable price of $2.50 in a restaurant. But actually, the purpose of his trip was pristinely capitalistic. In San Francisco, a consortium calling itself First California Import/Export Company had formed with the goal of securing the right to handle trade between the United States and Cuba as relations between the countries continued to thaw. A prime mover in the consortium was Dr. Carlton Goodlett, a physician and activist owner of the *Sun Reporter*. Goodlett and Jones had developed a close relationship, and Goodlett was generous in his public endorsements of the Reverend, some of which have a curious ring now. "I can spend a lot of time talking about this man who is concerned with the beginning of life, the alpha, but he also has a profound concern for the ending of life, the omega," the doctor told an audience around this time. "This is a man for all seasons." To Dr. Goodlett, Jim Jones had the Midas touch and, perhaps more important, the Reverend had a good relationship with Rosalynn Carter and Ruth Stapleton, the President's holistic sister. Amy Carter had even been to the People's Temple. Such contacts could be invaluable for the licensing of First California by the U.S. government. So Jim Jones was invited to be part of the consortium, and agreements about the percentage of profits which the Temple would receive, if First California secured the license to operate, were drafted. If Jim Jones was a Christian atheist, he was also a Marxist capitalist. He appreciated the nexus between revolutionary effectiveness and filthy lucre. (In the end, neither First California nor its competition, a consortium headed by Washington star Frank Mankiewicz, obtained the right to trade, because the Cuban involvement in Angola in 1977 froze Cuban-American relations once again.)

But the high point of Jones's Cuban trip, at least from the public relations standpoint, was a visit with Huey Newton, who was then a fugitive from American justice, having fled the country rather than face a murder charge in Oakland. Jones went to Newton's Havana apartment, accompanied by several of his sons and some of his aides. Although he had never met the Reverend before, Newton knew a great deal about him already; he had relatives who were members of the Temple. The two men greeted each other cordially, as comrades in the same vanguard. Jones had the style of these powwows down pat. A photographer was along to capture the summit for the Temple and Panther papers. In an aside, a Jones aide let Newton know that the Reverend Jones had not eaten in three months and was being fed intravenously. While it was a brazen lie, intended to elicit sympathy, Newton could relate to it. (No doubt, once again, the Temple researchers had done their homework.) Newton fasted for thirty days every year, and he knew from experience about the euphoric surge of energy that one gets (purportedly, I should say) after seven days without food. The fact that Jones looked well fed did not undermine the story for Newton. Solidarity, rather than skepticism, was his instinct.

After the picture-taking session, they sat down for six hours to talk in a darkened room of Newton's place. It must have been an extraordinary conversation, knowing what we now know. Dim as the light was, dark glasses masked Jones's eyes throughout, and the affectation made Newton uneasy: he had a prejudice against people who wear dark glasses in dark rooms, he told me later. They talked of Rhodesia and South Africa, of concentration camps the world over, and of Jonestown. Newton expressed an interest in visiting the settlement (but later the Guyana government refused him entry, not wanting to ruffle the American government). Newton liked the idea of a sanctuary in the Third World, since the Panthers had had the first in Algiers when Eldridge Cleaver was the "ambassador" of the International Section of the Black Panther Party, and his "Embassy" was accorded full diplomatic rights. (With the split between Cleaver and Newton, the privileged status ended, as the Algerian government closed down the Embassy. Christ defrosted Cleaver's icy soul, and the former revolutionary became a mod haberdasher.)

Soon enough, the air became thick with Jones's paranoia and despair. By paranoia, I mean not the "champagne of mental illness," as Dr. Goodlett later would call it in describing Jones, but a political virtue which Jim Jones had invented by that name. In the Temple newspaper that same month, above an article by the Russian poet Yevgeny Yevtushenko about eliminating war and developing a world humanitarian spirit, the headline THE POLITICS OF PARANOIA appeared. Huey Newton was ready to believe Jones's stories of harassment by the press and the establishment—although no political leader could have wished for better treatment from both than Jones was then receiving. Newton projected from his own situation. He understood the temptation of the revolutionary, in the midst of psychological warfare, to punish himself more than outsiders could ever do.

But it was when Jones first mentioned the term *revolutionary suicide* that Newton realized that they were talking past each other. Clearly, Jones knew where the term came from, but he was not quite onto Newton's meanings. The world was changing for the worse, Jones declared, and the only way to keep one's dignity was resistance by suicide. How could Huey maintain hope, Jones wondered rhetorically, with all the evidence of demise and atrocity about? Rather than accept the inevitable slavery at the end of the process, one must take one's own life.

This was not, of course, what Huey Newton had meant at all in his codification. Here was a philosophy of helplessness and melancholy, the very reactionary suicide he had argued against. Only in situations of extreme bondage, he felt, would turning the knife on oneself be justified. Otherwise, it was not only self-murder, but "a waste of a good knife." Yet a curious code of etiquette was at work in Havana. Jones was under Newton's roof, and an argument over the right-headed position on his concept was not what Newton cared to engage in at that moment. Tactfully, he spoke of hope. True, things were changing for the worse, but there was no inexorability about the trend. Idealistic hope was the very basis of one's existence, the spur for true and effective reform, and one had to keep that faith. Jones would have nothing of it. The situation was hopeless, he declared, and thereafter he went off to his business meeting.

Several weeks later, the front page of the *People's Forum* would carry the picture of Jim Jones and Newton displaying hearty solidarity, but more than a year after the meeting, with Newton back in the United States to stand trial, as Jones sat upon his azure throne in Jonestown, touching on the great moments of his life, he would speak of Huey Newton with contempt. All other revolutionaries but Jim Jones must be denied.

"In Cuba, Huey was living like a hog. His apartment was the dirtiest pigsty I ever saw. He was sitting on his ass, doing nothing, and honestly I spoke more Spanish in one day than he had learned in three years. That's what you get with these revolutionaries who won't adjust, who have to be in the limelight all the time. That's adventurism. I'm one revolutionary who can adjust!"

[2]

The sun was sinking low over the Orinoco Delta, as Claude Broomes and I kept strengthening the platoon of empty Banks Beer bottles, lined up in straight ranks on the desk of his Mabaruma shop. I was amazed at how many of the delicious brews I could consume in this climate without feeling the least effect. We talked amiably of things American, for, despite his tranquillity as the lord of the Kumaka estate, he retained a lingering curiosity in the events of the homeland. Fourteeen months in this lovely, enervating spot was long enough to sap most of one's interest in the outside world. The main news he awaited was of a part for his Harley Davidson 750, which stood idle and forlorn like a piece of statuary outside his dusty doorjamb. Even his father, the Honorary Consul for the Midwest, seemed powerless to expedite the part's arrival.

Fourteen months. I made a quick calculation.

"Then you were still in Chicago in September of 1977?" I asked.

He nodded.

"Did you by any chance meet Dr. Ptolemy Reid then?"

"Sure," he replied. "I did all the driving for him on that visit. He's a longtime friend of the family."

"Do you remember any calls about the People's Temple when Dr. Reid was staying with your family, and a visit from the Temple lawyer, Charles Garry?"

He did remember: something about trouble in Guyana, something about a "white night" in Jonestown. The incident was important. Dr. Ptolemy Reid was the Deputy Prime Minister of Guyana. From the inception of the Temple's missionary settlement in his country in 1974, Reid had been the Guyanese government official charged with overseeing the Temple's operation in the North West, and in the course of these duties became Jim Jones's chief advocate and protector within his government. He was a graduate of Tuskegee Institute in Alabama, with a doctorate in veterinary surgery, and his first cabinet post had been as Minister of Agriculture.

Reid's record of importing Americans for agricultural projects in the bush has been ill-starred in the past decade, but it is hard not to have a measure of sympathy for him. As a matter of principle, he believed that agriculture was the key to his country's survival, and it was never easy to persuade Guyanese to move from the thinly developed coastal plain into the hostile interior. At a Pan-African Conference in 1970, Reid's boss, Prime Minister Forbes Burnham, made a speech portraying Guyana as a sanctuary for political outcasts of the Third World and included black activists of the industrial world in his invitation. The first experiment for the sanctuary was a group of some two hundred American black militants who wished to found an agricultural project, or so they said. But once they were in the country, they hung out more in the rough bars of Georgetown than in their bush barns. It turned out that many were wanted for serious crimes in the United States, and they soon became a dreadful embarrassment. After some shooting on the streets of Georgetown, in a country where the possession of a firearm (under the law) is a virtual impossibility (unless you were Jim Jones), Dr. Reid personally deported them all.

Then came an outfit calling itself "Global Agri," which conned Reid and the Guyanese government into believing the company was serious about large-scale farming. The government put a considerable appropriation into that scheme before the rip-off was discovered. Then the Guyanese tried schemes without any ideological basis. A consortium of Texas cattlemen, for example, formed a plan for massive clearing of the jungle in the North West, in the area that later encompassed Jonestown. The plan called for planting the soil in grass, and eventually oil palm trees, and turning the acreage into a fattening station. The soil in the jungle was known to be virtually sterile, where the nutrients were quickly depleted by deep plowing and the earth rendered barren. The area was, in effect, a desert in the guise of a garden. A joint Brazilian-Venezuelan study found that planting the cleared jungle in grass and grazing it held the meager nutrients in place the best. But in 1973, as the negotiations with the Texans were close to fruition, the nationalization of the giant holdings of the old colonial concern, the Bookers Company, and of the bauxite industry scared the Texas capitalists away.

With this background, Dr. Reid was skeptical of Jim Jones at first and moved cautiously. But the energy of the settlers soon became manifest. Their productivity and imaginativeness in animal feeding and the conversion of waste for fuel were quickly demonstrated, and Reid was won over completely. This was the way he hoped other Guyanese "pioneers" would operate. Once captured, Reid accepted uncritically the argument of his constant visitors from the Temple: they were harassed by political enemies and the press because they had challenged the American system at its core by avowing socialism and proving that American outcasts could form in Jonestown a Utopian paradise. From Reid's experience in the Alabama of the early 1950s, the arguments had that start of recognition.

In September 1977, Reid, along with two other cabinet members considered friendly by the Temple, was in the United States for the signing of the Panama Canal treaties. From Washington, he had flown to Chicago for a social visit with his old friend, Dr. Edward Broomes, the Honorary Consul and the representative for the modest Guyanese community in East Chicago. Not long after the Deputy Prime Minister arrived, the telephone at the Honorary Consul's residence began to ring continuously, and the woman at the other end, identifying herself as Marceline Jones, frantically insisted that she must speak to Dr. Reid on a matter of life and death. Reid was irritated at the intrusion.

"Yes, yes, I know what they're talking about," he said with a wave of the hand. "I know what's going on in that place [referring to Jonestown]. But I'm too busy a man to bother with this now. Just ignore the calls," Claude Broomes heard him say. Soon after, Reid went off for a lighthearted shopping spree in the Loop.

These desperate attempts to reach Dr. Reid on September 10, 1977, were the culmination of a two-week crisis in the jungle. They were the harbinger of what happened over a year later and brought both American and Guyanese officials into the knowledge of just how dangerous Jim Jones was. The crisis began on August 26, 1977, when in San Francisco, Superior Court Judge Donald King gave a preliminary ruling, granting custody of John Victor Stoen to his mother, Grace, and ordering Jim Jones to appear in court. (The Temple lawyers did not even appear at the hearing.) But since Jones was beyond the jurisdiction of the California court, the order could not be enforced without a similar finding in the courts of Guyana. By radio, Jim Jones was informed of the bad news.

In the days that followed, the hysteria in Jonestown built, carefully controlled by Jim Jones. The happenings each day in what would later be called "The September Siege" were thoroughly innocent—innocent to the rational mind. But Jones and his pilgrims had withdrawn from reality: their paradise in the wilderness was a threat to the world as they saw it, so rooted was it in racism. A vast conspiracy was afoot to destroy them because philosophically they felt the world could not stand the success of Jonestown. Every visitor from the outside was suddenly an FBI or CIA agent in disguise. The events that followed must be viewed through Jones's dark lenses.

On August 27, a policeman named Potmore arrived at the camp and took particular interest in a garbage pit in the back part of the settlement. Potmore's interest stemmed from a report that digging the pit by hand was a form of punishment in Jonestown, but the policeman found the sides of the pit freshly covered with a backhoe. On August 28, the Regional Minister for the North West of Guyana arrived and conducted a "critical tour of the grounds," as the Temple organizers saw it. Then came a "Caucasian man," claiming to be from Nova Scotia, calling himself Clavel, asking specially who John Stoen was. The Temple had Clavel detained by the friendly local constable, because of his suspiciousness. On August 30, Jeffrey Haas, Grace Stoen's attorney, arrived in Georgetown with the California custody order, and this news was conveyed by radio to Jones from the Temple's Georgetown headquarters. Also on August 30, Richard McCoy of the U.S. Embassy arrived at the camp, asking among other things to see John Victor Stoen. McCoy protested firmly, however, that his office did not get involved in custody disputes and that he simply wanted to verify the well-being of the child. On September 2, an East Indian, claiming to be a cattle expert, came to the camp, asking the unusual question of what the Temple would do if Cheddi Jagan, the opposition leader, came to power. To the Temple it appeared an obvious trap to test loyalty to the government. On September 4, two Temple staff members in Georgetown, Harriet Tropp, Richard Tropp's sister, and Paula Adams, Jones's courtesan, posed as tourists at the Tower Hotel in Georgetown and initiated a flirtatious conversation at poolside with Jeffrey Haas. Tropp identified herself as an art history professor from Columbia and plied Haas with a series of questions. From the start, Haas guessed, by their curiosity, that the women were Temple members, especially after one of them, who had identified herself as "Kim" was called "Pat" by her companion. At this point Haas found the game amusing, and he was open about his mission to Guyana. He would have John Victor Stoen by the end of the week (four days away), he told his suitors.

Innocent happenings? In Jonestown, they were the signs that the death struggle was upon them. Then September 5. Carolyn Layton, once wife to Larry Layton, later mistress to Jim Jones, always in the female inner circle of Jones's leadership, described the day like this:

> September 5: Jim's cottage. Jim was standing near his dresser and a shot whizzed through an open window just missing his head by inches. This was about 11:30 p.m. We tried to imagine why a good marksman would have missed and some thought that it would have been easy to hit him if the person were a fairly good marksman. We were not sure if it was harassment or if it was assassination. The fact that it was within inches made us fear the latter.

Instantly, Jones's shrill, hysterical voice was on the loudspeaker, proclaiming a state of siege. Members ran to the Pavilion in the center of the community, and from there deployed around the perimeter of the camp with cutlasses and pitchforks. The country of Guyana was turning fascist, Jones screamed. The Temple's friends in the government, particularly Dr. Reid, were out of the country and the right-wing elements had chosen this moment for a coup. Sheets of rain poured down on the frantic defenders in the rain forest. Children, women, and old people stood their posts through the night ready to repulse the fascist intruders. In San Francisco, the news was received on the radio and rushed to Charles Garry, the Temple attorney, who by chance was then holding a news conference on Temple legal business and declaring that a government conspiracy existed to destroy the Temple. "I don't know what's lying in the weeds," he was saying, when an associate whispered the report from the jungle. Solemnly, he passed the word to the reporters, more evidence of the conspiracy, and the next day headlines appeared in California: JONES SHOT AT TWICE IN SOUTH AMERICA.

Indeed, shots had been fired around his house, but by his own sons. In the damp, fetid night, contemplating Garry's news conference in San Francisco, Jones himself cooked up the scheme. It turned out to be more dangerous than he had planned, however, because his sons *did* turn out to be poor marksmen, and one member of the inner circle, a Vietnam veteran, was nearly hit in a cross fire. At last, in his separation from the real world, he could get away with his farce. Years before, in Ukiah, he had staged his first assassination attempt on himself, and then had miraculously smeared his hands across the incarnadine mess on his chest and the wounds had closed. Thereafter, he proclaimed, "I am the only God you've ever seen, with blood gushing out of his chest, who after the nurses put their fingers in the

bullet holes, just wiped his hand across his chest and closed them."
The stigmata. The modern brother of St. Francis of Assisi. A glass case,
he announced, would be built in the Ukiah Temple to display the
spattered, holey shirt, but the Ukiah police heard of the incident and
demanded every piece of evidence for a criminal investigation, and the
shirt had to be quickly hidden away. Under the microscope in the
police laboratory, the savior's blood on the holy shroud might have
been discovered to be Heinz's tomato catsup. Now, finally, Jones did
not have to worry about such meddling. But why did his following not
consign more importance to this transparent fraud? To me, it has
always been the most haunting question, made all the more frightening by the answer given me by a Temple loyalist who remained loyal
well after the apocalypse.

"If the September siege was faked," she said, "his purpose was to
unite the people. Whether it was faked for effect or real didn't really
matter to me. I never asked. There was always the possibility that it
was real. I trusted his judgment that it was for a good purpose. The end
justifies the means, and if it took a staged event, then so be it."

This hideous leap of faith revealed again the religious structure of
the Jonestown experience. The pilgrims in Guyana had come to their
heaven on earth, and there they basked in the grace and the closeness
of their secular God, Jim, the only God they could touch. At the dinner
table they performed their sacrament of gratitude: "I want to thank Jim
for . . . Without you, none of this would be possible. Without you, I
would be back in Detroit [etc.]." To doubt him was not so much
disloyalty as sacrilege. Their presence in this sole multiracial paradise
in the world was justified *by faith alone.*

But this suspension of skepticism, this total faith in Jones, even if he
were engaged in preposterous fakery, perfectly mirrored in reverse the
Christian's faith in Jesus Christ. The heart of that faith, some
theologians consider to be the refusal of idolatry and the constant
doubt of all claims made by man on earth. In traditional Catholicism,
salvation comes through good works, whereas traditional Protestant-
ism argues that even an endless string of good works cannot guarantee
entrance into the Kingdom of God. For Martin Luther, the Christian
hope must exceed good works and be rooted in faith alone—but faith
in the transcendent God, never a mere mortal. With the suspension of
all skepticism, with the heightened idolatry of Jones, with no sense of
irony about the fallibility of their leader, Jonestown became a demonic
parody of the Kingdom of God. In the Bible (Luke 18:18), the ruler says
to Jesus:

"Good Master, what shall I do to inherit eternal life?"

"Why callest thou me good?" Jesus replies. "None is good, save one,
that is God."

But with heaven achieved on earth, with God constantly walking in their midst, there ceased to be any motivation toward discipline or good work or striving toward a "sky heaven." Without motivation, with all safeguards against idolatry gone, terror inevitably enters.

In Georgetown, meanwhile, the attorney Jeffrey Haas had been working to secure an execution of the California order granting Grace Stoen custody of John Victor in the courts of Guyana and thence to return to California with the child in hand. Technically, all that was involved for a writ of execution was for the Guyanese constabulary to recognize that the United States was a civilized country, with a fair justice system, for the order to be deemed valid. In a Washington briefing before he left the United States on Pan Am Flight 227, the State Department had assured Haas that there would be little problem with the validation. In Georgetown, this sentiment was echoed at first by the acting American Ambassador and by the Foreign Minister and Solicitor General of Guyana—all of whom Haas met soon after he arrived in the country. The government of Guyana supported almost everything Jim Jones wanted, the Foreign Minister told Haas, but the Stoen case was not political. The custody case should not be allowed to blemish U.S.-Guyanese relations, the Solicitor General avowed. But a day later the attorney received word that for technical reasons the Solicitor General could not execute the custody order himself —evidently the United States had been determined not to be a civilized place—and Haas would have to work through the Guyanese court. The Californian instantly retained local counsel, and a writ of habeas corpus was filed. On September 7, knowing nothing of the mood in Jonestown, Haas, along with a marshal from the Guyanese court, flew to Port Kaituma to serve Jim Jones with the habeas writ. Accompanying them was the brother of Kit Nascimento, the unctuous propaganda minister for the Guyanese government. (Nascimento's presence, incidentally, was partly motivated by anger. He was a devout Catholic and continued to harbor a seething resentment against Jim Jones for the fraudulent healing service that had so demeaned the Sacred Heart Church three years before. But he also sensed that Jim Jones was dangerous, and he was concerned for Haas's safety.)

The party approached Jonestown by jeep. At the gate, they were met by two Jones aides, one of whom was Maria Katsaris, Jones's pimply twenty-two-year-old mistress who lived in Jones's house with him and who had become John Victor Stoen's surrogate mother. In a cordial enough tone, Katsaris was sorry to disappoint the visitors, but Jim Jones was "down by the river" and had not been in the settlement for two days. As the dismayed delegation proceeded out the gate to return to Port Kaituma, their jeep driver burst forth that it was all a damn lie, that Jones had met that very morning in Jonestown with two immigration officers whose jeep had passed them on their way in. So they sped forward to catch the immigration officers and finally caught them on the outskirts of Port Kaituma. In a roadside confabulation, the officers confirmed their meeting with Jones only an hour before and complained of his arrogance. He had made them wait two hours before he would see them. Would they return to Jonestown, Haas asked, and help him complete service on Jones? The officers were horrified by the suggestion. Jones was too powerful. He had frightened them as he sat listening to their business solemnly, projecting an intensity and an ethereal concentration, his eyes masked completely behind his infernal dark glasses, throwing questions at them occasionally that kept them off balance.

"There are political implications to this thing," one official remarked. They did not want to be involved.

The following day Haas briefed the American Embassy and the Guyanese Solicitor General, and the day after he appeared before a Guyanese judge to report his reception in Jonestown. The judge was furious at what he heard and quickly set out a procedure for substitute service, ordering Jim Jones to appear in court on Saturday, two days away. The judge made arrangements for an army plane to fly Haas and the marshal the following day to Port Kaituma with an escort of an army officer and a high police official. If Jones made himself scarce again, the order was to be served on aides, and if they did not accept the papers, the order was to be tacked to Jonestown buildings.

Once again, at the Jonestown gate, the expanded delegation was met by aides, one of whom Haas recognized as Harriet Tropp, who a few days before had posed as the inquisitive and flirtatious art history professor from Columbia at the Tower Hotel. Now, there was no pretense to cordiality, no flirtatiousness. Tropp's demeanor was hostile, and behind her, several beefy males leered at Haas menacingly, uttering what sounded like oaths under their breath. Jim Jones was "in the field," it was announced, so Haas handed the papers to Tropp. She let them fall on the red soaking clay and then kicked them contemptuously. The dutiful marshal picked the papers from the mud and proceeded to the nearest structure, as he had been instructed, tacking them to the side. No sooner was this done than the hectors tore them down, referring to them as "trash and garbage."

"Can't you see we're trying to keep this place clean around here?" one grunted.

For the frazzled marshal, the final humiliation came when, during one of these tense exchanges by the cage side of the camp's pet chimpanzee, Mr. Muggs, the primate urinated on him.

Toward the end of this charade, Harriet Tropp announced that since the police were present, she wanted to report that Jim Jones had been shot at on Tuesday, and she wished to file a complaint against *Jeffrey*

Haas! But the marshal piped up that on Tuesday they were told that Jim Jones was not at the camp and had not been so for two days. Well, maybe it was Monday, Tropp floundered. It was a mistake, and the police officer took the initiative. He insisted that he be taken to Jones's cabin to see the bullet holes. Shamefacedly, this was done, and no bullet holes were discovered in the house. One imagines the touchable God hiding in the bushes until the policeman repaired to his jeep.

On Saturday morning, September 10, no Jim Jones appeared in the Georgetown courtroom. Instead, before the scowling judge, the court's marshal and attorney Haas told of their treatment the day before. Now the issue was clearly drawn. The judge issued a bench warrant, ordering John Victor Stoen removed from Jonestown and placed in the custody of the Georgetown court. More important, he issued an arrest order for Jim Jones, citing him for contempt of court. The matter was perfectly straightforward—or so it seemed.

To the rational world, it was straightforward; to Jonestown, apocalypse. In San Francisco, the Temple radio operator was instructed to move to the emergency shortwave channel, high on the twenty-meter band, reserved for ships in distress and military communications. Instantly, it was clear that a momentous decision had been reached. Jones had followed his normal parliamentary practice: making the decision himself, then calling his followers together to announce the shape of the situation and what he recommended, stating compelling reasons for his point of view and dramatizing the hazards of any other course of action, thus leaving no room for criticism or discussion. Only he possessed the facts. In the jungle, there was no way to test the truthfulness of what he laid out. Then, to display democratic method, a vote was taken, and the covenant established.

To Marceline Jones, who now frantically took over the microphone in Geary Street, the eerie voice of Jones; fading in and out from the stratosphere, pronounced their decision. The community had voted, and the consensus was unanimous. They would not allow their leader to be arrested, nor would they allow John Victor Stoen to be taken from the camp. It was a matter of principle. The arrest order was illegal, the service improper, or so his "distinguished" Georgetown attorney, Sir Lionel Luckhoo, had told him. If they allowed one member of the group to be taken, there would be others. It would set a precedent. Where would it stop? The most profound assurances from "high government officals" that this action would never happen had been violated. Their enemies had waited until their friends, especially that "great humanitarian" Dr. Ptolemy Reid, were out of the country. A coup was under way. The fascist elements of Guyana were taking over in the absence of the good democrats. Why else would an army plane have brought in the marshal to serve the court order?

Jones talked endlessly, deliriously. As time went on, more complicated and ghastly scenarios occurred to him. He seemed to think them up with each passing hour, as if he perceived a need to keep the following from getting bored. He would gladly go to jail or even turn over John Victor, he told San Francisco, but the community had voted against it. "I offered to make that painful sacrifice, but the people said no. The morale could not stand it," he said. "I counseled with all seven hundred people here [two hundred émigrés were still to come]. Their vote was unanimous. The decision is not to sacrifice one person, and that I not be arrested. I don't give a damn about going to jail. I'm ready to die. Please let my friends know that. I have guilt that I'm not in jail with the kind of corruption that I have seen in capitalism." His sacerdotal voice rose and fell with a paced resignation.

There were only a few options left to them. He ordered his California compatriots to go to all lengths to reach Dr. Reid in Chicago: to have him call off this "illegal" action by the Guyanese courts or implicitly to face the prospect of seven hundred deaths in Jonestown. Further, all Third World countries should be contacted to see who might take the entire community to a safe haven, free of harassment.

"We want to move out together. We want a ship to pick us up if there's a country that will give us asylum. We will not move out separately. We want a place of asylum for us and for those in the States who wish to be shed of racism . . . perhaps in Tanzania, maybe even in Uganda. That chap there [referring to Idi Amin] can stand up for what he believes in, and I admire him for that."

But if Reid could not be reached, and a Third World country did not dispatch a ship, he wanted the press gathered together around a telephone radio patch in Charles Garry's office, so he could make his last pronouncements and celebrate with them, and all who might be listening on the emergency channel around the world, as it were, his Eucharist. By beaming his Last Rite around the globe, he seemed to want to do Christ one better. Continuously, he asked if this was all being recorded for posterity.

"We may not live through the night," his icy voice warned. "We cannot endure this harassment. Night after night, day after day. We cannot endure it. We cannot possibly endure being shot at. Please explain that to them. It might be the only opportunity. Or to return to the United States without harassment, whatever. Grant us peace. We want to live in peace. We don't want to abandon the struggle. . . ."

On and on, for more than four hours, he spoke. At one point in the horrid night, he herded them all like sardines onto their shrimp boat, *cudjoe,* nearly sinking it to the ooze of the Kaituma River. Occasionally, as if to give credence to the imagined siege, Jones punctuated his monologue with shrill orders to his troops—feeble seniors and small children—deployed once again in the darkness and the rain, on the edge of the forest, gripping pitchforks and machetes.

"Keep down there to the left; that's where the snipers were spotted."

"Take those lights off people's heads, keep calm. Whatever you do, don't take offensive action. We only want peace. Act like pacifists!"

Earlier, he had commanded that if black troops invaded in the coming hours, they would not fight back, because there had already been enough black victims in world history.

In the radio room in San Francisco, tortured Marceline struggled to guide her mad husband away from his calamitous course and to keep control of herself. The efforts to reach Dr. Reid had failed, and she shuddered each time she had to report the failure to her husband on the radio. The other women in the room, Terri Buford and Deborah Blakey, frantically and tearfully were trying to reach diplomats and the press. But it was Saturday afternoon. Few were home. Those who were reached undoubtedly received the message of crisis and invasion in Guyana with mystification. Some evangelist in the jungles of South America, about to be attacked by Guyanese troops over a custody problem? Threatening the suicide of himself and his followers? Requesting asylum in the socialist world, or anywhere? It was a bit too bizarre, not the kind of thing one would want to deal with on a day off. But the Temple operatives kept reporting to Jones in the jargon of modern communications and of modern military and public relations efficiency that his machine was working smoothly.

"I hope this is all being documented," he commented, "in case we don't have an opportunity later."

"Roger, Roger, WB6, MID/8R3, the tape is running," the flat, professional voice of Terri Buford assured him. The press had been called, but they were slow in gathering.

"We might not be alive much longer," Jones responded. "Maybe that will get the press along a little quicker. By this time, you should have been able to contact God Almighty himself." Even at his magniloquent moment, the atheist slipped back so easily into religious words. He referred to the community as the congregation, and assured them that Jesus Christ taught socialism and his disciples practiced socialism in heaven.

But night was coming. Each time Jones remarked on the approach of darkness, it suggested the shivering, inexorable approach of the cataclysm. The staff members in San Francisco worked on another tack of contacting the friends of the Temple in the Bay area, so that perhaps their comfortable words might soften Jones's purpose. California Lieutenant Governor Mervin Dymally and San Francisco Assemblyman Willie Brown were unreachable. Dr. Carlton Goodlett was finally reached in New York and a phone patch to him was set up. Goodlett's advice was to forget about friendship with various high Guyanese officials like Dr. Reid, and for Jones to demand his rights as *an American citizen*. It was clear that the good doctor had no more appreciation of what was going on in Guyana than anyone else. To Goodlett, Jones responded, trance-like, with passive forbearance: "Life is the heaviest burden to give your people. To live for them . . . oh, it is much easier to die for them than to live for them." Goodlett blandly conveyed his support and sympathy.

At length, Angela Davis and Huey Newton were reached and agreed to talk with Jones and his congregation by phone patch. They were told only the surface facts: that an illegal arrest warrant had been issued for Jones and that the community was possibly under attack. "They have decided to stay there until the situation improves, or they will die," Terri Buford told Angela Davis. But with both Davis and Newton, the imperative was to support a fellow "radical" in need, and the facts of the situation appeared unimportant. Davis leapt to the easy explanation that the trouble in Guyana had something to do with that custody case the San Francisco papers "had so distorted." Over the radio, Jones was assured that both "Angela and Huey were putting out feelers for asylum in some other socialist country," but of course, they were doing nothing of the kind.

With Angela Davis finally hooked up, Jones told her of the assassination attempt by a sniper with a high-powered rifle and telescopic lens (the weapon seemed to get more sophisticated with each telling), and of the arrest order, and then asked her to speak to the congregation. Her soothing words came easily.

"We are very deeply obligated to you for what you have done to further the fight for justice, to further the struggle against oppression, to further the fight against racism," she said. "I know you're in a very difficult situation right now, and *there is* a conspiracy, a very profound conspiracy designed to destroy the contributions which you have made to our struggle. When you are attacked because of your progressive stand, we feel it is directly an attack against us as well. . . . We know you are going to win, and in the final analysis we're all going to win."

Jones asked for a jungle ovation for "this true champion of the people," and it crackled over the radio to her. From Huey Newton, this exponent of a very different brand of revolutionary suicide, the situation made no sense. Revolutionary suicide over a six-year-old boy? It was ridiculous. But he too responded not only dutifully but with Panther chutzpah. Guyanese officials should know that if they did anything to Jones, there would be a response from the Black Panther Party in the United States, as if an invasion of Panthers might be launched from Oakland. But at least Newton counseled Jones not to do anything "rash."

The undulating harangue from Jonestown picked up again, fading in and out, as if Jones were speaking from an echo chamber down a metallic wind tunnel, his voice coming through the high-pitched, fire-alarm-like hum of the airwave, often dropping behind the static. Endlessly, he repeated the themes of conspiracy, harassment, and the imminence of a heroic death. He told again for his congregation the story of his relationship with a woman called Grace, as if it were now a parable of womanly treachery in a modern Apocrypha.

"You know the background of these conspirators, unleashing their lies. One of them, named Grace, said she was never a follower, but we remember how well she threatened us, don't we? [Cheers] We remember how she tried to hurt us with lies, and hurt our cause with lies, don't we, congregation? [Cheers of yes]

"Now, I related to this woman called Grace and out of it came a son. She didn't bother to tell that, and the press did not bother to tell that: a beautiful son named John who looks like me, and I told you all about that, didn't I? [Cries of yes] Way out in the fields, let them know also! [Far away cheers] She told me to take the child. She put the child in my hands and said I don't want him anymore, and he heard it.

"They [referring to his enemies] think the way to get Jim Jones is through his son. They think that will shut me off, or cause me to die, before I give him up. And you decided that that was what we would do. That's quite an accurate appraisal, is it not? [Cheers; shouts of 'that's right']

"And the woman named Grace abandoned the child, John. She left our church for a long, long time. She went away with a man to L.A. and then in September last year she came to the L.A. church and pretended she was on the inside. . . ." And the parable ended with a denouement of theft and treachery. Not quite as grand as the story of Moses perhaps, but epic nonetheless.

At the end of it, the concerned voice of the information minister in Jonestown, the former television man from Modesto, California, Michael Prokes, broke in. "Did you get that?"

"Roger, Roger, loud and clear," San Francisco replied. Prokes's fine sense for good material was always vigilant.

But the orator was tiring, and when he tired, his meanness showed through. He protested that some of his following wanted to die too quickly, but *he* was holding them back. *He* was very, very calm. Then in a gratuitous gesture of cruelty, directed only at his wife, Marceline, he put on his sons. The nineteen-year-old boy Stephan, Marceline's only natural son, told his mother that they were trying to work things out there, but that he was ready to die. "Now I know this is the way I want it, Mother," he murmured. Jimmy Jones, Jr., the black adopted son close in age to Stephan, came on next and echoed the point. "It's hell out here," he told Marceline. "I'd rather die than go through hell."

Marceline tried to hold on. "If only you and your dad would just kind of hang in there for a few days," she struggled to say. "The other is so *final*. You're so brilliant, all of you, and you have so much to give to this life."

Jim Jones snatched back the microphone, scolding Marceline for being so emotional.

"I'm sorry for being so emotional," she apologized, muffling her sobs, "but it's awfully hard not to be."

"Night is coming, Marceline," his gelid voice said, "and we can't endure another night of this."

"But Jim, I am your wife. I've been your wife for twenty-eight years, and there have been many bad nights. I know of the pain and the suffering you've gone through for socialism, for economic and racial equality. I know about the beautiful child, John, and I know why he was conceived [a sacrifice for socialism, Jones had always said]. As painful as it would be for me not to see any of you again, I would not ask you to change your stand. I can only say that I have great admiration for you, the kind of person you are. I only feel sorry for a world that does not appreciate it. Do you copy?"

"Roger, right, I copy you, darlin', and seven hundred people here have copied you too." In the Jonesian scheme, there was no room for private sharing, even at the moment of death. "I want to say that I've been happy being married to you. You've been a faithful wife, but, most important, you've been a true humanitarian. I admire your bravery. I can't tell you how much your dedication means to me, and to all the people." He might have been thanking a dinner speaker at one of his "Man of the Year" testimonials. He commanded her to continue. It was good for the congregation to hear this love of him expressed. She did.

"It's hard for me to believe, though, that what has been started there is going to have to be sacrificed," she said, weeping openly now. "That the children that are so brilliant and have so much to give to this life, to the Third World, are going to have to be sacrificed because of hate and fascism. But I'm with you 100 percent."

"Thank you, darlin', for your loyal words," he said condescendingly.

But the Event must move forward, and Jones was not pleased with the mention of sacrificing children. It was a slip that needed redressing. Marceline was talking about how circumstances sometimes worked against them. It was just circumstance. . . . He cut her off sharply.

"Do you understand how a socialist country works? The Minister of Justice could have stopped this from happening. We were given assurances that we would have sanctuary here. . . ."

"Please, please, give us some time," Marceline wailed.

He patronized her. "My good wife, if you don't get control of your emotions, you can destroy *the greatest decision in history*."

But Jones was not entirely in control of his own emotions either. He repeated over and over that he had been up for four days without sleep. When he said, "We cannot endure another night of this," his voice betrayed the meaning that *he* could not go on. But he seemed to be getting nowhere. From San Francisco there was no word that a panting press was gathering or that Dr. Reid had been contacted or that his political friends in the Bay area were responding to his fantasy of siege. Finally, he broke.

"I hope the conspirators are satisfied," he said coldly.

From San Francisco, Terri Buford fed his ego. "Roger, Roger, I'm sure they're enjoying every minute of this. I'm sure this is very well planned and organized, and like you say, trying to hurt little children is the best way to hurt you."

"Be sure to make this appeal to good people, no matter what their political views: we've represented the United States so well. Not one, but dozens of people [here in Guyana] have told us: 'We always hated Yankees, but now we love them.' Get that across. . . . But we're under terrible, terrible pressure. Get that point across. . . ."

"Roger, Roger."

"We just can't stand that pressure. For God's sake, find some country that will give us asylum. For God's sake . . . for God's sake. . . ." His voice cracked. "For God's sake, we're tired. . . ." The pitch of his voice climbed an octave into a wail, and then into a deluge of sobs. "We're tired. We're tired."

With no change in her voice, Buford talked to give him a chance to regain his composure. "Roger, Roger, we've got people all over the place trying to find a country which will let people live a cooperative lifestyle in peace," she lied, as if that were the issue anyway.

"We're ecumenical," he continued. "We don't have property. We believe God is love, and love is socialism. We cannot love unless there's equality. The highest worship to God is to serve fellow human beings. God is love, and love is God. How can we really love unless everybody's equal? We're not trying to impose it on others. There's no feeling here that we're messianically sent. We're just a simple apostolic society, that anybody with a sensitive eye and ear couldn't help but appreciate."

He had caught his second wind, and he would go on for another two hours.

[3]

The forces of fascism never arrived that day to take John Victor Stoen away or to arrest Jim Jones. Later, the Guyanese judge on the case would protest that the custody order was never executed in Jonestown because the court did not have the facilities to care for a small child. He would offer no explanation as to why Jim Jones was never arrested.

The explanation instead came nine months later in an affidavit filed in San Francisco by Deborah Blakey, who had been in the radio room on Geary Street during the September siege.

"The September crisis concerning John Stoen reached major proportions. The radio messages from Guyana were frenzied and hysterical. One morning, Terri Buford, public relations advisor to Reverend Jones, and I were instructed to place a telephone call to a high-ranking Guyanese official who was visiting the United States and deliver the following threat: unless the government of Guyana took immediate steps to stall the Guyanese court action regarding John Stoen's custody, the entire population of Jonestown would extinguish itself in a mass suicide by 5:30 p.m. that day. I was later informed that Temple members in Guyana placed similar calls to other Guyanese officials."

Later, Deborah Blakey would be more specific. The wife of Prime Minister Forbes Burnham had been one official to whom the suicide threat was delivered. So the astonishing ploy worked. The legal pressure on Jones relaxed, and Jeffrey Haas went back to San Francisco empty-handed. As of September 1977, the treatment of the People's Temple within Guyana was a political matter to be handled at the highest level. As of this date, regardless of what it would say later, the government of Guyana, particularly the Prime Minister and the Deputy Prime Minister, knew exactly how explosive a group it had within its midst. So too did the countless shortwave radio operators around the world who monitored this crisis on the emergency channel. As of this date, the American Embassy in Georgetown knew that the clear-cut judicial directives of the Guyanese court system had been scrapped in the Stoen case, because they were so informed by Jeffrey Haas before he departed, and that Jim Jones's power within the Guyanese government had risen to the level of a separate principality. The threat of suicide had worked, but it had *always* worked, a Temple survivor would later tell me, always until U.S. Congressman Leo Ryan refused to be intimidated fifteen months later.

The effect of this crisis on Jones was crucial. It was "the setback of all time," he called it. Although he had succeeded in avoiding arrest in September 1977, the notion that he would be arrested if he ever left Jonestown became firmly implanted in his mind. It went beyond a notion to become an obsessive fear in the months ahead. In the fourteen months that followed, he left his settlement only once: to attend a concert of the Temple band in Port Kaituma, where he was certain of the constabulary.

He was trapped, and once he felt trapped, the end was inevitable.

"Once he became a prisoner in his own compound, the die was cast," one of his closest associate ministers would tell me later. "It became not a matter of how, but of when."

S I X

Tricking
the Natives

[1]

I N REACHING for his paradise in the jungle, Jim Jones was rooted in three millennia of ecclesiastical history. Harvard theologian George Williams has written that, as a tool of interpretation for church history, the concept of the garden in the wilderness equals that of the frontier for American history. The refuge in the desert has always been a state of mind as well as a state of nature. "It can be taken alternatively either as a state of bewilderment or a place of protective refuge and disciplined contemplation," Professor Williams wrote in his work *Wilderness and Paradise in Christian Thought.* "The millennial tutelage of Scripture had charged the wilderness with epic significance and theological meaning. The wilderness had become, in fact, a complex symbol of significance both for corporate and for the personal expression of Christian Life."* The Hebrews celebrated the conversion of Sinai's dryness into fertility. The dove led Jesus into the wilderness for his Temptation. The search for the New Eden has been constant. These are themes basic to Christian faith.

But the longing for paradise in the wasteland has positive and negative connotations. As Williams remarks, the pilgrimage to the beyond can express both the grace and the wrath of God, his protective as well as his punitive providence. It can be a place of salvation and covenant, but also of confusion and damnation. If it can be heaven on earth, it can also be the Lord's testing ground, or worse, a banishment, followed by dissolution, then chaos, then endless aimless wandering, finally, the dominion of the Devil. The very precariousness of the wilderness garden is central to the concept. But then, so too is the search for it epic and dangerous and heroic.

---

*From *Wilderness and Paradise in Christian Thought,* © 1952 by George Williams (New York: Harper), p. 4.

All of this appealed to the grandiose core of Jim Jones's personality. As early as 1960, Jones saw the destruction of America coming in two ways: through racial turmoil and through nuclear holocaust. His vision was to create a mixed congregation which expunged racism and then to take it to the safe refuge in the wilderness, which would escape the nuclear conflagration. He sought to convince himself and his following that the world could not bear the success of this powerful idea of harmony and sanctuary, that the mightiest governments on earth would array to destroy them, so penetrating was this beam of godly profundity to the essential depravity of the world. That his commune lasted only two years, as compared, say to eighty years for the Oneida settlement in upstate New York, many of whose cooperative ideas and sexual practices were comparable to the Temple's, goes to the weakness of Jones's spirit, with its strong element of self-pity, to the shallowness of his commitment, to the obsequiousness and ultimate enslavement of his following. With his spectacular ego, he longed for a shortcut into the history books, especially as he learned in 1978 that he was dying.

His favorite book in the Bible was Isaiah, this blend of religion and politics, with its elements of destruction, redemption, flight, salvation, and apocalypse. There he found his references for the destruction of the fattened nations:

> Woe to the crown of pride, to the drunkards of Ephraim, whose glorious beauty is a fading flower, which are on the head of the fat valleys of them that are overcome with wine!
>
> Behold, the Lord hath a mighty and strong one, which as a tempest of hail and a destroying storm, as a flood of mighty waters overflowing, shall cast down to the earth with the hand.
>
> The crown of pride, the drunkards of Ephraim, shall be trodden under feet, and the glorious beauty shall be a fading flower and as the hasty fruit before the summer.

> Isaiah 28:1–4

Jones also found references for the doctrine of a second exodus, the flight from an oppressive Israel into a new Egypt, through the desert to the promised land:

> The wilderness and the dry land shall be glad, the desert shall rejoice and blossom: Strengthen ye the weak hands, and confirm the feeble knees. Say to them that are of a fearful heart. Be strong, fear not: behold, your God will come with vengeance, even God with a recompense; he will come and save you. Then the eyes of the blind shall be opened, and the ears of the deaf unstopped; then shall the lame leap like a hart, and the

tongue of the dumb sing with joy. For waters shall break forth in the
wilderness and streams in the desert; . . . and a highway shall be there,
and it shall be called the Holy Way.

Isaiah 35:1–8

and the doctrine of a new nation, "born at once" (Isaiah 66:8) and of
comfort:

For the Lord will comfort you; he will comfort you; he will comfort all
her waste places, and make her wilderness like Eden, her desert like the
garden of the Lord.

Isaiah 51:3

and of expectation:

The voice of him that crieth in the wilderness: Prepare ye the way of the
Lord, make straight in the desert a highway for our God.

Isaiah 40:3

and, at the appointed time, of return, with vengeance, to purify the
decadent "civilized" world:

Draw near together, ye that are escaped of the nations: they have no
knowledge that set up the wood of their graven image, and pray unto a god
that cannot save.

Isaiah 45:20

Even in the style of his early ministry, wearing a red vestment on the
stage of his church, he took his reference from Isaiah.

Why are your clothes red and your garments like those of the wine
presser? The wine press I have trodden alone, and of my people there was
no one with me. I trod them in my anger, and trampled them down in my
wrath; their blood spurted on my garments and I stained all my clothes. I
looked about, but there was no one to help. I was appalled that there was
no one to lend support; so my own arm brought about the victory.

Isaiah 63:2–5

Perceiving himself as Isaiah's modern instrument, his hair black as a
raven's, shaving with a razor (Isaiah 7:20), he began to work toward his
vision. In 1960 he had been in Cuba, attempting to recruit forty black
families for his Temple who might be willing to go to Indiana. He
chose Cuba, he told one prospective candidate, because in 1960 he felt

that poor American black families would not be so easily convinced as Cubans, who might be finding the austerity and economic chaos of the early Castro rule unpleasant. His technique then, as always, was persuasion by repetition and exhaustion. One recruit told of Jones keeping him in his Havana hotel room from 7:00 a.m. to 8:00 p.m., talking without break. Part of the indoctrination went like this: "We will purchase buses and homes; there will be stores, so the people will have enough clothes. The Cubans will work on farms. They will be laborers. The people in the United States will keep their outside jobs, and they will provide money. The more we expand, the more money we'll have. You'll want to be in the church when you see all the money. We're going to have different races living together, eating together. No racism. No oppression. Everyone will be happy." In 1960, this was a radical and inflammatory idea, but also an unworkable one. For this particular recruit, the taste of the People's Temple was like the first sweet bite of a persimmon, before the alkaline sourness puckers the mouth. He soon found himself a virtual prisoner of Jones once he got to Indiana, and finally fled to New York on a ruse. In America, escape was possible.

A year later, Jones announced to his Temple that he was taking a year's sabbatical to search for their final sanctuary in the world. He considered going to Africa, but discarded the idea because of distance and language. First he went to Hawaii, but with Pearl Harbor, the islands were hardly a refuge from nuclear attack, and, besides, everyone wants a sanctuary in Hawaii. From there he traveled to Brazil, via British Guiana. A news report in the *Guiana Graphic* of October 21, 1961, pictures Jones with his family above the caption CHURCH BLAMED FOR REDS' RISE. By spending money on air-conditioned churches and big houses, ministers were promoting the rise of Communism, preached Jones, the secret Communist. The lucre could be better spent on developing countries like British Guiana. Evangelists were the special hypocrites. "Those preachers are wealthy men and should not take a cent from people. It's all robbery," and he cautioned the Guyanese about sending money to such frauds.

In Brazil he settled for eight months in Belo Horizonte, an inland city of over a million in eastern Brazil and the capital of Minas Gerais state. Here the vision of the jungle sanctuary gelled. To support himself and his "rainbow" family, as he called his eight multiracial sons and daughters, he worked odd jobs, one in a laundry, another for three months as an investment salesman. But he was not very adept at selling investments. Curiously, his boss found him too shy. Still, he projected an air of mystery. His house saw a constant parade of nighttime visitors, and during the day he left well attired with his briefcase in the morning and returned late at night. Always he avoided going into specifics about what he did. When he claimed to be a retired army officer, the suspicion grew that he was an intelligence agent of some sort. Once when he made a rare visit to the investment company office, he opened a briefcase full of checks, made out to him, clearly donations from Indiana and in amounts large enough to handle a purchase of land. To neighbors in Belo Horizonte, his dream of a jungle refuge for the poor and the oppressed was clearly expressed. He spoke often of racial integration, and as always made much of the persecution he had experienced in the United States, telling one Brazilian that, for his beliefs, he had been *stoned*, like St. Stephen, the first Christian martyr after whom he had named his only natural-born son. But he complained that Brazilian blacks were suspicious of him, and it was not easy for him to break this down. So he set about distributing food willy-nilly to whoever came to his house, and even ran an advertisement for the service in a local newspaper, offering spiritual assistance in the bargain.

But in the end, Belo Horizonte found his vision unappealing, and in February Jones moved to Rio de Janeiro. He tried teaching English in a private school, but on the first day of school he showed his students a picture of his family, apparently to test their liberalism, and was fired at the close of business. Again, he drifted into investment brokering and began doing social work, under Catholic direction, in the *favelas*, the hillside slums of Black Orpheus. He spoke openly of being a Marxist, a strange boast for an investment salesman who claimed also to be an ordained Baptist minister and who hardly possessed an intellectual grasp of economics. His show of dialectical materialism, once again, was simply to distribute food to the poor.

To one who knew Jones during his Brazilian sabbatical, the Reverend became progressively preoccupied with the promiscuous life of Rio, especially the kissing on the streets, the nudity, the propensity to urinate openly, and the presence of homosexuals. On the surface, the preacher projected the image of the upright, frugal family man, so dedicated to the principle of racial harmony that he had poignantly adopted black and Korean children, thus atoning in his personal life for the military and racial sins of his homeland. But the ends justified the means, and one of the means was sex. In his delirious depravity at the end of his life, lying naked on his bed in the jungle heat, taking his injections of five tranquillizers simultaneously, ministered to by his mistresses, calling teenage girls in to gratify him sexually by fellatio, and unable to urinate without being supported by his sons, sometimes for two hours or more, due to his raging prostatitis, Jones recalled his Rio sacrifices:

"[The Ambassador's wife] took a shine to me. We had all those kids to feed, and there was no funding. The Brazilians had tried to make a go of this orphanage and school, but they did not have any resources, and I became the principal food resource.

"So this Ambassador's wife offered me a pile of money if I'd fuck her, so I did. There is nothing to compare with the kind of revulsion felt when you're lying next to someone whom you loathe. And I loathed her, and everything she stood for: for the arrogance of wealth, the racism, the cruelty. I puked afterwards, it was that bad. But I got the money and I bought food and took it to these children. Only I made that bitch go with me, so she could see the other side of life. And when these half-starved, black and brown children reached out to touch her dress to thank her, she snatched her skirt away, lest they contaminate her lily-white self. . . . I could've killed that bitch, could have killed her. . . ."

Thus was born his high-blown concept of "revolutionary sex," and he even found biblical certification for it in the teachings of Paul. Seventeen years later, on July 1, 1978, he explained the doctrine once again to his Jonestown audience. His drift rested for a moment on his Temple courtesans hard at work in Georgetown. What did Paul say?

"Paul said you should present your whole body as a living sacrifice, wholly and acceptable to your God . . . and what is your God: Communism! When they couldn't get males into the Party, white women had to go out and find black males and fuck 'em into the Party. That's principled. If you don't understand that as principled, you don't know anything about revolution. Got good black leadership in the party now, and they were fucked in by white women who chose to give their bodies. So if it would save you, or promote a revolutionary cause or this movement, you should give your vagina, your penis, your asshole, if it's called for, and if you can't, then you're not a dedicated Communist." As was customary with these strange concepts, he turned the point around to his own sacrifice, his own denial. *He* could never get pleasure in sex. "I don't know how to selfishly use anybody. I don't know how to do that. I've always seen myself in the role of giving. If I receive anything, it won't be for long, because the giving will be outweighing the receiving."

If the remoteness of the Brazilian jungle attracted Jones, the politics of the country were a lure at first, as well. In the early 1960s, the President of Brazil was the leftist João Goulart, who had been moving his country steadily toward socialism by demanding radical changes in the Constitution. Neighboring British Guiana was attractive for the same reason. In September 1961, Cheddi Jagan was clearly the most popular politician in the colony. His People's Progressive Party (PPP) had gained power. At first, U.S. reaction, encouraged by the British, was to work with Jagan, despite his Communist leanings. But in October 1961, Jagan visited Washington, and from statements on television and to President Kennedy, the Administration grew highly skeptical of this romantic Marxist and sent him home without firm aid commitments.

This was the time of obsessive preoccupation with Cuba, the first Communist regime in the Western Hemisphere, with its growing ties to Moscow. With the volatile situation in Brazil and British Guiana, a second Communist regime began to look like a distinct possibility. Whereas in Brazil the hedge against Communism was a strong military, in British Guiana there was no rightist opposition. The police functions were controlled by the British colonialists, and the competition for power was between an avowed Marxist Jagan and an avowed socialist Forbes Burnham. The struggle between them was not so much on intellectual as on racial grounds, with Jagan representing the rural majority of East Indians and Burnham the urban blacks.

In February 1962, race riots broke out in the colony, a state of emergency was declared, and Jagan was forced to call in British troops to quell the disturbances. Later a commission of inquiry convened and failed to ascribe any blame to a particular faction, calling the events an "act of spontaneous combustion." It is not clear when the American CIA first entered the situation, but in May 1962, Forbes Burnham went to Washington. According to Arthur Schlesinger, Jr., in his book *A Thousand Days,* Burnham was thought to be "an opportunist, racist, and demagogue" before this visit, but his arrival on the scene swiftly changed the view. Schlesinger found Burnham an intelligent, self-possessed, reasonable man, insisting quite firmly on his socialism and neutralism, but stoutly anti-Communist. "Burnham convinced the Administration that he would temper racial animosities in his country, and broaden his base to include East Indians." As a result, Schlesinger wrote to Kennedy: "[A]n independent British Guiana under Burnham (if Burnham will commit himself to a multiracial policy) would cause us many fewer problems than an independent British Guiana under Jagan." In the months ahead, as an American diplomat in Guyana told me after Jonestown, "John F. Kennedy became the virtual head of the British Guiana desk at the State Department."

For the next year and half, as British Guiana moved toward independence from British rule under the helm of Cheddi Jagan, there were persistent strikes and race riots. Some time later, *The New York Times, The Sunday Times* [London], and columnist Drew Pearson documented the pivotal role of the Central Intelligence Agency in Jagan's eventual ouster. The CIA's station chief in Georgetown was Richard Welch, who operated under diplomatic cover as the number-two man in the Embassy, with the title of Deputy Chief of Mission (DCM). (Welch was murdered in 1976 when he was CIA station chief in

Athens.) Under him, two agents, William Doherty, Jr., and William McCabe, worked through the American Federation of State, County, and Municipal Workers and channeled money through the Gotham Foundation of New York to Guyanese labor organizations, who were busy fomenting the growing chaos. *The Sunday Times* reported that the CIA also operated under consular cover in Guyana. The American intelligence activities were undertaken with the full knowledge of British Prime Minister Harold Macmillan, and in coordination with British intelligence, according to *The Sunday Times.* By October 1963, the British had in the chaos their pretext to suspend the Constitution and, one year later, Forbes Burnham assumed power with a coalition government. "As coups go," wrote *The Sunday Times,* "it was not expensive: over five years, the CIA paid out something over £250,000. For the colony, British Guiana, the result was about 170 dead, untold hundreds wounded, roughly £10 million worth of damage to the economy and a legacy of racial bitterness."* But for Drew Pearson, the American columnist, and doubtless for most Americans at the time, the operation was a smashing success:

"The United States permitted Cuba to go Communist purely through default and diplomatic bungling," wrote Pearson. "The problem now is to look ahead and make sure we don't make the same mistake again. . . . In British Guiana, President Kennedy did look ahead." Pearson reported that in the summer of 1963, Kennedy met with Harold Macmillan "only because of his [Kennedy's] haunting worry that British Guiana would set up another Communist government under the guidance of Fidel Castro. If this happened just before the presidential election of 1964, and if at that time a Communist Guiana began seizing the Reynolds Metals aluminum operation and other American properties, Kennedy knew the political effect would be disastrous."†

For Jim Jones, working in the slums above Rio de Janeiro in late 1963, the political turmoil across the border in Guyana was probably remote, but the tradition of intense CIA activity in Guyana would later fit nicely into his "politics of paranoia." Meanwhile, in Brazil, the military was on the verge of a coup against the Goulart regime, and Jones prepared to fly home to Indiana. By his own testimony, he "got out of there just in time." He could build no model of millennial harmony in a country ruled by a military dictatorship, no matter how safe it was from a nuclear war between the superpowers, and in his projection of his own self-importance, he saw himself as a target for a

---

*From *The Sunday Times* (London), April 16, 1967.
†From syndicated column of March 27, 1964, © 1964 by Drew Pearson.

new right-wing regime. "You know, I didn't just hand out food in Brazil," he told his chronicler in Jonestown. "I'd given assistance to various underground people, and I preached Communism openly." International intrigue fascinated him, and it blew up his ego to think that American officials might find him a figure to keep tabs on. "Questions were asked at the places I visited, and AID officials questioned one Brazilian family extensively about my activities. AID must've played a significant role in CIA activities." But then, with uncharacteristic modesty, he added: "Of course, I know it's easy to get caught up in phantoms." It was one of the major understatements of his career.

He left Brazil shortly after John F. Kennedy's assassination, and shortly before the first of a string of military regimes took over in Brazil. Arriving back at his Temple in Indianapolis, he announced to the congregation that Brazil would not be an appropriate place for a sanctuary, given its turn to the right, but that British Guiana looked very good. In his absence, however, his church had become rife with dissension. An associate minister with a Pentecostal background had undermined Jones's teaching of integration and brotherhood; and it would take Jones some time to patch up the dissension, to move on to his next staging area in Ukiah, California, before he could think once again about his Isaiah destiny.

In 1970, four years after Guyana's independence from Britain, he returned to Guyana again. The year 1970 was a pivotal one in Guyanese-U.S. relations. Since independence, the diplomacy had been cordial, but in 1970 Burnham started a more dramatic course toward nonalignment and socialism by establishing diplomatic relations with Cuba. Under the terms of Public Law 480, the United States suspended all AID as a consequence. Also in 1970, Guyana left the British Commonwealth. Relations with the West declined steadily in the years that followed. The giant Booker interests of Britain were nationalized. In 1974 the American aluminum holdings of Reynolds and Alcan were taken over. Anticipating nationalization, Union Carbide had pulled its manganese operation out of Matthews Ridge and Port Kaituma so rapidly that it left behind massive steam cranes—now rusting behemoths overtaken by the jungle on the outskirts of the village—along with its cream-colored washing plant at the Ridge and its tippler at Port Kaituma to fall apart with the years. In the socialist construction of the government, Union Carbide was often used as a prototype of how capitalist interests gouged the country of its wealth and then abandoned the country abruptly, leaving only a great gaping hole in the ground.

In this climate of declining cordiality, Jones returned for a third time in late 1973. This time he brought with him a letter of introduction to

Ptolemy Reid, the Deputy Prime Minister, from Claude Worrell, Guyana's Honorary Consul in Los Angeles.

The Worrell endorsement portrayed Jones not as a blathering evangelist, terrifying his flock with hell and damnation, but as the leader of a large, committed following who were ready to put their considerable skills at the behest of Guyana, and whose philosophy paralleled that of the Cooperative Republic.

The nadir of U.S.-Guyanese relations came in October 1976, when a Cuban airliner, en route from Havana to Caracas, crashed in the Caribbean, killing seventy-three persons, including eleven Guyanese. Fidel Castro charged the CIA with responsibility, and Prime Minister Forbes Burnham took up the familiar refrain. The United States was trying to destabilize Guyana and other "progressive" Caribbean governments no longer with words and verbal exchanges, but now with acts and deeds. "This I know," Burnham told an audience. "The friends of the CIA, the people that are harbored by the CIA, the people that have been encouraged by the CIA, the people who had guns from the CIA to invade Cuba in 1961 are responsible. He who is without sin put up his hand." Small gratitude from one who owed his own career to the CIA. And then, with the tired rhetoric to which Jim Jones would later give a different cast, the Prime Minister said: "We will rather die on our feet, than live on our knees beneath any imperialism."

The U.S. State Department reacted with uncharacteristic harsh words, calling Burnham's charge of U.S. complicity "bald-faced lies." The U.S. Chargé d'Affaires was recalled. For three months the United States was represented by the chief consular officer in Guyana, Richard McCoy.

In the midst of this sharp exchange, Jim Jones wandered into the offices of the *Guyana Chronicle* in Georgetown. The local writer who received him and later wrote a promotional story about the agricultural project in the North West, found Jones dapper-looking, "more like an American playboy than a religious leader." During an interview that lasted more than an hour, Jones suddenly announced that he had booked a seat on the very Cuban airliner that was sabotaged, but changed his plans at the last moment—another Jones revelation, without doubt. "They've tried to kill me three times in the U.S.," he told his interviewer, and he expressed particular bitterness toward the CIA. The story spread quickly among his flock. So many times before, he had claimed to prevent serious injury to one of his following by revelation. Many members pinned red "prayer clothes" sanctified by Jim on their person, to keep them from harm's way. Now the CIA had tried, and once again failed, to assassinate Jim. As if to reward his intuition, he promoted himself now to the title of Bishop Jones.

Jones's campaign to ingratiate himself with the Guyanese government moved into a new phase during his October 1976 visit to Guyana. Temple representatives met with Forbes Burnham when the Prime Minister visited Port Kaituma, and a week later the Temple's information minister, Michael Prokes, who in two years would play such a prominent role in the last of Jim Jones, wrote a letter to Burnham. The four-page letter, a blend of socialist politics such as might have been written by Uriah Heep, began with Bishop Jones's disappointment not to have met the Prime Minister personally, but he "was working in the fields when we received word you were coming." But on the next trip Bishop Jones made to Guyana, the letter continued, he would be accompanied by leaders from "high echelons of the American government and the church," including the Lieutenant Governor of California. It reminded the Prime Minister that Bishop Jones was responsible for investing $4 million in Jonestown, that his church had a personal membership of over 100,000, that Jones was a top leader of the 2.2 million membership of the Disciples of Christ (as if to suggest that Jones really had a following three times the entire population of Guyana), that in Jonestown over 10,000 citrus trees had been planted. The numbers seemed to multiply geometrically with each relating. It pointed out the absolute support and loyalty of the Temple to the ruling party and the fact that everywhere the Bishop went in the United States he spoke of Guyana as a model of socialism. "If you are attacked, the [Temple] intends to fight on behalf of Guyana, if you wish our services. The Bishop has told his following that he would prefer even death than to see a good socialist government like yours destroyed." The rhetoric of Burnham and Jones had now gelled.

But of the Bishop's next visit to Guyana with his notables, Prokes wrote: "Naturally, it will help immeasurably if Bishop Jones is received as a dignitary, which he cares nothing about because he detests anything that looks like social climbing. But he has a lot of prestige in the States. In fact he is influential and respected among virtually every segment of leadership in the U.S. . . .

"Jimmy Carter [the presidential candidate] requested a meeting with the Bishop because he told our staff that Jim Jones and the People's Temple is all he has heard about since his wife met and dined privately with our Bishop. He was supposed to meet this past week with Carter, but Bishop Jones thought it was more important to come to Guyana, and so he asked to meet at a later date. He was not overwhelmed by Carter's request, though since talking to your foreign minister he hopes it represents the possibility of a change in leadership approach. . . ."

There were at least two big lies in the letter. Rosalynn Carter never dined privately with Jim Jones, but had met him at a large political gathering, and husband Jimmy never requested a meeting with Jones.

But Rosalynn Carter had called Jones after Jimmy Carter's nomination in 1976, and Jones was at his charlatan's best as he surreptitiously and illegally taped the conversation. His language veritably dripped with respect and helpfulness. How touched, how deeply moved he was that she would take the time to call, so moved that he was almost speechless, and "as a preacher, I don't usually lack for words." How much he appreciated her Christian ethical background and "broad liberality in accepting other religious perspectives." Anything she needed, he would be glad to provide, for he was 100 percent behind them. Radio spots? Television? Articles in the *People's Forum?* "We're going to win. We're going to win," he reassured her. Had he met with Ruth Carter Stapleton, the candidate's evangelical sister? Rosalynn Carter asked.

"I've read of her, with a great deal of admiration. If she's ever on another speaking tour, we would be more than honored for her to come our way. I like her approach. She has such a sane emphasis on spiritual healing and such a deep commitment to ecumenicity. . . ." He thanked her again for calling. "Your slightest wish is our command," he said.

"I really appreciate that," said Mrs. Carter.

"God's blessings be with you," he signed off.

With the Prokes letter to Prime Minister Burnham, the Temple realized that it was onto something. Nearly two months later, when Jones prepared to return to Guyana via Cuba for his visit with Huey Newton and the promotion of his import-export scheme, his chief aide, Timothy Stoen, tried to prepare the way. Writing to Fidel Castro, Stoen upped the figure of the Temple's active membership to 250,000, made it the single largest church in America, and "respectfully" recommended that Castro consider making the Jones trip a *Visit of State!*

Calling the Bishop Castro's most influential ally in America, citing Jones's constant condemnation of the CIA, particularly its tactics like the bombing of the Cubana airliner, referring to the way Guyanese officials treated the Bishop as the *real* American ambassador in their country, Stoen suggested that a State visit and a State tour, with the appropriate courtesies of course, was in order.

Modesty never handicapped the Temple requests.

[2]

In the trips I made to Guyana—the eight days there in the immediate aftermath of this tragedy, and the four weeks of February 1979 —literary allusions rattled around constantly in my head. The characters of Conrad and Evelyn Waugh, Graham Greene and D. H. Lawrence, Trollope, Sir Walter Raleigh, and even John Milton were my companions, and I soon found that this had its disadvantages as well as its advantages. Before I left for Guyana the first time, I saw Jones and his demise as a novel in real life, one of those rare public events which possess the essential elements of compelling fiction: mystery and horror, a primeval setting, a theme close to the raw, primordial instincts of man, a plot stretching belief and imagination, and a villain of satanic power who had used arguments I cared about on race and Vietnam and social progress to produce this ghoulish spectacle. The story tapped my morbid fascination, but it also questioned my political rootedness. Was the Jonesian calamity simply the *reductio ad absurdum* of 1960s thinking and practice?

Confronting real, rather than imagined, horror forces one to discard instantly the extravagant, and often pleasurable, emotions that good horror literature induces. Suddenly, in the midst of this human and political disaster, there was no training, no preparation, no insulation available. I matched the animal faith of Jonestown with animal apprehension and fear of my own. The unexpected telephone call, the message at the hotel desk from an unknown person, the creepy feeling of being watched and followed, if not by government agents or violent, conscienceless religious zealots, then by knife-bearing thieves ready to drag you into the slum even the police feared to enter. In cultivated outsiders, this mood in Georgetown induced the strangest behavior. A perfectly suave, worldly reporter from a major magazine found himself barricading his hotel door with a flimsy desk and chair at bedtime. Other reporters could not sleep for the Jonesian wraiths dancing in their heads. Still others found themselves paralyzed before their typewriters. For me, housed as I was in a room by the blue mosaic pool of the venerable Tower Hotel, with the trade wind gnashing the spiny fronds of a palm outside through the night, the vision of Graham Greene's *Comedians* fleeted in and out of my mind—a vision of an intellectual's body floating in the hotel pool.

Not long after my trip to Jonestown, when the incident was receding to the inside pages of American newspapers and reporters were gratefully departing Guyana, I wandered to the Park Hotel for a final beer with a journalist friend. Instantly, when I saw him, I knew something was wrong. He waved me to his room and sat me down amid his half-packed bags, as if to brace me for what was coming. He had had a visit from an old Guyanese who was a stringer in Georgetown for a number of newspapers around the world, he announced ominously, and now he knew the full story behind Jonestown. But he would not write it. He would not tell his editors he knew it. He wished only to wash it out of his mind as soon as he was able, and he meant to flee this backward place as fast as he could.

"I've given him your name," he said of his informant, a dubious favor at best, "and told him that you will write the definitive book on this subject. He will contact you at your hotel. If you want it, you will get the full story. I have just heard it, and I've sent the man away. If I were you, I wouldn't take it either. It will make you the most celebrated writer in America, and you will die for it."

I felt a nervous laugh rising from my belly and controlled it. My friend was a cynic, but this time there was no familiar upturning around the corner of his mouth, no posturing. He spoke of listening to the old man and feeling the terror start in his head and descend through his body to his toes. He directed me to take notes, ordering me to write his name, not on top, but on the inside of the notebook, where it would not be noticed if the notes were found. The image of the hotel pool popped back into my head. The return of the Temple angels to visit revenge on hostile writers was foremost in his mind.

For several days I waited anxiously to hear from this aging oracle, and when I heard nothing I finally made my way to Carmichael Street to see Mr. Paul Persaud, "the pundit of Georgetown." At his well-appointed three-story house, I struggled with the gate latch and heard a high-pitched voice call out to me by name. He had been expecting me. In the basement, the old man sat behind a desk, radio beside him blaring the afternoon news from Trinidad, an old-fashioned pen scratching away on a piece of paper in large, rounded script. His frame was diminutive. I guessed he weighed no more than one hundred pounds. Above his odd, angular East Indian face, his black hair seemed to be cut bowl-fashion: his barber, no doubt his wife, snipping closely around the ears and leaving the long strands on top to cascade in unmanageable curls down the side of his head. He had a habit of constantly pushing the copious forelock back over his head, as if in irritation, as he talked. His head shook with age and with the cadence of his words.

"There's been a car crash today, and eight East Indians were killed," he announced languidly as I entered his open-air basement office. "The Indian press will want to know about that, but I'm a lazy reporter. I'll file it tomorrow perhaps."

But we both knew that was not the incident I'd come to discuss.

Over time, I would have a number of conversations with Persaud, and, fairly or unfairly, I came to view him as the incarnation of Petit Pierre, again from Greene's *Comedians*. Petit Pierre was a journalist in the Haiti-set novel, and his exact connection to the atavistic regime of Papa Doc was never quite stated. He always delivered bad news in the most unctuous, charming way, and whenever he was seen wandering up the driveway, the protagonist of the novel shuddered. By contrast, Paul Persaud never conveyed information directly.

"Don't ask me any direct questions, chief," he'd say many a time. He suggested rather than declared, using riddles and rhetorical questions to imply delicious secret knowledge. How do you explain one-half million dollars in crisp notes found in Jonestown, without the smallest notation of their existence? How could it be that a community of Americans was up there dealing with the Russians, spouting socialist rhetoric, without the FBI and CIA infiltrating the place at the highest levels? Can you see the Temple befriending the Soviets without both the U.S. and Guyanese authorities knowing about it? And he played roles. You're Burnham. You want development. Your politics are racist. Here come eight hundred blacks and a sprinkling of whites. Would you risk letting it be known that you turned away such a group? You're Cheddi Jagan. As a child of the Soviets, would you press for a Jonestown inquiry if you knew the Temple's relationship with the USSR?

"What was the relationship?" I asked, the straightforward American.

"Don't ask direct questions, Jim."

And he was given to grandiose pronouncements. "Jim Jones may have been a rat and a Communist, but he was no fool. He made complete asses out of everyone he met. Jim Jones did what the entire U.S. government, with all its power, could not do: he succeeded in breaking up the Guyana-USSR friendship."

Often when I went to see Persaud, I would stand in line, as he held court for others: the Brazilian Ambassador ("Don't ask me about Jones's stay in Brazil in 1962–63, chief," he would tantalize me later), a Canadian diplomat, the head of the local Muslim movement. Their tones were always hushed as I approached, and they left quickly after I appeared. In the year before the disaster, Temple members had been part of Paul's court. They would often come and spin their tales of conspiracy and harassment, and in the wake, he had spoken for over five hours to the three who had escaped alive from Jonestown with the money and the guns. Why had he spoken to them? He had gotten to the bottom of the story, but he too declined to write it, not then anyway, perhaps later. Someday, he promised, he would write it up, make just a few copies, and give one to me. Just then, however, he was too busy with his daily stories, like the automobile accident that would concern the Indian press, or with his daily humor column in the *Guyana Chronicle*, a collection of vaguely off-color homilies, like "The respectable husband never finds pleasure in cheating on his wife. But since he is respectable, who else can he cheat!" or "No wonder Solomon was the world's wisest man. He had more than three hundred wives to advise him." Or he was busy with the fawning, sweet-puff profile of Prime Minister Burnham in the *Chronicle* on the anniversary of the country's independence. My curiosity about what Paul knew soon turned to irritation, and not long after I was warned about his connections. Later, he was asked, or so he claimed, to testify about what he knew to a U.S. congressional investigation, but he turned them down. "I'm a reporter, Jim," he said, as if that explained all. With a fay wave of his bony hand, he disparaged the poor American newsman whom he had so terrified. "It's too bad about Jack," he said. "If you're going to be in this business, you've got to accept the occupational hazards." It sounded like a warning . . . or a threat.

"If the government likes you, there are a lot of things they close their eyes to," he said once, referring to Jim Jones. And what, I inferred, were they capable of if they didn't like you? I had also been warned about the government's potential for violence. In the early 1970s, a Guyana University biologist named Joshua Ramsammy, who was organizing the tenants of the slums, Tiger Bay, was shot from a car in front of the open-air market, in broad daylight before hundreds of witnesses. The license plate was noted, but suddenly the government closed the records of the automobile registration office. Still, the car was eventually traced to the office of Hamilton Green, the cabinet member who in 1979 was coordinating Guyana's Jonestown task force and whose wife, Shirley Field-Ridley, was the Information Minister, dealing with me and the foreign press in her mice-infested office. Field-Ridley, an intelligent, English-educated lawyer, turned aside any inquiry concerning the Temple's ties with her government. Her refrain for all was that the Jonestown affair was a bizarre episode between Americans, having nothing to do with Guyana, and she bristled at the manner in which her country was being painted as the spitting image of a backward Third World country, full of lazy and uncaring people. Her uncooperativeness, of course, had done as much as anything to create that backward image.

But in the swirl of international publicity in November and December 1978, the real spokesman for the Guyanese government was the unctuous propaganda minister Kit Nascimento, whose training in public relations at Boston University—training in making the significant sound insipid—was put to the ultimate test. (Within Jonestown, Nascimento was referred to as yet another in the ranks of the CIA.) Beyond stressing time and again that the disaster was totally an American happening, and turning aside, as best he could, questions about his government's intimate ties with the People's Temple, Nascimento tried manfully and without the slightest success to engender interest in the economic basis for Guyana's invitation to Jim Jones. Nascimento hoped, rather bleakly, that Jonestown would focus the attention of the world on the "economic fragility of the Third World."

Just as in the days of Anthony Trollope, the fate of Guyana still hinged on sugar. Thirty percent of its foreign exchange earnings comes from sugar exports, but in the years 1975–79 the world price of sugar plunged from sixty cents per pound to seven cents. The labor and agricultural cost of the government-managed industry was over thirty cents per pound, and the simple equation led to the simple conclusion that Guyana was a country which, in the middle and late 1970s, went broke. High sugar tariffs which protect U.S. sugar growers made it impossible for Guyana to enter the U.S. market, and a crippling strike of sugar workers in 1977 hastened the economic collapse.

Besides sugar, the other major resource of the Guyana economy is bauxite. Guyana produces over 80 percent of the world's supply of calcine bauxite, used in the manufacture of refractory bricks for steel production. With Jamaica, Guinea, and Australia, Guyana competes with its metal grade bauxite, used for aluminum. But with metal grade bauxite, nature once again is the country's enemy. The shallowness of the water along the Guyana coast, due to the silt deposits from its great rivers, makes it impossible to move raw bauxite in large quantities from the deposits in the Berbice and Essequibo rivers over the coastal bar. So the mineral must be shipped out inefficiently in small ships. Jamaica, Guinea, and Australia do not have this problem of access. It takes four tons of bauxite to produce one ton of finished aluminum, but an aluminum plant must have a large source of electric power, and there is no such plant in the country.

"Why," Nascimento asked, "would a country like ours feel it necessary to invite a group like the People's Temple in to help us develop our interior? The answer is that we inherited from our colonial tradition a narrow-based economy, centered on sugar primarily. We are governed by forces largely external and beyond our control. The manipulation of the commodity market from abroad throws our economy into confusion. We get desperate and the result is that we grab what we can. We develop what we can with whatever is available at the time."

These arguments carry some weight. In contrast to the "golden handshake" that the Netherlands gave neighboring Suriname upon independence in 1975 ($1.7 billion in grants and soft loans over a fifteen-year period, resulting in a booming economy across the eastern border), Britain's handshake with Guyana was far less warm. Guyana was the third of the Commonwealth Caribbean "big four" to achieve independence—(Jamaica and Trinidad and Tobago preceded it; Barbados became independent six months later)—and its radical political tradition made Britain loath to sink much money into its former colony. The nationalization of large British holdings in the early seventies, particularly the Booker's Empire, made the British even more shy.

So, with no working capital at independence, dedicated to socialist principles, which scared many a potential investor away, the victim of the wild fluctuations in sugar prices, and unable to develop a high technology aluminum industry, Guyana took, in July 1978, the last remaining option to get its fiscal house in order. It signed a standby arrangement with the International Monetary Fund. Negotiations with the IMF had been going on for some time, and in the country's 1977 budget the requirements of the stringent IMF terms were anticipated. Imports of nonessential foreign goods were slashed, and local products were substituted where possible. Domestic yams, for example, replaced Irish potatoes. Many essential items were simply dispensed with altogether. On the radio in February 1979, in a display of democratic criticism, a questioner said passionately: "From the Minister of Trade, I demand the truth, the whole truth, and nothing but the truth: when are we going to get cheese in the country again!"

The sense of deprivation and breakdown was everywhere: no Xerox paper for photocopying at the police station; ink secretly smuggled in for an underground newspaper; terror at the Tower Hotel because of a missing thermos bottle; a Chinese restaurant open at noontime, but not for dinner, due to the paucity of Chinese ingredients; no natural gas to pump water to the third floor of a downtown apartment house. The IMF agreement required that wages be held down to the point where the Guyanese government was forced to renege on its promise to raise the minimum wage of sugar workers from G$11 to G$14 a day, or from U.S.$4.10 to U.S.$4.80. The professional class was forced into mandatory savings with a new Widows and Orphans Fund, expanded to include female professionals, previously exempt, and higher contributions to a Trade Union Pension scheme.

Through all this, Prime Minister Forbes Burnham tried to console his people with the promise that economic recovery would come in three years. But his talk was tough at the same time.

"Neither reduction in expenditure, nor increase in revenue, nor greater savings will ensure stability and growth in our economy, unless these measures are accompanied by increased production, improved management, and a sense of national discipline. This is a task for which all Guyanese, whatever their jobs or occupation, bear individual and collective responsibility," he said in 1978.

The refrain of sacrifice and discipline was constant, the exhortations against sloth and self-indulgence oft-repeated. I went to hear Burnham speak on the ninth anniversary of Guyana's transition to a republic. The occasion was held at the sport stadium on the outskirts of Georgetown (it must be a hard field to compete on, since the surface is asphalt). Contingents of youthful military and paramilitary groups marched smartly into the stadium, with chests puffed out in a manner one might find at a Boy Scout jamboree. Trucks carrying steel bands circled the rowdy crowd to lend a festive air. The audience was almost exclusively black, with only a sprinkling of the majority East Indians, for Republic Day is really a celebration of the final victory for Burnham's racist policies. When the entertainment went on, somewhere in the procession of steel bands and Africanized dancing there was a brief, obligatory interlude, when a lovely East Indian girl in a peach sari came on to sing an exotic, singsongy ballad from old India to the wild undulations of a sitar. The black audience found the music hilarious and shouted scornful catcalls. Behind the podium, from which Burnham would speak, the dignitaries from the ruling party sat attentively with the diplomatic corps. A couch had been moved in for the Prime Minister and the Deputy Prime Minister, Ptolemy Reid. I sat amid a delegation of scrubbed North Koreans, all in white short-sleeved shirts and small Kim Il Sung buttons.

Burnham arrived in his green Rolls-Royce. Drums rolled, the heels of the honor guard clicked at the loud British commands of the sergeant major, and the band played the song of the republic. I heard the words ". . . To foil the shock of rude invaders who'd violate her earth. . . ." Comrade Leader was a massive man, projecting well the mark of authority. But when the time came for him to speak, only the comfortable ruling clique behind him clapped enthusiastically for his message of discipline and sacrifices. He spoke his words in a precise, Anglicized cadence, trying to be inspirational at the start, welcoming groups from all parts of the country: Berbice, the Courantyne, the North West, the dry savannahs of the Rupununi, but a drunk kept shouting out epithets at him from a distance to the great delight of the section around him, and so Burnham welcomed a few "animals from the jungle known as Georgetown," as well. His threatening tone underscored his power. He would rail against the "jokers," the "Ananiases" and the "Sapphiras," the "rascals" and the "charlatans" who survived the independence. "Massa day done," he declared.

In general, his speech was a turgid lesson in perilous Third World economics, and it boiled down to the reality that there wouldn't be cheese and potatoes in the country for some time to come. "It is part of the colonial pattern, whether we are literally or metaphorically colonial, that things like vertical integration of industry should not take place in countries like Guyana, because such vertical integration would represent to our former bosses an area of competition with their own industries in the so-called developed world." But the economy was in trouble, and so the government needed to turn to projects with an immediate return, specifically agriculture. It was a matter of priorities. "What do we have in Guyana which can yield relatively quick returns? We have rich land. . . . In Black Bush Polder [the breadbasket of Guyana, as it were], if you have an akya stick and you are walking very slowly, the stick will grow. That is an indication of the richness of our soil and the greatness of our agricultural potential."

Perhaps the soil was that rich in Black Bush Polder, but it was not true in the North West District, where Jonestown was situated. But here was one reason why Jim Jones's presence in Guyana was attractive. He was part of the quick return policy of the struggling, racist regime.

In the unruliness of the crowd that night lay the disaffection of Burnham's people and the uncertain situation of his regime. But his problems could not be explained away entirely by the classic Third World dilemma or by the harshness of the IMF terms. In the last three elections in Guyana, the general elections in 1968 and 1973, and the referendum vote on July 10, 1978, to change the Guyana Constitution, reports of fraud were widespread. A referendum vote in 1978 was particularly suspect, because the main issue of the election was to determine whether the government could prolong the present parliament indefinitely without holding a general election, essentially creating a one-party state. The ruling party, the People's National Congress (PNC), held a two-thirds majority in Parliament. Its leadership was almost exclusively black, and its support made up of the black, largely urban constituency, which comprised 40 percent of the population. Cheddi Jagan's Marxist opposition party, the People's Progressive Party (PPP), catered to the generally rural East Indian majority, as stated earlier.

Had the July 10 referendum changing the Constitution not been voted in, general elections would have to have taken place in October 1978, and it was by no means clear that the Prime Minister's party could have maintained its two-thirds majority in Parliament. But the government staged a massive advertising campaign, making the symbol of a "yes" vote a house, and of a "no" vote a mouse. All along the revetment walls which hold back the ocean from flooding Georgetown (which is below sea level), "Kill the Mouse" slogans were scrawled in huge letters. Nonetheless, three-fourths of the Guyanese lawyers opposed the referendum. There were attacks on opponents of the referendum, including one upon the national poet, Martin Carter, who was thrashed by thugs in front of the Parliament building. The opposition PPP declared a boycott of the referendum vote. On July 13 the government announced that the ayes had carried the election with 97.8 percent of the ballots. Later it was revealed that only 14 percent of the population had voted.

The International Commission of Jurists, based in Trinidad, studied the referendum vote in detail and declared it to be "massively fraudulent," and that the ruling party could maintain power in the future only by widespread electoral cheating. The electoral practices of the Burnham government became a matter of increasing concern to Western governments which supported Burnham, particularly the United Kingdom. In January 1979 the *Financial Times* of London reported that Britain was debating a cut in aid to Guyana "to persuade the government of Mr. Forbes Burnham to adopt more orthodox political practices." But the only alternative was the Soviet-aligned PPP of Cheddi and Janet Jagan.

This, then, was the political and economic environment into which Jim Jones moved and was able to create his state within a state. Guyana needed his money, needed the energy and skills of the Americans in a hostile jungle desert, needed these Americans on the disputed border with Venezuela as a buffer against military invasion. And the government persuaded itself that Jones and his movement were politically like-minded.

While he played to the socialist and racial rhetoric of the Guyanese government, he also brought them impeccable credentials from the establishment of the American government. The Temple prepared a pamphlet which had in it the following endorsements:

I am grateful for the work of the People's Temple Christian Church in defending the First Amendment guarantees of freedom of the press, in managing the drug program, and in running the ranch for handicapped children. Knowing of the congregation's deep involvement in the major social and Constitutional issues of our country is a great inspiration to me.

Walter Mondale

Your commitment and compassion, your humanitarian principles, and your interest in protecting individual liberty and freedom have made an outstanding contribution to furthering the cause of human dignity.

Joseph Califano, Jr.
Secretary of Health, Education, Welfare

It is indeed encouraging to me to find that citizens such as yourself remain deeply committed to the vital freedoms which the First Amendment guarantees, and are sensitive to governmental actions which erode them.

Sam Ervin, Jr.
U.S. Senator

It is only through the hard work and commitment of persons like yourself and those in your church that our great social problems will finally be overcome.

Warren G. Magnuson
U.S. Senator

Citizen power has always been one of my watchwords, and I am glad to see it in action. The work of Reverend Jones and his congregation is a testimony to the positive and truly Christian approach to dealing with the myriad problems confronting our society today.

Hubert Humphrey
U.S. Senator

The People's Temple Christian Church sounds almost too good to be true. I cannot praise its membership too highly. You are truly practicing Christians in the finest sense.

Mike Gravel
U.S. Senator

And so it went, like a catalogue of the liberal political establishment: through representatives in Congress like Bella Abzug and Ronald Dellums, to mayors past and present, Joseph Alioto and George Moscone of San Francisco, Richard Hatcher of Gary, Indiana; to heads of civil rights organizations like Roy Wilkins of the NAACP; to the stars of the American radical community: Dennis Banks of the American Indian Movement, Angela Davis and Huey Newton, even Jane Fonda. Fonda had attended one Temple service, and although she was only briefly introduced to Jones, she was impressed with the makeup of the congregation and their devotion. Soon after, she became the target of the letter writing shop of the Temple, which asked for a thank you note from her to Jones. Fonda complied:

[I wanted to] tell you again how deeply moved I was by the experience that Sunday—the atmosphere, the obvious need you have so remarkably filled in thousands of lives, how humanly, passionately and articulately you have redefined the role of the church, Christ, religion—I also recommit myself to your congregation as an active and full participant, not only for myself but because I want my two children to have the experience. . . .

In the months that followed, Temple members shadowed Fonda and her husband, Tom Hayden, wherever they spoke publicly, importuning the activists to sign additional letters of support which were already typed for their signature, including statements of outrage at the proceedings to wrest John Victor Stoen from Jones. While Hayden and Fonda sensed something "clearly wrong" with all of this, and broke off contact, Jones in his Temple meetings was claiming the recruitment of "an Academy Award winning actor" whom, of course, he refused to name.

But the Lieutenant Governor of California, Mervyn Dymally, a native of Trinidad, was the most constant supporter. When the Temple was attacked in *New West* magazine, Dymally hastened to its defense. In October 1977, with Jones in Guyana, Dymally wrote to Prime Minister Burnham that the American government and the American media were trying to discredit one of the most dedicated activists and finest men he ever knew, and that this conspiracy to eliminate Jones was backed by a huge amount of money.

In early February 1977, Jones had returned with Lieutenant Governor Dymally and was treated with the honors that his information minister, Michael Prokes, had requested. Prime Minister Burnham received Jones and Dymally as significant American leaders and his Foreign Minister, Frederick Wills, was present. The report in the *Guyana Chronicle* afterward projected the aura of a high-level summit. The private meeting centered on the relations between Guyana and the United States, the report said, as if indeed Jones was now serving as the unofficial American ambassador. It mentioned the recent "private" meeting between Jones and Mrs. Carter and Walter Mondale. "The Bishop made his personal support of the Carter-Mondale ticket contingent on the assurance that the new administration would pursue a noninterventionist policy, particularly with respect to Guyana. The Bishop said he was given that assurance by both Mrs. Carter and Vice-President Mondale." Following the meeting at the Prime Minister's residence, Deputy Prime Minister Ptolemy Reid hosted a luncheon for Jones and Dymally, to which the top Guyanese ministers of state were invited. By mid-February 1977, well in advance of any hostile publicity about the People's Temple in California, Jim Jones had succeeded in portraying himself as a politically powerful operator and as a heavy investor in a country, broke economically, with narrow options for attracting foreign capital given its socialist and nonalignment policy, and its insignificance in world affairs. Under such circumstances, Jones was perfectly suited to create his state within a state. Any threat to control the affairs of Jonestown could be met by the threat to pull out of Guyana. In 1977–78 that was a portent Guyana could ill afford.

Prime Minister Forbes Burnham met with Jones personally only on this occasion, but the People's Temple made the most of it. A picture taken of Burnham, Jones, and Dymally (with Foreign Minister Wills in the background) was cropped to dispense with Dymally, and the altered picture began to appear in Temple promotional materials, with the cut line: Jim Jones meets with Prime Minister Burnham, when Burnham *visited Jonestown recently!* On the working level in Georgetown, Temple staff members conducted their business primarily on the cabinet level. Overall charge of Jonestown, which consisted mainly in helping Jones get what he wanted, was left with Deputy Prime Minister Reid, but frequent meetings were held with the Minister of

Foreign Affairs, the Minister of Home Affairs (who had charge over police), and the Minister of Education. It was always implicit that Jones had Burnham's support, and upon occasion the Temple operatives met with Burnham's wife, Viola, who was an active political force in her own right.

Further, when Jones's legal problems over the custody of John Victor Stoen developed in September 1977, with Jones now technically under the control of the Guyanese justice system, the Temple hired two lawyers in Georgetown with the closest ties to the Prime Minister. One was John Clarke, an eighty-four-year-old Georgetown barrister and Burnham's own law partner. He advised the Temple on financial as well as legal problems. When the question arose of how the Temple's money in Guyana might be best invested, Clarke was quick to advise that the best way would be to make investments in his (and the Prime Minister's) law firm, Clarke & Martin. He guaranteed an interest nearly six times that of the government bonds. The other attorney was Sir Lionel Luckhoo, who was given chief responsibility for the custody case. Luckhoo was Burnham's personal attorney, and he had an exalted reputation in the country's sleepy establishment. He had been knighted by Queen Elizabeth and appeared in the *Guinness Book of Records* as the most successful criminal lawyer in the world, for having successfully defended over two hundred murder clients. Devoutly religious, author of such books as *Dear Atheist* and *God Is Love*, as well as one on horse breeding, Sir Lionel wrote a column every Sunday for the *Guyana Chronicle* in which he was a faithful apologist for the regime's policy of hardship. In a column after the Jonestown demise, he referred to Jones as a "Satanist," but it did not prevent him from continuing to serve as counsel to the survivors.

In the fall and winter of 1977–78, a skilled and highly efficient lobbying effort was run from a commodious three-story house in the outlying neighborhood of Georgetown known as Lamaha Gardens. Georgetown had never seen anything quite like it. Energetic, highly disciplined, and dedicated young Americans, most of them female, were constantly knocking on official doors. They always came in groups of two or three, and were always aggressive, direct, and highly emotional. They pandered to the philosophy of "cooperativism," which the Guyanese saw as the underpinning of their "revolution." And with some ministers who seemed susceptible to flirtatious overtures, much was made of Temple parties and dinners. When it was mentioned that eighty-four-year-old John Clarke had liked the looks of a Temple girl, it was carefully noted in a memorandum to Jim Jones.

Whatever sexual encounters the female Temple members had with Guyanese government officials were well planned. Jones's most effective courtesan in the playful, television-less atmosphere of

Georgetown was a wiry brunette with a flat monotone for a voice named Paula Adams. Like so many of the visible figures within the Temple, Adams had a story of having been healed of some illness by Jones, hers an unspecified female disorder which had persisted for over a year, until, purportedly, Jones healed her before the congregation. She had been one of the original seven "pathfinders" for the Temple in Guyana, having arrived in 1974 and lived in a house in Port Kaituma as the land was cleared for Jonestown. But in Georgetown she found her real calling. Once on an early trip to Guyana, Jones had singled Adams out to a group of the faithful as his "professional prostitute" and had held up her wrist adorned by a gold bracelet, given her by a government official. "You see what can be accomplished," he cooed. She had had a number of well-planned liaisons, but while her voice may have oozed with the carmeline tones that Father Morrison knew, her overtures were not always roundabout. "She asked me to fuck her," the publisher of the *Guyana Chronicle* told me. Her main achievement, however, was her relationship with Lawrence Mann, the Guyanese Ambassador to the United States.

Mann was something of a bon vivant, married to a mathematician, but he seems to have genuinely fallen in love with Paula Adams. They pursued their affair openly—not that this was out of the ordinary. When Mann visited in Georgetown he took Paula Adams to social functions as his companion. When he entertained American diplomats at his Georgetown house, Paula Adams served the tea and cakes. It became widely known that in classic blackmail fashion (or *whitemail*, as it was called in Jonestown) Adams made tape recordings of their bedroom encounters, which were turned over to Jones. But for once, Jones was wildly naive, because in Caribbean society, particularly in high government circles, it would be more a topic of concern if the Ambassador was *not* having an affair than if he was. Mann's voice in Guyanese policymaking was never important, but he knew a great deal, of course, and he was a favorite of the Prime Minister's. Mann was treated by Burnham as the son Burnham never had, as one American diplomat would describe it. The Ambassador's affair with Adams never tarnished his career. Never was it treated with anything other than amusement, even in the aftermath of the Jonestown disaster. Indeed, Jim Jones corresponded directly with Prime Minister Burnham about the affair on two occasions in 1977. In one letter, at a time when Jones was well pleased with his dealings with the government, he referred to the affair as a healthy thing, but later, when Jones was under heat on the Stoen custody case, he claimed that Ambassador Mann was raping one of his Temple members. On a trip back to the United States only weeks before the disaster, Paula Adams confided to a friend that Lawrence Mann was really more in love with

Jim Jones than with her. She could always get "Bonnie" Mann to do what she wanted, she said, but Jim Jones had taught her how. For he had occasionally been on an extension phone by her side, as she talked intimately to the Ambassador, and Jones had whispered directions to her, such as, "Now, tell him that you love him."

But if sexual liaisons were not damaging, disloyalty to Comrade Leader was, so Paula Adams taped Ambassador Mann's political chitchat as well, and at the right time, in August 1978, to engage in a little "whitemail," she wrote a letter to Burnham detailing each disloyal comment. Dated August 8, 1978, a critical juncture for the Stoen custody case in the Guyana court proceedings, the letter admitted to Prime Minister Burnham that Adams had been taping her intimate conversations with the Ambassador . . . out of sheer loyalty to the Comrade Leader, of course. For pages, stories of the Ambassador's transgressions were conveyed to the Prime Minister: Mann's violent nature, his poker playing, his hedonism, his gossip about high-ranking members of the government, his preference for life in the United States. Jim Jones and the Temple would continue to report any ambassadorial indiscretions to the Prime Minister, Adams wrote, for the Temple was well pleased with Burnham's *clean-up* program.

After the Jonestown disaster, Prime Minister Burnham professed to know nothing about the People's Temple, but in fact, since the middle of 1977, he had received frequent long, intimate, and detailed letters from Jones and his aides, sometimes every day for a stretch. Always the Temple espoused "undying loyalty" to Burnham and his party, as it described Temple problems or fears, passed on gossip of disloyalty or intoxication or sexual kinkiness about officials major and minor, such as the minor official's wife who did not stand when the Guyana national anthem was played. In many of these letters to Comrade Leader, the Temple's theory of life and death was openly espoused.

September 26, 1977: We had considered going to other locations: we had invitations from other nations, to go so we would not have any future fear about survival.

December 20, 1977: [Some Guyanese officials] make us feel short lived. We live only one day at a time, but we can't help but wonder what we would face if and when you and a few of your top ministers are not on the scene. . . . We wanted you to know how much we appreciated your friendliness, as well as that of your wife, Dr. Reid, and Minister Mingo. We felt as if we were treated with genuine respect and that helped us considerably, because of our feeling of not having a future.

March 18, 1978: We had caught the Foreign Minister in silly, little lying games, but we still like him because he highly regarded you and interpreted you in an intelligent manner to us. We had been getting all kinds of diametrically opposed views on what your attitude was, vis-à-vis our movement. It seems that a lot of people like to stir up mischief. . . . We need guarantees that our freedom and survival won't be hampered by the machinations of a few racists abroad.

We keep hearing rumors that this or that person will be the next Prime Minister—names other than Dr. Reid. We would have no confidence living under the administration of one person who appears interested in your position. We are not religious, but one thing Jesus said is a valid guidepost: "No man takes my life. I'll lay it down on my own terms." When you stood up to Kissinger, we heard all kinds of complaints. Jim Jones, however, chose *that* time to bring his sons here with him, as they wanted to be present and if the U.S. came to destroy, as with Dr. Allende, he and his sons wanted to die with you. We have been through so much hell-attempted assassination, church and senior citizens homes burned, that it has certainly steeled our backbone for dying.

March 23, 1978: We recognize that to some our approach towards life and death is an enigma. We have even heard that we have been called insane. No doubt, such a misinterpretation stems from a lack of comprehension about our attitude towards living, and especially, dying. We do not fear death. Rather we would be proud to die for what we believe—proud to have our death meaningful. Cuffy [Guyana's Nat Turner] set limits on the usurpation of his freedom, and gave his life. Vietnamese monks burn themselves for a just social cause—not some perverse "weird" sense of martyrdom, but because they felt the cause they were dying for was far more significant than their individual existence. Death in many ways would be a welcome relief from a life of pain, responsibilities, and pressures.

So Prime Minister Forbes Burnham, the chesty Comrade Leader, knew very well the nature of the American pioneers, but pondering the benefits, he was prepared to take the risks.

Jones's other tireless worker in Georgetown was, of course, Sharon Amos. Amos had been with Jones from the early days of the church in Ukiah. She was aggressive and highly educated, the bearer of a master's degree in psychiatric social work from the University of California, and she had always been attracted to strong men. In 1977–78, when she handled "public relations" for the Temple in the city, she had her three children with her. Two of the three were the issue of one Deneal Amos, who had set himself up as a small-time guru and con artist in northern California during the 1950s, his concept: a combination of Zen and basketball. But Sharon Amos had left him when Jim Jones crossed her vision. She was not particularly attractive: four feet eleven in height, with heavy legs and stringy blond hair, and despite her pleasant voice, her overly aggressive demeanor not only came as a surprise to

Guyanese officials but alienated many of her own companions as well. After she was gone, her mates referred to her methods as being typically Jewish, although she was Protestant by upbringing. She could burst into tears with the speed of a two-year-old, and perhaps more than any other Temple member she had the makeup of a fanatic.

Notwithstanding the fact that she possessed none of Paula Adams's sensuality, Sharon Amos developed a strategic relationship with the Chief Justice of Guyana, Harold Bollers. The Chief Justice was responsible for the assignment of judges to particular cases, and should any problems with a case develop (say, with the Stoen custody case), Bollers had the authority to take it over himself. During 1978, it was not unusual to see Sharon Amos with the Chief Justice at Saturday night dances in Georgetown hotels, the leading form of weekend entertainment for the Guyanese elite. Once Bollers even suggested to the Cabinet that if a Cabinet wife was ever indisposed for some official function, his friend Sharon would make a superior substitute.

If "revolutionary sex" underpinned Jones's Georgetown operation, it was only one of many "strategies" the Bishop used to solidify his jungle demonocracy. He had taught his workers that lying, or laying, in a good cause was only the means to a higher goal. It was only a *strategy.* The concept of political strategies was a holdover from the radical movement of the sixties, but Jones had carried this concept, as so many others, to its ultimate, twisted extreme. By calling falsehood and treachery strategy, the moral negativeness of the process was neutralized. That was the beauty of being a real revolutionary.

Sharon Amos wrote prolific memoranda to Jim Jones on the activities of his Georgetown operation and, taken together, they reveal the intensity and the success of the contacts—although it is always possible that Amos elaborated in her memoranda to make her look better in her guru's dark eyes. Here are some of the topics and personalities.

A memorandum dated March 22, 1978, concerning a meeting with Guyana's Foreign Minister, Frederick Wills, reads:

"He [Wills] talked to Dr. Reid. Reid said that Wills is being quoted around as giving assurances to PT. Reid accused Wills of saying too much to PT. Wills said, 'You think that I'd tell a group of people like PT government secrets?' He used the rhetorical question to avoid admitting one way or another. . . ."

"RE John Clarke (Lawyer in the Prime Minister's firm). John likes girls. He is 84 years old. Don't waste time with him, [Wills advises] his interest in your group would be women. Wills himself is attracted to ———. He keeps talking about the fact that her matter-of-fact voice on the phone made him stop smoking. Said if he were 20 years younger, he would go after her."

In another memorandum, concerning a meeting with Vibert Mingo, the Minister of Home Affairs, Amos wrote about Mingo's views on the Stoen case.

"If Stoen's lawyer were here, and approached the court for J's arrest, the Marshal of the Court would have to execute the warrant. . . . He said that if the PM [Burnham] had dealt with the matter of John Stoen when it first came up, then the court wouldn't be involved, but now the PM can't interfere in the case. . . . He said he might see [the judge in the Stoen case] at a cricket match, and then he would bring up the matter."

Six days later, after another meeting with Wills, Amos conveyed his advice concerning Jones coming into Georgetown and avoiding the authorities.

"Re JJ coming to town, he [Wills] said that if he does, get authority from Mingo. If a private citizen tried to start anything against JJ, we could send him back to Jonestown. JJ should be unpredictable, set appointments, and then switch them at the last moment. . . . If JJ comes to town, the opposition could say there are warrants out for this man, and it would look like JJ is flaunting the situation. However, if the [ruling] party could live with the pressure from the opposition, it will be all right. We should check this through Mingo."

Another meeting in March, this one with their lawyer, Sir Lionel Luckhoo: "We asked why the PM would see us in the U.S., but not here. Luckhoo said the PM felt it would be different over there."

Another memorandum mentioned the chief of the Guyanese police, Lloyd Barker. ". . . Monthly booze for Barker. I think he'll see through this (but I could be wrong, and we'll do it if it will help with him). Maybe it should be staggered though, so it's not so regular."

Another mentioned a meeting with Viola Burnham, the Prime Minister's wife: ". . . told her that JJ thought very highly of what she was doing for women, and she said she hoped she could live up to that."

Finally, there was a memorandum, dated May 19, 1978, which reported a meeting with the "pundit," a reputation that Persaud loved. It was vintage Paul: humor, innuendo, suggestions of inside information, and fatherly advice, contradictions, cynicism, and grace.

"Paul Persaud is 65," Sharon Amos wrote Jones. "We asked if he would come to dinner sometime, and he wondered how we know he loves to eat. He doesn't drink, by the way, but says he has a reputation for being a drunk because he makes offhanded humorous remarks and shakes his head while he talks. I think he could be a good source of info, because he's been around for a long time. . . .

"Said he'd gotten negative stuff on us, but says the Prime Minister likes us. There's a fine line between character and reputation, he said, and in our case, we have good character and a bad reputation. But anyone who has a reputation for being progressive, productive, and humanitarian, is going to make enemies, and we were victims of human behavior. He wondered if JJ comes to town, because he would like to meet him, but he didn't seem interested in going to the project. That's for young people, he said.

"I made some confusing comment about the CIA, and Persaud said the Prime Minister asked him once how he could be sure that Persaud wasn't CIA. Since he worked as a stringer for *Time* magazine, he said it was tough to deny he wasn't Agency.

" 'Well, chief,' Persaud answered, 'journalists *and Prime Ministers* are always the prime suspects, aren't they?'

"The Prime Minister simply smiled."*

Or that's what Persaud said the Prime Minister said . . . or that's what Sharon Amos reported to Jim Jones that Persaud said the Comrade Leader had said . . . and who was to know any more what the real truth was? The argot of Georgetown suited Jim Jones perfectly.

---

*Quotations on pp. 165–67 come from Associated Press memoranda.

SEVEN

To Russia, Wistfully

[1]

DURING THE "seven-day siege" in September 1977, when Jim Jones came within a hair's breath of exterminating his community the first time, after staging a mock assassination attempt on himself with his sons as coconspirators, he ordered San Francisco to find another place of asylum for his endangered, precious commune of impotent rebels. Within his magnificent fantasy, he imagined a slew of Third World countries breathlessly ready to receive his motley group, possessed as it was of high ideals and simple brotherly mission. He was assured that Angela Davis and Huey Newton were frantically working to find the next safe haven, and that soon enough, an ocean liner would arrive beyond the great silty delta of the Orinoco to spirit them away to a new paradise. Perhaps, then, Jones could still distinguish between his doleful rhetoric and the realities of the world, but I doubt it. The two had become joined with his arrival in his Sinai in South America, far as it was from the imperfect world of good and evil mixed, and compromise abounding. He was too highly evolved for this world, and his epic mission too good for mere nations to tolerate. His persecution had become the stuff of legends.

Even in Guyana—this no-count country at the very maw of the globe—his enemies had managed to trap him. With the life and death struggle to keep John Victor Stoen, he had rounded out the full dimension of his nobility. He was a superman with magical gifts, a Triton among the minnows, his mission pure, bound up with the affliction of the forgotten multitude. His peons basked in his Infinitude, rejoiced in his Beneficence; and now, they would poise their existence on the lofty principle to save John Victor, this son of Jim and child of the world, save him from this unfit mother, this woman called "Amazing Grace," and this "transvestite" imposter of a father, this man, no, this sterile Judas queer called Timothy. If idealism can be

168

viewed as an emotion solely, separated from the truth or reason, Jim Jones and Jonestown swelled with it.

Still, the great ocean liner had not arrived in September, and no other country, Third World or otherwise, had leapt to invite Jones, if indeed any had actually been contacted at the point of crisis, coming as it had on a weekend. Anyway, Jones had found immediate relief from the legal pressure in the custody case by more mundane than sublime means. Nevertheless, in October 1977, a Temple disciple in San Francisco did sit down to write some eighteen countries about relocating the commune. The selection of countries was diverse and revealing, for it reflected both the sentimentality and the naiveté of the People's Temple. Albania and North Korea were two Communist countries investigated, but the inquiries were posed through the simple-hearted method of asking the U.S. State Department about the possibilities. It is difficult to imagine the Temple being very happy under the smiling countenance of Kim Il Sung or Enver Hoxha, and it is doubtful that those gentlemen would have permitted Jim Jones a state within their state, nor respected the sanctity of his truckfuls of dollars. The Temple also contacted Finland and Sweden, curious places for eight hundred or so black Americans, as a few black deserters had found out during the Vietnam era, and a number of African countries, including troubled Mozambique and Angola. Once again in the case of Angola, then immersed in civil war with Cuba as a major player, the Temple communard submitted his inquiry through the U.S. Department of State. The country officer for Angola at the State Department replied in a letter dated October 18, 1977, which he must have written tongue in cheek:

> The Department of State can of course not speak for the Government of Angola. However, we would certainly not consider it advisable for Americans to plan to establish a settlement in Angola at this time. The country has been immersed in civil war for several years. Moreover, the United States has not recognized the Government of Angola, and thus we have no Embassy in that country, nor is any other country representing our interests there. Thus the U.S. Government would be unable to assist Americans who encounter any difficulties in Angola.

As the Jonestown story would unfold, that last line would carry considerable irony.

Other improbable choices were Bangladesh—picked perhaps for its reputation for starving children and natural disasters—and Turkey —its jails could be a problem. But the most curious of all was the Temple inquiry to the United Arab Emirates. Perhaps the preacher was attracted to the biblical imagery of the desert, but Jim Jones of Arabia? Somehow, the picture of him strutting imperiously about in a gleaming aba and kufiya headdress, casting his sights to a horizon frayed by oil derricks, is somewhat out of focus although Lawrence of Arabia before had loved the desert because it was so "clean." And yet, an exodus to an Islamic refuge might have been as stageworthy in its rejection of the white-imaged Christianity and hostility to the West going back to the Crusades as an exodus to a Communist state.

None of these inquiries bore fruit, however, and Jones began to concentrate on a more deliberate strategy closer to his new home. Among those who had turned down Jones's plea for immediate asylum in September was the Soviet Union. At the time Jones scoffed at the Russian's spinelessness. In Jonestown, he told his chronicler:

> The character, the spine is gone in the Soviet Union. Perhaps it is, perhaps it isn't. Their thrust of late in Africa is promising. But I'm disillusioned when people tell me they wouldn't consider under any circumstances taking six hundred or eight hundred measly people who want to escape oppression. I don't understand. Carter's mouthing human rights in Russia every day, and they won't take a thousand people? I don't know why they wouldn't want to take us. People with no place to go. That's why I don't buy it, when I'm told you can't take six hundred people to Russia. Let's try.

The Soviets would not take the community instantly, but they left the door open. They conveyed the impression that the Temple might be able, over time, to earn its way in. In November 1977, five Temple representatives attended the sixtieth anniversary celebration of the Russian Revolution at the sprawling Soviet Embassy grounds in Georgetown, and this raised a few curious eyebrows in the Western diplomatic community. The chief contact for the Temple in the Soviet Embassy soon became Feodor Timofeyev, whose official title was Third Secretary of the Soviet Embassy and Chief of Press Operations, but whose duties were later revealed to be somewhat broader. In early 1978, the Soviets made their first propaganda use of Jonestown, writing about the commune for Tass. In part the article read:

> Its founder, Rev. Jim Jones, tested all the promised "good" of American democracy. After being sure that his attempts to find justice in America were in vain, Jones called a vanguard of his supporters to leave the "Free World" where they had failed to find a place. "I have chosen Guyana," Rev. Jim Jones told the Tass correspondent, "first of all because this country is socialist oriented and is working toward the establishment of socialism for the most just and human society in the world." . . . After being in Jonestown, one can hardly believe that everything was created in one or two years. The inhabitants of Jonestown are creative, they love work, and they celebrate life. They demonstrate real care and concern for children and seniors alike.

Temple literature was quick to make use of the Russian connection. In a letter dated March 14, 1978, addressed to all U.S. congressmen, reference was made to the Soviet interest: "Even Russia's *New Times* magazine has praised [our] work and done so in spite of our strong support of Russian people of Jewish descent, an obvious disagreement. We receive letters weekly from Russians. In fact, several overtures have been made from Russia, which sees our current harassment as a form of political persecution."

No congressman paid the least attention to the Temple's March 14 letter, nor should one have, necessarily, for it took the form of a printed handout which arrives by the bale on Capitol Hill, a single-spaced diatribe with its important lines about defection buried deep in political rhetoric. But in retrospect, the letter was highly significant, both for its oblique reference to "overtures" from the Soviet Union, implying embarrassment to the United States if the overtures were accepted, for its consequence of locking the Temple into an intractable position, and for its closing lines: "I can say without hesitation that we are devoted to a decision that it is better even to die than to be constantly harassed from one continent to the next."

In the early spring of 1978, the meetings with Timofeyev were becoming a weekly affair. Each time they met, Timofeyev turned on a radio in his office, as if to frustrate the imperialist bug in the room, lending an air of high intrigue to the conclave. The talk was becoming substantive. The Third Secretary acted as an advisor on a number of Temple problems, but the conversation always returned to the topic of a grand exodus from Guyana to Russia. In mid-March, Temple staff member Sharon Amos reported to Jones the following on a meeting with Timofeyev:

—Timofeyev said that he feels that the risk for Jim's life if he came to town might only be 10% but it is not worth taking/he felt verbal assurances are not enough, should have something in writing from the court
—regarding negative press, he said that if former members have turned against the church, he would like to know why they have changed
—he has tho never seen anything like our paper in Capitalist society, it is totally correct/often papers have something wrong in their position but not this one
—it would help if we had material showing concrete support of people like Angela Davis
—regarding the need for exodus, quick transference of money/he doesn't see the need for such a situation developing right away, not within a year at least
—regarding a possible delegation going to the USSR, he said it was a possibility that could help, no problem getting visas at any time, but

when asked if it would be possible to arrange meetings with officials, he said that would have to be coordinated and might take a little bit of time/he is waiting for response back from Moscow to the letter we sent to Moscow a week ago with our requests

—he said that it was a difficult thing to arrange (exodus), but when I cried and said "it would be very painful for the door to be shut against children," we adults don't matter so much but we need safety for our children, he said that the USSR had taken in 5000 Spanish children (from Spain) and had been taken care of and then returned later to Spain/so he felt it was worth pursuing*

By its own testimony, the American Embassy was only mildly curious about these contacts. Ambassador John Burke was predisposed to feel that the Soviets were toying with Jones, making their customary "mischief," and the Timofeyev meetings were treated in that vein. But how can one dismiss the publicity coup that the Russians would stage in the defection of a thousand American Communists, most of whom were black? Consider the publicity that the defection to the United States of a single Bolshoi Ballet star generates. With Jim Jones and his crew safely in the Caucasus Mountains, his demonology befogged in reams of propaganda, the Soviet publicity could right the balance of all the Baryshnikovs and Nureyevs and Godunovs who ever defected to this country. For it would not take a brilliant propagandist to argue persuasively that the ballet stars were lured solely by capitalist lucre for selfish reasons, while the Jonesians defected from lofty philosophical persuasion. Still, the American Embassy would argue officially that it made "no effort to monitor the association."

That was not, however, entirely accurate. Richard McCoy, the American Consul in Georgetown, had very good contacts within the Guyanese police force. As Chief Consul, it was he who provided visas to the United States—a golden bargaining tool in a country where so many Guyanese viewed America as the promised land—and McCoy used the tool freely to keep well-informed. Later in the spring of 1978, he raised the issue of the Temple's Russian contacts with Sharon Amos, Jones's lobbyist in the Guyana capital, by the by. The Temple could talk with whomever they pleased, invite anyone to Jonestown they wished, but wasn't it just a bit inconsistent with their stated policy of simply wanting to be left alone in peace? Upset at being challenged, Amos replied defensively that they were just trying to be friends with everyone. Then, taking the initiative, Amos charged the Consul with being a CIA agent. McCoy had had enough.

"So what if I am!" he barked back at her in an attempt to maintain his own sanity and took some pleasure in the stunned look on her face. "Get off this CIA kick. They're not interested in you."

---

*Courtesy of Associated Press.

Whether that was a rhetorical flourish or fact is hard to know. Earlier, when Amos had suggested to Timofeyev that McCoy was CIA, the Russian had responded defensively.

"If we look at it that way, we'd say that two million Americans were CIA!" he said.

In any case, by this time the CIA should have been interested. In these spy games between Soviet and American intelligence agencies, played with particular relish in remote places like Guyana, the agents usually knew who their opposite members were. McCoy, for example, had good reason to believe that Timofeyev was a major in the KGB. In the spring, the two would have a civilized lunch.

"Are you really going to take all these people?" McCoy asked Timofeyev with undiplomatic directness, referring to the exodus rumor.

The major just laughed. "These people are crazy," he replied in his best Peter Ustinov English.

If Timofeyev thought they were crazy, his behavior in the coming months was strange indeed. Talk of scholarships in Russia for Temple members began to be discussed. Perhaps the Temple band and the Temple basketball team could go to Russia on a "cultural exchange," the Temple delegation forming a "scouting mission," as Jones phrased it, scouting the next "haven within a Communist paradise." Jim Jones could go with the delegation and pursue negotiations with Soviet officials in Moscow. In early May, Jones considered attending an international conference in Warsaw as part of a contingent of American Communists. The arrangements were made through Albert Kahn, General Secretary of the Communist Party USA, and Kahn proposed that Jones travel to Moscow after the Warsaw conference for a week's vacation and discussions with Soviet officials. But the pastor demurred at the last moment.

During the spring, as the Russians and Americans got better acquainted, three things about the Temple attracted the Soviets. First, of course, was the propaganda bonanza that a thousand defections to the Soviet Union might comprise. It would be an epic event. Evoking the Cherokee trail of tears, Jones often referred to their "trek" of six thousand miles from Indiana to California to Guyana. Now he could add on another five thousand miles. But from the Soviet standpoint, a mass defection could point up the hypocrisy of President Carter's human rights policy, and Jim Jones was quick to offer himself—after exodus—for speeches on human rights all over the USSR.

Second, the Russians became fascinated by Jones's unique method of using religious techniques to spread atheism and socialism.

A March memorandum from Sharon Amos to Jones on a Timofeyev meeting read:

—[Timofeyev] said it is truly amazing JJ can take religious people and make them atheists because that is something USSR is having trouble with and they'd like to benefit from how JJ does it, because he must be brilliant and if they could have people use his techniques it would be helpful

—I mentioned that JJ also wrote Errors in the Bible and we used to give them out/he said USSR had analysed every word in the Bible and have lots of books showing contradictions, but it is more the one-to-one communication that is needed. . . . In the USSR they have a one-one situation of one religious person to every one atheist, and they still can't get it done.

In another such discussion with Timofeyev, Sharon Amos said, "I came [to the Temple] with a Bible in my hand and a white brotherhood card. I was very religious, but it is from that type of background that Jim has educated us to what we are today, and I'm a positive atheist."

"Don't say you're a positive atheist," Timofeyev corrected her. "Say you're an atheist. Nothing is positive. We have gotten rid of religion in our country, but there are still at least 10 percent religious people in the country."

"That's good," Amos said agreeably.

"That's not good," Timofeyev retorted.

"Well, no," Amos backtracked, "I mean by comparison to the United States, where 90 percent of the people are religious, it's good."

The last attraction was the Temple fortune. Timofeyev must have struggled to maintain a good Communist's composure when the communards talked of their millions. By spring, discussion of a transfer of the Temple assets to Soviet banks had gotten down to the mechanics of it. Jones thought that the Russian Orthodox Church might make a good guise for his money, so that he could maintain the tax-exempt status for his money in the United States! Timofeyev, in turn, started to promote Russian-made helicopters and speedboats, especially the boat with underwater wings which could travel fifty miles an hour, lending a certain James Bond quality to the negotiations, as if the archenemy Timothy Stoen were a real-life Blowfield, whom they might pursue in fantastic, high speedboats through the streams and eddies of the Orinoco Delta. The Temple fortune should be kept in dollars, rather than converted to rubles, the Russian diplomat stated forthrightly. As time passed Jones was offering that $3.5 million be transferred as the first installment, then the entire fortune in one package. But as problems arose later, Jones realized that his money was his best bargaining chip. His representative suggested to Timofeyev that the Temple buy $5 million worth of Soviet equipment and supplies, but that it be held in the Soviet Union for the Temple's arrival.

On April 13, 1978, Alexandre Voropaev, a Tass correspondent, was scheduled to make the first Russian visit to Jonestown. In her classically thorough way, Sharon Amos schooled Jones for the impending visit. Voropaev was trained as a linguist, rather than as a writer, and therefore, wrote Amos in a memorandum, he was probably KGB. Additionally, she reported with evident distaste that Voropaev's wife, who would accompany him to Jonestown, painted her nails and wore makeup. Voropaev himself drank and smoked, and was a male chauvinist, but the Temple apostles should be tolerant of Communists not as highly evolved as they. "Of course it's important to balance praise of JJ and [Jonestown] with the more inclusive mention of our commitment to USSR and to world Communism—as they will be watching for hero worship [personality cultism]," the Amos memo read.

Three days before the Voropaevs arrived, Jones held a nightlong discussion in the "Town Forum" on the question of an exodus to Russia. The mood was quiet and friendly, and the Bishop seemed to be enjoying himself. Toward midnight, a young woman named Ruby rose to ask several important questions.

"If we went over to Russia, would they try to use us as pawns to threaten the U.S.?" she asked haltingly.

"They don't seem inclined that way," he replied. "If they'd wanted to use us as pawns, they'd sure got busy [by now.] They want to be extremely careful about being seen with us. They want to be sneaked in, when they come [to Jonestown]. I think they've been genuine . . . most concerned and considerate." He broke his sentence to accept a plate of food, as the audience sat without, but he assured them that it was cold, and that he was not enjoying it.

"Another thing," Ruby continued, "I'm sure they've heard about our white night stands, probably not in detail. But what if they were in camp with us, and something didn't go right, just what would they think?"

"I like your dissent, Ruby. That's the way we grow," he answered, munching on his cold morsels. "She makes a good point. She ought to be in strategy. I don't know that they've heard of our tactics. They don't know the full extent of it. Nobody knows the full effect. They don't know how mean our white nights can be. If we go to Russia, though, we will have to be productive, and we'll have to assimilate. We're not going to demand that everything go just our way. So I've made the offer [of compromise]. That's why I like Guyana. We can have our own independent government, our own sovereign existence. It's not likely that we'll have that any other place in the world."

If the Russians had not heard specifically of white nights, Jones's curious term for the night of ultimate crisis when they might die in mass suicide (it had first been "black night" but changed when that term was thought pejorative), they were certainly apprised of the Temple's death wish. As early as March, Amos was telling Timofeyev that the group would die rather than give up John Victor Stoen. Later, it was death rather than live under capitalism, if Guyana should move to the right. With time, as Jones became impatient with the slowness of Moscow's responses to his overture, he took to threatening.

"Why can't we lead principled lives?" he wrote the Soviets. "Either we need to be dropped into Mozambique where we can fight or be taken to the USSR as a model of principled people. If we are too hot to handle, get us into Mozambique so we can die for something we believe in."

They were in total solidarity with the Soviet Union, he wrote, "but one action could trigger this movement to its death."

By the summer, Feodor Timofeyev was raising maddening technicalities. The Temple's request for asylum had not been specific enough. How many wished to make the exodus? What were their ages and skills? Overtly irritated now by the constant flow of tears from the Temple staffers, he once sternly rebuked Sharon Amos for a display, saying he had cried only once in his life: the day his mother died. The tearful Templeite replied that it was one thing to cry for oneself, quite another to cry for hundreds, whose future was in their hands. Another time, he chastised them for their injudicious use of the telephone, saying that an American diplomat had asked jokingly at a social function when the Soviet doctor planned to go to Jonestown. The whole Soviet Embassy was upset by this breach of confidentiality, he said, and as the memo to Jones described it, "he would have to tell Moscow this in his report, and they would have to take this into consideration when making any major decisions." No doubt, this caused more tears. Timofeyev was also having some difficulty explaining to the Kremlin about John Victor Stoen. Again a Sharon Amos memorandum described this: "[Timofeyev said] it would take pages and pages to explain why JJ had intercourse with this diabolical woman and that it might have been a frame-up from the beginning, and that Russians don't understand such a thing very easily anyway, about having intercourse with a woman out of marriage."

"Well, why should they have a problem?" Amos replied. "Lenin had a mistress, and he worked very closely with her and his wife."

"I've never heard this," Timofeyev replied in surprise, according to the Amos memo. "I've been studying biographies of Lenin since I was 8 years old, and haven't ever read that!" (No doubt because the state frowns on talk of Lenin's well-documented relationship with two mistresses.)

In any event, Timofeyev thought it would be better if Jim Jones himself explained to the Kremlin how John Victor Stoen came to be.

Jim Jones began to doubt that the Soviets were taking him seriously. So, he sovietized Jonestown still more. On the night of an equatorial full moon in August, intensive classes in the Russian language began. To receive their nightly gruel, which by now consisted mainly of rice and gravy, a member was required to mouth a hearty "How are you?" or "Good evening" in Russian, as well as answer a question or two on the news from Radio Moscow, asked by the "supervisor of political enlightenment," who stood at the head of the food line. Friday evening classes in Marxism-Leninism were instituted for the older members, taught by Jann Gurvich. Among other subjects, Jann gave instruction in the new Soviet Constitution, promulgated in 1977, with heavy emphasis on Articles 49 and 50 under the chapter entitled "Basic Rights, Freedoms, and Duties of Citizens of the USSR." Article 49 stressed the right to criticize the shortcomings of state programs, "Persecution for criticism is prohibited. Persons guilty of such persecution shall be called to account." And Article 50, spoken in Jonestown to evoke images of the civil rights era, guaranteed Soviet citizens "freedom of speech, press, and assembly, meetings, street processions, and demonstrations." The streets and squares of Russia, as well as the radio, press, and television, the Constitution read, were put at the people's disposal for this purpose. One could almost see the Temple members in some Black Sea city square swaying in protest against the latest five-year plan, singing "We shall overcome."

Also in August, Jones required the news from Radio Moscow to be typed verbatim every night. His typist usually finished around midnight and walked the copy to the West House, passing it to one or another of Jones's two mistresses who lived with him. The following morning, the camp awoke at 6 a.m. to the sound of the morning news and commentary by the Bishop. This was in accordance with Jones's message that the Temple would have to earn its way into Russia. "When the top leadership of Russia comes here, they want to see a very productive place, a beautiful landscape, a lot of smiling faces, with a heavy amount of news, and speaking Russian as well as you can." Soon, in an economy of words, he began to refer to the time when "the Praesidium" would come to Jonestown.

"Some of you are frightened that you'll never learn the language. But they will allow us to have a commune of our own there. So it will not be so important that you speak Russian well. But there will be students who want to go on to other opportunities, schooling or off to Africa to help with liberation. There will be a million opportunities. The sky is the limit, my darlings. But you who are fearful, don't worry. You'll learn enough to get by. Anyway, in the Soviet Union, the second language is English. Everybody practically knows English. They speak

English from nursery school on up. That's how important English is to them, because their principal enemy is America."

The Soviets, he reassured them, were fascinated by the Temple movement. Not only did they see Jonestown as a model Communist community, but they were spending $1 million a day to try to understand his paranormal magical faculties. For a second, he must have thought the figure was not impressive enough, and he changed it to $2 million a day. Later, it would become $3 million a day.

The planning for the grand exodus went forward. The camp intellectual, Richard Tropp, prepared a report on locations in the Soviet Union suitable for relocation, settling on an area called Krasnodar, south of the Caucasus Mountains on the east coast of the Black Sea, as the Temple's first choice. Second choice was Azerbaijan SSR, very near the Iranian border, but perhaps for political reasons, they might have to settle for "pioneering areas" of the northern Himalayas, in the vicinity of the China-Pakistan-Soviet border. With this information, Jones sought to reassure his flock, especially his seniors, that the community was headed for something comparable to northern Florida, not the Siberia of their minds. At a "People's Rally," perched upon his green wooden throne and drinking his iced soda pop, he described their "total exodus to freedom." They would go to the "non-black soil regions" near the Black Sea, but they were not to worry: the region was tropical and balmy where oranges and tangerines grew.

"We would be the first community ever accepted from America in the Soviet Union," he confided. "Of course, we have to pass before some scrutinizing eyes, but there's no question it can be done. They're going to profile us, not to see if you have a jail record, but to make sure that there's no CIA people here. That's natural. It'll take some months to get that done. In the meanwhile, we've got to work this place to the fullest.

"In the Black Sea where they have oranges and tangerines and it's very warm, you people won't be able to jump right in there. They know that. But they care enough for a black, interracial model communist community that they will have buildings already set up. Heat would be provided, so there's no question about seniors. It's slightly colder than here, but it depends on the time of year. But don't get nervous. Any place where there are oranges and tangerines isn't going to be much different than here. They have a little snow like Redwood Valley, but it barely stays on the ground. They even have some places that are almost like Guyana. But we can't ask them for the resorts of the Soviet Union, right?"

"Right!" came back the animal response.

"All we can ask for is free medicine—that's what all Soviet citizens are guaranteed. Free surgeons. Free dentists. Free eye doctors. Free education, and almost now, free housing. Free telephones. Now they want twenty of us to go by the end of the year. But I'm telling you this right now, from the heart. Some of you musicians don't know apple sauce about Marxism-Leninism. I better start hearing some Marxist-Leninist talk from you soon, or you're not going!"

If the climate of Russia was one ghost that needed dispelling, the paucity of black people there was another. A Soviet film had been shown in Jonestown, and not a single black face had appeared in it. Some communards muttered about this, and of course, the muttering got back to Jones, as all "negative thinking" was supposed to. From his microphone in his house, his voice was washed over the houses and fields.

"I hear some complaints that there's not enough black people in the Soviet Union. There happen to be thousands of black people there. They just don't live in any one specific neighborhood. The reason that there's not millions is that the Russians did not engage in slavery. The Russians never took in black slaves. That's in their favor. There's one hundred fifty different racial and national ethnic groups, one hundred fifty. That's about as many different races and nationalities as you can find in the world. And they want us for the very reason that we are black and Indian; they want black and Indian Communists.

"Racism is the second highest offense of law there. If you use a racial slur, they haul you into criminal court, not civil." Not only that, Aleksandr Pushkin, "their greatest writer," was black, Jones declared. [Pushkin's great grandfather had, in fact, been a black general in the service of Peter the Great, but whether that made the writer black is a hard call. Jones did not mention that Pushkin was better known in his time as a Moscow nobleman than a black man.] "So you'll have more freedom there than you have here," he continued. "But if you get to the Soviet Union, and you don't want to stay, they certainly won't make you stay. You will have the privilege to go back to the United States, to Babylon, to suck on the great beast called America, to die in a concentration camp, to be blown up in a nuclear war, in the United States, where there'll be no underground shelters and cities like there are in the Soviet Union. That's your privilege."

As the heavy emphasis on news became heavier during the summer of 1978, Jones instituted tests at nightly sessions to make sure the communards were absorbing his lessons. He must have been disappointed in his results. After his morning news and commentary broadcasts, the news summaries were posted in the camp library, and members were expected to read them, if they had not got it all the first time. By the summer, many members' benumbed minds were tuning out his diatribes, and they found the tests hard.

• What did Venezuela have to say about Nicaragua today? "To

Marxist-Leninists, people who believe in liberation, it would be encouraging," Jones said, trying to be helpful.

- Name some of the major fascist dictatorships in the world. "Fascism, you'll remember, is the last stage of capitalism, when the state takes over with repressive force of violence and coercion. The executive becomes a dictator under martial law, and usually establishes concentration camps. The USA has de facto fascism. Fascism de jure is where it's called such: military takeover, black people in concentration camps or gas ovens. So name some of the major fascist dictatorships in the world? Fascist: f-a-s-c-i-s-t. You should be able to get at least one, because I just named one." This must have appeared to some to be a particularly hard question, since Jones at the time was claiming Jonestown was going through its Stalinist phase, and his leadership representing the "dictatorship of the proletariat."
- What did the Soviet Union recently achieve in space?
- What did the Chinese defense minister have to say about nuclear war today?
- What anniversary is China celebrating today, and what did the Soviet Union do about it? "What the Soviet Union did showed their tremendous compassion and desire for coexistence," Jones nudged.

But occasionally, Jones's religiosity and his Communism got confused in the execution. One night at a People's Rally during a test, he was berating the assemblage for their complaints about the food, scoffing at the way they "bled" him with their notes about their petty problems, causing him pain in his mind and body. This was an affront to his own infinite, unmatchable Goodness (which in the socialist dominion of Guyana had replaced his former Godliness).

"People don't like goodness, it makes *them* have to be good," he instructed. "If you see goodness in someone else, it means only one simple equation: you've got to be good too. Folk don't want to be good by nature. Their animal instincts are opposed to being good. They want to be like a goddamn bunch of fighting wolves in a pack. They want to dominate, to kill and not be killed. They want to rob. They want to drain. . . ."

And then he switched gears abruptly. "And that's why Mao said . . . What was the basic premise of Mao? Mao said there's only one way a revolution can come. Do you know, Millie?"

The decrepit, seventy-four-year-old black woman in the front row twisted in embarrassment as the microphone was put in front of her. "The only way you can . . . you can keep it is being peaceable and being honorable," she guessed.

"Oh, shit, Mao Tse-tung said that? No, no, no, no. He's the head of China, the head of the revolution in China, marched six thousand people on a Long March. . . ."

Millie hung her head. "Oh, I had my mind on something else," she shuffled.

He tolerated her. "OK, what did Mao say about bringing on the revolution?"

"Onliest way you can bring it on . . . is by killing," she proclaimed tentatively.

"Well, that's OK, I'm going to let you pass," said the lenient teacher. "But he had a nice little phrase that everybody should know. Change comes . . . what?"

Millie stumbled some more.

"Change comes through . . . what?" Jones said, more forcefully.

". . . by the barrel of a gun," Millie said in triumph.

"That's right, senior. That's good. Because you, by rights, would have every reason to forget some things. Change comes through a barrel of a gun, said Mao Tse-tung. This place would be a paradise tomorrow if every department had a supervisor with a submachine gun . . ."

The assemblage applauded.

". . . there'd be no shit here. Everybody'd work. There'd be no trouble. The Guyanese government's been suggesting that we get armed, so we can enforce our laws." He came back to Millie. "Thank you, dear. You pass."

In early September 1978, Jones announced that the Russians would soon be paying Jonestown a visit. Three weeks passed, however, before arrangements became firm. In Georgetown, Timofeyev seemed to be balking, telling Sharon Amos not to get hopes up for an exodus. So in Jonestown on September 22, well after 2 a.m., Jones cut a tape for the Russian diplomat. This was the fourth month of elevated temperature, Jones confessed, with a reading of 105 degrees in the past few days. He was taking cold showers and constantly getting alcohol sponge baths.

"I desire at this point particularly with my health the way it is to go to the Soviet Union to set up a collective there. . . . But I hear now that there may be no possibility of this. We'd like to know. We are not a people who believe in delusions or illusions. If we are to die, then we wish to know that we are to die. . . . If the Soviet Union is out, I don't think I can make it. I'm a man who believes in Communism. I'm probably more Soviet than some, in fact I know I am. I don't want any games between us. So I would like from you just a direct response. Are we or are we not welcome in the Soviet Union?"

But to his community, he did not convey his desperation. To them, a Soviet exodus was to remain a sure thing, the bird in the hand.

Finally, on September 29, word came that Timofeyev and a Soviet doctor would arrive the following day. A certain sense of euphoria prevailed in the camp. Not only were the Russians coming, taking the commune another step toward that final exodus to freedom, but alternatives had surfaced. A beautiful country in Africa had invited them in as well, Jones told them, but "for security reasons" he declined to name it, underscoring again his Dostoevskian mystery and authority. (The country was Ethiopia.) The camp, as he had stated many times before, operated on a "need to know" basis only.

And Cuba loomed suddenly as a possibility. Since the early part of 1978, the Georgetown contingent had been negotiating with the administrator of the Cuban Embassy as well, one Alfriedo Ferreira; and Ferreira too had heard his share of the Temple will to die. But he would have nothing of it. In August he had commented to Sharon Amos, by her testimony, "that it would be a waste for us to die as fodder for the capitalists when it wouldn't be the right time to have any useful effects." The Cubans had told Amos that the chance of an exodus there was less than 50–50, unless there was an emergency. Then exodus could be quickly arranged. But of course, Jones had told his community nothing of these odds. "Our future is bright, my darlings," he cooed.

The early part of the evening on September 29 was spent on the Cuban opportunity, but it had its uncertainties. Would the Cubans take his old as well as his young, his blind as well as his fit? For *his* loyalty was pure; he knew *his* own morality, but he could not be sure of anyone else's.

"I'm not now going to start splintering off those I want to take care of. It's all or none. That's my motto. . . . Whoever's refused, I'm staying with them, and dying with them. I'm not going to change that, because that would be immoral, and I couldn't live with myself. My morality is all I've got. I'm not good-looking. Gave all my money away. All I've got is my principles."

And then he fell easily into his aphorism:

Some come a blind, some come a halt, some lame,
But all come callin' their Father's name
And Father treats you just the same.

So the Cuban morality would have to be tested. He smelled opportunism in the Cuban offer. Perhaps they would try to split up the group on the dock. If Cuba was their choice, they had better make their stand on the boat.

"I can't tell you what is going to happen when our boat gets there. You can have a white night in the harbor. We can do that. Set the son of a bitch afire if they refuse to take somebody. . . . Don't think it's that easy to get someplace you want to go. What's that old saying? Bird in the hand worth two in the bush. I see the Russian bird and the Cuban bird as the two in the bush. . . ." No, he corrected himself. He had the Russian bird in the hand.

The discussion went on and on. As the clock moved toward 1 a.m., he brought forward his elderly to express their faith and devotion in him to sway the vote as he wanted.

"Father, you're the greatest and the most wonderful . . ." the old woman began.

"Just a quick vote, sweetie, 'cause it's getting so late, people can't think," he interjected. "What do you want to do?"

"I want to go back to San Francisco, or wherever the devils are who're worryin' you, and kill all of them."

Earlier in the evening, he had stressed that vengeance was not a Communist principle but this time vengeance served. "Thank you, honey," he said, and turning to the secretary at his side who kept the notes (for historical purposes?) he said, "Put that down, with her name." He called for the next one.

"Dad, you brought us all this way. Spent all this money. Now some go one way. Some another. We done forgot who our leader is. We don't need nobody else, we got all we need. I'm gonna follow my daddy. My sister told me, they're tellin' us out here, Jim Jones making a fool out of you seniors. I said, well, I'm glad to be his fool."

Jones cut her off. He did not like the mention of the enemies. "Good as he is, your Father has not been able to communicate it to all the people. Anybody accuses him of making fools out of seniors has to be a . . . barbarian. Next."

"Dad," said the black septuagenarian, "I came here because of the principles you stood for, and that's what kept me here. So when I voted for Cuba, I voted for the children, not for myself. . . ."

"No need to explain your vote, honey. I've been with you a long number of years. What do you want to do with your life?"

She too wanted to go back to kill the enemies. It made him sentimental.

"We got some beautiful people here," he said. "She's been with me twenty-odd years, going on thirty now. But I'll tell you one thing, all these seniors standing up here testifying they'd like to go back and kill our class enemies, I think I'd just as soon fight it out on the ground we got."

Applause rippled over the congregation.

"I ain't leaving these people," his voice rose. "I don't care if they're blind, halt, lame, paralyzed . . . or crazy. I'll be with 'em on that ocean vessel when it comes. They say some of us are mentally ill. Some of my best workers are mentally ill. I'm not sure you don't have to be mentally ill to be a Communist. You have to get sick mentally about what's going on in the world, and have to have a healthy degree of paranoia. OK, who's next?"

The testimonials became standard. "Daddy, this is the onliest freedom I ever had. In my life. When I went to the church, I made up my mind to follow you wherever you go. I'll be with you until the end. If I can't go with you, daddy, I'll lay down my life to die."

"Thank you, darling. I see you mean it. If she does that, the Communists won't know what to do with it. But she's real. She's real."

A white teenager rose to testify. "I don't really want to go to Cuba," she said pointedly. "We've got people here who would do things that the Cubans wouldn't permit. If we went to Cuba, we might not be able to protect them."

"That's true, honey," Jones responded. "Their laws are strict. We've got people here who can only be controlled by a very tight structure. That may be one of the reasons Guyana lets us stay in a cooperative. They say, hey, we can use these people politically. It's worth it. But I don't think we want to release all these American ghetto folk in our streets. Better let them stay up there in the North West District, and let Jim Jones kill himself trying to keep 'em good.

"In Cuba, every block has a committee for defense of the revolution, every square block. You don't start any gossip there, honey, because they report everything. Once they didn't report and damn near got destroyed at the Bay of Pigs. They were tortured under Batista, so they know what fascism is. They believe reporting is an honorable thing, and in this place, some of you still don't believe it. In the socialist system, you're reporting to protect the people, whereas back there in the USA, you're reporting to protect the police. So our police here have to be efficient and humble. Can't walk around here all gaudy-like. We're not pigs. We're representatives of the people."

"Another reason for not going to Cuba," said the witness, "is that we might have trouble getting some of our people from the States into Cuba."

"That'd have to be worked out with me," Jones said, with passion again. "If we can't get our people in, I ain't going. I'm too tired. Fought too many battles, struggled too long. I've been true to all of you. I ain't gonna start being true to 99 percent of you now. I'll be true to 100 percent or I'm gonna slit my throat with my own fingernail tonight. I'd rather be dead or tortured and I am being tortured. [Applause again.] And I'm not going to live with a tortured conscience."

The elaborate idolatry proceeded, with the debate shifting to the question of whether Cuba would allow Jones to become a great leader of the world revolution or whether Castro's jealousy would prevent it. Another witness drew the issue as a choice between training and education of a professional ("There are lots of professionals in the world") versus training "in principle" that only Father could provide ("There are only a few principled people"). She opted for Father's principle. Questions were raised of whether Cuba would allow them—dependent as they were on Jones's infinite Goodness and beneficient leadership—to remain intact as a group.

"We'd have to make a case intellectually to the Cubans that we had to stay intact," Jones responded. "But if problems arose, if they started to harass us, well, hell, we can white-night one place just as well as another." The congregation rustled with excitement, as Jones's voice lowered into a guttural, basso profundo laugh. "Right on," he congratulated himself.

The time for the vote arrived, and he asked for the hands of those who wanted to go to Cuba. A few tentative arms rose from the congregation. Once declared, a few ayes were informed by Jones that they were voting to go to Cuba "whether I go or not." Off the stage, the few were counted. Someone included Edward Moore, a fifty-two-year-old Louisianan.

"Edward Moore? Which way is Cuba, Edward?" Jones hurled out, his laugh rising shrilly. "Down at the north end of the cooperative, you say? . . . Over that way? . . . Oh, out by the piggery? . . . Northwest of the piggery? . . . What's that, Hazel? . . . Northeast of the piggery, I got you." His high-pitched cackle cut the humid, still night air, and the assembled saw that they could laugh too.

"Now listen you people who voted for Cuba, you need to make more points, because you're an honest dissenting minority. You're beautiful people, you dissenters, and we respect you, but you've got to be more persuasive. . . . But if any of you voted for Cuba because you're afraid of dying. . . . I say, KEEP ON MOVING . . ." and he swung into a civil rights song. They joined him, swaying, possessed.

It was past 1 a.m. now, and one could feel their fatigue and their love. He managed a final pep talk. Socialist classes would be held the following night, instead of at the usual time. The place must be spic-and-span for the visitors. "Park-like" settings out on the porches, buildings washed, grass cut, for their chance of getting to Russia depended on the community's appearance. He wanted everybody active: quilting on the porches, reading by candlelight under the houses, nobody idle, lots of smiling faces.

"And when you go by him, give him a salute. How do the Soviets salute, left hand or right?" he asked. Confident answers came back both ways. "Wait a minute, we got to have this right, because one way is Trotskyite and the other way is correct. Let's find out. Anyway, they'll be impressed with that, because they're coming expecting religion. That's why we need to compensate. When you see him, smile. Say, greetings, comrade. Hello, comrade. So happy to have you with us, comrade. Comrade, Comrade, Comrade, Comrade, Comrade, you hear. Don't say 'brother.' How many will say comrade now?"

"COMRADE."

"Everybody say Comrade."

"COMRADE!"

His joviality drifted away, as the organ swung gracefully into a soft adagio behind him, as it might in a thousand small churches in America. His words of benediction, his comfortable words, came slowly, rhythmically, hypnotically, movingly.

"Love you. I *do* love you. Think of the victories we won on taxes over the state of California. We won over the Attorney General. We won over the government of Guyana to keep our doctor here. That took a white night. A white night paid off. It paid off. And I hope some of you got a little more knowledge of yourself. If you didn't you ought to be sorry. . . ."

He paused for the organ to swell briefly into fortissimo and return again pianissimo.

"Peace and love. . . . We'll use the left hand for salute until I tell you otherwise. . . . I love you very much. Now, as you go down the path, think, please, on healings, on blessings, on protections I've given you. On the people I've saved from jail, people whose lives I've saved when you were paralyzed, on homes I've kept from destruction. Nobody to love you . . . Father cares. Father cares. You can tell it in his voice, he cares. . . . He cares, and he'll be with you all the way. . . . Good night, my darlings. Good night, comrade. Good night, comrade. Good night, comrade."

He blew kisses to them as they filed out of the Pavilion. "Peace. Peace. Peace. . . . Remember don't call me Dad. Call me Comrade as long as the Russians are here. Comrade Jim. Comrade Jim, you hear. And Comrade Marceline. Each cottage teacher, I want you to emphasize that tomorrow. Peace. Peace."

A vigilant disciple whispered something into his ear. "Oh, yes. I want all those Soviet pictures up too. All over the camp. Lenin. All over this place . . . Lenin, and . . . what's his name, that other old fool. . . ."

"Marx," someone helped.

[2]

Feodor Timofeyev arrived the next day and stayed for two days. A hefty man of about five feet nine, with blond, wavy hair and a gregarious, outgoing disposition, he brought with him Dr. Nicolai Fedorovsky, the physician at the Soviet Embassy in Georgetown, whose specialty Sharon Amos had described as "raising people from the dead." While Dr. Fedorovsky spent hours with Dr. Larry Schacht and the medical staff, examining the more critical medical cases including that of James Warren Jones, Timofeyev toured the delights of Jonestown. True to his practice, Jones invited the Russians to his cottage after dinner for a marathon discussion, and this one lasted until 5 a.m.

The following night, October 1, Jonestown threw a banquet of sorts for its guests. In the middle of the Pavilion, at the head table as it were, the visitors dined well on spareribs and chicken, dressed with edo greens. Around them, the communards had their normal rice and gravy, with some chicken bits mixed in for appearance. (Later, Jones would make much of how he ate the ribs only so as not to make a "scene," but they had made him sick. "I can't stand seeing you people [deprived], knowing how you like ribs or how you like a piece of pie. But you should be glad you didn't eat that stuff. Everyone who ate that special food got the running shits.") After the meal the entertainment began. Timofeyev seemed particularly to enjoy the Moms Mabley routine, simulated by one of the black senior citizens, and to Jones, this showed the Russian was no prude. But the program of music, comedy, and dance had its climax in a song by Deanna Wilkinson, the Aretha Franklin of Jonestown, a number of her own composition called "1981." With slow measures in the high range of the organ behind her, she belted out the gospel.

In 1981, everything will have changed.
You will see, you will see, you will see
You stand in line with your passport to sign
And the government says no to your kind.

You will walk down the street
Not a friend you will meet
All your friends are gone
And locked in Santa Rita

America was not what you thought it would be
We have seen
We have seen
All her lies

Your family has died
For America and its lies
All your life, all your life
You have been deprived.

Yes, in the fall of the year, in 1981.

Timofeyev clapped heartily and whispered his impression to Jones. In 1981, he confided, he doubted that any Temple communards would be able to leave the United States for Guyana, or any other place, given the trend toward fascism in America. Jones nodded enthusiastically —it was the kind of thing he might have said—and then rose to the tumultuous cheers of the throng.

"Thank you, comrades," he said, raising his hand for quiet.

"For many years, we've let our sympathies be publicly known: that the United States government is not our mother, but that the Soviet Union is our spiritual mother and. . . ." The audience rose instinctively with long sustained, sports palace cheers. "It's amazing that we got by so many years saying it. I have spent hours with this great man, Feodor . . . Feodor [he had a little trouble with the pronunciation] Timofeyev, and in him, I have found no contradictions and no discrepancies. After so many hours of the kindest benevolence from Comrade Timofeyev, in which he fulfilled our highest hopes and noblest expectations, we were not mistaken in allying our purposes, our destiny, with the destiny of the Soviet Union." Again, cheers halted him, for they knew his inflections; they knew the significance of his pauses, and when their response was expected. "We have served many a guest in this community, but for the first time, *this* guest wondered, 'Are we being given special treatment?' and we replied yes. . . . And he said, we want to go through what you go through. Eat what you eat. Enjoy what you enjoy, and sacrifice with you, if it's necessary. . . . And now I give you, Feodor Timofeyev, the consular and chief of press for the Embassy of the USSR."

For Timofeyev, facing this audience of glowing, expectant black faces, as they waited to be transported by him as they always were by Jones, must have been a memorable experience. All his training served him poorly for once, for it is doubtful that such agents are schooled regularly in the rhythms of Pentecostal American religion. One could feel his ill ease in the nervousness of his high-toned laugh, and even in the awkwardness of his bear hug for Jim Jones on the dais, before he took the microphone. He was no orator, at least not in English, but he began on the right foot by greeting them in Russian, and they responded boisterously, as if they all had understood him.

"On behalf of my Embassy, I send my deepest sincere greetings to the people of the first socialist and Communist community of the United States . . . in Guyana and in the world," he said in swollen-tongued English and Jim Jones led the cheers. "It is a great privilege to see, as an eyewitness, what I've heard from representatives of the People's Temple in Georgetown, about your successes and the development of your project. . . . And now, the Soviet Press and the Soviet People will know much about this wonderful, so-dear-to-us community."

His start was not bad, but when the major moved into an extended and tedious history lesson about the development of socialism in the Soviet Union, even Jones found it difficult to identify the applause lines. Timofeyev spoke to them, "Communist to Communist," about the October 1917 Revolution, the first time "working class peasants, intelligentsia, and soldiers" had combined under the guidance of "our dear Vladimir Ilyich Lenin" to begin a new era of socialism in the world. (The assembled must have had difficulty in identifying with working class peasants, intelligentsia, or soldiers.) He spoke with feeling about "our glorious victory" in World War II, "what we call the Great Patriotic War" and of the twenty million Russians lost. "But we protected the whole world from the fascism and the imperialism." Through these difficulties, beset as they were by bourgeois forces, they had grown and finally had arrived at "the epoch of the socialism." In a different epoch, Lenin had told the youth to study and study how to build the socialism and the Communism, not only to know the theory, but to apply it in their lives.

"And I'm very happy that I saw here in Jonestown the full harmony of theory, created by Marx, Engels, Lenin, and the practical implementation of some fundamental features of this theory, under the leadership of my comrade Jim Jones. . . . I have heard that people came together with Jim Jones, because they trust in the idea of socialism and in the equality of Marxism-Leninism. We share with you all that idea, and since you are socialists in heart and mind, you share the socialist history. We thank you very much that you call us your spiritual motherland."

He wished them every success in their great and difficult task. "You've done a lot, but you should do more in the future." They should make their community one of the best, "about which any person in America can dream." Six weeks later, many Americans *would* dream about Jonestown in the rustle of the night.

With that, and thanks for their hospitality, he sat down, and Jones grasped the microphone, plunging into the heroic bars of the Soviet national anthem, his voice cracking and quavering on the high notes.

United forever, in friendship and neighborhood
A mighty people shall ever endure
A great socialist Union shall live through the ages
A dream of the people, this fortress secure.
Long live the Soviet motherland
It was built by the people's mighty hand
Long live her people, united and free
Long live this socialism state.

Breathless, Jones thanked his comrades. "This gentleman said something last night, comrades," he continued, "that I cannot quote here, because it might embarrass him, but he said something that gave me more peace than ever before. I knew, after I heard his words, I didn't have to worry about my family in Jonestown anymore." Heartfelt cheers met that.

"The meeting is dismissed. Peace and love, comrades."

But the evening was not quite over. Timofeyev rose for one last gesture.

"We would like, from our heart, to present this book, entitled *For Life*, which is dedicated to the foreign policy of the Soviet Union, and shows the different epochs of our struggle for peace and disarmament, and stresses the solidarity of the different peoples of the world. In my behalf, and in behalf of my colleagues, I present it to comrade Jim Jones, the great fighter for socialism and for peace."

Long after, when the cheering dribbled away, they broke into a high-spirited song with the words, "We're a Communist and we're glad, We're a Communist today, a Communist all the way. . . ." The music was punctuated with the claps of the thousand, but it is unlikely that Timofeyev knew the score had been borrowed from The Baptist Hymnal.

When it was over, Jones commanded them to salute him, and they did so, with their left hand, a salute Jones said, from Jonestown.

"Jonestown, Soviet Union."

———————————≻⊣ ⊢≺———————————

The following night, Jim Jones would go on for six hours, until well after 2 a.m. There was much to relate, tests to be given, exhortations to deliver, people to threaten, a trial to conduct. They were closer than ever to the history books, and one could sense Jones's elation. Early in the session as he conducted a news test (How much does a black person in the United States earn in proportion to a white person? One-half? One-third? One-eighth? "It's no complex fraction," Jones declared. Describe the situation in Chile today. A leading question), his speech was badly slurred. He parceled out delicious snatches of his nightlong negotiation with Timofeyev as if they were chocolates. For starters, he promoted the Russian, no longer simply a consular, but the real Ambassador of the Soviet Union, not simply Chief of Press in Guyana, but for all South America.

"The Soviet Ambassador was spellbound, simply fascinated by us, a little threatened even by our goodness and our lack of elitism," he confided in them. "He said, Jim Jones took the church and used it to bring people to atheism! We haven't been able to do that with the Soviet Union's churches in fifty years, and we control them! We cannot get them out of their religion. But to be humble, some of *us* are not out of it. Of course, my paranormal factor confuses things. It confuses me. When I raise someone from the dead, it troubles me. But that doesn't make me believe there's a loving God. It's a long jump from my power to believing there's something loving up there, because if there was, he'd of left us alone and never made us make this trip in the first place. . . . How many blacks are shot, and there's no Jim Jones round to heal them! So we can't talk enough about the goodness of Communism, and I know we can't talk enough about the goodness of your leader. Jim Jones is Goodness. He is Communism embodied."

And Dr. Fedorovsky had told him, so he said, that he was the man to wean Russian Pentecostalists away from their faith.

"You could convert our Pentecostalists, [the doctor] said, and I could! We know how to sing. We know how to put in the emotion and the heart. You, Comrade Jim Jones, would appreciate Russia, because you would not take it for granted like a lot of our people. . . . Yes, I replied, we'd kiss the ground."

By Jones's telling, there had been much talk about the evil of America and much sentimental talk about the Soviet motherland. Timofeyev had entrusted him with the most secret information that the CIA was cloud-seeding in Guyana to cause too much rain and therefore destroy the Guyanese harvest. In Georgetown, U.S. diplomats were whispering on the cocktail circuit that the Temple was comprised of "a thousand Baptist child molesters." The United States was threatening Guyana to cut off all aid unless the Temple was dismantled and kicked out of the country. "See how evil the system is! You got a wicked country to deal with, honey; it's a *wicked* country. You better thank your stars that you hit here." But after 5 a.m. that morning, Timofeyev had grown softly sentimental. Four things, he had told Jones, were most dear to the Soviet people: peace, love, Communism, and Moscow. Moscow? " 'Because that city represents all that is equality, all that is just.' And I said, there's only two things I disagree with in the Soviet Union. I would never have admitted that Stalin made any mistakes, because the United States never admits mistakes. And I never would have given up Austria [after World War II]. 'I like you, Comrade Jim Jones,' he replied. 'You're a very frank person.' "

Amid this chummy comradery, Jones would have them believe there had been great substance. Timofeyev had promised that "a move against the People's Temple was a move against the Soviet Union." That had been the news that made Jones feel secure about the future of Jonestown. Arrangements were made for clandestine contact in Morse code on the shortwave radio in the event of a "U.S. invasion" of Jonestown. It was a kind of "early warning system," he told them, and through the coded radio contacts, the communards would know where to go, who secretly to meet to slip away to freedom. Once again, in the fantasia of his mind, the vision was magnificent, Soviet warships diverted from the Persian Gulf perhaps.

But meanwhile, they must work extra hard to make Jonestown an ideal.

"Now we've got to make this a model, because we want to be

approved by the Praesidium when it comes in. We must make this the best. He [Timofeyev] can champion our cause. He's already got the clear signal . . . I said, we want to speed it up, and he replied, it takes time. The process takes time, comrade." But wouldn't it take five years to become a Soviet citizen? For the Temple, Jones reported Timofeyev as saying, it could be a matter of nine months. And what about the relatives who were hounding them from the States, or the U.S. consuls who invaded their community every three months?

"Not in the Soviet Union [he told me]. They will see your representative in Moscow. We will assure them that you are alive. They will never come near your community. There are certain places in the Soviet Union where the U.S. Embassy cannot go, and where you'll be settling, they won't be allowed to go."

What about their social security checks? Timofeyev must have found this concern for a double dole amusing in a discussion of high-minded, principled defection and asylum. As Jones told it, Timofeyev responded with jolly good humor, "fat fellow" that he was.

"In the first place, I want to tell you, Comrade Jim Jones, we're not interested in your checks. The Soviet Union is a rich country."

"But we wanted to have $40 million for the Soviet Union," Jones said.

"Oh, Comrade Jim Jones, we don't need your $40 million," Timofeyev replied, Jones trying lamely to reproduce a Russian accent, but it came out more Latinized. "We are a rich nation. All we're interested in is productivity. All we want is you Communists!" (As for the social security checks, they could use them as toilet paper. The audience roared at the thought.)

So they must put so much work into their community, make it flower, make it grow, so they could leave it as an ideal.

But were they up to the challenge? It was time to berate them for their sloth, for their lingering bourgeois thinking, for their residue of America love.

"Some of you still got Americanitis. You've been ruined, some of you asses, you've been ruined by American capitalism, and you don't like to change your structure. You want peace when we're still in war. We shouldn't expect to have a light schedule until we get our people free."

He launched into the way the North Koreans worked, sixteen hours a day, rebuilding a society with beautiful cities in twenty years after it had been leveled by American warplanes. In a film he promised to show them, you could see the discipline as well as the joy, the sunshine on the children's faces. "Kim Il Sung calls them the kings and queens of our revolution. They're our gems; they are our future." (Years before, Jones had adopted a Korean daughter—no doubt as atonement for the sins of his country in Korea, but by October 1978, this adopted daughter, Suzanne, had deserted him and had joined the ranks of "class enemies.") But North Korea was a bit remote from Jonestown, and it was getting late. People fell asleep in the congregation before him.

"Wake up, please!" he barked. *"Wake up your neighbor!"*

He did not intend to send his musicians to Russia unless they were better at prattling the party line, he said, returning to an old theme. Special classes in Marxism-Leninism for musicians were to be formed.

"They [the Russians] love us for being teetotalers. Last time [on a trip] we got no further than the mouth of the river, and some people were taking liquor. I'm not going to have it! I'm not going to have some slob go over there, representing us, and get soused, because the Russians drink, and some CIA may be at a public function. There'll be thousands come to hear us in Moscow. If you fuckers drink and can't open your mouth and talk Marxism-Leninism, you're not going. . . . *Shift, please* [They were going to sleep on him again]. . . . You haven't got much time. You've got October, November, December, that's it." If they could not be genuine Communists, at least they could put up a better appearance. He reproached them for not acting *as if* they knew the answers. "When we have guests and I ask questions, put up your hands whether you do know or don't know, as if you had knowledge. You'll not be called upon if you don't know, for it will be directed, orally or by letter, who is to answer."

His calm and rage flowed like sea swells. Timofeyev had loved the song "1981," he reported softly. " 'I like that song,' he said. 'It's a sad song, but I like it. It's very true, when they say, No to your kind.' " In 1981, Jones's Timofeyev predicted, no American would be able to leave America. Jones set up his oratorical straw man. Moving into his best mammy pantomime, his voice raised and crackling: "That ain't gonna happen to me," he mimicked.

"What do you mean it ain't gonna happen to you, fool nigger?" his hate burst forth. "Paul Robeson was the best actor, the best singer in the world, and they took his passport and told him he couldn't leave America. He went totally mad. His mind snapped. So don't you wait too long, honey. You're not Paul Robeson. Some of you were beautiful yesterday, but today you are dumb asses." Back into the mammy voice he went. " 'I don't see no black people in your films.' You idiots! How in the hell are you going to see black faces in a country that did not engage in buying black slaves? That's outrageous to make that man get up here and talk about race. It's disgraceful. . . . He was a friendly man and he took it, but I wish some of you would learn to keep your mouth shut! We're going to watch for you next time . . . with a shotgun!"

His intimidation of the stupid and the outspoken always received an ovation, as peers searched the crowd for the guilty among them.

If they cheered him as he commanded and expected, he feared silent resistance. He feared the quiet dissenter who *knew* how to keep his mouth shut, the tiny mouse of a defector in all of them. In this sense, he faced the classic anxiety of any totalitarian. Even on the night of October 2, buoyant as he was about the "assurances" of Timofeyev, he trembled at the story of an aging member, a black man in his seventies who had openly talked of visiting his relatives in the States one last time. Thus, after his soaring flights and gyrations for five hours, after a test, after his enthusiastic fleshing-out of his private talk with Timofeyev, it was after 2 a.m., and a Jonestown trial began.

Several witnesses came forward to testify to the old man's unfortunate supplication. One witness was kind, telling the "jury" of a thousand that the man had no "anarchy" in his heart. But a younger female was harsher. In a piercing, angry voice, she reported him as saying, "I really want to get away from here, and by Christmas, I will be gone."

"That may be true. That *may* be true," Jones said ominously, and then leveling his stare at the stooping, slave-figure, said, "By Christmas you want to be gone?"

Pathetically, the old man spoke, barely audible, imploring, "I will ask you. Can I make a trip to see my peoples?"

"By Christmas, you'd like to be gone!" Jones said, his voice rising.

"I'd like to make a round-trip ticket . . .," the man tried.

The Bishop would have nothing of it, and he moved into his scriptural cadence. "I'm asking you one question. You have listened here to me many times, and I do not intend to repeat myself now. I have established myself on this proposition, and I have made myself unequivocally clear. I've moved now from an administrative socialist office into the Office of Savior. Do you want to go home . . . what you call *home* . . . by Christmas?"

The slave trembled before the Savior. "Naw, naw . . ." he muttered, lapsing into terrified gibberish.

"It's a fearful thing to fall into the hands of the living. . . ." He paused, unwilling to say *God*. Deep in the audience, someone muffled a giggle at the pathetic sight. Jones's rage soared, but he kept his steel stare leveled at the target. "Some find this humorous. I do not. I am now in the Office. I have the power to send you home by Christmas . . . but it won't be on Trans World Airlines."

His eyes closed. His hands folded, as if in his Office, he was trying to control the vengeance of a wrathful angel. The conclave froze in the presence of his hideous power.

The old man spoke. "You just take anything and make a big thing out of it."

"That's not a small thing," Jones shrieked. "That's *blasphemy*. It's *blasphemy*." The old man mumbled something. "*It's blasphemy!*"

Jones cut him off. "They may find good humor in your babbling, but it's *blasphemy* to talk about going back when you've not been given approval. You want to go back by Christmas? You can. You can. You can float back!"

"Right," responded the jury. Again, Jones fell into hushed, trembling meditation. After a long pause, he spoke with icy words . . .

"If I cease meditating for you, you won't need to go home."

Again he paused.

"You understand how many things are wrong with you?" he asked, and then his revelation burst out. "Blindness faces you early. Death faces you early by liver. Death faces you early through diabetes. Death faces you early through your kidneys. Do you want to go home?"

Humiliation was complete. "No," the old man said.

"Then be seated and shut your mouth and don't be in my face anymore."

The old man melted into the audience, and as quickly as Jones had entered the Savior's Office, he left it, his tone reverting to the next administrative order of business. But only temporarily. For this silent resistance had made his rule so precarious that magic and authority were his last resorts. Fear of his "gift"—his power over life and death—was the last thing that bound them to him. The idea of America lingered. It had to be destroyed, overtly now.

He had made up new words to an old song, he announced. He would have them learn it and be ready to sing it "upon command." The old song was "America the Beautiful." Carefully, slowly, he spoke the new lyrics, once, twice. The organ played a few opening bars, and then they belted it out in the jungle night air.

O beautiful for spacious skies, for amber waves of grain
For purple mountain majesty, above the fruited plain!
America, America, socialism shed Thy Grace on Thee
And crown whatever good you have with brotherhood
    (You need it badly)
From sea to shining sea.

The dreamy strains of the organ tarried for his benediction. "This organization is your salvation," he said softly above the melody, the pastor of comfortable words, the prophet of grand visions. "America, we don't like to think of you as a desert wasteland, as I have seen you in a prophetical vision. I've seen your cities melt before my eyes. I saw it first in Indianapolis years ago, and so we can sing. It is not the American people or the American landscape we oppose. It is the false system that does not represent the people. We represent the people. And now . . . turn to your neighbor and give him three miracles. . . .

How many miracles have you seen since you've been here? Raise your hands. . . ." They complied, all, as if they had knowledge. Satisfied, he moved into the closing hymn.

"Have faith in your God. Have faith in your God. . . ."

[3]

After the Timofeyev mission to Jonestown in early October, the tone of the communications between the Russian Embassy and the Temple became direct and fruitful. The transfer of the Temple fortune now became an imminent prospect, with Timofeyev advising the Temple on the manner of withdrawal of the funds from Guyana. He was concerned about the loss of interest that might be involved in taking the money out of the country and about the possibility that the U.S. dollar might be devalued. Fearful that the Temple withdrawal would strain the good relations between Russia and Guyana, Timofeyev advised the communards not to tell the Guyanese bankers, for God's sake, that the money was being withdrawn because the group was emigrating to Russia. Timofeyev cautioned them not to introduce "tears and emotion" into their dealings with Soviet bankers. For the first time, he was informed of substantial Temple monies in Swiss banks. Ironically, the question arose of whether the Temple intended to open a short-term external account or make a long-term deposit.

Because the Soviet diplomat was so concerned about the effect of an exodus on Russian-Guyanese relations, the discussions often centered on a ruse for the Temple's departure which would not be embarrassing. Jones found in the turn to the right in the 1978 Venezuelan elections the perfect excuse: he could simply tell Guyana of his fear of armed conflict and his unwillingness even to contemplate the thought that his family might fall again under capitalist rule. There turned out not to be time to air this proposal fully, but when Timofeyev joked that he had friends in Venezuela too, suggesting it did not matter what country ruled the North West, Jim Jones did not find it funny.

Still, many problems remained. But at least the manner in which the question of emigration was to be resolved now clarified itself. A Soviet delegation (which Jones referred to in Jonestown as the "Praesidium") would visit Jonestown. Then later, Jones would take his scouting mission to the Soviet Union, preferably in the winter of 1978–79, so the winter climate of the new paradise could be examined. Perhaps by May 1979, a final decision could be made. May was set as the target date for the transfer of the fortune. The matter, Timofeyev now told Sharon Amos, was being considered on the Politburo level.

Jones wanted the process speeded up. Perhaps as they waited for the Politburo to act, the Russians would arm Jonestown. Timofeyev tried to hold back this eagerness by saying the delegation from the USSR could act on all this, whereas he could only inform.

"That might be too late," Sharon Amos told him.

On the afternoon of October 16, 1978, a heavy, tropical shower pummeled Jonestown, and many residents took shelter in their cottages. As the storm swirled about them, a restful musicale commenced over the public address system, first appropriately enough, with Beethoven's First Symphony, continuing with the romantic, Strauss-like strains of a concerto for guitar and orchestra by Spanish composer Salvador Bacarisse. Midway through the Bacarisse concerto, as guitarist Narciso Yepes began a controlled arpeggio, the shrill, breathless voice of Jones cut into the music and the patter of rain.

"ATTENTION! ATTENTION! *Ia Khochu mir.*"

His tentative Russian bespoke his desire for peace, but high-tension details preoccupied him. In the past twenty-four hours, there had been three suicide attempts, one by a teenager who had drunk a dangerous dose of gasoline. Such behavior was selfish, said the tired voice, the voice of an old man now. They must keep themselves alive to register a lethal blow against capitalism, *when the time comes.* Anyone who succeeded in taking his life in such a self-centered fashion would revert five hundred generations. But if anyone was having such feelings, they were to give their names to the radio room and get medication to "elevate" their mood. For good socialists to let down the heroes: Paul Robeson, Patrice Lumumba, Stephen Biko. . . . So many sad stories.

"Oh, this is horror, this horror of horrors," he moaned. "That we would let down people like that. If you're feeling sorry for yourself, why don't you think of the little baby somewhere who's screaming? . . ."

But the suicide attempts were only half of it. A woman escapee had just been caught after wandering aimlessly in the jungle for two and a half hours.

"The next time a person tries a foolish maneuver like this, we're not going to break production. We will not bother to take thirty people from our work force. We're going to get the police. The commander of the Guyanese Defense Force, the head of the army and the air force, is a dear friend of ours . . . and the head of the police, we'll just turn you over to them. If you got to Georgetown, the Guyanese authorities would return you to face our structure and discipline. Now that the U.S. Embassy has been embarrassed, they will return you also.

"So you can take your chances with the tigers and the snakes and the bugs. You cannot survive in the jungle, unless you have a guide like myself with intuition. You don't understand its danger. I cannot begin to tell you what a tiger can do to you. One blow from his leg can break your whole spine and neck, not to mention he can eat you. Snakes out there can make your leg nothing but a mass of ulceration. Check it out in the medical office. Your eyes go blind, you become paralyzed, snakes that can kill in twenty minutes. There are crocodiles that can devour you in one gulp. Frogs you just have to touch, and you die. Spiders of all sorts. They have some fevers here you can't even imagine. Quicksand just beyond the East House that will swallow you up over your head. You are insane if you think you can betray this movement. You'd be better lost in proverbial hell than in this jungle.

"You must stop this negation! You're bringing on tragedies. I love you, but I must be stern in defense of the lives of our children. . . . The only way it can hurt is from within. Security measures must be implemented immediately! In every cottage, heads of committees for the defense of the revolution must step up their activities, so we can be aware of these renegades of anarchism who have not died out to self-centeredness and egocentrism, who cause us further pain and loss of production and put further strain on your Father's health. I cannot afford this! I have not had any sleep for five days. I cannot stand this! If you care about the one who loves you more than anyone who has ever lived on earth, who has put his life on the line for all of you, you will stop this.

"Anyone not reporting negative talk or action the instant it happens will go to the New Brigade immediately, no *ifs, ands,* or *buts.* Anyone who tries this again will be dealt with in the most severe fashion. Every supervisor is responsible for reporting the exact time back to work of your people, or they will face the discipline of the Entire Democracy of this Town Forum. We will have no more of this!

"I don't know why anyone would want to leave the body of socialism. Anybody would be a fool to leave my protection, but do not overuse that protection. I'm the only one who has it. Maybe someday, the Soviets who are spending $3 million a day will reveal what it is. But it's a hell of a value to you. . . .

"Do your gratitudes, because your protection is in proportion to your gratitude. Here you don't have to worry about concentration camps, honkie police coming down your alley, looking at you with hate, arresting you for no reason . . . or genocide . . . or nuclear war that will kill 212 million people in twenty minutes. Here you have clean air and clean water. The heat brings out the toxics in your body. We have here natural herbs that cure everything. Papaya skins can cure ulcers and cure cancer. It's in the news this morning that race tensions in fascist USA are the worst they've ever been since the emergence of the Ku Klux Klan. The air is so bad there that it's comparable to smoking three and a half packs of cigarettes a day. Chlorine in the water causes cancer. You can't eat the meat because sodium nitrate in it causes cancer, as well as all the chemicals that the capitalists put in the food to extend shelf life, so they can make their big profits. So let's keep our gratitudes high!

"Tonight, there will be a curfew after the meeting. We have been informed by the Soviet Ambassador that Venezuelan bounty hunters cross the border every night. So you must be in your cottage after meeting. At quarter to eight tonight, Soviet language classes begin. You must be in your seats at quarter to eight, because security will be through the buildings, looking under the beds, everywhere. I demand that roll be taken. If you are not there, we will deal with you. . . .

"Insecticide committees, empty all garbage cans now! Replace the lids on them! As I look around the project, I don't see people using fly swatters! Get them out now, while there is a bit of a rain. They'll come inside. Go after them with a fierce battle! The flies are worse than we've ever had. We had them practically down to nothing. We used to have no mosquitoes at all. So we want to take heart earnestly. Anyone seen not using a fly swatter will be brought to question in People's Rally tonight!

"Now, the next time we have a full moon on the sixteenth of the month, I want you to think of the beauty of swimming in the ocean at moonlight. And disregard any fear for it. Counteract the fear with pleasure. I was right in my revelation about the low cycle on the sixteenth when nations have fallen around the world. But by our mental power, we can rise above even the effect of lunar tidal waves. We're 98 percent water, but we can counteract even the pull on our water system with positive thought. Remember on the sixteenth I saved. How many miracles I performed on the sixteenth! We've had breakthroughs on the sixteenth. No major disasters have affected us on the sixteenth. So it is important that you remember these things.

"All right, the rain has stopped. Back to work! Back to production! All units back in usual points of surveillance. Listening posts in every cottage. Step it up, please. Step it up, please. . . .

"I thank you, and I love you very much."

The next time the moon was full and it was the sixteenth of the month, Congressman Leo Ryan had landed in Guyana to investigate the charges about Jonestown.

———————————<>—<———————————

November 18, 1978, 5 p.m. Eight miles away, on the cinder airstrip at Port Kaituma, Leo Ryan and four others lay dead. As the debate of his last Town Forum began, Jones did not know this yet. He knew only that one of his following had gone with the Congressman's party to shoot the pilot of the delegation plane and bring it down in the jungle.

"What's going to happen here in a matter of minutes is that one of those people on the plane is going to shoot the pilot—I know that. I didn't plan it, but I know it's going to happen." He *did* plan it, for his mistress Maria Katsaris, who never acted without his approval, had given the authorization. "They're gonna shoot that pilot and down comes that plane into the jungle. And we better not have any of our children left when it's over. Because they'll parachute in here on us . . . I've never lied to you. I never have lied to you . . ." on he went, liar to the end.

From the assembled, a sixty-one-year-old white woman, Christine Miller, rose. Intelligent, articulate, neat in dress, and handsome for her years, she was a former probation officer in Los Angeles. Six months before in her self-analysis letter, Miller had written to him of her unhappiness in Jonestown. "I'm used to traveling, and I can't do that here. I'm used to doing what I want to do when I want to do it. It seems I'm in a cage like a bird." Now, she challenged him in their democratic process of collective decision-making.

"Is it too late for Russia?" she asked.

"At this point, it's too late for Russia. They killed. They started to kill," he answered, referring to his angels at the airstrip. "That's why it makes it too late for Russia. Otherwise, I'd say, yes sir, you bet your life. But it's too late. Once we kill anybody . . ." He paused, straining for the metaphysical. "I've always put my lot with you. If one of my people does something, that's me." He patronized her. "Christine, you've always been a good agitator, and I appreciate it. I like agitation, because you have to see two sides of an issue, two sides of a question . . ."

In the past, she had often pushed the debate along. Had he put her up to it this time? With two sides to every question, in their scheme, his opponent had to be trounced—visibly.

"I say, let's make an airlift to Russia," she asserted. "That's what I say. . . . Nothing is impossible, if you believe."

"How are we going to do that?" he responded. "How are you going to airlift to Russia?"

"I thought they [the Russians] said if we got in an emergency, they gave you a code to let them know." What about those assurances from Timofeyev, those guarantees about which he had been so expansive, the ones that had set his mind at ease about the future of his people?

"No, they didn't," he confessed. "They gave us a code that they'd let us know. . . . Not *us* create an issue for them. They said that *if* they saw the country coming down, they'd give us a code." So it had been speculative. There had been no real assurances. He was on shaky ground, but he was still master of appearances. Turning to an aide, he postured, "We can check on that and see if they'll take us *in a minute,* but otherwise we die. I don't know what else to say to those people. . . . But to me, death is not a fearful thing. It's living that's cutthroat."

"There are too few people who left for twelve hundred people to give their lives," Christine Miller insisted, referring to the fourteen refugees who had fled with Ryan earlier in the day.

"Do you know how many left?" he asked.

"Maybe twenty-odd. That's small in comparison to what's here."

"What's going to happen when [the twenty] get on the plane and the plane goes down?"

"I don't think it will go down."

"You don't think it will go down? I wish I could tell you you're right, but I'm right. . . . That plane will come out of the air. There's no way you can fly a plane without a pilot."

"I wasn't talking about *that* plane," she argued. "I was speaking about the plane for us to go to Russia."

"To Russia? Do you think Russia's gonna want us? . . . Do you think Russia will want us with this stigma? We had some values, but now we don't have any values." So it had come to that. They were all common criminals now, and he, their crime embodied.

"I don't see it like that," she held on. "As long as there's life, there's hope. That's my faith."

"Everybody dies. Someplace that hope runs out, because everybody dies. I'm tired of being tortured to hell. That's what I'm tired of. Tired of it."

They were all tired, but they had the strength to applaud.

"Twelve hundred lives in my hands. I'm going to tell you, Christine, without me, life has no meaning." Again cheers drowned her. "I'm the best thing you've ever had. Once I have to pay, I'm standing for people. They're part of me. I cannot detach myself. No, no, no, no. I never detach myself from your troubles. I have always taken your troubles right on my shoulders, and I'm not going to change that now.

"It's too late. I've been running too long. Maybe next time you'll get to go to Russia. The next time around. I'm talking now about the dispensation of judgment." He was moving again into the Office of Savior, of Destroyer. "This is a revolutionary suicide council . . .," the council of one. "We have no other road. I've listened to you. Right now, I'm making a call to Russia. What more do you suggest? I'm listening to you. If there's one slight bit of encouragement . . . I just now instructed him [beckoning to an aide] to go and do that. We will put it to the Russians. But I will tell you the answer now, because I am a Prophet."

But it did not take a prophet to know the answer.

"It's over, sister, it's over," a male voice shouted at Christine. "We made a beautiful day, and let's make this a beautiful day." The place resounded in cheers.

"I'm speaking here now not as the administrator. I'm speaking as a prophet. I wouldn't step into this Seat and talk so seriously if I didn't know what I was talking about. An immense amount of damage is going to be done. I cannot separate myself from the pain of my people. You can't either, Christine, if you stop to think about it. You can't separate yourself. We've walked too long together."

"I know that, but I still think as an individual I have a right . . .," she started.

"You do, and I'm listening," he injected.

". . . to what I think and what I feel. We all have a right to our own destiny as individuals. I have a right to choose mine, and everybody has a right to choose theirs."

"I'm not criticizing that."

"I have a right to my own opinion," she said.

"I'm not taking it from you. I'm not taking it from you."

He had others to do that. A man spoke from the side. "You don't know what you're talking about, Christine, about having individual life. You're only standing here, because of him."

If it was too late for anything, it was too late for talk of individuality.

Minutes later, someone whispered the news from the Port Kaituma airstrip to Jones, and with its announcement, there would be no more talk of Russian airlifts. As the final ritual began, he called for Annie McGowan, the seventy-year-old black woman, born in the Mississippi Delta, a charwoman in East St. Louis for many years before she came to him. In McGowan's name, the bulk of the Temple fortune had been shifted to two Swiss banks located in Panama City, Panama. Accompanied by Maria Katsaris, Jones's mistress and financial secretary, McGowan had made frequent trips to the banks abroad, their last trip coming only two weeks earlier. At this moment, as the wails began around them, Jones had the presence of mind to execute legal documents. Dutifully, Annie McGowan signed the covering letter put before her.

Dear Mr. Timofeyev:

The following letter is a letter of instructions regarding all our assets which we want to leave to the Communist Party of the Union of Soviet Socialist Republics. Enclosed in this letter are letters which instruct the banks to send the cashiers checks to you.

I am doing this on behalf of the People's Temple, because we are Communists and want our money to be of benefit to oppressed peoples all over the world, or in any way that your decision making body see fit. . . .

With the enclosed letters you should have no difficulty in receiving the checks upon the mentioned maturity dates.

Cooperatively yours,
Annie J. McGowan

This letter was rushed to Jones's cabin, where Maria Katsaris put it together with three other bequeathing letters. Later, upon their examination, the Guyanese police concluded from the manner of the typing and the position of the dates on the page that all four letters had been prepared *before* November 18, although three of the four were dated as such. One bequeathing letter was dated November 6, 1978, around the date when Congressman Ryan decided finally to make the trip to Guyana. The evidence pointed to premeditation, as if Jones had found in the Ryan visit a pretext for the "one glorious moment" he had described three years before to his congregation.

"I'd just as soon bring it all to a gallant, a glorious screaming end, bring it to a screeching stop in one glorious moment of triumph . . ." than to endure the attacks of his enemies, he told them in 1975, well before he had any real enemies.

At Jones's cabin, Katsaris frantically packed two suitcases with the contents of the safe. Together with the four letters, her passport, and that of Annie McGowan, she crammed in over $1 million in American and Guyanese currency. Three young, white communards were summoned to the cottage—when it mattered, Jones trusted only whites—told of their mission to get the suitcases to "the Embassy," and sent on their way. But the suitcases soon proved too heavy, and one of the couriers buried over $500,000 in a chicken feed bag near the piggery and another $48,000 in a nearby banana grove. When the three made it to the railway tracks for the rickety train that traveled between Port Kaituma and Matthews Ridge, they discarded the second suitcase. Meanwhile, in Georgetown, the Temple headquarters was informed over the shortwave radio of the final ritual. A Temple staff member cleaned out the safe there as well, about $35,000, and rushed it to the Soviet Embassy.

Over a week later, railway workers would find the discarded suitcase, and in what must have been quite a sight in a country where the minimum wage is approximately five dollars a day, and where the American dollar brings three times the official exchange rate on the black market, they split up the loot. Soon enough, the local police caught wind of the transaction, and to their astonishment, they were able to recover over $300,000 from various Amerindians in the area. But how much was in that suitcase by the tracks will never be known. Three weeks later, a riverboat captain set out from Port Kaituma for Venezuela with over $50,000 in American greenbacks, presumably to change them on the black market. But he was found dead just over the border.

In Georgetown on December 6, 1978, the *Guyana Chronicle* published the first word of the link between the Temple and the Russians. Only then did the Soviet Embassy turn over to the Guyanese authorities that paltry and embarrassing fraction of the Temple fortune intended for them, the mere $35,000, their short-lived reward for their yearlong flirtation with this dangerous, obsessed, brilliant, and in the end, very sick "freedom fighter."

EIGHT

Mirrors
and
Prisms

[1]

WHEN *New West* magazine published its attack on the
People's Temple in August 1977, an attack for which
Grace Stoen was a major source, Timothy Stoen appeared
horrified. Ever ready to come to the defense of his spiritual leader,
Stoen, by late August, was making headlines in upstate California with
the announcement that he planned to file an $18 million lawsuit
against *New West* and a small-town weekly that had echoed the
magazine's charges against Jim Jones. In announcing his plans for the
libel suit, Stoen was quoted as saying, "I'm a street fighter. I must show
the world that the [media] cannot wrongfully hurt innocent people
without being brought to account."

But between August and November 1977, Stoen made a startling
turnabout. On November 18, 1977, the California court officially
granted Grace Stoen custody of John Victor Stoen, and who should
curiously be joined in her appeal but her erstwhile husband, Tim.
Timothy Stoen's own account of his apostasy, like so many accounts
by Temple members, past and present, was supremely unsatisfying. He
would say that he had been withdrawing emotionally from the Temple
for two years (Grace would later say it took her six years to get out of
Jones's grasp), that he had attended meetings with less frequency, that
it had dawned on him slowly that all the church's altruism did not
assuage one glaring truth: Jim Jones created in his members a profound
sense of unhappiness and guilt. Simultaneously, he felt his old
bourgeois instincts returning, his old "taste for elegance." He wanted
to read again. He wanted to listen to jazz and to have his old Porsche
back. He wanted relief from this constant preoccupation with the evils
of the world and free time to follow a few frivolous desires for a change.
It had dawned on him that rebels are rarely happy and content. He
wanted all these things, and yet he could not discard his Jones-instilled

guilt for wanting them. For one desire, however, he could not apologize: he wanted this child, John, who bore his name, and in whose upbringing he had taken some hand, back in the United States.

For weeks in September and October 1977 he wrestled with what to do with his life, escaping to a room in New York's Chelsea Hotel. He came to the realization, at least by his own narration, of his gullibility and naiveté. He saw that Jones was offering the impossible: there was no certainty in the world; one could not live without skepticism; the individual had to accept ambiguity and danger; there was no such thing as Jonesian security.

The first steps of his withdrawal were tentative. While he disavowed naiveté, he held onto the naive notion that Jim Jones would never resist the decision of the courts to the end, would never flaunt the courts openly. At first, Stoen could not fathom the idea that the presence of John Victor Stoen in Guyana would become the principle upon which Jim Jones would stake the existence of Jonestown and the lives of his followers. In joining with Grace, Stoen still could not challenge the goals of the Temple. As he moved into opposition he maintained the critical blindness of separating goals from tactics and strategies. On the day the California court delivered its verdict, he wrote to Jones asking that John Victor be returned in a week, but he was quick to promise that he and Grace would raise the child in interracial, giving surroundings rooted in the highest teachings, as if that would persuade Jones to let the child go. In his letter, Stoen even wished for the success of his mentor, hoping that the goals they once held together would be realized at Jonestown. It is no wonder that Jones felt he could still browbeat his old lieutenant.

But the methods of Jones were now the issue—methods, of course, that Tim Stoen knew perhaps better than anyone else alive.

He had heard that Grace was being discredited before John Victor's eyes, a practice deeply disturbing to Stoen, which he felt was emotionally damaging to the child. In this November letter, Stoen demanded that the practice be stopped at once and that the boy be told of the depths of his mother's love. The apostasy of Grace and of himself, Stoen wrote, had nothing to do with the validity of Temple goals.

In the Bay area, meanwhile, a number of parents had become increasingly concerned about the silence of their children from Guyana, or worse, the apparent efforts of Jones to split his followers from their blood ties. In one instance, a fifteen-year-old girl who went to Guyana without her father's consent or prior knowledge wrote to her grandmother, reprimanding her for inquiries about the girl's well-being: "I'm sorry to hear that you called the radio station," the letter concluded, "but since you did, I will not be writing you any more." In another instance, that of Maria Katsaris, Jones's mistress and by now the surrogate mother of John Victor Stoen in Jonestown, her father, Steven Katsaris, a Ukiah psychologist, traveled to Guyana to see his daughter. Once there, Katsaris was told by Sharon Amos that Maria did not wish to see him because in the past he had sexually molested her! (Katsaris would later go to the lengths of taking a lie detector test to prove the charge false. Not to be outdone, Maria would later describe the supposed sexual abuses in the most graphic detail to the Temple lawyer, Charles Garry.) Katsaris's first fruitless trip to Guyana was in September, but he returned again in November 1977, and finally was allowed to see his daughter . . . in the presence of three Temple members. She exhibited the classic signs of sleep deprivation and her demeanor was cold, hostile, threatening. Before her father, Maria was transformed and unrecognizable.

In still another instance, this one in December 1977, parents of two teenage boys traveled to Guyana with their attorney, bearing a California court order for the return of their younger son. They were informed that Jones had held a "council meeting," and it had decided that "it was best that we [the parents] not see or talk to our sons."

The news of Timothy Stoen's apostasy spread to these distraught parents rapidly, and in January 1978, a group calling itself Concerned Relatives gelled around this prize "defector." In the first half of 1978, the group grew to about twenty-five members, but with Stoen's knowledge and legal professionalism, it also grew in the confidence that something could be done about their problem. Stoen argued that not much would be required to get a response from Jones. The Bishop had a propensity for overreaction. (To a fellow Concerned Relative, Stoen commented after the apocalypse: "I never thought he'd overreact *that much.*") At last, the Concerned Relatives had a leader who knew most of the Temple secrets, who had legal skills, and who knew the organization's "pressure points." The Stoens' battle for John Victor would become the main thrust of the group, for Tim Stoen argued that Jim Jones's credibility with his following now rested on the proposition that "they'll never get John Victor away."

Into this arena of confrontation between the People's Temple and its opposition, U.S. authorities entered as referees in a significant way in January 1978. Before that date there had been sporadic contact. Richard McCoy, the boyish Chief Consul in the Georgetown Embassy, had visited Jonestown for the first time in August 1977. Through the fall he had had frequent visits from Sharon Amos and her inevitable companions, always probing, always pressing McCoy to go on record in support of Jim Jones in the custody case. McCoy took a strict stand of neutrality.

In the American Embassy, the People's Temple "problem" was viewed as consular as opposed to political, but the two sides of the diplomatic mission were soon joined. So long as the Temple remained a member of the Guyana Council of Churches, which it did till the end, it was entitled, in the official view, to the protection of the First Amendment, safeguarding religious freedom. The Guyanese government conferred the privileges of a religious group on the Temple throughout. Furthermore, in Guyana, the Temple was largely beyond the reach of the American legal system, at least until such time as *hard evidence* of U.S. law violations was gathered. If American citizens were in fact being held hostage by Jones, American diplomats could assist any self-avowed hostage in his escape from Jonestown, but essentially the blanket charge of the Concerned Relatives was a matter for the Guyanese constabulary to investigate. If the Temple was proven to be violating international fire-arm laws by smuggling guns into Guyana, or if it were defrauding the U.S. government on welfare or social security payments, or if it were violating communications laws by a misuse of its amateur radio communications between San Francisco and Guyana, the group would form a legitimate subject of official inquiry. But, taken together, the scope for action by American authorities was limited. The American government would operate only around the fringes of the problem—by mandate and by choice.

Besides its fundamental protection under the First Amendment, the Temple received critical support in a backhanded way from the Privacy Act and the Freedom of Information Act. Both laws were the outgrowth of the Vietnam era and the Watergate scandal and were intended to protect individuals and organizations from government spying and harassment that might have political, as opposed to legal, motivation. From the time that the Temple retained the services of activist attorney Charles Garry in August 1977, it had complained —and Garry had willingly echoed the complaint to the press—of a vast governmental conspiracy against them. As one of his earliest counsels, Garry urged the group to employ the Freedom of Information Act to uncover the conspiracy. A list of over eighty federal agencies was compiled, starting with the obvious law enforcement agencies and moving to obscure offices of military intelligence agencies abroad. Throughout the fall of 1977, FOIA requests for any information in official files on the Temple were prepared for the individual government offices. All the agencies were responsive, but much to the Temple's disappointment, every response was negative. Although there were in fact hundreds of State Department cables pertaining to the Temple, the Temple requests did not harvest a single document from the State Department or any other agency.

In early December, again under the guidance of Garry, Privacy Act requests were filed by every member of the Temple community, then about twelve hundred. Under the Privacy Act, the government would be required to produce any document in government files on that individual. Once again, the People's Temple did not receive a single document from the government as a result of this work.

What the Temple did not know was that these requests had a substantial intimidating effect upon American diplomacy in Georgetown. In early 1978, the U.S. Embassy informed the Department of State that documents did exist in its files on selected individuals and began to gather the papers together. On March 23, 1978, the relevant documents, including some twenty Embassy cables, were sent to Washington, presumably for delivery to the People's Temple (although the State Department never got around to processing them). From early 1978, a mood developed in the Embassy that virtually no document relating to the Temple could be kept secret. Embassy officials began to think that Jim Jones would always be relatively current with Embassy thinking and action. From December 1977, extreme caution and strict legality were emphasized. As a matter of policy, diplomatic reporting on the Temple became strictly factual, eschewing speculation or analysis. As a State Department report on the disaster later described it, the Embassy was "obliged" to follow "a cautious policy that stressed impartiality, objectivity, accuracy, adherence to strict legality, and insistence on hard evidence as the only basis for action."

In the end, the Embassy was so cautious in its actions that it became impotent. Later, it pleaded that it was victimized by an "array of constraints," placing major blame on the Privacy and Freedom of Information acts. Its mode of operation was to leave any serious discussion of action to undocumented oral discussions, which could not be touched by the two acts. But oral discussions easily float out of a bureaucrat's busy mind. The result was that important negative impressions or unsubstantiated concerns, formed by the diplomats who dealt with the Temple, never appeared in official communications and, therefore, never gave the Department of State, if it was ever inclined to order action, adequate information to guide the Embassy in Georgetown. But it is hard to judge who was less inclined to action, the Embassy or the department, for in general the Temple was considered, as one diplomat characterized them, "a bunch of dingbats."

It was as if the Embassy ceased to be an Embassy and became a judicial tribunal. Diplomacy or, more precisely, the diplomatic duty to protect Americans in jeopardy abroad, was made to fit strict rules of judicial inquiry. The Embassy began to see itself as the impartial judge between two opposing bizarre groups, each of which hurled the wildest threats and whispered the weirdest innuendos at one another. The bizarre stories about Jones from Stoen soon became matched in kind by stories from the Temple that Tim Stoen was a "transvestite." For good measure, Stoen was also charged with being a CIA agent. All of this was speedily labeled propaganda in the American Embassy. The charges against Jones, served up by Stoen or the often irresponsible California press, became hearsay.

The Embassy simply wished the whole problem would go away. Well, not quite. Never far from the diplomats' minds was the portent that Jim Jones might leave his community precipitously, either from illness or by proving himself a charlatan. Ambassador John Burke came from the Midwest, and the image of Elmer Gantry was strong in his thinking. He never dismissed the idea that Jones might be a fraud and abscond one night with his people's loot. In the event of Jones's departure or worse, his death, the Embassy would be faced with the mountainous job of repatriating more than one thousand Americans. In its bureaucratic concerns, the Embassy found that prospect hideous.

In the critical period between August 1977 and August 1978, the operational officer for the U.S. Embassy was the Chief Consul, Richard A. McCoy. In his mid-forties now, McCoy had made his way into career diplomacy by an unusual route. Raised in New Jersey, he had quit high school before he ended his sophomore year to go to work. In 1952 he enlisted in the Marine Corps, and on active duty he was able to get his high school diploma. After his hitch in the Marines, part of which was spent as an Embassy guard abroad, he entered Cornell College in Mount Vernon, Iowa, and after graduation returned to the military, entering air force officer candidate school and emerging as a counterintelligence officer in the Office of Special Investigations. After six years in the air force, during which he proudly cites a few big security cases he cracked, he entered the Foreign Service at the age of thirty-two. Easygoing and enthusiastic, almost undiplomatic in his spontaneity, devout in his Catholicism, strict in the raising of his two teenage sons, McCoy was an unlikely target for the charge, made and then discredited in the aftermath, that he had had sexual liaisons with the Temple girls of Georgetown. For starters, he never found them very attractive.

McCoy had arrived in Guyana as Chief Consul in August 1976. Several months later, when the Cubana airliner was sabotaged, and Prime Minister Forbes Burnham charged the CIA with complicity, McCoy suddenly found himself as the ranking American diplomat in Georgetown, since the Ambassador and Chargé d'Affaires were pulled out in protest. During his three months as acting ambassador, McCoy met Jim Jones for the first time, when Jones came to introduce Mervyn Dymally, the Lieutenant Governor of California. McCoy found Jones well-spoken and pleasant enough, projecting sincerity in his beliefs and dedication in his work, but lacking in any humor (a quality nearly all Temple members shared). The conversation lasted over an hour, with Jones dropping the names of his purported buddies, Walter Mondale and Rosalynn Carter, and charging that the CIA was after him. McCoy paid little attention. He viewed the meeting as a courtesy visit for an American politician, and this boastful, domineering preacher of the fringe, whose community in the North West then numbered no more than thirty Americans, did not make much of an impression.

In the three more meetings that McCoy would have over the next year and a half with Jim Jones, the pattern of his first conversation changed only in degree. McCoy heard the same charges of governmental conspiracy each time, as if it were a cassette which Jones played for him mechanically. August 30, 1977, was McCoy's first visit to Jonestown, and it bore the first hint of possible beatings in Jonestown. Arriving in Matthews Ridge, the Consul was told excitedly of a Temple member in the infirmary with ugly lacerations on his back, claiming to have been beaten in Jonestown, to have escaped, and who was now pleading for safe passage back to America. McCoy immediately took a local policeman in tow and proceeded to the bedside to take a statement, prepared to go from there to Jonestown to arrest the guilty party. But at the infirmary, the Temple member turned out to be a barely literate street black in his early fifties, who exhibited stammering fear and suspicion toward McCoy, as if he finally found himself in the presence of that CIA agent Jim Jones had warned them all about. Directly, the patient changed his story, asserting that the cuts on his back had come from hauling rough-hewn lumber, not from beatings. His only request was to go home. In Jonestown, McCoy presented the problem to Jones, and the pastor adroitly and loftily offered to pay the man's passage home, underlining that anyone in his mission who wished to return home was free to do so at Temple expense.

This episode had two consequences. It would convince McCoy that any Temple member who was truly being held hostage in Jonestown could find a way through the jungle to safety, if the desire were really there. Second, McCoy would use the case as an example to other concerned parents to show that members were free to return to the United States at will.

On January 4, 1978, Grace and Timothy Stoen arrived in Guyana to push the writ of habeas corpus for John Victor that lay idle in the Guyanese courts. Now, McCoy found himself smack in the middle of two contending parties, and the air became thick with charge and countercharge.

On January 11, 1978, McCoy made his second visit to Jonestown. This time, its purpose was threefold: to speak to twelve members, including Jann Gurvich, whose relatives had expressed concern, to check on a number of older citizens who were receiving social security benefits (to establish that they were alive and receiving the payments directly), and to have a good look at John Victor Stoen. His technique on this visit, as well as on his other three, was standard. He prided himself on his ability to put people at their ease, and this was, after all, not a criminal investigation. He felt he must exhibit the American virtue of fair play and the legal standard of innocence until guilt was proven. Besides, he knew by now that hostile confrontation would not only be counterproductive, but also could fit into the Temple theory that he might be some sort of "provocateur."

In one form or another he asked these questions: How are you? What are you doing? Are you being well-treated? Do you wish to leave? Are you being held here against your will? Have you been mistreated in any way? What are your plans for the future? Have you heard from your family in the U.S.? Are you satisfied with your present life in Jonestown? McCoy also devised ways to talk at random with the commune's citizens, in order to determine whether answers were forced and rehearsed. To keep his relations cordial with the Temple operatives in Georgetown, the Consul acceded to their demand that advance notice be given before a visit and that a list of names of those he wished to interview be given. But, as general practice, McCoy devised an open and a *reserved* list, the latter not given to Sharon Amos and containing the names of those about whom the most serious allegations had been made. Jann Gurvich was on the reserved list for the January visit. Further, the Temple was told that as long as allegations of abuse persisted, consular visits to Jonestown would continue quarterly. The Embassy felt that the quarterly visit constituted diligent monitoring without giving credence to the Temple's charge of "harassment."

On this visit, as on the others, McCoy spent about four hours in Jonestown. He sensed nothing amiss. The older members, "seniors" as they were amiably called, were all neatly dressed and spoke to him without apprehension, expressing satisfaction with their lives. The diplomat found their answers to be spontaneous and apparently unrehearsed. Some hostility surfaced from the inner circle when he passed letters from relatives directly to the communards, and Jones himself seemed somewhat disconcerted when McCoy asked to see Jann Gurvich. Startled, the Bishop pointed to a nearby tent where school classes were under way, but protested, "You didn't tell me that you wanted to see her." McCoy simply pivoted on his heel and walked to the classroom. Jann turned to him with apparent surprise at seeing a stranger, but she responded breezily to his questions, without any of the apprehension he might have expected. In the brief interchange, McCoy pointed to his car, saying he had a Guyanese official with him, and if she wanted to go home, she could do so immediately under his protection. She smiled and demurred graciously, even with a touch of condescension. Back at the Embassy several days later, McCoy wired

Louis Gurvich that Jann "appeared well and happy and enthusiastic about her teaching duties." Her happiness seemed somewhat beyond the diplomat's ability to judge in the few minutes he spoke with her, but the cable relaxed Louis Gurvich's anxiety for a few months.

McCoy's official report to the State Department also accented the vibrance and achievement of the commune. Cabled several days after the visit, it read in part:

The Consul is convinced on the basis of his personal observations and conversations with People's Temple members and Guyanese Government officials that it is improbable that anyone is being held against their will in Jonestown. At no time during his conversations with People's Temple members did he sense that individuals were fearful, or under duress or pressure. They appeared adequately fed and expressed satisfaction with their lives. Some were engaged in hard, physical labor repairing heavy equipment and clearing fields, but this is normal work on farms. . . . There are competent X-ray technicians at the site. The Consul was alert to possibility that attempt might have been made to stage a favorable scenario for his visit, but given conditions at the community, does not believe that this could have been done. Work and life appeared to be going on in a normal fashion. Persons with whom he talked in private—some of whom were those allegedly held against their will—appeared spontaneous and free in their conversation and responses to Consul's questions. Also local GOG [Government of Guyana] officials who visit the community frequently and often without advance notice told Consul that they have never received the impression that anything strange was occurring in the community. In short, there is no hard evidence available.

At about the time that McCoy was clearing the slate for the department, two events contradicted the tone of his report. Diligent Ms. Amos came for a visit, accompanied this time by Marceline Jones. Ambassador John Burke had ordered McCoy always to have another diplomat present in all future meetings with the Temple representatives, another example of his growing caution, because the Ambassador feared the Temple would claim McCoy said things for which his consul would have no corroborated defense, again a legal thought. So on this occasion the Deputy Chief of Mission, the number-two man in the Embassy, John Blacken, joined the conversation. In the heat of considerable passion, prodded by the presence of the Stoens in Georgetown, Sharon Amos delivered the first direct threat of mass suicide.

"If they take John Victor from us," Amos said, "we will all sit down and die. We'll all commit suicide."

"Don't give me that!" McCoy cut her off sharply. "I'm not going to listen to such a thing." The Stoen matter was in the courts, he said, and if the courts decided in the Stoens' favor, an orderly transfer of the child would take place. In his mind, the Consul attached no particular importance to Amos's comment. Perhaps she was threatening a hunger strike or some such traditional 1960s strategy. He viewed the comment as a psychological ploy, and his view never changed in later discussions both at the Embassy and in home-based consultations at the Department of State. All talk of suicide was nonsense. The Amos threat was not reported to Washington.

Meanwhile, Grace and Tim Stoen were matching Sharon Amos in diligent vituperation, as they called on government officials and diplomats around Georgetown. But on January 13, 1978, Guyanese officials abruptly informed the couple that their visas were canceled and that they were to leave the country within twenty-four hours. Upon inquiries from the American Embassy, it was learned that the expulsion order was issued by the Temple's friend, the Minister of Home Affairs, Vibert Mingo, but initiated by the ideological aides around the Temple's chief advocate in the government, Deputy Prime Minister Ptolemy Reid. The Embassy quickly prepared a formal diplomatic protest to the Minister of Foreign Affairs, Frederick Wills, another Temple friend. He took the matter directly to the Prime Minister, Forbes Burnham, but Burnham at least was still maintaining a distance. He angrily called in Mingo and upbraided him for making Guyana look ridiculous in American eyes. The expulsion order was rescinded forthwith, and the Stoens were allowed to stay in the country for another five days. The consequence of this episode, however, was to demonstrate to the American Embassy the extent of Jim Jones's inroads into the top level of the Guyanese government. The political wing of the American Embassy was now joined with the consular.

On January 26, Sharon Amos came again to the Embassy and presented McCoy with an affidavit, signed by Tim Stoen in February 1972, in which he declared Jim Jones to be John Victor Stoen's real father. But before he left Guyana, Stoen told McCoy that the document was false, and that *he* was the real father. McCoy found the whole matter a royal mess and began to look for ways to maintain his own sanity. But the dimensions of the dispute were now drawn.

Shortly afterward, *San Francisco Chronicle* columnist Herb Caen was given the same document and published it in his customary chatty style. The Stoen-Jones dispute had become deliciously San Francisco in nature. The city had had trouble with bishops before, of course. Bishop James Pike had left his post as Episcopal Bishop of California after he announced his misgivings about the Virgin Birth and the Trinity, and faded into a Judean desert in 1968, never to be heard from again. His successor, Bishop C. Kilmer Myers, also became notorious, retiring as

Bishop with the public announcement that he had become a "vulnerable and sinful human being" as he admitted himself to an alcoholic's clinic. So a custody fight between a preacher and a father, the leader and the apostate, was perfect for the Bay area newspapers. Caen made the most of it. First, he quoted Tim Stoen's lawyer: "I think that when Tim signed that affidavit he really believed Jones WAS the father of his son. He no longer believes it. I think he was hoodwinked." Then, a reaction from Grace's lawyer, Jeff Haas: "What affidavit? I've heard that Jim Jones is sterile." Finally, Charles Garry, Jones's lawyer: "I've seen the boy, and he's the spitting image of Jim. Jim sterile? He has fathered a child since the boy was born." Herb Caen affectionately entitled his column on this matter "This Old Town."

———————⊃◁ ▷⊂———————

With the political office of the Embassy now focused on the dispute, the number-two man, John Blacken, traveled to Jonestown on February 2, 1978, taking along a visiting diplomat from Washington, the desk officer for Guyana in the State Department. Blacken and, later, his replacement, Richard Dwyer, were the highest diplomatic officers to visit Jonestown during the last year of Jim Jones. (Ambassador John Burke specifically eschewed visiting the community, fearing that the Concerned Relatives would interpret a tour as favoritism to the Temple.) Even though his contacts with Temple members were infrequent, Blacken seems to have maintained a relaxed manner with them. A month later, as he prepared to leave his post in Guyana for Washington and an appointment to Ambassador Andrew Young's staff at the United Nations, Blacken bade Sharon Amos goodbye at the Embassy. In her report to Jim Jones on the farewell, which of course might have contained a touch of elaboration, Amos described giving Blacken a wood souvenir and how he kissed her goodbye. They talked about Andrew Young, the provocative statements to which he was prone, and their frequently controversial consequences.

"Anyone who does anything decisive gets into some difficulty," Blacken replied (according to Sharon Amos). Clearly, Amos interpreted that as an oblique compliment to the Temple, and she made much of Blacken's statements of pleasure at what the Temple had accomplished.

Probably he was merely being diplomatic, for in early February Blacken had listened carefully in his lengthy chat with Jim Jones. Jones made his familiar complaints, but they were not delivered with the shrillness that indicated irrationality to the diplomat. Blacken was impressed, as all had been by the neatness of the community and its achievements of clearing and cultivating the jungle desert. He saw no evidence of mistreatment. But, for the second time in three weeks,

Blacken heard the threat of mass suicide. On this occasion, during a discussion of the Stoen case, an aide around Jim Jones remarked that they would all die before they gave up John Stoen.

Thus, as of early February 1978, the menace of self-extinction had been mentioned directly to the Chief Consul, a ranking political officer (twice), and the Washington-based head of the Guyana desk at the U.S. State Department. Admittedly, the notion was unfathomable, unfathomable as an American idea, unfathomable in the modern world. To be sure, the decree to be ready to die for one's country or one's beliefs was as common as lice and modern armies, but one's political leaders defined for young and old the cause for which the supreme sacrifice was necessary. From the psychological standpoint, was there any difference between the Marine at Hamburger Hill in Vietnam and the Temple member surrounded by the demons of Jim Jones's creation? Both were programmed to die. Perhaps the Marine was the sadder case, especially if he had no emotional understanding or interest in why he was in Vietnam.

What of a Vietnam veteran who had faced death both in Vietnam and in Jonestown? What would his attitude be? There was at least one of those, and as the U.S. Embassy focused lamely on its problem, the veteran approached his Father's throne to testify about his commitment.

"Dad, in 1968 and 1969, they sent me to Vietnam to fight a war I didn't know anything about. I had no principle to die in that war. You've saved my life so many times, Dad, and I'm living on your time. All I have now is this life of my own, and I would die for you right now, Dad. I'm willing to face the front lines with you right now."

Still the notion was unfathomable. The only possible historical parallel was Masada in A.D. 73, when 930 zealots killed themselves before the Roman soldiers overran their mountain fortress. But to do the same over a six-year-old child when the only soldiers surrounding them marched in their heads? It was ridiculous. Nonetheless, by the Embassy's own construction, that only *hard evidence* was "operationally pertinent," by February 2, 1978, three key diplomats had direct knowledge of Jim Jones's epic threat.

But on his February 2 visit to Jonestown the diplomat John Blacken had been more deeply struck by something else. Jim Jones asserted that he was an agnostic. This fit more into categories Blacken could understand, for the Temple enjoyed rights and privileges under the First Amendment and other laws that protected religious expression of any kind. So surprised was Blacken by Jones's comment that he evidently made something of it in official conversations and on the cocktail circuit. Soon enough, it got back to Sharon Amos, and she leapt on the problem. In a report to Jones, she wrote:

Re rumors from American Embassy about JJ being an atheist:

—He [McCoy] said it was his policy not to say anything about Americans to Guyanese.
—said John Blacken did tell him that he was surprised that JJ described himself as an agnostic; he told John that JJ was moving away from the stereotyped Christ to be more interested in following Christ's life and once in a while doubted the very existence of God.
—Dick [McCoy] didn't know, however, that John would mention that in town as he said John was very sophisticated in knowing what to say and what not to and he didn't think John would say that.
—when I called him [McCoy] back and told him that it was him that we were told was talking about J being an atheist, he said it was untrue.
—he had said before this second call that he would discreetly find out who was the one in the Embassy that was talking.

(McCoy later would officially deny through the State Department that he had ever offered to find out who was gossiping.)

This matter went to the core of Jones's fraudulence. He postured as a great radical to the Huey Newtons, but he longed for the ear of the establishment politicians. He engaged in sacrilege and promoted idolatry, but he cried foul when authorities suggested he be denied the protections of a religious group if he was only a social philosopher. He proclaimed himself a Marxist and an atheist, but bragged of his Midas touch and declared that "service to my fellow man is the highest service to God." And he hated it when people gossiped bad things about him. He wanted it every which way. That nearly a thousand Americans would follow this magnificent hypocrite with his mumbo jumbo to the ends of the world, and then to the end of their life, shifts the question to who they were, and what was the nature of American society in the 1970s which could make this poppycock appealing.

[2]

The Front and the Reality. For all Richard McCoy's pride in himself as a relaxed and effective investigator, he and other diplomats, visitors, and eventually the press that came to Jonestown in 1978 were no match for the elaborate staging that greeted them there. Later, a minor aspect of the Jonestown denouement would be the State Department's recommendation that its consular officers be trained to detect signs of "mind control" or "coercive persuasion," but there is unlikely ever again to be such an isolated situation, and even terms like *mind control* indicate the subjects were spouting a line against their will. In general, that was not the case in Jonestown. But people were beaten. Some did desperately want to leave—the very things McCoy was supposed to be uncovering. While the Consul and the other American diplomats were deceived enough to write favorable official reports, there lingered in their minds a suspicion, a disquieting uneasiness that was beyond their power or inclination to resolve. That would be left to a flashy congressman who had no patience with bureaucratic or diplomatic obfuscations, and who was prepared to use power and guile on the same plane as Jim Jones. Only in Congressman Leo Ryan did Jim Jones finally find his match.

To create his Front, Jones had a hard task, for it required his zealots to unlearn many of the rote responses that had been beaten into them over months and years. For the Bishop was clever enough to know that diplomats or journalists, intent to discover a scandal, would come with a stock idea of what a concentration camp should look like, of how prisoners so incarcerated would talk, of how a Hitler-like or even Eichmann-like commandant would speak and be treated. As a consequence, Jones and his advisors put considerable thought into managing the impression that this was basically a nonpolitical cooperative experiment, grounded in the Christian ideal of a sanctuary, dedicated to sharing, led by a forceful but unpretentious Midwesterner. If there were deficiencies, they should appear to reside on the field of naive, scout-camp idealism.

Once the strategy was decided, it was practiced and rehearsed. Special classes were held for those who had trouble relearning, with Jones often playing the role of the diplomat or the reporter or the secret FBI/CIA man, and playing it very well. A tape was made on how to greet visitors, and those who failed the test in the role-playing sessions were required to listen to it over and over. First impressions were important, so when visitors came, the gate was taken down. It was to be referred to as the front entrance. The dwellings in Jonestown were to be called cottages, residences, or apartments—not barracks. Near the camp where the children played in a waterfall, the spot was not to be called Camp #1 but the cathedral. The three-story tower at the far end of the cottage area was dubbed the pagoda; slides were angled to its first tier, giving it the appearance of a children's playground; it was a windmill, or wind generator, and a place during the hot season where the vigilant watched for forest fires. The name of the camp was Jonestown, not freedom land or promised land; a community, not a family. The Bishop was to be addressed as Jim, or even Blackie or Ole Buddy—never Dad or Father, his place in their emotions as simply "the best friend you've ever had." At all cost, they were to cut away his "aura" for the day that outsiders were there. Visitors were to be told Blackie lived somewhere in the cottage section, but that they had been warned by the government not to say exactly where because of the assassination attempts against him.

"Believe he's God?" the tape ran. "I'd laugh at that one. Ha. Ha. Ha. Some colorful little lady might say, I don't believe there is a God. I'm a Liberator, a Savior, but you don't tell that. You don't cast pearls before swine. You say, you don't have to believe in God to be in this community. . . ."

They could admit belief in spiritual healing, but only after medical science had been exhausted. Cancer? They were to stick to what had happened to them personally, but they could say records existed of healed cancer patients before and after. Visitors were free to study the public record. Marriage and divorce were matters of free choice (they were not to mention the "relationship committee" which had to approve a heterosexual or homosexual companionship), and as a point of information, he told them that a divorce took three months in the Guyanese court. But residents were not encouraged to hop around from mate to mate, because in a cooperative that caused strife. They kept their own passport, personal papers, and money. ("Where do you keep your money? You could say, where do you keep yours? Please, sir, that's a personal matter.") If someone died, why, of course, they called the local officials and executed the will. If loved ones wanted the body, it could be sent back. They could travel where they wanted on outings, like to Georgetown, but in general they were all to prefer the country life. If someone wanted to leave, well, there were plenty of paths out, a free train, airports in two directions, boats traveling down the river constantly. Security guards? Weapons? Beatings?

"Look shocked! Anything crazy they ask like that, look shocked . . . or puzzled. Security guards? What have you been doing, sir, reading some wild nightmare stories? Science fiction?"

When it came to complaints, they had not heard any. Oh, there's always one complainer who would probably complain in heaven. Entertainment was to consist of good, wholesome movies, television, and documentaries, but no ghost shows like *Dracula* that gave the children bad dreams or crime shows that glorified violence. No physical violence existed in the camp. Children had ceased to fight one another, because they believed in rewarding good behavior. Nothing about being on the floor or public services [the Jonestown terms for trial and punishment], please, unless the Bishop decided otherwise. When the occasional child acted out, he was denied a night or two of television. The news came from Voice of America, Radio Netherlands, news magazines sent in from the States, and the *Guyana Chronicle*, but in general they didn't get involved in politics.

"Are you Communists? We're not in politics. Only believe in sharing. We admire the Jewish kibbutz and enjoy this form of nonviolent communalism.

"Don't criticize the USA. Things we've been saved from: muggings, gangs, racism, drugs, rape, happen in any urban center.

"Which is best: socialism or capitalism? Say, I'm no politician. Nations will have to live in peace together. In a world of nuclear bombs, no point in talking better or best. We all had better learn to get along with one another.

"So you think nuclear war will come? I'd say, anything's possible after Hitler's Germany. If your back is to the wall, you could say, everybody in the U.S. is talking about nuclear war, but I didn't come over here for that reason."

As for the delicate area of the food they eat, they were to begin by naming the meats. If they had forgotten them, he gave them a litany: pork, ham, fish, chicken, beef, even special meats like labba, the wild bush pig, and, on two occasions, even wild bush cow. "It was very tasty," they could editorialize. For God's sake, mention rice last. They loved the fresh fruits and vegetables, especially because they had no chemical preservatives.

Did people go naked? "No sir, we don't have a nudist colony here," he said with a chortle (they didn't). "We're pretty democratic, but we haven't quite voted *that* in yet. Add a cute little flare to it now and then," he told them, and then he gave four praises and a treat to the girl who suggested putting an *M* and an *F* up on the two entrances to the latrine. He hadn't thought of that himself.

In general, they were to look the questioner in the eye and smile a lot. Be friendly, never be intimidated, but bear in mind that most people were as dangerous as serpents and seldom harmless as doves. Don't answer quickly, and if you couldn't say So-cial-ism or par-ti-ci-pa-tory democracy, don't say it at all.

So they were lined up before him, and he became the interrogator.

"How's the food here, madam?"

"The food is wonderful," came the cheery reply.

"Wonderful? I don't know what wonderful is. What kind of food do you have?"

"Well, we have cornbread. We make our own bread. We have rice. . . ."

"Oh, Christ sakes, don't name rice first, *please.* They say we never eat anything here but rice. Chicken, pork, eggs, fish. Come on with the meats first. What kind of pastries and sweets do you have?"

"Oh . . . they're good. . . ."

"Too slow. Too slow. Say, we got candy, pastries, pies, peanut butter. We make our own peanut butter. Doughnuts. Fresh doughnuts every day. Pudding, cake, peanut fudge, popcorn balls. No, maybe we better not get into that. They might ask me for popcorn, and I ain't got enough to give 'em. Banana bread. Say, we got anything a modern bakery would have. OK. You pass. Next . . . Do you have any parasites here, sir?"

"No, I never saw any."

"You wouldn't sir, because you can only see them under a microscope. Anybody ever been treated for worms?"

"Not that I know of."

"What I would say is: our doctors are on top of that. We clear up worms in no time, but just to be safe, we don't go barefoot. Next . . . How's your health, sir?"

"Health's fine, gained more health since I've been here. Had bladder trouble in the States, and I'm not suffering from it here."

"Good. You didn't say I healed it. You're just not suffering from it here. I'd say, I have better health here, not more health though."

"Better health."

"Yes, maybe it's the good water, or the good food. Don't have any sodium nitrate. How many know what sodium nitrate is?" A sprinkling of hands went up. "Will you *please* tell your neighbor what sodium nitrate is . . . ? OK. Why did you come here, young lady?"

"Reason I came was racism."

"Well, you look pretty good, young woman. How did it hurt you?"

"There was trouble in school. . . ."

"Can't you say, I was about to get in trouble because of my hostility. You should be the first to think of that . . . OK, pass. What are your political beliefs, madam?"

"I don't have any political beliefs."

"You have no beliefs at all, woman?"

"I believe in my own beliefs."

"What are your beliefs?"

"Social . . . Social . . ."

"Oh, God, if you can't use a big word, say, believe in living together and sharing. What are your religious beliefs then?"

Silence.

"You should avoid reporters like the plague, honey, because you don't think well on your feet. Just say, hi. I don't mean you're dumb. Some people think better in writing. Some better on their feet. Just stay away from 'em, OK . . . ? What kind of entertainment do you have here, sir?"

"We have a band and dances. We play cards and bingo. . . ."

"You *ought* to say movies and TV right up at the top, much as you watch. Some could mention the library first, but not all. Looks superficial, but you ought to mention the library before cards. Next. How many hours do you work, sir?"

"Eight."

"What's your shift?"

"Seven to six."

The place burst into laughs and catcalls.

"By my last count that makes eleven. Got to watch these reporters. They'll trip you."

"Eight to five," someone yelled out from the audience.

"No, don't say that," he answered. "If you say eight to five, and they see people walking down the path at 6:30, somebody's going to get in trouble. . . . Where'd all the money come from to build this place, sir?"

Silence again. Jones shook his head in exasperation.

"We're in trouble. You ought to know all these questions. I've told you to learn 'em. Seems like you're hesitant to speak, sir. What's the problem?"

"I don't remember," mumbled the voice in shame.

"I'm sick of you people!" His voice rose angrily. "It's so easy for you to sit back and let Jim Jones do the thinking. What are you hiding, sir? How did you get all this money? Must have taken millions of dollars." (To the press, the Temple members had to appear to have a choice about turning over their money to Jones.)

"I don't know the answer to that, Dad."

"*Shut your mouth!* You didn't hear anything tonight. You just called me *Dad.* . . . How does anybody make money? Bake sales. Old clothes sales. Rummage sales. Offerings . . . Usually you're a pretty good liar. You just don't have the sense to back it up. Abraham Lincoln said, 'No man's got a good enough memory to be a successful liar.' "

On and on it went, for hours. And so, when a fair-minded diplomat like Richard McCoy or, later, a frightened reporter like Don Harris of NBC came to Jonestown, asking politely if residents were happy or being well treated or wanted to go home, it was a pushover.

The surface challenge of answering a few soft questions from outsiders *correctly* was a pushover, that is, but what of those few, or many, who, if asked by Richard McCoy about wanting to leave, were ready to hop in the Consul's Land Rover and speed away to freedom —what of them? No amount of training in the Temple doctrine in the rehearsals could ensure their correct responses in the real interview. For the impulse to defection, Jones needed the stronger antidote of Prophet's power. Before Him, they must toady, quivering with fear and awe, knowing that He was connected on some plane far beyond their comprehension—if not heaven, then hell—if not hell, then the more secular circles of hit squads or Mafiosi or revolutionary justice.

On a night not long before a consular visit, Jones displayed his power in all its diabolical magnificence. It was the night after his mother had died in Jonestown—that heroine of the revolution, as he referred to her, even though she had rejected his message and doctrine. It was as if his mother's death energized his evil soul, for he restrained his passion, delivering his threats with soft exultance. He had halted her decline into slobbery paralysis in the final hours, he told them, but it had been difficult, for she was not receptive to his magic, and, as such, he could not save her altogether. He fought her resistance to him as best he could, but she was stubborn, strong-willed, and she did not want to listen. On her deathbed, as he had tried to work with her, she had repeated again that she could not be a child to him, like all the rest. A mother could not be a child to her son, and it was hard to teach "sweet, lovely old dogs new tricks." When she passed away, he had presided over the packing of the box and the hammering of the nails just right and the careful spading of the earth, and he had suffered.

For them, there was a lesson in it. Those who did not follow his instructions, who rejected the touch of his hand, then swollen from his own arthritis, as if it were a "rubber glove filled with water," should not expect him to pull a "stunt" at the last moment, to pull something from his wondrous "grab bag," for their very recalcitrance begged for hypertension or diabetes or other dread consequences. Still, when they passed away as well from defector's disease, he would still love them as he had his own mother and exercise the same tender care in their interment. Even though she had rejected his message, she had still worried about his problems. In those last months of decline, those who had told her of their petty difficulties had helped to kill her. Her first major attack had come after two had tried to escape. They then must share in the responsibility for her death, they who were lower than reptiles, lower than the primates. For she worried too much about those she loved, and he had the same problem.

His worry at the moment was their social security checks. The fascists in the States had placed a "hold" on their mailing (temporary as it turned out, a misinterpretation by postal officials of the Social Security Act, and soon remedied), but he knew how to deal with that. His seniors might just put on a fast, and the authorities would have to come out and make them eat.

"We'll tell it on the radio. We'll tell it all over the world. We'll fast until we get our money. We have a right to do that."

They cheered, and he quieted them with "Peace. Peace."

"Before we starve, I have some other things in store, but I won't tell them over the radio. We have to keep our little trade secrets. We're not going to stand here and starve to suit the fascists. A fast will make them nervous. We'll make headlines in certain parts of the world, even if the capitalists ignore us. And even they will take notice when we get into the second, third, and fourth stages of it. Because I got it all laid out. Some of you in the relationship committee are thinking about who you want to marry, who you want to fuck. I got a lot of plans too. But I ain't thinking about fuckin', I'm thinking about rapin'!"

Their roars of approval soon quieted again with his "Peace."

"Oh, we've got different distinguished people who want to visit us, investigate us. I've got all kinds of programs for them, and they're worked out from A to Z. It depends on what kind of birthday party, or anniversary party they want."

At their cheer this time, his loathing for them burst out.

"You're so naive. You don't even know what Jim Jones is all about. You can't even follow him. You haven't even smelled where he's at yet, much less follow him. You don't know who he is. If you didn't get a real good look at him, you wouldn't know who he looked like. You haven't got next to him. But I got *all* kinds of plans. They better release that damn money, because I don't die easy."

He was hitting his stride. They shouted for more, more of his Being, more of their nothingness. He ate it up.

"You who are stupid piss-ants and reptiles, who are lower than the primates, you can make whoopee if you want, but your whoopee makes me sicky . . . *peace, peace.* . . . You make your whoopee, while I do something that's far more significant, because I know exactly what's going to take place. I've made some *big* plans, honey, both here and there and everywhere. Lots of plans. Um huh. Um huh. I just have to gargle over that radio and all hell breaks loose. Just one word to one person, another word to another person, and it sounds like aimless little talk about the sun shining. If I start that conversation, the whole world's going to know we came along. . . . So watch it. I can get anything I want to buy, and I know how to buy it. I got people back there who don't act like socialists, going around wining and dining. You'd think they were some high classy-chassy in the social set.

"You gonna commit treason? You better know who you're dealing with! It don't pay to mess with someone's got a *live wire.* Because after we're all dead over here, you might go to a social party, after you got your little thirty pieces of silver, for selling out the greatest people on earth. You might walk in with the Judas tribe, and wife of Judas might be one of the ladies I'd laid to make a socialist. She might give you slow poison in your champagne. You fuckers, I like to look at you now, because you don't know how clever I am.

"I made plans for [your] treason long ago, because I knew I couldn't trust nothing, only Communism, and the principle that is in me. I knew I couldn't depend on the arm and the leg, so, honey, I never put all my eggs in one basket. I've rolled my balls in many places. . . . Right . . . You figure that out if you can. . . ."

And then he slid exuberantly into a little Democratic Party jingle about "Happy Days Are Here Again."

"So think about it, honey, when you think about selling out. You go back to New York, you won't be safe. Go to Pennsylvania, to California, to Miami, you won't be safe. You say, our enemies are getting by. But all I have to do is go. . . ." He clicked his tongue. "I've made long, long plans to take care of these enemies. You better hope I keep talking to you, because when I stop talking to you, when I start calling up my aces in the hole, it'll be dangerous business then.

"I'm a Man of Steel, though I feel every ache and pain. I didn't waste my life down through all these years to see it come to nothing at the graveyard. Oh no, you're not going to just put a little shrine out there for me next to my name. I didn't sweat and bleed to see this movement come to nothing. This is part of the historical procedure, part of historical change.

"So you can't park me out there next to my beloved mother, and think you can get away from me. I've got lots and lots of tricks up my sleeve, honey, and it won't make any difference if we all lay down our mantle. That old song used to be a lie:

> Low in the grave he lay
> But up from the grave he arose
> With a Mighty Triumph o'er his Foes.

No, no. Look out, because I got weapons you can't see. I've gone through hell and high water. I've sacrificed. You think I'm going to let somebody betray that? Mum huh. I ain't gonna forget. No sir. Anybody got a question about that policy? It's a fair policy. Everybody understand it? Then be careful. . . . Because Santa Claus is checking his list, going over it twice, seeing who's naughty and who's nice. . . ."

It would be their last Christmas with this malevolent Santa Claus, eleven months before the distinguished visitor, Leo Ryan, arrived for his birthday party, but the plans for that celebration had been laid long, long before, from A to Z.

N I N E

Phantoms
Large and Small

[1]

IT IS SAID airily and with broad acceptance that in modern
American "cults," the minds of members are programmed, but I
am inclined to believe that the human mind is more beautifully
complex than any computer box will ever be. No computer will ever be
devised that can decide at some critical juncture that it does not like
its program and suddenly throw the whole mess away, along with the
programmer, starting afresh on its own. Nor is it likely that this
renegade machine would decide that its new program should be to
track down and destroy its evil old programmer. Dissent is not an
option for a machine.

I have tried to imagine a situation in which I would gather in a room
the nine dumbest people who ever loved me, and over a period of time,
make them do in concert an absurd thing which is not only against
their interest, but downright harmful physically. I cannot imagine it.
This problem of cults cannot be simply a matter of stupidity. Perhaps,
then, it is solely environment. What if I were to have in my room
terrifying engines of torture: great cylinders filled with warm, dark
water in which to immerse my subjects for hours, without light,
suspended in time and space; or terrible poisonous snakes to wrap
around their bodies when they were bad; or hideous barnacled paddles
to beat them; or more modern military field phones to wire their
genitals and "ring them up"—if they talked out of turn. Surely, they
would escape from me with a steady loathing at the first opportunity.
So it cannot be only a matter of fear and power. Perhaps I could deprive
them of sleep for days and put them on a few grains of rice swimming
in gravy-like water for a time, and then when they cried uncle dangle
steak and onions if they would only follow me. Wouldn't the dumbest
among them find me a monster? Maybe then I could win them by
orating for hours, weeks, months, and wear them down simply by

226

repetition and superior stamina. With this, no doubt, they would be disoriented and exhausted. Perhaps their last shred of dignity and confidence would be shattered. But would it be enough? I doubt it. So it cannot be a matter of weakness, either. For them to listen, my drift would have to appeal to their emotional center. For them to put up with all of this, I would have to strike to the very quick of their being.

And what if I did? What if my subjects were open to my message —"suggestible," as the psychiatrists call it. Would that be enough to make them my robots? Would they be stuck in that track where all action is instinctive and predictable, taken without thought to consequence, expunging all possibility of remorse later? If so, it follows that these subjects would have achieved an insect-like will and could not be held responsible for any action. Their defense for performing absurd or criminal acts would be that they existed totally under my tyranny of "coercive persuasion."

Sometime after the Jonestown disaster, I lunched in Georgetown with Dr. Hardat Sukhdeo, a fine American psychiatrist of Guyanese extraction who was a bona fide expert in "cult behavior" and who had come to town to testify in defense of Larry Layton. Dr. Sukhdeo found himself with a difficult dilemma. He did not rest comfortably in supporting Layton, who had come so close to killing four people at the Port Kaituma airstrip, but the psychiatrist felt strongly about the "principle" that brainwashing expunges all individual responsibility. Layton was Jim Jones's to wind up and send anywhere to do anything Jones wanted, according to Sukhdeo, and Layton would never have guilt about these missions afterward.

My reaction was sharply negative. What difference, then, could there be between Larry Layton and, say, William Calley at My Lai? Was Calley not "brainwashed" just as thoroughly by military training and the broad policy of free fire zones? If so, Calley too would avoid accountability, as, indeed, his defense had argued, unsuccessfully.

But Dr. Sukhdeo pressed me with details of "cult behavior." Had I not noticed the mannequin manner in which Temple members walked, or their stiff, contorted posture as they sat, or the odd construction of their dreamy speech? I had noticed none of these things. The cultists were all, he said authoritatively, in a perpetual trance. Cognition of atrocity was impossible for them. A person beaten in their presence was not hurt, but helped to correct his deficiencies. A poisonous snake wrapped around a recalcitrant member's neck was not a snake, but a necklace. The underground black box, in which antisocial members were placed to modify their behavior, was not cruel punishment, but a "sensory deprivation" chamber, certified as salutary by a hundred mental hospitals in America. The only hope for the survivors of Jonestown was to "deprogram" them quickly and "resocialize" them in the rich and ambiguous reality of American life.

With the last, I could not quarrel, except for the language, but while I found much of Dr. Sukhdeo's perspectives provocative, I soon wondered whether his resocialization program would be for the best. He believed in the psychiatrist's omnipotence and felt that under hypnosis he could make any individual perform as he wanted, not just the "suggestible" ones. Turning the argument personal, he claimed he could turn me into a killer. He could put me in a hypnotic state and simply suggest that the Indian waiter who was then serving us the tasteless cassava cakes was about to kill me, and I must kill him first. He would lay a gun on the table, snap me out of hypnosis, and when the poor waiter came with the oranges, I would inevitably shoot him dead. I did not believe it, nor do I believe it now, but I was not about to let him prove his point. At the very least, I know better than to allow such a professional, even such a gentle and trustworthy one, to put me in a hypnotic state in the first place.

Dr. Sukhdeo consulted with the Secret Service and the FBI in the aftermath of Jonestown, and as a reward he demanded to know what books on mind control the FBI had found in Jim Jones's cottage in Jonestown. Curiously, the FBI could provide him with no titles. I think there is good reason. One starts at the wrong place altogether, if Jonestown is viewed as simply the most magnificent mind control laboratory of the 1970s, just as one errs if the world is viewed as a giant sanatorium.

Jim Jones was the singular product of the last thirty years of American history, and his following was the blend of disaffected blacks and whites for whom modern America provided no answer in religion, political action, or education. His overwhelming success in California, where he built the single largest Protestant membership of any church in that state in little more than four years, dramatizes the void he filled. His success was deeply rooted in the general failure of the 1970s. Without Richard Nixon, without the Vietnam War, without the demise of the civil rights movement or the departure of the traditional church from social action, without the current trend toward self-concern and hedonism, there would have been no Jim Jones.

How quickly the country leapt to the view that Jones was a charlatan gone mad in the jungle in his personal apocalypse, taking down with him followers who were the mind-programmed dregs of our society. This is the only palatable stance for the majority of Americans who were well-adjusted in the 1970s. Madmen are to be dismissed; the dregs of our society are better done without. For many Americans, Jonestown was a metaphor for what they, in their hearts, would like to see happen to the California "cultists," the drug addicts, the hopelessly poor and old, especially those who were black, for so weighing down the society. The very word *cult* separates a group, voluntarily so, from the rest of the society's experience. No wonder the People's Temple fought the word so vehemently.

America called Jonestown a horror story, but this view—the charlatan and his cultists, fit only for the psychiatrist's couch —detoxifies the real horror. I have listened for hours to Jones's voice, felt his presence and his magnetism and in the end his banality, studied his unique blend of politics and religion and magic. I talked with the Temple devoted, for whom even the ghoulish spectacle of the final demise had not cracked the lessons, however twisted, which Jones taught. They are far from the robots I first expected. And I have talked to despairing parents like Louis Gurvich, some wallowing in unjustified guilt over how they might have raised their children differently, parents who had found themselves powerless to shake the hold of the Jonesian spell.

For the devoted and the disenchanted alike, Jones touched the quick of their belief and their helplessness in a passive age of cynicism, making them vulnerable as most of us no longer are to political and religious messages. Once touched, they were held by his compound of authority, mystery, magic, and message. If the 1970s saw a myriad of strange cults and brief-lived fads, especially among the young, it was because America had no central social mission. It was a time for the country to rest and to forget. Forget Vietnam. Forget "civil disturban-ces." Forget Watergate. With the country's duty defined so passively and negatively, there was little center stage on the American scene to appeal to that basic human yearning to have a purpose broader than oneself. For those in whom this yearning was strongest, in whom cashing in on America's wealth was not enough, only sideshows were available.

It could have been different. The 1970s could have been the Second Reconstruction in American history, an active, inspiring attempt to bind up the nation's wounds, to care for those who had borne the pain and the defeat of Vietnam and for those who had resisted it as immoral, to ensure that those for whom the civil rights struggle had been waged were not left in a void after the gains of the sixties. Jim Jones was onto something important. The brilliance of his appeal lay partly in his persistence with the old, hope-inspiring rhetoric of an active angry age, after most had abandoned it and many were bored with it, partly in his distortion and defiling of Christian theology within the context of a Beethovian mission for the poor and the oppressed, partly in his effectiveness in exercising power with the radical and the established alike, partly in the excitement of claiming to be a Communist in America, especially if you masqueraded as a fundamentalist preacher.

But as much as anything, his power lay in the symbolism of his movement. Its millennialism or its Communism was not unique; there have been many socialist Utopian experiments before, many far more noteworthy. Its uses and abuses of religion for ulterior motives are common enough. The real difference was in the idea of a successful community which broke down racial, age, and sexual prejudices. With the success of Jonestown, a whirlwind would sweep the world, he convinced them. Had Jones drawn the line there, he might have been a minor social philosopher after all, for to see the personal interrelationships at the Temple was to see something unique in America. Never did the Temple operate on the personal charm of Jim Jones. He had very little of that. Many in Jonestown disliked him personally and thought him authoritarian and had felt that way for years. But he was the leader and must lead, and the overbearing quality of his personality did not mean that the follower could be "anarchistic" in response. With Jones's authoritarianism equated with leadership, dissent with anarchy, escape with defection, the system was very well worked out. But it operated on the plane of belief and commitment, and brainwashing does not describe what was at work. If the apostles of Jim Jones held on to their beliefs with Jonestown intensity, they were right: there was no place for them in modern America. Nor does mind control describe the control Jones exercised. As a result, Jonestown was very difficult to escape, for those who did escape, and in the end destroyed Jones, never questioned the overall purpose of what Jonestown was trying to say.

The question remains: was Jim Jones sincere? If one defines sincerity as the congruence of avowal and actual feeling, as Lionel Trilling has, the question is beyond me, for so public was Jim Jones, to the extreme of public depravity, that it is impossible to know his true feelings as he ranted for the mass. Certainly, his early success was rooted in a lie and a chimera: the Communist in preacher's clothing. But the success of building Jonestown was rooted in a sincere vision, a unique amalgam of Christian, Communist, millennial, and civil rights ideas. Without his self-destructive ideas, without his utter contempt for his following, without his obsession with his own greatness and supernatural power, Jonestown might have endured. He was no more a devoted Communist than he was a devoted Christian, but he was the true Alienated Man in an age when alienation had ceased to be fashionable. He saw himself as a "strategist/speaker," and his brilliance in the managing of people. As a master of strategies and games, played with such inferiors, his grandest strategy was personal: to carve for himself a place in history. In that lay his ultimate insincerity. He claimed a pure loyalty, but in using his poignant following in his personal design, to make an allegory for the future with their lives, an allegory that they could never understand, he established his ultimate insincerity. In that, as well as in the fertile ground of the 1970s in America which spawned him, lies the real horror.

To say, as the Guyanese coroner's inquest had, that Jim Jones was criminally responsible for 912 deaths is certainly true, for without his insane direction, without his systematic dehumanization of his following, without his design for this isolated laboratory of totalitarianism, November 18, 1978, might have passed as just another forgettable anniversary of Chester A. Arthur's death. Apart from the browbeating behavior of the volatile magistrate at Matthews Ridge who produced the judgment he wanted, the difference between an official verdict of criminal responsibility for Jones and of suicide is important, indeed crucial, more for history than as a matter of law. For it began the process of judgment on a note of condemnation. Had the verdict been suicide, then these deaths were easily and conveniently dismissed as irrelevant to the wider world, the just elimination of a madman and his collection of outcasts, the just fruit of blind obedience. Only the psychiatrists' questions of how "suggestible" individuals can be "programmed" into robots might hold some vague interest for a few.

In the aftermath of the Event, Americans turned to psychiatrists for understanding, as if in the argot of our times only they had anything significant to say about the Event. Predictably, they delivered with their determinist explanation that left no room for choice, no room for free will, and no room for the dignity and intelligence of man. If the victims of Jonestown were robots, they could not think for themselves and, therefore, in Cartesian terms, they had ceased to exist as human beings long before they lined up for the potion. But the films of Jonestown, the physical achievement of the place, interviews with survivors, even the most faithful, belie this robot theory. Robots can have no responsibility for their actions.

The crime of Jonestown calls on us to stretch our old modes of Aristotelian responsibility. In his work *The Question of German Guilt*, Karl Jaspers defined four categories of guilt. Criminal guilt applies to acts capable of objective proof which violate unequivocal laws. Political guilt applies to acts of leaders and to acts of a citizenry for the consequences of policy, arrived at together. "Everybody is co-responsible for the way he is governed," Jaspers wrote. Moral guilt makes every person morally responsible for all his or her deeds, including the following of orders, and here jurisdiction rests with the person's conscience. And finally, metaphysical guilt, according to Jaspers, posits a solidarity among mankind, which makes each human being co-responsible for every wrong and every injustice in the world, especially for crimes in one's presence or with one's knowledge.

"If I was present at the murder of others without risking my life to prevent it, I feel guilty in a way not adequately conceivable either legally, politically, or morally," Jaspers wrote. "As human beings, unless fortune spares us such a situation, we come to a point where we must choose: either to risk our lives unconditionally, without chance of success and therefore to no purpose—or to prefer staying alive, because success is impossible."*

While all of Jaspers's categories are apt, together they do not encompass Jonestown. If the atrocity is mass suicide, and my own suicide is a part of the wider spectacle, is my own death an atonement? Can I say to myself, this absolves my shame, this rights the balance sheet and is just punishment, and society has no more interest in the matter?

Clearly, the Jasper concept of guilt is not broad enough. Jonestown requires a concept akin to metaphysical responsibility, having no legal color which leaves a residue of responsibility beyond one's own death. That concept is complicity. In complicity, the shadowy underside of guilt, there is the certainty that despite brainwashing, despite the isolation and the blind loyalty to this demon, the participants all, even at the last moment, had a glimmering awareness of *choice*. Perdition was total.

[2]

In mid-April 1978, Jones found a new excuse to keep the commune in a fever. On April 13, the *Ukiah Daily Journal* published an editorial about the Concerned Relatives group which concluded with these lines: "One father has even threatened to hire mercenaries to raid Jonestown and 'liberate' his son by force. Trouble that could lead to an international incident may lie ahead." Here was a splendid diversion from the slowly encircling process of the Stoen proceeding, having the added value of providing the stuff of a red alert. Sharon Amos took the matter instantly to the Guyanese Foreign Minister and to Richard McCoy. As always, the Temple wanted it both ways: it would charge the Embassy with harassment, provocation, and infiltration by intelligence agents, and partiality in the Stoen case, but at the same time it demanded the protection for the powerless as *American citizens*. McCoy struggled to maintain his diplomatic poise. Only the Guyanese constabulary was empowered to protect them from invasion, he asserted, but he seriously doubted that any soldiers of fortune could make it through the dense jungle from Venezuela to Jonestown anyhow.

---

*See Karl Jaspers, *The Question of German Guilt*, © 1947 by Dial Press Inc. (New York: Dial), p. 32.

What had started as a metaphor in California became a reality in Guyana. The politics of paranoia had become the politics of self-pity. In their minds, their enemies took on monstrous stature, gained green beret expertise and Mafioso cruelty, had enormous bankrolls, and, if one looked out to the community's perimeter to the massive, entangled forest of greenheart trees, one could almost see the commandos lurking about amid the animal sounds and rustles. ("They're out there!" he screamed often. "They're out there every night!") Nothing tested this phantasm. The angry, frustrated statement by a distraught father quoted in the Ukiah paper suddenly translated for Jonestown into a well-equipped cadre of Vietnam veterans poised on their perimeter.

As far as I am aware, only Louis Gurvich in New Orleans, far from the rarefied atmosphere of the San Francisco Bay, ever pursued executive action to retrieve a loved one from Jonestown. Only he among the distraught relatives had the money, expertise, and contacts to launch an expensive, high-risk commando raid. Within the small group meeting at Timothy Stoen's house, the subject had, in fact, been discussed but instantly discarded, if for no other reason than the abhorrent fact that mercenaries were a figment of Jones's imagination and the Concerned Relatives did not wish to operate on Jones's level—at least not on this question.

Still, the general controversy over the People's Temple had attracted a few crackpots, and one of them was Joseph Mazor, a tall-tale teller and ex-convict, with a long record for passing fraudulent checks, a "paper hanger" as they are quaintly called. On the up-and-up side of things, Mazor made his living as a private investigator, and in 1977 he had been retained by several apostates to recover property they had deeded to the People's Temple. With Mazor's appearance on the scene, the Temple's propaganda machine turned this small-time swindler into a giant villain who in the end would probably command the assault of mercenaries on Jonestown. Mazor was not a private investigator, the Temple asserted, but really a "special agent for Interpol—the Nazi-infested international criminal police organization begun in Hitler's Germany!" No doubt, Mazor adored this grandiose notoriety, and he responded with relish. For Temple ears, he spun the tale that in September 1977—was it during or after the September siege?—he told it both ways—he led a team of two, no, four commandos to Guyana, prepared to kidnap not only two children of his clients, but the entire complement of one hundred eighty children in Jonestown! Steadfastly, as Mazor told it, they crept through the jungle with their high-powered rifles and grenades strapped to their belts. There had to be a diversion, and from nowhere Venezuelan rebels appeared all around them in the jungle, popping their rifles off in the air and creating a frightful panic in

Jonestown. The detail sneaked closer and at the perimeter, to their complete surprise, they did not find reconnaissance towers and barbed wire befitting a bona fide concentration camp as they had supposed, and so did not have to use the superduper wire cutters they had brought along. Relieved, they slipped into the camp quietly and snatched only the two children of their clients—a kind of philosophical compliment to Jonestown for being a benign rather than an evil place.

To hear this skelly-eyed private dick tell this story, with his deep voice and air of secretiveness, as I did in May 1979, is an experience. The Temple and Mazor deserved one another: Jones needed a villain and Mazor needed the notoriety. When Mazor let it be known that he was chartering a 727 to take people out of Jonestown, Jones had material to work with in his nightly sessions. Finally, Jim Jones had his "terrorist" in the flesh, one who was delighted to play on the prismatic plane of imagined revolutionary heroism. By late spring, Tim Stoen and Joseph Mazor had gravitated toward one another, and in Jonestown it became well known that the Stoen-Mazor operations were in the stage of advanced planning.

Actually, in the early spring of 1978, Stoen's group was preoccupied with much more traditionally American methods of redressing their grievances. It was working on a petition to present to the press and public officials which the group called "Accusation of Human Rights Violations by Reverend James Warren Jones Against Our Children and Relatives at the People's Temple Jungle Encampment in Guyana, South America." The Temple's March 14 letter to all U.S. congressmen, alluding to a suicide covenant, spurred the effort, for the Concerned Relatives were the only individuals who noted the reference and took it seriously. During this period, Stoen arranged to have a shortwave radio installed at Berkeley, so that the Temple communications could be monitored.

Several days before the *Ukiah Journal* editorial about kidnapping appeared, the Concerned Relatives presented their petition to the press. Taken as a whole, the document was powerful and moving, and in the end it was accurate in its major details. Organized as a legal brief, with appropriate appendices of hard evidence, the document cast its plea within the context of the United Nations Charter, as well as the constitutions of the United States and Guyana. The main elements of the *J'Accuse* were four: (1) Jones had threatened mass suicide; (2) he had employed mind-programming techniques to destroy family ties, to destroy belief in a transcendent God, to cause contempt for the United States; (3) he had created a concentration camp by confiscating passports and stationing guards; and (4) he had deprived his following of the rights of privacy, free speech, and free association. But the section on the threat to die was particularly noteworthy. Quoting the March 14 letter, the accusation read: "We know how exact you are in choosing your words, and there is little doubt that this letter was dictated by you, since it has been your policy over the years to dictate all letters sent to government officials on Temple stationery." Had the decision already been made? the accusation demanded to know. Who was consulted and did anyone dissent? By what moral or legal justification could Jones make such a decision on behalf of children? Who besides Jones would decide when the point to die had been reached?

The launching of the accusation hardly met hopes of a media splash. Brief stories appeared in the San Francisco press picturing a Concerned Relative handing the accusation through the chain-link fence at the rear of the Temple. San Francisco yawned.

But it was heard loudly five thousand miles away in Guyana, and on April 18, 1978, the answer came. A message to the press arrived via radio phone patch at the offices of attorney Charles Garry in San Francisco. The sender was Harriet Tropp, Richard Tropp's sister and one of the three attorneys in Jonestown, although Jones stood by her side in the Jonestown radio room throughout the transmission, whispering instructions. The Concerned Relatives had now publicly threatened "to hire mercenaries to illegally enter Guyana and use whatever means necessary, including armed attack and kidnap, to capture relatives in the People's Temple community," she said. "These hired guns will violate laws and resort to killing and mayhem to fulfill their contract." At long last, this showed the true terrorist nature of the Concerned Relatives group. She demanded to know where their money came from. Previous attempts by armed agents to assassinate Jones and kidnap children had been thwarted, she claimed, but the public should see the cruelty and evil behind "the base, nasty motives of these public liars." It was a classic example of how these disciples had become prisoners of their own overblown rhetoric in the jungle. But more menacing, the side reference to self-extinction, made first by Sharon Amos to the American diplomats, then committed to paper in the March 14 letter to congressmen, now in mid-April became overt policy:

[A statement has been issued] to the effect that we prefer to resist this harassment and persecution even if it means death. Those who are lying and slandering our work here, it appears, are trying to use this statement against us. We are not surprised. However, it seems that any person with any integrity or courage would have no trouble understanding such a position. Since it is clear that the persons who are plotting so actively to destroy our organization have neither integrity nor courage, we are not at all surprised that they would find it offensive. Dr. Martin Luther King reaffirmed the validity of ultimate commitment when he told his Freedom Riders: "We must develop the courage of dying for a cause." He later said that he hoped no one had to die as a result of the struggle, but, "If anyone has to, let it be me." And we, likewise, affirm that *before we will submit quietly to the interminable plotting and persecution of this politically motivated conspiracy, we will resist actively, putting our lives on the line, if it comes to that.* This has been the unanimous vote of the collective community here in Guyana. We choose as our motto: not like those who marched submissively into gas ovens, but like the valiant heroes who resisted in the Warsaw ghettos. Patrick Henry captured it when he said, simply: "Give me liberty, or give me death."

If people cannot appreciate that willingness to die, if necessary, rather than to compromise the right to exist free from harassment and the kind of indignities that we have been subjected to, then they can never understand the integrity, honesty, and bravery of Peoples [sic] Temple nor the type of commitment of Jim Jones and the principles he has struggled for all his life.

It is not our purpose to die; we believe deeply in the celebration of life. It is the intention of Jim Jones, and always has been, to light candles rather than curse the darkness, to find and implement constructive solutions rather than merely complain about problems. But under these outrageous attacks, we have decided to defend the integrity of our community and our pledge to do this. We are confident that people of conscience and principle understand our position. We make no apologies for it.

Again the press paid no attention. Talk of Patrick Henry from Guyana was a bit too farfetched, even for the San Francisco press, and besides the air was becoming so thick with verbiage about a steamy Gulag Archipelago and grotesque depravity that it was all best forgotten. What was once a heroic mission for the downtrodden had now become a seedy little holy war, involving a tight nexus of questionable figures. The once vast conspiracy by the U.S. government to smear and destroy the Temple was now reduced to the modest efforts of Timothy Stoen. But Stoen drew one important conclusion from the events of April. The strength of his little band lay not in what they did, but in Jones's amazing overreaction to virtually any criticism, for his very power rested on exaggeration. It would not take much to get a reaction from Jonestown.

Meanwhile, the accusation was tailored for Cyrus Vance, the American Secretary of State, and Forbes Burnham, the Prime Minister of Guyana. In transmitting the petition to Secretary Vance, Stoen's exasperation was evident: "I wish there were some way to convince you that the situation in Jonestown is desperate," he wrote. But his demands of the State Department were naive and unrealistic. Among them, he entreated Vance to station U.S. Embassy personnel in Jonestown around the clock to protect U.S. citizens there.

In the end, it did not matter what Stoen demanded. His petition was never read by Secretary Vance. It bounced around various departments in the State bureaucracy. No functionary did more than scan it, much less recommend any action. The State Department's attitude toward this messy little problem was ossified. It was in the middle between two sets of crazies, and since nothing could be determined as true under their self-professed and unattainable standard of "hard evidence," diplomats looked away. Later, in the turgid language of a State Department report in 1979, the matter was left on this murky note: "The most that can be said for the handling of the [Concerned Relatives] petition was that at the working level . . . it was read and thereby added to the general fund of information."

While Stoen tailored his petition for Vance and Burnham, the apostles in Jonestown prepared responses to the accusation point for point. Under the pressure of the accusation, the Temple felt forced to refine the full scope of its alienation. More overtly than ever, Jonestown now claimed to be a Communist collective. Regrettably, there was the need to screen mail for possible outside sabotage and to make sure that Jonestown residents did not make inflammatory statements to their dense relatives. "Frankly we consider this necessary because it is obvious that many people in the United States do not understand the workings of a Communist collective, and statements which are of themselves quite reasonable for a Marxist-Leninist, would throw a bourgeois relative into a frenzy." There was a need to assert the principles of Marxism-Leninism over family ties, and to modify antisocial behavior by hard labor in the fields in a "New Brigade." There was a need to have "centralized" decision making. "Jim Jones has never made a decision that ran contrary to the wishes of a substantial majority of the collective. . . . The collective operates on consensus, much more than majority rule. Jim, as spokesman for the community, will voice a decision made by the collective, but will never arbitrarily *create* a decision by himself." (In retrospect, *arbitrarily* seemed to be the important word.) Never had Jim Jones claimed to be an "anthropomorphic" God. Upon occasion he claimed to be God, equating God with *Good*. This was the "technique of transference" for the religious (mainly the elderly) who found the doctrine of Communism too shattering to swallow at first. Jones was simply equating the best in humanity with deity, thus forming "a bridge between the theistic and atheistic perspectives." But that was in the past, when he needed to make "the masses" sit still with religion, so that they would also hear his political ideology. But now that they were a collective in a socialist community, such statements about being God or Good were no longer made.

Trading accusations with the Concerned Relatives point for point was not entirely satisfying for Jim Jones, however. There had to be some twisted personal reason why Timothy Stoen seemed so driven to destroy him. Amid the slapstick and pathos of it all, Jones, in fine 1970s fashion, set a camp intellectual to the task of compiling a psychological profile of Stoen, which was written but never used. Had America not lived through Watergate or the Pentagon Papers or the fascinations with the CIA or the fad of psychohistory, it is doubtful that such an idea would ever have occurred to the Bishop. As if Stoen were really Daniel Ellsberg or the Ayatollah Khomeini, and he the Jonestown Intelligence Agency, the Temple author set to work. The profile postulated that Tim Stoen as a younger man was consumed with the ambition to land the ultimate symbol of male power: the presidency of the United States, and he carefully charted out his road to the prize. With this mania, he attached himself to a real "man of power," not to mention wisdom and principle, Jim Jones. But here "the fantasy of power met the reality of impotence"—the latter begets the former, the document hypothesized—and Stoen's "transvestitism" was laid bare. But in his moment of ultimate desperation, he found a way out of his dilemma: "He manipulated a situation to have the very *genes* of his ego-ideal (and power-ideal) implanted in his wife, and thereby *become* Jim Jones through being the 'father' to Jim's own offspring."

Lest this be thought to be lowbrow stuff, the analysis contained lofty universals:

> Stoen's battle is now a very desperate one, since it has been now revealed that, all along, he was fooling. Not only fooling the public about his "son," but fooling . . . himself. His affidavit is a most interesting document. It is full of ironic truth. It accurately tells of his inability to be a "father" and of his desire that Jim Jones be the surrogate for his own thwarted desire for self-perpetuation.

> The lust for power and authority is one of the strongest urges in man. It is perhaps his most fatal urge. It is closely aligned with a kind of desire for *immortality* which, to many men, is identified with a desire to have progeny, to perpetuate their genes, to prove their manhood, their virility. Again, the strength of the urge cannot be underestimated, as many socio-biologists have demonstrated. It is *primal*. It helps explain why Stoen, a seeker after earthly fame which he knew he couldn't have, tried another way to assuage his compulsions by conniving to "kidnap" the genes of an individual he regarded as the person he wanted to be, or who "possessed" the secret of potency and power he couldn't find within himself because, as a deluded and narcissistic man, he could never begin to fathom it: he was looking for it in the wrong way, seeing it in terms of a *selfish*, rather than a *selfless* desire.

In his desperate repudiation of his former ego-ideal, Stoen was trying to "rehabilitate himself from the self-condemnation" of his admission regarding John Victor's true parentage. Stoen's claim to the "spiritual" as well as biological fatherhood of John was another "pathological symptom." "Now there is only one course left for Tim Stoen as he writes the last act of his own personal tragedy: to put his entire being into getting his 'son,' to kidnapping the genes of Jim Jones, even if it means trying to kill him, or sacrificing the happiness of the child. . . . The real tragedy here is the way Stoen is trying to use and abuse a child in a desperate game to rehabilitate his own reputation, and to victimize, in the process, a truly magnanimous man who tried to help him through the psychological morass which Stoen could never extricate himself from, and upon whom Stoen has turned with a monster vindictiveness."

How familiar this psychological mumbo jumbo sounds! How often have the faddish psychiatrists and psychohistorians foisted these labels on political figures of the seventies: Ellsberg, Nixon, Carter among them. And yet, with its pseudomedical tone it rings with profundity. Quite independently, it would not be long before the Concerned Relatives would commission their own "clinical diagnosis" of Jim Jones. The diagnosis discovered that the Bishop was a "paranoid, psychotic, egocentric megalomaniac."

This is the sound, as opposed to the substance, of truth—a technique Jim Jones learned very well from the America of the 1960s and 1970s. Pseudomedical terms have replaced basic human emotions. Ambition, dedication, conviction, joy and discontent, the will to dominate, the difficulty of freedom, the temptation to blind submission, yearning and remorse, good and evil, love and hate, honor, shame, and, yes, guilt—these human emotions have lost their meaning. For answers to complex personalities and unorthodox behavior, we must have psychiatrists' wisdom. If the Temple's psychological profile on Tim Stoen, or the Relatives' easy medical box for Jim Jones is sick, the cue came from the age.

[3]

On May 10, Richard McCoy traveled to Jonestown for his promised quarterly visit, taking with him the new Deputy Chief of Mission at the American Embassy, Richard Dwyer. A large portly man with that blanched indoor look of a functionary, eyes peering out through small horn-rimmed glasses, Dwyer was a Hoosier who had grown up only one hundred miles from New Harmony. His upbringing had given him a lifetime interest in Utopian experiments, and so he came to his new post eager to visit Jonestown and this modern-day Robert Owen. Dwyer had, of course, been thoroughly briefed in Washington before his departure for Georgetown on the sticky Stoen case, and he was well schooled in the State Department's position of impartiality amid the nasty accusations which hung in the moist air.

While McCoy went about his consular duties of interviewing six communards in his relaxed fashion, Dwyer got the tour. He was shown the display of Jonestown dolls which were by then being marketed in Guyanese stores, and he spoke to selected residents, listening diplomatically to the prepared spiels. One always did a lot of polite nodding in dealing with the Temple apostles. At a nutritious lunch, the Jonestown Express played jauntily for his entertainment. The community's achievement impressed Dwyer. As a sophisticated man, with twenty-two years as a career Foreign Service officer, he contrasted what he saw with a Potemkin village, (the sham villages which the eccentric Prince Potemkin had constructed in the Crimea to impress and delude Catherine the Great). Dwyer concluded that Jonestown was much more than that. Yet through his visit he wondered how such a large group of Americans could be content to live this dour, removed life over the long haul. The place had the flavor of a Boy Scout camp for him, lacking, at least overtly, the ideological fervor of a kibbutz. Once the initial blush of novelty wore off, how could the followers be motivated? He was anxious to ask Jones about it.

Dwyer spent much of the visit locked in conversation with the Bishop. Jones spoke at length about the dark furies which pursued him.

"Perhaps I'm paranoid," he offered.

"If you can say that, it must mean that you still have some perspective," the diplomat replied, in a comment that chilled him when he recalled it. To himself, Dwyer would think what a wit once said, "Just because you're paranoid, doesn't mean the bastards aren't out to get you."

When he was not railing against the furies, Jones spoke of his jungle achievements. The words rolled out of him in the form Dwyer recognized from the Temple press releases. Clearly, the Bishop was not a man for detail. He talked of their kitchen's discovery of cassava fudge, but needed a cook to explain the recipe. He made much of a converted washer-dryer that dried diapers with wood gas, but needed an aide to tell Dwyer where the contraption was located. But of people, he spoke naturally and often movingly, pointing out various individuals who crossed his gaze, telling their stories of defeat and redemption. Crudeness spliced his drift, and this surprised Dwyer, who came expecting a more sanctimonious tone. Much was mentioned about socialism and Communism, but softly.

"We want to be good Americans, a credit to America and to Guyana," Jones said, as always trying to assuage rather than alienate the powers that were.

As usual, the diplomats left Jonestown with far more on the positive than on the negative side of the ledger. McCoy had seen everyone he wanted to. The number of new buildings that had been constructed in the four months since he had been there impressed him. He went anywhere in the camp he wanted, without the least restriction. Perhaps the upbeat responses of the subjects he interviewed were not genuine, but again he could not *prove* that. Once their plane rose from Port Kaituma's cinder airstrip, Dwyer directed the pilot to bank lazily over Jonestown so that he could take pictures from the air. On his mind was the chance that hidden roads snaked to hidden buildings on the periphery of the camp, but when the films were developed, his photo interpreters discovered none.

As the diplomats arrived back in Georgetown with nothing new or damaging, in San Francisco the Temple was preparing a press release with the headline: US GOVERNMENT REFUTES CHARGES AGAINST PEOPLE'S TEMPLE. At last, the group had acquired an official State Department document which supported their position. Containing general guidance for reply to letters from Concerned Relatives, the first paragraph of the document read:

> As part of the traditional and internationally sanctioned protection services, officers of the American Embassy in Georgetown, Guyana, periodically visit the People's Agricultural Temple located at Jonestown, Guyana. These officers have been free to move about the grounds and speak privately to any individuals, including persons who were believed by their family and friends to be held there against their will. It is the opinion of these officers, reinforced by conversations with local officials who deal with the People's Temple, that it is improbable anyone is being held in bondage. In general, the people appear healthy, adequately fed and housed and satisfied with their lives on what is a large farm. Many do hard, physical labor but there is no evidence of persons being forced to work beyond their capacity or against their will.

On May 12, Richard McCoy looked up from his desk to a most remarkable sight. Before him, alone, stood Deborah Layton Blakey, who had come to Georgetown a month before. She was a darkly attractive young woman of twenty-five, and theretofore, as the Temple's financial secretary, had projected a confident, sharp-tongued deportment. But on May 12, 1978, she was in a highly nervous state. She wanted to go back to the States, she blurted out, but she must have the help of the U.S. Embassy to do so, and she must leave immediately, on the first plane out. Her Temple colleagues would surely try to stop her.

Of all the families whom Jim Jones touched and destroyed, the Layton family provides a microcosm of Jones's satanic method. For within its bounds and its marriages outside, the family contained an angel killer and an apostate, several Jones mistresses, and a matriarchal pawn, whose first acquaintance with political atrocity had been Hitler's Germany. If there is any real heroism in the Temple saga, it is that of Debbie Blakey.

Deborah and Larry Layton were the children of an eminent Berkeley biochemist and Lisa Layton. The latter was the product of an aristocratic Jewish family which had been in banking for over two hundred years before Hitler came along. Her uncle, Dr. James Franck, won the Nobel Prize in physics in 1925, after he discovered laws governing the impact of the electron on the atom, laws that were important in the inevitable chain that would lead to the atomic bomb. In 1933, Franck, a Jew, was presented with new Nazi laws which would force him to dismiss from his staff any non-Aryan. Refusing to comply, he resigned his professorship in Göttingen and published a courageous attack on the new legislation. Within weeks he fled Germany and ended up in the United States. During the Second World War, Franck gravitated into the company of atomic scientists like Edward Teller and Enrico Fermi in the atomic bomb project in Chicago. But after the war he led the protest of conscience by scientists concerned about the consequences of using the new weapon. In the Franck Report, published in 1946, he and others urged the government to consider the use of the bomb a cataclysmic political matter and not simply a larger, more destructive military weapon. So the clash of science and conscience was deep in Deborah Blakey's heritage.

Meanwhile, as the roundup of Jews began in Germany, Lisa Layton's parents sent her to America, and not long after she came to this country her parents were arrested and placed on a train to a Nazi concentration camp. On the journey, they swallowed poison pills and were removed, unconscious, from the train. They recovered from the poison and made their way through Italy to the United States.

Lisa Layton, meanwhile, went to Pennsylvania State University, where her uncle was teaching at the time, and there she met her husband, Laurence Layton, who was then finishing his doctorate. In the 1950s, Dr. Layton was lured into the field of weapons research as well, working both in nerve gas and missile development. But this work weighed on his conscience, and in 1957 he resigned and joined a Department of Agriculture laboratory near Berkeley. Still, Dr. Layton's past would remain a constant source of guilt and liberalism for him, as America moved into the turbulent 1960s, and it would give Jim Jones a real handle on Lisa Layton and the Layton children.

Young Larry Layton was the first of his family to fall under Jones's spell. In 1968 he found himself in Redwood Valley, taking significant doses of LSD, smoking marijuana habitually, and facing a 1-A draft classification. His application for conscientious objector status had been turned down. His induction was imminent. So when members of the People's Temple approached him, he and his wife, Carolyn, were happy to attend a meeting. At the meeting Jones called Layton out by name and warned him that if he did not get rid of the marijuana he was then growing in a flowerpot in his apartment, he would get into considerable trouble. How had the preacher known about his habit? In any event, Layton dutifully destroyed the plants after the meeting, and several days later the local police miraculously came to his home, making inquiries about marijuana. Layton was instantly a believer in Jones's prophetical powers. The conversion strengthened when, after Layton joined the Temple, "Pastor Jones" wrote a letter to the state draft board which resulted in a reversal of its earlier decision and the granting of conscientious objector status.

Not long after he joined the Temple, Layton's marriage went awry for the strangest of reasons. Pastor Jones announced to his congregation that he had fallen in love with Carolyn Layton and, indeed, had "related" to her, and she had "compensated." A divorce was quickly arranged, and Carolyn Layton would become Jim Jones's first official mistress. Later, she had a child by Jones, named Kimo, and Larry Layton went on to marry another Temple member, Karen. She, too, subsequently would be taken as a Jones mistress.

Indeed, Jones's relations with Karen Layton provided an apocryphal legend of his selfless use of revolutionary sex and his gigantic sexual powers. He told the legend often, how this "blue-eyed, balmy-eyed bitch" came to him, after she had been babied by a black minister and taught to feel that she was something special. This feeling of special-ness was dangerous to the movement, but the movement needed her connections. So he, "the maestro of revolutionary sex," took her out to the briar patch and lay with her for eight hours, the pain so bad that he carried the scars on his knees from that day. It was as if the crown of thorns had moved to his loins. But she grew, and he could now depend upon her, but unless you have a revolutionary purpose, you'd have to be a masochist to go through an "eight-hour fuck."

In the aftermath of Jonestown, it was only on the sexual level that Larry Layton could manage the least stirring of resentment toward his leader. Yes, he was a little jealous of Jones for all his women. Why were all the women in love with Jones? "He was the leader," Layton replied. But, according to Layton, Jim Jones "used sex to keep people from committing treason. That's why he took up with Carolyn. It was not self-centered. He was making people more dedicated socialists." Besides, Layton added, "romantic love is a delusion."

Deborah Layton Blakey was six years younger than her brother, Larry, and she followed him into the Temple in 1971. Jim Jones officiated at her marriage to Philip Blakey, an English Quaker, but the pastor ordered the couple separated immediately, and Philip Blakey was subsequently sent to Guyana as one of the early pathfinders.

Through Deborah and Larry, Lisa was brought into the fold in 1974. Of all his followers whose background this guilt artist manipulated, Lisa Layton's vulnerability is perhaps the most poignant and bizarre. In her escape from Nazism to her wealthy intellectual life in Berkeley to Jim Jones, some critical alarm slipped. Early in her infatuation with Jones, she began to sleep on the floor of her hillside home. Soon she forced her husband to sell their Cadillac. Valuable household possessions began to disappear. A divorce followed in 1975, and the family house was sold at a high price. Lisa took a considerable share of the profit and turned it over to the Temple. Her former husband would estimate that in the end she had given the Temple over a quarter of a million dollars.

Amid the constant preoccupation with cancer and Jones's ability to cure it, Lisa Layton became obsessed with the fear of the disease, and, in time, the fear became a reality. By the late spring of 1977, when Jones left for Guyana, the cancer became acute. By radio, Jones sent word to her that he could heal from Guyana, that she should hold on, for his powers extended beyond his touch and line of sight to celestial relay. For a while she waited for his wonders to work, but eventually she decided on the temporal route. After a lung was removed she repaired to Guyana. At first she had a cabin of her own in which to recuperate, but soon enough, with the pressure of housing, she was moved into one of the Jonestown board and batten dormitories with other "seniors."

By the middle 1970s, Deborah Blakey became part of Jones's inner coterie of young, white, and occasionally attractive women. She had been present at Jones's first suggestion of mass suicide in January 1976, had watched Grace Stoen testify then that she would prefer to see John Victor die like that, lest he have to fend for himself in the cruel world out there alone. She had watched a respected member of this inner circle challenge Jones at the first rehearsal: "Forget it, I'm not going to die," he had said—but she did not know that this dissenter was really a shill, whose dissent was planned in advance by Jones to set up a loyalty test. Dutifully, she had drunk the grape juice, and when she had not expired in the forty-five minutes as Jones predicted, she, like others, wrote to Jones at his request about the effect the experience had had on her. Jones cast his rehearsal in the most valiant terms. He needed to know the depth of their commitment. Were they ready to go that far for someone else? How deep was their selflessness? The response he wanted was that they had felt strengthened by the experience, that a feeling of freedom passed over them, free of the fear of dying, that they felt secure and ready to face death. The decision to die itself, its heroism, its beauty, the idealism of the act itself, increasingly possessed them, pushing aside any discussion of the reason, the justification for doing so. As it did so, it would represent the final triumph of means over ends. To die for what? The *what* was receding in importance. To die into nothingness: the play was becoming absurdist.

As part of the inner cadre, she was also well aware of Jones's method of sexual bonding, bonding to him and him alone, that was becoming increasingly central to the pastor's plan for control. Larry had had two wives taken from him, and Jones had sired a child by one of them. Indeed, Debbie would see the first treason from the Temple take place shortly after the first suicide rehearsal, over this very issue of sex. Eight black members wrote to Jones that they were leaving not because of him, because "to us you are the finest socialist and leader this earth has ever seen." But what had happened to socialism? And what had happened to his professed belief that only in black people was there energy and hope for the world?

"You said that the revolutionary focal point at present is in black people," the traitorous letter read. "There is no potential in the white population according to you. Yet, where is the black leadership, where is the black staff and black attitude? Black people are being tapped for money, practically nothing else. How can there be sound trust from black people if there's only white nit-picking staff, hungrily taking advantage to castrate black men? Staff creates so much guilt that it breaks the black spirit of revolution (if the blacks have any). There's no revolutionary teaching taught the way it used to be. At one time you told us to read, yet now staff comes in to steal books from those who have them. All the staff concerns itself with is sex, sex, sex. What about socialism? How does 99 1/2 percent of People's Temple manage to know zero about socialism?"

The absence of vibrant, young black leadership, the loss of revolutionary underpinning bothered these traitors, but it was the singular depravity of the Temple in early 1976 that these blacks felt an ultimate unfairness not to themselves but to Jim Jones! *He* was being disserved by his staff. He had to "fuck" members of his white inner circle of men and women (Grace Stoen, Carolyn Layton, Karen Layton, Tim Stoen, Mike Prokes mentioned among them) to keep their loyalty. "The thought of [the staff's] demanding your sensitivity and dedication in such a manner is grossly sick," the letter read, but that the Bishop might be depraved did not occur to them. "You came to the people giving them the greatest reason to live, the greatest reason to die, the greatest reason to fight—socialism. However, you can't do it all. You can't move unless your followers realize the necessity to shape history themselves."

Curiously, these points never struck home for the rest of his black followership. To begin with, its accent on individualism was heretical. Nor did it shake the loyalty of Debbie Blakey. During the September 1977 seige she had been in the radio room at the San Francisco Temple on September 10, 1977, when Jonestown nearly became a mausoleum the first time around, and she had been one who tried frantically to reach Deputy Prime Minister Ptolemy Reid of Guyana, then in Chicago. Rather, it was the experience of Jonestown that finally moved her across the critical boundary into apostasy.

If ever Jones worried about the loyalty of Deborah Layton Blakey, he must have consoled himself with the thought that in her case he had the securest of handles. In Jonestown he had Lisa, dying of cancer and in need of love and care from her family, along with Larry and her two sisters-in-law, Carolyn and Karen. If family hostages were not secure enough, he also had spread the story that once Debbie had caused him a heart attack, when they were in bed together—the trauma caused by a note she presumably sent to him reading: "I will love you whether you are a communist or a fascist." To the assemblage of the Temple, Jones had exclaimed: "That's the *worst* thing anyone can say to me."

And yet, in the passion of her later apostasy, she professed shock at the things that greeted her in Jonestown when she arrived there in December 1977, as if suddenly a totally new situation was presented to her, far different from anything she had seen in six years in the Temple. She was horrified that Jones spoke incessantly to them over loudspeakers, day and night, in their cabins and even by remote control as they toiled in the fields. The punishments transfixed her, especially "the learning crew" and "Big Foot." The "learning crew" was the euphemism for the brigade of recalcitrants who had committed some transgression against the Temple. They were housed in a separate building, and they learned by performing hard labor at double time. Constantly watched by armed guards, they were forbidden to communicate with the faithful. She cringed at the torture she witnessed. Once, Jim Jones divulged the escapade of a member who had intercourse with a Georgetown pharmacist when she had been on a mission to get drugs. As Jones lavished the audience with the details, Debbie Blakey watched in horror as members leapt from their benches and beat the woman with their knuckles bloody and senseless at his feet.

And Big Foot. Once again, Jones's derivative attentiveness to his world was manifest. In the 1960s and early 1970s, the California press was laden with stories about the legendary Neanderthal with a humanoid face and hairy body, some eight feet tall, graceful in movement, shy and frightened in disposition, who emitted a putrid smell. The creature's name was Sasquatch, or Big Foot, and he lived in the mountains of the Northwest. The last official sighting came from two anglers in 1972, when Jones was amazing his audiences in Ukiah. But in the jungle the legend needed alteration, and it happened that a certain jaguar was seen many times hanging around the perimeter of Jonestown. On one occasion it got one of the encampment's dogs. So Jones decided that the cat should be captured, and when the crew went to find it, the beast peered contemptuously at its would-be captors from a tractor seat and then scampered away into the forest. When Deborah Blakey arrived in Jonestown, a visit to Big Foot had become the ultimate punishment for naughty children. Off they would be taken into the dark viny trees at night to a well near Jones's cabin. Two men would be swimming deep in the pit, and slowly the child would be lowered, with the splashing and the animal sounds below him more excited with every inch closer. To escape the creature's embrace, the child was required to shout his apologies to "Father" in reparation for his sin, and if Father did not think the screams loud or sincere enough, a second lowering was in order.

For less severe transgressions there was "the box." This was the inspiration of the principal of the Jonestown school, Tom Grubbs, who had majored in psychology at the University of California and had even done a little graduate work. He brought with him to the jungle an old psychology textbook from his school days and there found a reference to the sensory deprivation box used in behavior modification. In October 1977, Grubbs wrote Jones a memorandum proposing the construction of such a box to deal with tough disciplinary problems. At first, the remedy existed aboveground, reminiscent of *Bridge Over the River Kwai*, but later was placed in the dark recesses of a root cellar. In January 1978, the remedy had a curious transformation. With a member "on the floor," in a nightly commune meeting, Jones ordered that the box be brought in, but instead of the box all expected, lieutenants brought a coffin to the Pavilion, and the guilty party was placed in it. For one who watched this spectacle, the terror was nauseating, for she recalled being placed in a drawer by her parents as an infant. But in March 1978, the box was eliminated, for one of Jones's lawyers in Jonestown advised him that this might be bad *legally*. The use of physical and psychological violence decreased markedly thereafter. The fear that the Concerned Relatives might catch wind of the practice asserted itself. But the absence of terror had its consequences. The followers seemed to become more rowdy and undisciplined. Comments were made that members could not respond to Jones's velvety love, only to his thunder and lightning. The better he treated them, the worse they acted. It sounded like something a psychologist might say about his white rats.

At what point Deborah Blakey began to see these techniques as torture (rather than "counseling"), overwhelming the lofty purpose of

Jonestown is not clear, but six weeks before she stood before Richard McCoy in the American Embassy she began to plan her escape. She could confide in no one about her plan, for she knew the testing procedure. Any report of escape intentions was to be given instantly to Jim Jones. He often sent people out to say treasonous things, only to test if the listeners reported them. In her tenure in Jonestown, Debbie Blakey had seen a small child turn his father in for whispering plans to leave Jonestown, only because the boy thought it was a test of *his* loyalty. So the first problem was to get to Georgetown, and this Debbie Blakey accomplished in April by securing the post of financial secretary in the Georgetown headquarters at Lamaha Gardens.

As she stood before McCoy six weeks later, part of the tremulousness in her voice came from Jones's oft-repeated claim that he had a spy in the American Embassy. But McCoy moved speedily. He ordered an emergency passport to be prepared, and as it was, he listened to his first direct hard evidence. All the consular visits to Jonestown had been staged, she confessed, but, worse, new and frightening events were beginning to take place, particularly rehearsals for mass suicide. Still, she harbored no ill will against the Temple and wished only to escape Guyana quickly.

So spooked by the entire Temple case was the Embassy by this time that Ambassador Burke and McCoy felt it entirely possible that this was a Jones setup. As the day of May 12 proceeded, the Ambassador decided that instead of McCoy writing a report on Blakey's confessions, which would be secondhand and *hearsay*, Blakey herself would be asked to sign a sworn statement. This was to be a hedge against her recanting later, which might make the Embassy look ridiculous. McCoy wrote the statement out, focusing on the rehearsals, and the following morning Blakey signed it. But in an action so symptomatic of the diplomatic behavior throughout, the statement was promptly put in an Embassy file and not removed for six months.

Debbie Blakey was escaping in the nick of time. In the days before, memoranda were being written to Jones about her irritable, "pissy" behavior, and had Jones gotten them in time she would have been yanked from Georgetown in an instant. When, on May 12, she disappeared from Lamaha Gardens, the crisis was on. By chance, as she was escorted by an American diplomat through last-minute details, she encountered an associate at the Georgetown post office, and a well-practiced exchange took place. Why didn't she say she was leaving earlier? Jim would have let her go. All he asked was that a dissident tell him what was wrong, so he could correct his mistakes. Wouldn't she at least make one last trip to Jonestown to tell Jim why she was leaving? Would she at least speak to him over the radio? A letter to him, then?

No, she would do none of these things, she replied, but if they would take a pencil, they could send this message to Jim. She had no grudge against the church; she was just tired. She thought it unfair to have a crisis when there wasn't one, and others were getting tired as well. People cannot live on a string. She wanted simply to settle down. She respected Jim's beliefs, but the Jonestown structure shocked her: the constant confrontations, the learning crew, the fear of treason. She promised not to get involved with the Concerned Relatives, but, graciously, she suggested that the radio codes be changed.

"Why?" she was asked.

"You know, because I'm leaving," she replied.

One last time the Temple apostle asked the defector if she wouldn't tell Jim directly by phone. It was the least she could do. This time she agreed. Off the colleague scurried to arrange a telephone-radio patch to Jonestown, and when she returned, the Embassy car, with Debbie, was gone.

By coincidence, Richard McCoy was returning to America on May 13 for consultations, and so the following day, on the bumpy ride to Timehri Airport, Debbie Blakey had the protection of two American diplomats. She knew her mates would be at the airport for one last attempt to stop her, and they were. Until the last moment, she sat in the Embassy car outside, terrified, with the American Consul. When finally they made for the plane, her way was blocked near the customs officer by her former colleagues, including her sister-in-law Karen Layton. It would ease the mind of the One who loved the most, the One she had caused to have a heart attack, if she would keep in touch, it was said amid tears. She could imagine how distraught, how sick at heart he was at the news. And what about her mother, Lisa? She owed her mother more than this. Don't tell her, Blakey snapped, and reached out to them for a final loving embrace.

On the flight to New York, Deborah Blakey elaborated on the horrors of Jonestown. Besides more details of suicide drills, she spoke of arms smuggling, diversion of vast funds to foreign banks, Jones's total control over his following. Why could the disenchanted not slip through the jungle to Matthews Ridge, the Consul inquired, returning to his old conviction about the ease of escape? Jones had convinced them that Guyanese officials would return any who tried, she replied. Why had no one accepted his invitation to leave in his company on his consular visits then? There was no confidence that one man could accomplish the feat, she said, and, furthermore, how did they know that he was not the spy in the Embassy Jones claimed to have? What should she do? Should she go to the press? There was irony in his reply. Previous press reports had accomplished nothing, he asserted unabashedly. He advised her to go to *other* American government agencies to repeat her allegations—the Customs and the Firearms Control Agency of the Treasury Department perhaps. It crossed his mind that if she did not go to these agencies, he would do so himself, but the old code asserted itself. His testimony would be secondhand and *evidentiarily weak*. Perhaps he would be violating privacy laws if he did. So he rejected the idea. Besides, she could be a provocateur. His impression was of a woman whose identity was shattered, who was now placing herself in *his* total control, but what if she were planted to compromise him? Upon their arrival late at night in New York, he checked her into a Kennedy Airport motel, and then took a taxi all the way to a La Guardia Airport motel, so that even the appearance of compromise would be impossible later.

As powerless as McCoy felt himself to be, Debbie Blakey had finally convinced the Consul that there was something profoundly wrong in Jonestown. In Washington, he spoke to a number of officials about the new development, but either his presentation lacked force or its reception met glazed looks and clogged ears. The evidence was uncorroborated after all. Furthermore, on the subject of mass suicide, McCoy, the most knowledgeable of the diplomats on the case, continued to dismiss the suggestion as preposterous. If mass suicide was ridiculous, what merited fresh attention? Blakey was saying Jones had his followers under total control, not that he controlled them against their will. If his apostles followed him obediently, adoringly, foolishly, that was a matter for the Grand Inquisitor, not for the Department of State.

The Consul returned to Georgetown on May 23 and briefed Ambassador Burke. In diplomatic jargon, the mood at the Embassy now became one of "heightened uneasiness," but no effort was made to pluck Blakey's statement from the file and make something of it. Instead, in a manner that would later be described backhandedly as "exquisitely careful," Burke set about to draft a cable to the State Department requesting further *legal* guidance on the entire Temple matter. It was not a task that this cigar-smoking model of unflappability approached with joy. His interest in June 1978 was political reporting on the Burnham government's effort to ram through its referendum, which would obviate the messy need for elections. Furthermore, U.S. aid to Guyana jumped from $500,000 in October 1977 to $31.5 million by the summer of 1978, so there was much of *real* importance going on. The People's Temple was becoming more of an irritant than anything, taking up more than half the time of his Consul. Still, with so many bizarre stories floating about, it could not be ignored.

Burke's cable of June 6, 1978, was part analysis, part request, part cover. Jonestown's autonomy had become virtually total, it stated, and while it was understandable that Guyanese officials did not want to "bother" with an apparently self-sufficient and xenophobic group of foreign nationals, the lack of Guyanese political presence in Jonestown raised legal questions "which this mission is not qualified to answer." How could the government of Guyana be cajoled into exercising more control?

> It is requested that we be instructed to approach the government of Guyana at an appropriate level to discuss the People's Temple community and request that the government exercise normal administrative jurisdiction over the community, particularly to insure that all of its residents are informed and understand that they are subject to the laws and authority of the GOG [government of Guyana] and that they enjoy the protection of the Guyanese legal system.

To the lay person, uninitiated in the niceties of diplomatic intercourse, this seems a modest request: does an Ambassador abroad really have to ask permission from Washington every time he makes a contact with a host government? Despite the brouhaha that was later made over this ambassadorial cable and the department's response, the lay person would be right: it was modest, and this exercise really was not necessary. All Ambassador Burke had in mind, in the face of mass suicide threats and reports of concentration camp conditions, was that a Guyanese official be dispatched to Jonestown to give the residents en masse a civics lecture. No direct interference with Jim Jones's dominion was in Ambassador Burke's mind, no request to station Guyanese officials in the camp, or anything of the sort. Jones had successfully persuaded everyone that his place was not a town, but a private farm, and it was easier for everyone that it be viewed as such.

When the telegram arrived in Washington there was suspicion that Burke was simply "making a record for self-protective purposes," for with no new "evidence" presented—the absence of Debbie Blakey's story in the cable was glaring—and with a request for permission to conduct diplomacy for which Burke already had every authority, the department could not divine what this was all about. Still, a number of home base officers discussed the June 6 cable and three weeks later responded that until "evidence of lawlessness" was discovered, or *until an American citizen requested assistance,* no action by the Embassy should be taken. It might be construed as American interference in Guyanese affairs!

What this exchange of cables conclusively proves is that the diplomatic mission, by the way it thought, by its headlong embrace of constraints and legalistic interpretations, by its ineptness, could never have resolved the People's Temple horror. The legalistic approach had become a cop-out. The fact is that as of May 12, when Debbie Blakey appeared in their midst, there was plenty of firm evidence for strong action. With the paralysis of the diplomats, it would take a showy, grandstanding politician on the stage six months later to bring the tragedy to its final catharsis.

[4]

With the marriage of Larry Layton to Carolyn Moore in 1968, a fusion took place between the Layton family of Berkeley and that of the Reverend John V. Moore, a Methodist minister from Reno, Nevada. Two of the Reverend Moore's daughters, Carolyn and Annie, teacher and nurse, joined Jim Jones early on, and both had an intense interest in the world around them, fueled by the protests of the sixties and early seventies. Carolyn Moore Layton had majored in international relations at the University of California, Davis, and Annie Moore had marched in many civil rights and Vietnam protests with her parents, as well as participating in vigils for the California farm workers, before she began her nursing training. By their father's lights, they took their social commitment seriously, and this no doubt pleased him. They gravitated to the Temple for its overt struggle toward a more humane and just society.

As his daughters' commitment to Jones became all-consuming, there is much that must have been kept from the Reverend Moore, or about which he asked no questions. He would not know that his daughter Carolyn was the first sexual partner that Jones would confess openly to his church, after which a divorce was quickly arranged between Larry Layton and Carolyn. Nor would the Reverend know that his grandchild, Kimo, was of the union of Carolyn and Jones. Nor did he know that after Timothy Stoen left the Temple, Carolyn presided over the compromising letters department and was sent on secret missions to handle the transfer of millions of dollars of the Temple fortune to Caribbean banks. Instead, the Reverend Moore exulted in Jim Jones's construction of what Jonestown was: a cooperative of caring and sharing in the true New Testament sense, and he found in the Bible and in his religious vision much to paint a heroic, Christian experiment.

Not long after Deborah Blakey sought refuge in the American Embassy, the Reverend Moore and his wife traveled to Jonestown. They found their daughters blissfully happy, with Carolyn living in Jones's cabin with Kimo, along with John Victor Stoen and his surrogate mother, Maria Katsaris. Jones quickly saw in the Moores' visit a chance for counterpoint to the horror stories he correctly expected soon to see appearing in the California press. There could never be a denying that the Anti-Christ had created an impressive community. Indeed, the physical attractiveness and achievement of Jonestown, its closeness to the goodness of Christian teaching, are the very things that made it truly evil, for only with temptation can this story have a moral dimension. The Reverend Moore found Jonestown a miracle. With the sight of the old, black woman hoeing in her garden, the words of Micah (4:4) occurred to him: "They shall sit everyone under his vine and his fig tree, and none shall make them afraid. . . ." The freedom from fear, as the Reverend Moore meant it, was the fear abroad in the streets of American cities for the poor and the old. He knew nothing of the fear abroad in Jonestown. At work in the jungle was the heart of the church's self-understanding: "We who were nobody are now God's people." He meant the transcendent rather than the temporal Godhead.

When the Moores returned to San Francisco, a press conference was arranged at the Temple for them to describe their "amazingly beautiful adventure." They spoke enthusiastically of the achievements: the cleared jungle; the library of eight thousand volumes; the delightful meals of natural grain and vegetables rich in protein; the brilliant young doctor, Larry Schacht; the nurture of children and family life, generally; its "creative and wholesome ways." The San Francisco media came and went with heavy eyelids. The occasion had the feel of a rosy public relations stunt rather than the grand refutation of the charges that Jones desired, and the Moores' testimony went unreported.

Meanwhile, safe in San Francisco, Deborah Blakey considered what she should do. By her Jonestown conditioning, she distrusted U.S. government agencies and so did not act on Richard McCoy's recommendation to contact other authorities. In time, she was in touch with Grace Stoen and soon contacted Grace's lawyers. On her first visit to the attorney's office to tell her halting story, she rang the doorbell. Margaret Ryan, the associate of Jeffrey Haas, whom Blakey had come to see, was upstairs in the quaint four-story residence where she made her office and did not hear the bell. So Debbie Blakey sat down on the steps and waited for a full four hours on the stoop until attorney Ryan started past her at the end of the workday. Ryan found Blakey's timorous behavior and shattered identity withering.

But, with help, Blakey's confidence grew, as Grace Stoen's had before her, and in the classic fashion of the apostate, she swung so passionately into charges against Jones that she began to embellish his horrors, as if without the embroidery no one would believe her. She told of weapons, but instead of the archaic, rusting arsenal of a mere thirty-one firearms that were eventually found, she put the figure at two to three hundred rifles, twenty-five pistols, and threw in a homemade bazooka for good measure. There were rehearsals for mass suicide, but instead of the one she experienced in San Francisco, the September siege she heard over the radio, and the alerts and talk of harassment, she now claimed that the rehearsals took place at least once a week in Jonestown. And instead of Jones's ragtag guards, she conjured up the Orwellian military image of khaki-uniformed "security alert teams," which "swarmed" the camp. The food was rice for breakfast, rice water soup for lunch, rice and beans for dinner, and by February 1978 half the camp was ill with high fever and diarrhea. Strange that the American diplomats had never noticed this pestilence.

On June 15, 1978, Blakey executed an affidavit detailing her experience. Despite its exaggerations, the document remains the most important of this entire saga, for its poignancy, for its bitterness, and, in the end, for its prescience. Jim Jones had become obsessed with his place in history, the affidavit declared, and the ridicule he had received in the press had made him fear that he would be denied his niche. "When pondering the loss of what he considered his rightful place in history, he would grow despondent and say all was lost." His despondency became theirs. Life in Jonestown had become so wretched that members had become indifferent to this world. She thanked Richard McCoy for his assistance, but, given the stage-managed quality of consular visits, she asserted that investigative efforts were inadequate.

"On behalf of the population of Jonestown, I urge the United States Government to take adequate steps to safeguard their rights. I believe that their lives are in danger." But there would be no action. The affidavit was sent to the Department of State on its day of execution, and its receipt never acknowledged. No evidence exists that it was ever read carefully, much less acted upon. It was not even transmitted to the U.S. Embassy in Guyana. Like her earlier statement in Georgetown, this Blakey document repaired to the bowels of some State Department file cabinet.

In retrospect, the accent in the affidavit on the fatigue of the communards by May 1978 stands out, for this is central to my inquiry here on the nature and possibility of choice in the final moments. As a whole, the community was simply exhausted. In their weary minds, they could imagine Jonestown as a blissful place, if only Jim Jones had not been there. Exultance in His splendor had ceased. Few were still convulsed in ecstasy for his message. So many catharses had drained dry their well of strength and resistance that many began to long for the final catharsis. The majority began to block out what Jones said. Mechanically, they went through his political tests, seeking to give him what he wanted, and at all cost, to avoid his punishments or his verbal rebukes. By distrusting everyone, they became adept at searching out motives and hidden agendas. Some, who once had thought it would be gallant to die for what one believed in, now simply wished they were dead. Their agony lay in unconsummated threats. For many, it had become easier to die.

If they were simply worn out with him, he was worn out with them. Their sloth brought him to tears. They sucked and drained him dry. In Jonestown, he bemoaned their inconsiderateness.

"Yesterday, I went out to the East Field to watch workers there and I wept. I haven't cried in a long time, but I watched those workers for fifteen minutes and I wept. They didn't give a fuck . . . kickin' dirt, throwing things. They didn't give a fuck and I wept. Oh, the anxiety and hurt that I've had to bear! A proverb came to me, O Jerusalem, O Jerusalem, how oft I yearned to gather you under my wing, like a hen doth her brood, and you refused."

As always, he was a distorter and a defiler of the Word. The proverb he recalled was really Matthew 23:37, and if he had read the passage accurately and in context, it would not have comforted them. It spoke of Jerusalem as a place of false prophets, as the murderer and stoner of true prophets, the stoner of those sent to her. Jerusalem had rejected the Savior and in the verse afterward, Jesus warned:

"Behold your Temple is left unto you desolate."

[5]

In June 1978, as the *San Francisco Chronicle* prepared its story on the Blakey affidavit (which it would headline GRIM REPORT FROM THE JUNGLE), a reporter called the Temple for a reaction. A radio-phone patch was arranged to Jonestown, and across the airwaves the voices of Lisa and Larry Layton crackled with denunciations of Deborah. The mother charged her daughter with stealing thousands of dollars from her and supposed that Debbie was still on drugs. The brother said his "little sister" was telling a mountain of lies, because they were socialists and she was a thief, and so on and so on.

By mid-July, Lisa Layton was failing in a Georgetown hospital. She weighed eighty-eight pounds; her cancer had spread to her liver. In town, Larry's second wife, Karen Layton, stayed with her, consoling her by reading aloud a book about "the Nixon dictatorship." Karen Layton, by this point, was pregnant. Jim Jones had completed his rounds. After her stay in the hospital, Lisa returned to Jonestown to die slowly in the next three months of the disease she so dreaded, consumed with hatred for her daughter, cared for more and more by Larry, who spent his mornings in the fields and his afternoons with his mother. As she approached death, Larry became ever more frantic. Her condition was not caused by cancer but by the bitter seed of his little sister's defection, as Larry saw it, and when Lisa died he considered

Deborah responsible. High-strung always, Larry Layton disintegrated into permanent depression after his mother's death. In October and November, he was under constant sedation, taking Darvon morning and night for pain and Elavil for depression—the only one in Jonestown (other than Jim Jones) who received this combination of drugs. As usual, on the morning of November 18 he got his pills. In Larry Layton, Jim Jones had the perfect instrument, his best killer-angel.

The chain of events that day began with Larry Layton. It would end with a member of the Reverend Moore's family. Through the final ritual at the Pavilion, Carolyn Moore Layton stayed with her son, Kimo, in Jim Jones's cabin, as did Maria Katsaris, with her surrogate son, John Victor Stoen. As the wailing in the distance subsided, they were joined there by nine others from the innermost circle, including Karen Layton and Carolyn Layton's sister, Anne Elizabeth Moore. The inner cadre would be the only ones to have the luxury of a private, solemn last rite.

Outside the Pavilion, a tall, flat-faced, coal-black man of twenty-five named Stanley Clayton had managed to trick a remaining member of the security team who had brandished a crossbow at him into letting him by the outer ring of people. As the female security guard stepped back, drawing the crossbow at him, a loving look passed over Clayton's face, and he reached out to embrace her. He just wanted to give a last embrace to a friend of his who happened to be in an outer building. When Clayton passed her and saw his opening, he bolted for the bush and moved six hundred yards deep into the forest. There he lay hiding for over an hour, listening to the diminishing cries until he was startled by five shots, fired in slow, spaced sequence. After a long period of waiting he crept back slowly into sepulchral darkness. He would need his passport, and some money, if he could find it. Carefully, he made his way to the camp office, where he knew the passports were kept in a trunk. When he determined no one, dead or alive, was inside, he entered, going to the trunk. But he could not see. He turned on the light and frantically searched for his passport. Luckily, the passports had been filed in alphabetical order, and he found his in twenty seconds, switching off the light as he clutched the cover. As he moved toward the door in eerie darkness, he heard a terrific blast of a powerful firearm—a single crack in the jungle night coming from Jim Jones's cabin, followed by a throbbing, terrifying stillness. For five minutes Clayton remained transfixed in the office, listening for the slightest sound. But there were no more shots, and he dashed for the road to Matthews Ridge.

When the first Guyanese soldier entered the West House a day and a half later, he found thirteen bodies. Twelve, including the two boys, were dead from poison. But before the open safe, where more than $550,000 lay stacked, was the body of Annie Moore. Beside her were two weapons, one a Ruger .357 Magnum, one of the most powerful handguns made. Half her skull had been torn off from its blast. On a table lay a stenographer's notebook with four pages of her writing, her last pronouncement. Given the cataclysm of the moment, one might have expected some special inspiration, but the note was a banal reiteration of the familiar line: Jim Jones was love incarnate; Jonestown was paradise. It ended with the line, scrawled in red: ". . . We died because you would not let us live in peace."

Sometime later, the Guyanese crime chief, Skip Roberts, an American-trained professional, would come to the following conclusion about the final moments. With the inner cadre all dead in Jones's cabin, Annie Moore left the house to make one final round of the lost paradise. For the past three months, she had been Jones's personal nurse. At the Pavilion, she found him still alive, lying amid his victims in the attitude of rest, drifting away into a drugged oblivion from the fistful of pentobarbital he had just swallowed. Had Annie Moore come minutes later, she might have found him asleep or assumed he was dead, and he might have been alive the next day when the soldiers came. But he could still get words out barely, and he pleaded with her to shoot him. She made him comfortable, putting a pillow beneath his head and arranging his hands. Then she shot him behind the left temple. Turning, she saw other remnants of life. So she shot one dog, then shot the camp's chimpanzee, Mr. Muggs, twice, and then another dog once. Five shots. Then in disgust, she flung the weapon aside. Returning to the West House, she wrote her final note and then blew her skull off.

A week later, in Reno, Nevada, the Reverend John V. Moore assumed his pulpit as usual for his regular Sunday sermon at the First United Methodist Church. For his lesson, he chose two readings. Exodus 20:1–6 put forth the First of God's Commandments: there shall be no other Gods beside Him, for "I the Lord Thy God *am* a jealous God, visiting the iniquity of the fathers upon the children unto the third and fourth generation of them that hate me." And Matthew 25:31–46 was the motto of the People's Temple. Delivered at the Last Supper, Jesus' words blessed him who feeds the hungry, clothes the naked, ministers to the imprisoned, takes in the stranger, "for inasmuch as ye have done it unto one of the least of these my brethren, ye have done it unto me." The reward of this righteous behavior was eternal life. In these two lessons lay the contradiction of this man Jim Jones, who had claimed the Reverend Moore's daughters and grandchild, the contradiction of good and evil, of heaven and hell, of a merciful and a vengeful, jealous God.

And it was these contradictions which the grieving pastor attempted to resolve but could not. The commitment of his daughters to the downtrodden had been strong, the commitment he had encouraged, and Jim Jones's sensitivity to social justice as deep as any man's he had ever known. But from the beginning, he had cautioned his daughters about their worship of Jones, for it took the form of adulation reserved solely for "the Unseen and Eternal One." To disobey the First Commandment was to court disastrous consequences. To the sin of idolatry, the danger of heroic paranoia was added. In the Reverend Moore's last meal with Jones and his daughters, the air had been thick with talk of conspiracy, and no voice was raised to question the substance of these fears. Fear, preached the Reverend Moore, first controlled them, then overwhelmed them.

"Death reigned when there was no one free enough, nor strong enough, nor filled with rage enough to run and throw his body against a vat of cyanide, spilling it on the ground."

But how could there have been? To the grief-stricken pastor, good and evil stood in equipoise at Jonestown. The jungle experiment presented the eternal struggle between the forces of life and death, of building and destroying in the human race. Its failure is our loss, preached the Reverend Moore, for it showed the power of the death forces. It was a metaphor for the world. Are there people free enough and strong enough in the world who would throw themselves upon the nuclear stockpiles for the good of the world? "Without such people, hundreds of millions of human beings will consume nuclear cyanide, and it will be murder. Our acquiescence in our own death will make it suicide."

Perhaps that was Jim Jones's apocalypse, and perhaps in that negative symbolism the allegory has an element of nobility. But symbols contrast, and one must choose. For me, more powerful is the triumph of evil over good in this microcosm, the victory of the Anti-Christ, the squalid swamping of laudable Ends with disastrous Means. The Reverend Moore would talk of accountability for the nuclear warriors, but not the accountability of Jim Jones—or of his followers.

For in the end, they were not victims, but perpetrators.

T E N

May 13, 1978

[1]

I T WAS MIDAFTERNOON on May 13, his forty-seventh birthday, the day, he would tell his host later, that he died. May 13 was the day he gave up thinking he could communicate his Goodness to them. Somewhere high above Trinidad, as their plane sped toward New York, Deborah Blakey was beginning her story to Richard McCoy. In Jonestown, as Jones began the white night early, he seethed with the thought that she had picked his birthday to defect as a special twist in his suffering soul. But he was not ready to announce to them the real reason that they might die later in the evening.

It began in the alabaster heat of the afternoon, with the electric sound of the insects, the murmurings and small movements of things underfoot, the shimmering waves of the swelter rising from the banana fields, the kiskadees, with their necrotically yellow throats, hopping gregariously on the ground, and the carrion crows soaring overhead, all mixing with the voices and the static of their radio, talking breathlessly to San Francisco in "tongues," as he called their codes, lending an air of prodigious crisis. There had to be a good reason for their "stand" that day, and the Bishop conjured a trilateral attack. In Georgetown, the Minister of Health Affairs was demanding that Dr. Larry Schacht come to town for a three-month residence, so he could qualify for licensing. But Jones felt that he could not lose his young Albert Schweitzer even for three days. Over that issue alone, even this uncritical congregation might have balked at the inevitable lineup. But in San Francisco, the Concerned Relatives were peddling their accusatory petition again. A press conference was only hours away, where the Temple from Jonestown via radio would answer the charges yet again, to the profound boredom of the press. But a licensing dispute and yet another momentous press conference still needed bolstering, and so, at that very moment, Jones informed them, the Attorney General of the

259

United States had entered the case. He was deciding whether to come after John Victor Stoen.

To repulse this pincer movement, they were presenting their war demands. In Georgetown, the situation was uneasy, unsettled, dangerous, for their friend, the Prime Minister, was in Russia, and whenever the Prime Minister was gone, Guyana was a "land of emergency." One only had to consult history to know how many coups take place when the leaders are gone. They should recall that on that other terrible white night in September 1977, "when we came so close, my darlings," Burnham had also been abroad. They had been promised there would be no interference in their affairs, and wasn't it curious that the pressure on the doctor came just now? From "our" black and Indian origins, "we" are tired of broken promises, he told them, wrapping the cloak of epic struggle once again around their imagined problem. The doctor would not go to Georgetown, not for three weeks or three days. For anyone who even considered coming to Jonestown to get him, the implication would be very strong. They would come in at their own risk. And simultaneously, the "vast news conference" three hours hence over the radio would make the difference in what happened not simply with the measly Attorney General of the United States . . . but with the U.S. Congress! (His skill for making the smallest claim grandiose was boundless.) They should rejoice in the power of their revolution, for when the whole U.S. government came down on you like this, you knew you were doing something right.

With the radio crackling beside him, he drew the issue. He had made his decision. He would not allow the Attorney General to take away John Victor, for they had solid intelligence that the evil official was ready to shoot the child full of deprogramming chemicals, as if deprogramming were a chemical matter. He was beyond the point of crying now. It was time for decision, for action. There were options. He could slip through the jungle into Brazil or Venezuela and make his way back to Babylon to take care of the class enemies. Perhaps he would elicit the help of his Central American connections, some dictator or another. Then in America, depraved like the "fleshpots of Egypt," he could take care of the enemies and then die gallantly for "all the children of the world, for this Communist collective, and for Principle." Jonestown could be left in Mother Marceline's charge, and they would obey her . . . at the point of a gun.

His apparent successor stood by his side through this exposition, constantly taking his blood pressure, no longer the sugary sentimental conciliator. In the reedy, sharp voice of the dictator's handmaiden, she chimed in: "I'll tell you one thing: if you're counting on me letting you out, forget it. I would kill you before I'd let you harm one of these children [as if anyone had suggested that] . . . I'm telling you right now, it'd be a great honor to die for this cause tonight. I'd fight to the very last breath in my body against these devils." She shook with passion, in a voice aged overnight by thirty years it seemed, but who exactly the devils were stayed obscure. He patted her with a trainer's pride.

"We've been at this thirty years, and she's still ready to fight. That's a long time to be with a fighter. And some you aren't ready to fight now!"

In the rear of the Pavilion, the coaching of the various members who would answer questions from the San Francisco press (if any showed up) about their health and happiness began. Among the coaches were Richard Tropp, who wrote their initial statements, and Jann Gurvich. There was only a space of three hours to "press time." But it soon became clear that the coaching was not going well. Harriet Tropp, a lawyer and Richard Tropp's sister, called to him from the rear of the Pavilion.

"It's not going well, Dad," she announced.

"They're not trying hard enough," Jones roared.

"They're trying, but it doesn't come out natural."

A flunky jumped for the microphone.

"Don't you *dare* dispute Dad in a white night, woman," he hissed. "Don't you ever do that."

She recoiled with her sin. "I apologize, Dad. I'm truly sorry. I forgot myself," she said. It had been ordained that these graduates of law school, members of the California bar, and other professionals must remember that principle of silence in white nights more than the rest.

Jones tolerated her mistake this time. "They're not trying hard enough," he repeated. "If they really hated their relatives, it would come across. If you can't come across, you're a fucking traitor. You people say you can't do, you can't do. I stuttered and stammered as a child, couldn't get a sentence out. So you better talk back there, because our lives are resting on you. No mealy mouthing, either. It better come through strong. You better be getting with it, because if you don't, your ass is going to be kicked all the way to the learning crew, or, farther than that, to the psychological department."

He had tried many things to sustain at a peak the level of their hate toward their relatives. A month before during a "catharsis" over mercenaries, the entire community had filed before the microphone to describe what slow torture and death they would recommend for their kin in Babylon, and it had become a creative competition to see which of them could make the Bishop laugh the highest and longest with their ghoulish fantasies, most of which began with the sex organs. In the end, two suggestions tied for the prize. One ninety-year-old black woman had proposed to build a big white church, put all her relatives in it, and then burn it to the ground. And an eight-year-old boy had suggested killing his mother, cutting her up and poisoning the pieces, then feeding the bits to his remaining relatives. To that, the Bishop's laugh trilled uncontrollably from bass to contralto prestissimo for an endless set of measures. There was no joy in the percussive offensive sound, only triumph and bloodlust, as he contemplated the poisonous feast. The laugh hung high in the air, like contagious ether.

But now, at a serious moment, when it was no longer his form of entertainment, somehow the fire had left them. The first act of *this* passion play centered on a tawdry little interrogation of Stanley Clayton, the cook who would survive on cunning in six months. Clayton bore a special burden, which was the flip side of Jann Gurvich's. He was the nephew of Huey Newton, the high priest of revolutionary suicide, and a valid rebel. Elitists and elite revolutionaries alike had to be denigrated. Clayton's interrogation displayed not so much the banality as the seediness of evil, for he was "on the floor" for a high Jonestown transgression: only hours after his black companion named Janice had departed for Georgetown, he had lain with a white woman. It was a sin that put one more scar in the psyche of the white members, making them want to take blowtorches and sear their skin darker, as Jones put it. The moral of the interrogation was that they all had no more loyalty than chickens, certainly not as much as dogs.

Jones often thought of chickens, dogs, and domesticated animals when he wanted to teach his missionaries something important about themselves. In another moment, he lectured a child he saw remove the wing from an insect. "The world is so full of pain, son," he said gently. "Don't torture things. Because if you don't learn sensitivity for life young, you sure won't learn it later. I don't want to see any more of you kids stepping on bugs or teasing dogs, or we're going to tease *you* in the public service union." It launched him into his favorite theme. "I've got a strong sentimentality about animals. Take that anteater of ours some of you want to put back out in the jungle. You complain about its smell, but I'll tell you this. I'd rather smell some of these animals than some of you humans." His voice rose to receive their applause and then receded. "If you put that anteater out, it will die. A tiger will get it in nothing flat. When it climbs up on you, it doesn't want to hurt you; it just has such big claws. So you can't put it out. It doesn't know how to fend for itself anymore.

"That's the problem when you domesticize something. It can't function anymore in its natural habitat. When something comes to me, animal or human, I feel a responsibility for it, so can't we build a cage for that anteater?"

His metaphor escaped them, so he moved to chickens, always surer ground. No one seemed to mind his transitions anymore. "I can't even eat chickens. I've watched too many of them die. They die calmly if you love them, but you can tell instinctively that they know what's coming. They get excited. . . ." With disgust, he noticed someone sleeping before him. "OK, sleep on. I know it don't make any difference to you about chickens. But you know, there may be a step up some day. Someone might decide to chop your head off."

But that was in a calmer moment, as one judged calm in Jonestown, and now, in his "rage of love," it was Stanley Clayton's chicken-like infidelity that tormented him—so different, say, than a dog's loyalty toward his master. "Ever since as a child I saw a dog die, I wanted to commit suicide. It was the first time I felt guilt. But I still had some little dogs and cats alive, and I had to keep care of them, so I stayed alive for some thirty-nine-odd years more. Just little animals I stayed alive for, because I didn't know who was going to feed them, and I was *too young to know how to kill them.* . . . Then a little later, my mom needed me, and then some poor soul down the road, poor and minority. Then always blacks wanted me for their champion. It's always been that way. So you can do what you want to, while I do all the thinking, but I'm bored and disgusted and sick with you who do so little for socialism when you have such a good example to follow."

It was as if he needed Stanley Clayton to bridge the stations of his martyrdom in this last passion. So from the origin of his guilt, he moved back to Stanley. Why, he wanted to know, had contract killers once come after Stanley?

"I can't think why, Dad," Stanley mumbled.

"The gangland doesn't come after you just because you're Huey Newton's nephew. Who was after you?"

"I ran the streets a little, Dad."

"What'd you market? Did you sell dope on the streets?"

"Did a little of that, Dad."

"Shit, I'm just as black as you [at least his hair was] . . . and I'd starve to death before I pushed that stuff on any of my black or Indian brothers. I consider you a class enemy now, Stanley," and he turned away as members leapt from the audience and started beating on Clayton, tearing his shirt. But the tearing affronted Jones's chintziness. "Would you quit tearing Stanley's clothes!" he barked. "I usually win these goddamned white nights, and if we're unlucky enough to get through this one, he'll need something to wear. . . . But there'll be one come we don't get through. I'd like for a white night to come and not pass."

Clayton's cheated companion, Janice, was brought forward, as well as Dr. Larry Schacht. For after Clayton's sin had been discovered, it had been decided that Janice should "relate" to the doctor, so overworked and uncomforted as he was. The first act now had its triangle. Soon it came out that Stanley had tried one last time to make Janice stay with him, rather than flee to the doctor. Jones made him describe his move.

"In that last talk with Janice in the loft, Stanley, what were you trying to get accomplished? Don't tell me. I know. All that babified talk, you wanted her to feel sorry for you, so she wouldn't go with that doctor, weren't you, Stanley?"

"That's true, Dad."

"So you could get more nooky, right?"

"Yes, Dad."

"That line is so old, Stanley, it's boring. I can't image what the choice is between you and the doctor anyway. I've lain with women that made my skin crawl, men and women, but if I lay down next to someone, I would like to imagine that they were thinking slightly above the capacity of an ape. . . . The Office said *no* to one more chance, and you tried to con her into it. Did you make love that last time, Stanley?"

"No, Dad."

"Well, that's one breakthrough for woman's emancipation."

"It's clear Stanley is a homosexual," Dr. Schacht offered, a curious rebuke for one who had had his own episodes.

"It takes two years for a man to be honest about his homosexuality," the Bishop proclaimed. "I've had to do it for this movement, with great big football players, twice your size, Stanley, big bucks of men, and they oohed and ahed. I don't have to tell no street man like you about this, though, now do I, Stanley?"

"No, Dad, I've done that."

"Good, Stanley. See, you're growing," and then as if all the host had not heard, he repeated Stanley's admission of homosexuality. "That's good you can be honest about that. I've got a hell of a sex drive, and it's all oriented towards women. But if women had the proper pride, they ought to become a legion of Amazons, become lesbians, and never take a look at one of us. Because only then would they be capable of fighting a revolution. But you women get moony-eyed around men, you go crazy, and you can't do a thing for the cause. And you men are no different. All your intelligence goes to your balls. All you who are in love are in trouble."

They had arrived at the next station: his fantastic and selfless sexual prowess, their moony-eyed impotence.

"How long can he fuck, Janice?" he asked.

"About two minutes."

"Two minutes? Two minutes! Oh, you women sell out for such a pittance. OK, so you had a two-minute fuck, what else did you have in common? Did you ever go to college, Stanley?"

"I took a three-week college course once," Stanley mumbled.

"So here we sit in the middle of a white night, not knowing whether we're going to die tonight, being bored by a two-minute fuck and a three-week college course."

His gale of laughter swept over them, and when it dissipated he launched yet again into the apocryphal legend of his eight-hour heroics with Karen Layton. And then with Grace Stoen. And then with others, but "I won't tell [on] the black ones." Then an aide brought him the draft press statement, and Stanley got a moment's respite. Jones looked at the clock which he had set up beside him. Only two hours to doomsday, he said offhandedly. He mouthed the words of the draft written by Richard Tropp, and translated into oratory for them.

"We will be like the valiant heroes of the Warsaw ghettos, before we are through. If you can't understand that willingness to die, if necessary rather than compromise, then you will never understand the integrity, honesty, and bravery of the People's Temple. . . ."

He approved it and turned back to Stanley.

"Now, where were we, Stanley?"

"I was telling you about sex, Dad."

"*You* were telling *me* about sex, me, the maestro of revolutionary sex! Oh, c'mon, Stanley. What were we saying?"

"You were talking about your eight-hour. . . ."

"Why'd you remember eight hours, Stanley?"

"Well, me being only a two-minute driver, eight hours be more than I could strive for."

"More than you could strive for? You'd have to be a maniac to strive for eight hours, unless you were helping a revolution."

"That's true, Dad."

"I remember every painful minute of it. You people who believe in love, you're fools. You can't fuck for no seven hours. You women can't take no seven-hour fuck, and all you have to do is lay there. Only saw one woman who could take it, and she had to be a masochist. But she grew out of it, and she's a good revolutionary now. Hell, I can fuck fifteen times a day, and I've got to worry about all of you at the same time. But the only fuck I want now is *the orgasm of the grave.*"

He called for his wife to take his blood pressure, because he felt it rising. One hour and fifty minutes to go. He dared not take any more medicine, because he feared he might be too tranquillized when they arrived at the moment of history. So he called for a portion of brandy instead. Meanwhile, Dr. Schacht stepped in as fabulist.

"The other night, as Dad was pouring out his soul to try and save the likes of you, he had a small stroke. He couldn't see a thing, and later in the night he had three convulsions, three seizures. But he didn't bother you with that. Dad's been saying it for a long time: life is shit. Any life outside of this collective is shit. Every relationship is shit. You people who think you're loved. You're not loved, you're needed. All I want is to die a revolutionary death. And I don't want to get involved in a relationship that might sidetrack me."

Something in Schacht's narration touched Jones's sentimentality. He recalled the senior who had told him the nicest thing the other day, and how rarely nowadays he heard nice things from them. She had said if there were no enemies, she would still pick this place to end her life, because it was so beautiful. How sweet. How lovely of her to say that. Usually, their comments were different, and he slid into his flapjack mammy's voice again. " 'I didn't get my food today.' 'I didn't get the right medicine.' 'They made me wait five minutes in line.' That's all I ever hear."

An old woman in the back waved her hand to get her food.

"Don't worry, honey. They'll get the food to you. You'll eat before you die." That touched his funny bone, and he laughed, but his amusement shifted to melancholy quietly. "Never saw anything like it. They'd eat as they were lowered into the grave. Sometimes, I don't know where you people's heads are. . . . OK, Stanley, give us some news."

"How's that, Dad?"

"Give us some news, I said. Here I throw my voice away four or five hours a day, giving the news. . . ."

The fabulist jumped back in. "You ought to be grateful that Dad pours all this news out to you, so you know what's going on in the world. It's fantastic."

"Well, I've been back in the kitchen today, and I didn't hear too good," Stanley tried stupidly, knowing it would get him nowhere.

"That's OK, Stanley, it doesn't have to be today's news," Jones said leniently. "We'll give you *any* day."

"I try to keep up with it, Dad, but, you know, back in the kitchen. . . ."

"*Any* news, Stanley!"

"Zimbabwe?"

"Good, Zimbabwe. Where's Zimbabwe? Southeast Asia?"

"Naw, Africa."

"That's good. What part of Africa?"

"South Africa."

"OK, that's close enough. What about Zimbabwe?"

"They won their struggle over there."

"Four hundred fifty of their children were tortured yesterday. I told that on the news this morning. . . . *I can't live with this.* Marceline, take this blood pressure again. I think it's getting to the danger level. C'mon, Stanley. C'mon, man. I can't take this. What are we having this white night for?"

"We're having a white night, Dad, because . . . our enemies are walking around our building in San Francisco with some type of paper, protesting something. That's just a sketch of it, but I have this problem of hearing and. . . ."

Jones's breath was becoming progressively heavier on the microphone.

"Protesting what, Stanley?" he smoldered, low, ominous.

"Demanding that they get John Victor, but I didn't hear exactly. . . ."

"Who's coming after John Victor?"

"Tim and Grace."

"Not on your life. Tim and Grace come in here, they'd get their brains blown out. It'd take more than Tim and Grace."

"Well, the noise back in the kitchen. . . ."

"Hey, Stanley. Hey, Stanley," someone whispered from behind the podium, and Stanley fell for it.

"You fuckers are too stupid to deal with me," Jones said, close now, ever so close, to the brink. "He whispered your name and you turned around and you say you can't hear. . . . You people just tear me apart. You tear me apart. YOU'RE KILLING YOUR LEADER. The CIA hasn't been able to do it. I know what causes my blood pressure to rise. It's risen 20–30 points on both ends. . . ."

He snapped, bursting into cascading sobs.

". . . Oh, how I cried for the people in *Roots*," he sobbed. "When the Fiddler says 'free at last' as he lay dying, how I cried. I've been a slave all my life. Nothing I saw in that movie was as horrible as I've had to endure. To feel for a thousand people, to worry about them night and day! My heart breaks so many times every day, because I see so much that pains me, so much.

"This is a perfect society compared to the United States, but it was not what I wanted. I never thought we'd be faced with multimillion-dollar lawsuits. I've been in this *little prison* for nearing a year now. Made no name. Made no prestige outside, because the best way I could serve you was to stay out of the news and not be forging ahead in the limelight. But this is not my cup of tea. I'm a speaker. I'm a revolutionary, a tactical leader, a strategist. But that was not what was needed, because that would endanger our babies and our seniors. But I'm dead. You're the only thing that's alive in me, and that's dying.

"Some people have an unlimited capacity for evil, my darlings. I tried America, from one coast to the other. I took you around and saw that every city was the same. If I could have found one better than San Francisco, I would have taken you to it. I'd have liked to fight there. But we didn't have a chance to win a revolution there. All we had was a chance to see old people and children tortured. Here we can die on our own terms."

From his depravity to his cruelty to his sobs, he moved now onto the plane of the hypnotic, his clerical, teaching tone establishing itself, his soothing sounds rising and pausing with great effect.

"That's what Jesus said: No man, no man will take my life. . . . I will lay it down . . . lay it down when I get ready. Some Christians don't understand us because we're more Christian than they will ever be. . . . And Paul said that it's all right to give your body to be buried . . . but be sure you've got charity in your heart. Charity means Principle. What is pure love? Communism . . . In other words, Paul was saying, give your body to be burned. Set it afire, if necessary to convey a revolutionary message, but be sure you've got Communism in your heart."

His substitutions were often brilliant, but wherever the spirit of Jim Jones may now reside, St. Paul would probably like to have a little chat with him about the use Jones made of his doctrine. In Jones's mind, a secular image had invaded his rhetoric, an image of the 1960s had merged with St. Paul: the bonze in his orange robes dousing himself with gasoline before the American Embassy and setting himself afire.

[2]

The clock on the dais drew close now to the appointment with the press in San Francisco, and with the Congress of the United States, and with the valiant heroes of the Warsaw ghettos. He continued his bulletins on his blood pressure, as the radio squawked by his side, as the coaching of the witnesses proceeded in the rear, as Dr. Schacht delivered his lines as fabulist and Marceline Jones repeated her readiness to die because of fidelity to Jim and hate for the devils; and Stanley Clayton stood, head hung at the side, as whipping boy and comic relief. Having moved roughly through the stations of his sacrifice, the Bishop proceeded to a strange Eucharist: announcing that if worst came to worst, and they were all starving, he would offer himself to be cooked, as a living sacrifice, so they could eat, saying this while he drank his brandy alone, to calm his soaring hypertension.

It was the misfortune of several families to have arrived in Jonestown on May 13. With only thirty minutes to the fateful decision, he called them all up to get their views on what they were seeing. It would be some relief, he said, from Stanley's two-minute fuck and three-week college course. As they filed forward, he had his sons hold up a blanket, so he could urinate from his throne, and when the cackles rippled through the Pavilion, he chastised them for frivolity. White nights were so funny, part of their acting program, he hissed, but they should beware because the old fox was not blind tonight, and as he relieved himself he would be using eyes in the back of his head to watch them.

Several standard idolatries were delivered, and then it was the turn of the Parks family. Their conversion to Jones had come fourteen years before, when they followed him to Ukiah from Ohio. Before they left California to join him in the jungle, they sold their $16,000 home and turned over the proceeds to the Temple.

First to testify was Tracy Parks, aged ten, a wiry little girl with stringy blond hair, who had always found Jim Jones to be a nice enough man, but now she was seeing him act as never before. Still, despite her shock, she had a child's cunning, knowing instinctively from a life in the Temple what was required of her.

"I'm prepared to die for this family, for freedom, if I have to. Thank you, Dad," she said, her words coming in a gush, and they satisfied Jones. For now, he was on a critical point, one of the last problems that always haunted his vision of the last moment: would the parents balk when it came to the fate of their children? He had fortified his infernal doctrine of guilt with a special commandment for the children: they were never to feel pity for their parents, only hostility, because the parents had brought them into this evil world, and for that they deserved only eternal scorn. In the old days in California, Jones had forced his only natural son, Stephan, to beat him in services, to display the boy's hostility for his creation and to expiate the father's guilt. Time and again, Jones harped on the equation: good socialist children should despise their parents. Good socialist parents should constantly ask the forgiveness of their progeny for the sin of procreation.

It would be the special fate of Tracy Parks that her stay in Guyana began with this rote testimony . . . that later in the evening she would watch Stephan Jones wrapping a parrot snake around the neck of a retarded member, watching the poor woman go screaming out into the darkness . . . that the child would move like a mannequin through six months of agony, smiling when she was required to, mouthing the proper lines and never getting into children's discipline, and that as a defector on November 18, at the Port Kaituma airstrip, as they waited for Congressman Ryan to board a plane, her mother's skull would be blown apart by Temple riflemen, and before the child's eyes Larry Layton would shove a revolver into her brother's chest, pull the trigger, and the gun would misfire.

On May 13 her father, Gerald Parks, followed her in his testimony.

"I'm also ready to die, after forty-four years of contributing nothing to this life or finding any point or reason for it. There would be no glory in it. But as long as there is one on this earth that is not free, none of us are free. I'm prepared to die if need be."

No glory in it? In the twenty-five of his forty-four years spent with the People's Temple, he had made no contribution to life? There was a dangerous note of sacrilege in what he said. Jones feigned distraction with other matters.

"I'm sorry," he said, "I was listening to the radio and didn't catch all of that. If anyone has any questions from the audience of these people. . . ."

From the body of the audience, a close apostle shouted a question, clearly, precisely, as if the coming discussion had been well planned in advance.

"Would you take your daughter's life, if it came to that?"

Gerald Parks knew he was caught, knew that he had been chosen to receive public instruction in a Jonesian catechism.

"No, I'd give mine in place of hers," he said, all too honestly.

It was wrong, very wrong, but Jones knew he had to be careful.

"Hold it now, you've got on a sensitive point," he said softly. "You may not understand the gravity of that question, but all of our children have faced this. They will not be hurt by it. None of our children have caused difficulty by facing this thought."

It was perhaps his most grandiose conceit—to speak for the nearly two hundred children who had only begun to live. The fabulist knew to step in for him.

"You say you would lay down your life for your child," Dr. Schacht said. "The question is, if the fascists were coming up the road right now, and we were going to die in a fight, would you leave her for the fascists?"

"If it came to that, I'd have to take her life." There was nothing else he could say, lest they set upon him as they had Stanley Clayton. The multitude applauded his correct response.

Jones remained velvety smooth and loving. "Do you understand that?" he asked gently. "But she's old enough. How old is your child?"

"Eleven," Parks said, as if by adding a year to her real age, she might gain the privilege of choice.

"She passes the age then," Jones replied. "We fight at eleven. She would take up a cutlass and fight until she was dead . . . unless it came to an overwhelming invasion. Then we would gently put [the children] to sleep. They would not know what hit them. We're already prepared for that. A people who are really loving and a Father who is genuinely compassionate is prepared for all such emergencies. With such a melee, we have an arrangement here that every living soul can step out of life easily. So long as there is the alternative to make a mark, you fight. Remove the enemy's life and then your own. But they may try to set up the melee to be black against black, us against the black Guyanese soldier, and that fight would dishonor socialism. Then it's best just to lay down our lives, . . . and what's that called, congregation?"

"REVOLUTIONARY SUICIDE," they replied, like a collective bird's chirp.

"And why the children? Because the fascist's torture methods are so severe, as you saw in the *Day of the Jackal*," he said, giving Hollywood its due. "Any suicide for selfish reasons is immoral, and your history will be cursed and you will come back in some lower form. So suicide is unacceptable, except for revolutionary reasons. But our advanced seniors and our children will not go through the torture. We're not going to let them make a mockery of our babies, nor torture our old people. . . ."

His strategist's intuition told him that this was too cerebral, presenting them with too much to think about. He did not want them to reflect upon their fate, but to be constantly convulsed in passion. So he called for another witness to wash away the messy burden of choice with blind faith.

"How do you feel, honey? You may die tonight," he said to the elderly mammy before him.

"I'm a fighter, Father, you know that."

"Yes, darlin'."

"I've been in this family since 1971. . . ."

"I know, honey. I remember your song, because it used to keep me going."

"Yes, Father," she said, swelling with emotion, trying to contain her sobs. "When I came out of the States, I meditated so hard about people trying to hurt you. When they hurt you, they hurt me. You're the only father I have. This is the only family I have. I love you, Father."

"Oh, how I remember your song, darling. Sing it for us now. I haven't heard it for so long. Sing it, sister. That might just carry us through."

The words rolled out of her on tractor tires, big and powerful and cleated.

All the days of my life, ever since I've been born,
I never heard a man speak like this man *before.*
All the days of my life, ever since I've been born,
I came to Father as I was.
He give me a resting place, and he have made me glad,
I never heard a man speak like this man *before.*

He exhorted the throng to join her, and they were back in church again, swaying and clapping and belting it out, as they felt the transitory ecstasy pass over them. He led the chorus, adjusting the words to his liking. *Never heard a man speak like this socialist man before.* They repeated and repeated it, and in their frenzy, with the organ in the background to elevate their mood, he underscored the truth of the lyrics, touting their courage, their Principle, his majesty. "If we hold on, we'll make it," he soothed, intimating the first real hope for that night. But he felt sad too at those words, sad that it was so true that there was no man who ever spoke to them like this man before. But not sad enough to forgo hearing it again, hearing it louder, and back they went into it. Still louder, he urged, not just for them or for him, but for "a tactical reason." There was one enemy out there in the forest, he said, motioning grandly to the darkness beyond, that they had not caught yet, so let *him* hear it, let *him* know the army he faced. As Jones started into the first bars, he changed to Indian howls, the shrill yelps of terror as they slapped their mouths, pursed in a halo of righteousness, the righteousness of the hunted. The savage, staccato screams of a thousand carried out into the black immensity, sending the wildlife scurrying for cover deeper in the jungle. The frightful clamor lay somewhere between the braves of Geronimo and the hysterical, tongue-clicking women of the Casbah. It went on and on. He took a bullhorn.

"IF . . . YOU . . . MAKE . . . THE . . . MISTAKE . . . OF . . . TRYING . . . TO . . . COME . . . IN . . . AND . . . GET . . . ANY . . . ONE . . . OF . . . US . . . YOU . . . WILL . . . DIE . . . YOU . . . WILL . . . TAKE . . . ANYBODY . . . OVER . . . ALL . . . OUR . . . DEAD . . . BODIES . . ."

But from the dense, misty forest there was no response, not even an echo. The forest absorbed it, as all else, dully, indifferently.

In due course, doomsday came and went, but the white night lingered on. Toward midnight, Jones had ceased to fret about the Attorney General of the United States and the press in San Francisco. Only the results of their menacing threat against the Guyanese government remained to be recorded. Since radio contact to Georgetown was not possible at that moment (the United States was probably jamming them, he told them), he had sent armed minions to Port Kaituma to place a personal telephone call to Paula Adams. As they had agreed earlier, depending on how she refused the call—back in ten minutes or in twenty—they would know if they were really in trouble that night. If they were to die later, Jones suggested, they could do so with the comfort of knowing that the Temple had saved the price of a long-distance call to Georgetown. He continued his bulletins on his blood pressure, announcing the range of 170/130, an impressive diastolic rate at the emergency point, where stroke or heart failure or hypertensive encephalopathy might occur at any moment, causing him to keel over before their eyes. For some reason, this bulletin was modest in relation to past claims, for only a month earlier, as he drew the picture of mercenaries about to land in their midst, he had flashed them the superhuman reading of 480/130, the 480 being 180 points over the measuring capacity of a blood pressure apparatus. For the older members, who were constantly preoccupied with "their blood," these readings must have made their eyes bulge.

As time wore on, Dr. Schacht passed him various pills to control his stratospheric pressure, but they seemed not to have an effect, or he feared drowsiness at a moment of such import. Besides, he said, the pills cost too much. So he called for more brandy. Meanwhile, he ranged across the terrain of his saga. He had ordered a 350-ton freighter to be bought that day, so that they could make their exodus smoothly this time, without having to rely on the Russians or anyone else, and he evoked the old image of the September siege, when they had all piled on the shrimp boat, *Cudjoe,* nearly sinking it to the bottom of the Kaituma River. Coming in a few days was a boat with six months of provisions, 13,000 pounds of medicine, and enough military equipment to "keep people off this hill for some time." That was more "guarantee of life" than they ever had in the States, and one wonders if any of them did a double take. He paid Marceline the ultimate compliment, of being one white woman he could look at and think "nigger" right off the bat.

"Oooooh, that brandy's strong. They ought to have told me it was straight 90 proof before I drank a quarter of a glass."

Wistfully, he returned again to his sacrifice, how he lived in this little prison of his own making, while they could travel luxuriously to Georgetown and elsewhere. That was only one sacrifice of so many he had made, but they would never take John Victor: that was one sacrifice he would never make. Oh, how he wished for sleep, but his enemies never caused these white nights when he was rested, if he could remember when he had had rest. He longed for a pill that would allow him to sleep straight through just one night. Could they imagine what it was like to think you had slept and then to see that the clock had advanced only one solitary moment? If only he could quit feeling for just one minute, but then he loved them too much for that. Progressively, he became more cheery and more flighty.

"I'm drunk!" he declared, with a burst of his unforgettable laughter, and they applauded. "I could depend on you to clap, but don't start no shit. I'm on to you. I may stagger to get you, but I'm after you. Father's drunk and bleary-eyed, but he's *on the ball.*"

Suddenly, it was a love fest.

"Dad, I think you ought to get drunk more often, without people getting judgmental," someone prompted.

"If I got drunk more often, you'd die, but not necessarily in the proper order," he bantered giddily. He never missed a chance, drunk or sober, to trivialize the malignant destiny that awaited them. "No, I'm just chatting with you. I can't think of a soul tonight I don't like."

In fact, he thought one white night they might all get drunk on brandy because, as a point of information, he had enough brandy in stock to get them all drunk twice over. Over the months he had built the stocks by requiring every member to buy a bottle in the stateside duty-free shop on their way down. Maybe it would be the last night, and they would take part brandy, part sleeping potion.

"I'm an example and a sample of what it's going to be on the last night," he soared. "Wheeeeeeeeee . . . I see two Vincents in front of me and one's enough. . . . Laugh, Jeff, or your ass will stay on the learning crew."

His son, Stephan, sat at his feet. He offered the sullen enforcer a drink of brandy.

"What you need tonight is a good fuck, son," he said affectionately.

"You give me a good fuck, and I'll take it, but I'm not sure it'll be good." Stephan at least had the doctrine straight.

"Now that's a wise man," the father said proudly. "Because there're consequences, aren't there?"

The "old fox" was cross-eyed, bleary-eyed, drunk as a skunk, but they'd better be careful, because, drunk or sober, he knew how serious white nights were. Still, he felt guilt that he and Stephan were drinking, and they were not, but he made no move to remedy the situation. He felt so good that he might just tell every secret he knew, but he told them none.

"Goddamn you, whoever gave me this on an empty stomach, you did it on purpose. . . . Ha, ha—oh, yeah. If I drink it all up," he said, pointing to the bottle, "you people would not be protected. I'd be going through this audience seeing who'd be willing for a fuck."

They cackled. They poked one another in the ribs. A septuagenarian waved her hand from the back of the Pavilion.

"What is it, dear? You want to fuck? Oh, I feel relaxed enough now. Whisper to me, darling. . . ."

Suddenly, a wave of nausea overcame him. He called for the pail.

"Oh, no," he moaned. "What an unpleasant way for all this drinking to come to an end. . . ."

A nurse rushed to crouch at his feet, expectantly holding the bucket for him.

". . . You see, there's nothing good that doesn't have a bad ending . . . except socialism," he said, directing the nurse to shift the pail so he wouldn't see the bottom of it.

———————◁ ▷———————

So this night, the next to the last white night, loitered on, with the drunken leader reeling on the verge of vomiting, finally pulling himself out of danger of that ignominy by eating beans and okra, singing jingles about musical fruit and flatulence, rattling on about how few tomorrows they had, decreeing that they should write up for him what meaning this night had for them, but, at least, ceasing his comparisons to the valiant heroes of the Warsaw ghettos.

In the oracle of the Temple, May 13 would soon be transcribed as the night he died. His body lived on, painfully, but his will to transmit his goodness was dead. He was lethally dangerous from this day forward. But also, because the doctor had not been forced to Georgetown, and the Attorney General of the United States or the U.S. Congress had not—yet—come for John Victor, and the charges of their class enemies had been refuted, it would be written as another white night that had paid off.

After May 13, they were all living on borrowed time, sentenced, and then suspended in an indefinite purgatory, until the right moment presented itself for the execution of his grand design.

E L E V E N

The Last of
Jim Jones

THE VERY LAST of Jim Jones was played out, as much as anything, on the modern stage of our time. Into conflict came ambitious men who wished to carve their place . . . and hold it . . . in their different professions, and so it became a play of institutions at the end as well as men. In the diabolical achievements of Jim Jones, there were profoundly important issues. But as the forces came together to their unspeakable conclusion, issues were secondary to theatricality, politics and journalism and religion so entwined with entertainment that one hardly knows where to make a separation. And with entertainment, the demands of the audience, as perceived by the entertainers, are central.

What Americans require in the modern age of the politicians they will return to office, of preachers they will flock to hear and support with donations, of rebels who excite them, of television specials they will watch or newspapers that amuse them, of Hollywood movies they will pay exorbitantly to see, or of personalities they will follow in the "style" sections of their newspapers—all this is part of the Jonestown story, lending it, as Jim Jones might say, its metaphysical dimension.

Jones loathed America, but if he could have carried that loathing into disinterest for how he was viewed there, he might have proceeded with his experiment in atavism until it fell apart from natural causes. But he did care what Americans said about him. Much as he urged his following to forget the "beast of America," he could not do so himself. He wanted to be remembered in *American* history, to be an American hero of the Left, to teach America a lesson about itself. It was as if Moses was desperate to learn from Egypt what the gossip about him was on the steps of Pharaoh's palace. The fact that America had ceased to care a sou, and by his entrapment in the jungle and his declining health, the fact that time was running out fired his desperate vision of the final glorious moment. The tragedy of a maverick congressman was that in forcing his way into the den of Jonestown, he had no inkling of the different sphere in which Jim Jones revolved, not the sphere of higher evolvement and high principle which the Bishop proclaimed to his peons, but of regression into animal instincts.

[1]

Often it was said about Congressman Leo Ryan, in life and in death, that he was a loner, a man who danced to his own tune, or marched to a different drummer, or similar clichés that American politicians often reach for in begrudging testimonials for colleagues they do not like. He had come to Congress by the unorthodox route of the teacher, and once there, much of what he did was unorthodox. His democratic liberalism was traditional, his concern for the poor and the environment sincere. Yet, his style was brash and offhanded and showy to an excess, so much so that it often embarrassed and irritated many of his colleagues, even in that society on Capitol Hill of many flamboyant characters.

To be sure, he represented a "television district" of northern California, where a politician needed to go far beyond simple good service to his constituents to be reelected, where involvement in trendy and esoteric concerns pleased the wealthy and liberal and often superficial voters of San Francisco suburbia, where an attractive and abrasive style exhibited often before the cameras was essential. While his opponents always claimed he was in political trouble, Ryan had become used to winning political elections easily, including his three elections in Congress. Once he won a primary election on the Republican ticket as a write-in.

The relationship between political success and theatricality suited Ryan, and in the scorn with which he was treated by many of his fellow politicians there was an element of envious hypocrisy, for Ryan was a better actor than many in his manipulation of television to get what he wanted. (This hypocrisy reached full flower after Ryan was killed, when behind the fulsome oratory about "this great man and great statesman," "this esteemed and respected colleague," the prevailing sentiment in the privacy of the congressional cloakroom was that Ryan got exactly what he deserved.) Yet few doubted his qualities of perseverance and courage. His ability to adapt, to be ribald or highfalutin, outrageous or conscientious, gave him a chameleonic unpredictability that made him good at his way-out crusades. But it also cost him influence in Congress. He was not marked for leadership within the House of Representatives, nor was he good at influencing either his institution or the government in general to perform in the best interests of his district. Still, these very qualities which made him anathema to the political establishment of the Congress—his actor's impulses, his love for the television studio, his adventuresomeness, his determination, his essential curiosity—made him the perfect man to penetrate the elaborate fraud of Jim Jones.

Reared in Nebraska, Ryan had drifted to California after service in the Navy in World War II and had become a high school civics teacher. After a stint in municipal politics, he became Mayor of South San Francisco in 1962, and then a State Assemblyman for a decade. In the State Assembly, he refined his skill at devising personal missions that were sometimes dangerous and clandestine, and that projected him as a heroic and engaged politician to the voters and the press. In 1965, when Watts exploded, he moved in with a black family in the insurrection zone and taught as a substitute for two weeks under an assumed name. When he came out of the heat, he told the newspapers it was a "nightmare" but now he understood the frustrations that could cause the outburst. When conditions in California prisons were "the thing," and Johnny Cash was wailing his "Folsom Prison Blues," Ryan again took a nom de guerre, incarcerating himself in the prison for eight days. Among California's most ruthless criminals, he might have been killed at any moment, for the jockeying and testing between himself and the inmates was constant, as he told it later, and told it often. Pulling his time was bad enough, but going out into the yard was the critical juncture, the dramatic highpoint. His knees felt like jelly, "but I had to do it." The lesson?

"You really can't do your job if you allow yourself to be afraid. You have to put fear behind you," he said. But it is unclear how these missions translated into legislation which bettered the conditions in Watts or in Folsom Prison. The tedium of crafting good legislation was not his passion. On the wall of his Sacramento office hung a painting of a sailboat with the inscription, "I know which way the wind is blowing, but I must set my own course."

His tour in Folsom Prison helped make him congressional material. When another maverick congressman, Paul McCloskey, was gerrymandered south in 1972, after challenging Richard Nixon for the presidency over Vietnam, Ryan won election to Congress on McCloskey's vacated turf. But Ryan also saw his Folsom time as stageworthy, and he sat down to write a play about it. Called *A Small Piece of Sky*, it was not a good play and was never produced, for good reason. While violent and unpleasant interchanges between dangerous prisoners seemed authentic enough, his characters had no saving graces. It might have been better if Ryan had made himself the central character of the piece. That a politican would first stay in Folsom Prison incognito, then use the experience for political promotion, then write a play about it, smacked of slumming.

The leaden quality of his play did not, however, discourage Ryan's literary pretensions. In the last two years of his congressional life, he began a novel, whose working title was *Hydrogen Terror*. A roman à clef with an Andrew Young prototype as secretary of state, it was the old story of Arab terrorists placing small hydrogen devices in such historic sites as the Lee Mansion across the Potomac River and holding the government ransom. In researching the believability of the novel, Ryan went to the Lee Mansion and emplaced fake hydrogen devices in the eaves, just to satisfy himself that it could be done. He saw the book as a way to liberate himself from the shackles of a fixed income, but he did not have time to finish it.

In his six years in Congress, Leo Ryan authored one major piece of legislation. The Hughes-Ryan Amendment was passed at the height of the Watergate crisis, when the CIA's hand in the scandal was revealed with Howard Hunt's voice alterators and cockeyed wigs. The Hughes-Ryan Amendment transferred the oversight of the CIA from the blind and hawkish Armed Forces committees to the Foreign Affairs committees of both houses, a move which the agency fought vigorously. By most accounts, the amendment never should have passed, least of all at the insistence of a freshman congressman. But Ryan marshaled press interest and support in the nation skillfully. The achievement won him the permanent scorn of the CIA. His authorship of the amendment got him a seat on the Oversight Subcommittee and there he insisted, perhaps from his essential curiosity as much as anything, that the subcommittee be informed of all covert operations. After his death, conspiratorialists argued that the CIA had "set Ryan up" by not informing him of the danger in Jonestown, because the agency hated him so much. But no evidence surfaced to indicate that the CIA had any inside information.

The promise of his first term never materialized. His passion for the esoteric became his reputation; few in Congress could get as excited as he could about oppression in the Philippines or a United Nations university in Japan. In his third term, he was not only a member of the House Foreign Affairs Committee and busy earning the dubious honor of being the most traveled member of Congress, but he also assumed the chairmanship of an environmental subcommittee. Not long after he became the chairman, he announced to his staff that the subcommittee would shift its focus from the boring job of ensuring the efficiency and economy of environmental agencies of government to the staging of "media events." Congressional hearings, he let it be known, were really political theater. Thereafter, issues for investigation were chosen for their high visibility. His hearings became sound-and-light shows heavy on blown-up photographs, slides, and, hopefully, movies. To his committee staff, he described himself as an "antinuclear nut," soon focusing on the problem of nuclear waste. In September 1976, he held a hearing in San Francisco on the dumping of nuclear wastes off the Farallon Islands and had for display giant pictures of great "puff ball" plants of atomic proportions that evidently grew around the dump site. His accent on political theater drove responsible members off the committee and the quality of the staff work went into a severe decline. With the power of chairmanship, Ryan seemed to think he could investigate anything. Once he had to be talked out of an investigation of the Moonies as being pretty far afield from energy and environment. In his disappointment, Ryan remarked, "Well, *something* has to be done about those people."

Through his rocky public life, Leo Ryan had lived a tempestuous private life as well. Married twice, divorced twice, his second marriage to his secretary, he was the father of five children. He liked the company of attractive women and engaged in a search for the one woman who could share his lusty life of adventure and understand him "warts and all." It was a search never quite fulfilled. Like Jim Jones, he strongly preferred to have women as his closest aides.

In 1973 he put his mind to setting his affairs in order, amending an old will. The tone of the new will reflected his spirit and whimsy. In a curious way, it too bore faint connections to Jim Jones. For any who wished to find out what his life had been like, Ryan referred them to his family, who could provide "some interesting revelations—à la Boccaccio and Canterbury," an affectionate perspective, one must conclude, on the way he saw his Chaucerian earthiness and sensuality, his occasional glory and sometime ridiculousness. These family members could provide 98 percent of the story.

"The other two percent I take with me. . . . In that two percent is the greatest residual of joy and terrible pain." He asked his friends to gather around for a dinner to celebrate him, and, "Lord willing, I'll be there too with no concern for a hangover." For others, if there was to be a public service, he would appreciate "a reasonable rendition of the Navy Hymn," and for an epitaph he still liked H. L. Mencken's the best: "When I depart this vale of tears, if you have some thought to please my ghost, forgive some sinners and wink your eye at some homely girl."

Whatever he may have been as a legislator or a husband, here was a man who embraced life, who recognized his flaws and understood human emotions, who hated pretense and appeared to know when he was being pretentious. But perhaps more interesting than these jolly and piquant thoughts for the only congressman in American history to be assassinated was a passage earlier in the will:

"I'm truly sorry that I was born in a transitional age when I became one of the first, it seems, to discover that there is a planetary orbit to most people's lives, not a parallel track. We enter each other's gravitational pull for a time, and then are wrenched away—by death, or more often by force of circumstances and changing personalities. In the process, we cause both joy and pain, and experience more of the same."

Unlikely as it is that Leo Ryan had worked out very thoroughly any astronomical schema for personal relations like this, he was prescient about the gravitational pull that existed between him and Jim Jones. Force and counterforce were attracting one another inexorably, and out of their collision would come a tragic explosion.

[2]

Jim Jones began to deteriorate physically long before he found himself imprisoned in the oppressive jungle. But only there, removed from the care of medical specialists, obsessed by his inevitable martyrdom, terrified to leave his flock even for a day, did his illness overcome him. And yet, this very illness had become central to his precarious hold on his community. It was the source of their pity and the residual of their love for him. Often it became his goad to sustain, if not their love, at least their guilt-ridden paralysis to challenge him. For whatever visible distress he suffered, *they*, not the class enemies, were responsible. They were killing him, not the conspiracy. They must feel that burden in their pores, as he felt their disease in his. The spectacle of this volatile, sick man before them underscored his magical gift of paranormal healing. He could heal, because he took the disease of others into his own body, not curing it, but simply transferring it from their common body to his magnificent one. By 1978 the true believer might have seen this miracle of transference performed hundreds of times and might conclude that at long last, diseases accumulated over his selfless years were taking their final toll.

His flaunting of medical advice stretched back to his earlier days. He had always toyed with total exhaustion, never heeding counsel for rest. His hypertension was a constant condition. And he had diabetes, whose effects he was supposed to control by a diet of 1700 calories a day. But sugary sweet cakes and soft drinks were his weakness, and his cook and maid to the end, a seventy-six-year-old woman named Rose Shelton (also known as the "cancer lady" because she was the keeper of the chicken gizzards for the fake cancer healings), always oversalted his food. As a result, he would tell the community in the fall of 1977 that his blood sugar count was always forty-five, half that of a normal person, and that it caused him constant headaches, dizziness, "and frustrations like I want to knock the block off people, but I never do." Still, insulin drove him at an enormous pace, he said, and his condition made their whispers sound like CANNONS.

"You can't know that. I think I'll be put down in the history of this place, if there is one, as the tough guy. Nobody likes the tough guy. Some people like power. I hate it. I want to be the friend. You can see that, when I go down, and pat you, love you, cry with you. That's my nature."

By February 1978, he had developed a chronic coughing condition which he first called bronchitis, but soon realized that that sounded too mundane. By April, with the crisis over "mercenaries," he was posting them astronomical blood pressure rates. By May, rheumatoid arthritis was swelling his wrists and hands to the extent that one could barely distinguish the trunk from the appendages. In early July, he began his refrain about his legendary death on May 13, so any physical pain or disease he experienced was in the nature of gratuitous suffering. By midsummer, he had repaired to his bed and was seldom seen around the encampment during the day.

On August 8, 1978, he announced that he had lung cancer. It was with a great effort of will, he said, that he kept from coughing all the time. They should recall that he once healed his wife, Marceline, of lung cancer, as if to intimate that her disease was responsible for his. The time had come for heightened sensitivity and kindness, because they must begin to think about succession. Perhaps he had five years to live at the outside, he told them, but without an operation, only a few in one hundred were still alive for that long. If he could get an operation, he might be cured, but to go to Georgetown would be a great embarrassment to the Prime Minister of Guyana. To go abroad risked assassination. When he heard it, he was calm as a cucumber, he proclaimed, as if a burden had been lifted. But he would appreciate their stoicism. He did not want them to cry for him—the power of negative suggestion—and then, at this dramatic moment, he noticed before him a member so stoic about his announcement that she was nodding off to sleep.

"Well, that's very nice of you to sleep, dear heart," he raged. "I hope you die before I do. Because I don't want any of you left alive to worry the leader."

His outburst was short, and he returned to a calm narration of the several times in his life when he had healed himself. But his memory of those miracles was dim, now, . . . so Marceline remembered for him, especially the time, over twenty-five years before, when the doctors gave no hope for a recovery from stomach cancer, and he had walked away from it out of his global duty.

"For you alone, I know you wouldn't have anything done now," Marceline said. "But I can say for myself and the others, we're going to have a doctor come in here and look at your lungs carefully, and there's going to be surgery if that's what it takes. We're going to do everything we can to preserve your life. We're going to do it, and you don't have a choice."

Jones chortled tolerantly. "Oh yes I do. Mother's sentimental and she loves me, the highest love that a human being can have."

"Of course you have a choice," Marceline corrected herself. "But we're going to proceed to do what we can."

He ignored her.

"There's so much drain on me here. People stopping me on the path with their little problems. I am so dead tired. You'll never know how exhausted I am with this temperature. But the other day, I wanted to show you what I can still do. I got more of my heavy share of logs and carried them to the pile until I got knots in my shoulders. I was so foggy-eyed, I couldn't see in front of me. But I wanted you to know I love work. Nobody is above work. . . ." And then, in case there were any doubting Thomases in the audience, he offered to show them later the knots on his shoulders from his ordeal.

In fact, by this time, it had already been arranged for his friend, political supporter, and business associate, Dr. Carlton Goodlett, to come from San Francisco to perform a thorough physical examination. In the course of his long medical career, pulmonary diseases had been one of Dr. Goodlett's specialties. Goodlet arrived in late August to find his friend a mere shadow of his former self. For five weeks, Jones told him, he had had continuous fevers of 102–103 degrees, and only that day had he struggled out of bed with great effort to accord his old companion a proper greeting. When they got down to the medical details, Goodlett heard much more that disturbed him. A month before, a Russian doctor had conducted an examination, and while his diagnosis was inconclusive, had recommended a bronchigram, suspecting severe bronchiectasis. But Jones's mild cough and his unhampered oratorical powers seemed to rule that out. Further, bronchiectasis would not cause the persistent high fever, and Dr. Goodlett as well, without hospital tests, could not be sure of the fever's origin. He was, however, certain of one thing: Jim Jones did not have cancer, and yet, as disturbing as anything, Dr. Goodlett learned that Jones was taking a combination of powerful antibiotics: Terramycin, erythromycin, and ampicillin, which in concert were not only highly debilitating to the body, destroying needed defenses, but in a diabetic could actually invite opportunistic infections. Goodlett's preliminary diagnosis was that a chronic infectious process was eating at Jones's lungs, probably a fungus of some sort. Of particular concern was the possibility of coccidiodomycosis, a rare disease known as valley fever, which had attacked a few people in the Ukiah area during the years Jones was there. The valley fever seed might well have lodged in Jones's system and flowered when his defenses were destroyed by the antibiotics. The danger of valley fever was that it spread from the lungs to the central nervous system quickly; its symptoms were weight loss, fever, and weakness, with death often occurring within a year.

Jones must immediately leave the jungle for proper tests: Dr. Goodlett was adamant about that. "You're too valuable a man to treat yourself like this," the doctor urged. Jones wondered if the equipment for tests could not be flown into Jonestown. Impossible, Goodlett replied, and he proposed three alternatives. If Jones thought he could stay in the United States for ten days safely . . . He could not, so New York was eliminated before Goodlett's second breath. Havana or Moscow then. But Jones's terror at leaving poured out. In exasperation, Goodlett ordered Dr. Schacht to make slides of the stomach fluids, but when they were flown to San Francisco several weeks later, Goodlett found that they had been improperly stained to test for valley fever or any other fungus.

Several weeks later, in mid-September, Charles Garry, the Temple attorney, journeyed to Jonestown. Witnessing Jones's precarious physical condition, finding him incoherent, receiving the Bishop's fears about being arrested or assassinated, Garry paid visits to Guyana court officials, including Chief Justice Bollers, in whose hands the Stoen case now rested. From these local officials, Garry received absolute assurances that Jim Jones would not be arrested if he came to Georgetown for a definite medical examination. The attorney passed on the information that the Chief Justice was of the mind to dismiss the Stoen case, given the slipshod manner in which it had been handled. Garry also conveyed the word that Tim Stoen's lawyer in Guyana, Clarence Hughes, had represented Prime Minister Forbes Burnham's first wife in a messy divorce proceeding and so had no political standing with the present government. "You must get medical attention, and there's no way in the world that they will arrest you," Garry messaged his client. But still Jones did not heed the counsel. Clearly, by this time, his departure from Jonestown had ramifications far greater than his personal health. More than that, his physical demise was now bound up with his obsession of his glorious destiny. If he left Jonestown, not only did he risk a rebellion in his absence, but he also risked dying a common insignificant death and losing his chance for so much as a footnote in the history of the macabre.

In the late summer he began his descent into addiction. It started with a mild program: two Quaaludes and a shot of cognac. He mixed the brandy with soda pop and told his devoted that it helped his blood circulation and his heart. By mid-September 1978, the Quaaludes and cognac ceased their effect, and he advanced to liquid antianxiety and antidepressant agents, in various combinations and dosages, injected in liquid form into his veins: Elavil and Placidyl for depression which gave him a dry mouth (forcing him constantly to lick his lips, cow-like, with his tongue), Valium for anxiety, and the powerful Nembutal or pentobarbital, the hypnotic barbiturate. By early November, the level of pentobarbital in his kidney and liver had reached the generally accepted lethal range, but he had developed a great tolerance.

On the loudspeaker over the encampment and on the radio to Babylon, his voice was becoming increasingly frail, his speech increasingly slurred, his orders to San Francisco increasingly erratic and strange to his longtime communicants. On October 2, after the departure of the Russian doctor, Nicolai Fedorovsky, Jones announced that Fedorovsky had finally gotten to the bottom of his medical problem, that it was really hereditary emphysema. By then, however, added to his lung disease, whatever it was, his hypertension, his wild experimentation with sedatives, his growing addiction, his constant fever, his rheumatoid arthritis, came a virulent prostatitis. So difficult had urination become for him by early fall that he required catheterizing—his wife, Marceline, and sons holding him up by the shoulders for as long as three hours to accomplish a flow. On October 28, Dr. Schacht announced that Dad had had a heart attack and had been *dead* for three minutes. But, miraculously, he had revived, proclaiming heroically that he still had the strength to search out their enemies and kill them. Soon, Schacht said, Dad would struggle before the devoted.

By this time Jim Jones had become a medical freak.

On November 5, Marceline Jones was back in San Francisco and paid a call on Dr. Goodlett. She reported to him that her husband's temperature still soared uncontrolled. Goodlett exploded at hearing that his compadre still had not received the medical examination in Georgetown or elsewhere that the doctor had demanded. If Jones had been his patient in San Francisco, Goodlett said, he would have long since ceased to treat him. Not only that. It might now be too late. A man cannot have high fever for six months without permanent, if not fatal, damage. Jones was now a very poor risk, Goodlett declared. Marceline lamely made the usual excuse about her husband's fear of leaving the project. But this time Goodlett would have nothing of it.

"If the project can't survive his absence for ten days, it's not worth a damn anyway," he said. "It looks like he's just spinning his wheels down there. Either he's stupid or he's afraid something will happen in there."

Three days later, on November 8, 1978, someone tried to poison Jim Jones's food—or so he announced in a quavering, frail voice. It was the third time it had happened, and at that moment his technicians were studying the food under a microscope. Henceforth there would be surveillance in the kitchen.

"What kind of beasts do we have in our midst?" he cried. "But don't you worry, if you're guilty, we'll find you. I'm already narrowing my investigation. My feet may not be ready, but what I can put in my hands is." But with his fingers swollen to a clown's size, it is doubtful that he could pull a trigger still. There were other ways. "If I catch you, the court won't have any time to deal with you, because I'm going to hang you from the highest tree I can find."

He ordered the lights in the center of the Pavilion to be turned on, so he could see the whites of their eyes. "Fact is, I'd like to be a sampler of every bit of food that goes through this house," he said feebly. "Because I've got a resistance that's not ordinary. You think you're so smart, that you're dealing with an ordinary man. Somebody gave me enough [poison] to knock out a horse, goddamn you. You give me enough to knock out an elephant, and I'll still be there to beat your ass."

It was trouble enough to try to stay awake and alert to defend his people (and himself against his people, one could almost hear him say). Even now, there was a congressman who was a member of the *John Birch Society* who wanted to come to Jonestown. The preparation for Congressman Ryan's party had begun.

"My opinion is to tell him to stick it," Jones said.

Nearly two weeks later, in San Francisco, Dr. Carlton Goodlett watched the first television reports on murder and suicide in Guyana. From the pale, metallic cast to Jones's visage, from the way his skin hung flaccidly from his bones, from his estimate that Jones had lost forty pounds in the two months since his examination, Dr. Goodlett concluded that the Reverend Jim Jones would have died from *natural* causes in another ten days.

[3]

In the late summer of 1978, as he lay naked and feverish in his cabin, a fresh fantasy entered Jones's consciousness. He would become a Hollywood star along the way to his place in American history. He was encouraged in this notion by several new characters who entered his distant orbit at this time, feeding his ego by investing him with grand labels and flatteries, touting his experiment as the shape of the future . . . if there was to be a future . . . , firing his grand delusion by "confirming" the vast governmental conspiracy pitted against the Temple. The newcomers to the Temple trough were the notorious Mark Lane and his sidekick, Donald Freed, who had danced their way through the gut issues of the 1960s Left, the Panthers, Wounded Knee, Vietnam atrocities, and the titillating conspiracy theories about the deaths of John Kennedy and Martin Luther King, Jr., making movies, books, and dollars to the universal contempt of those who had worked with them. In the age of the docu-drama, when rebels were only gnats to the government establishment, and Hollywood was discovering the 1960s as safe turf, this duo had happened onto the lucrative entertainment value of radicalism. In effect, Mark Lane had brought the street theater of the 1960s off the streets and into the established institutional life of the nation. He had even run for vice-president once, on a ticket with Dick Gregory, the sometime comedian and political gadfly. To the 1968 campaign, Gregory and Lane had provided one bit of lasting comedy, when they came up with a mock-up of a dollar with Dick Gregory's head instead of George Washington's. It turned out to work in coin-changing machines around the country, and when the authorities got after them Gregory's retort had been, any machine dumb enough to give four quarters for a dollar with a black man's picture on it did not deserve respect.

If you were James Earl Ray or Huey Newton or Jim Jones, Lane and Freed offered you a package. Not only did you acquire a lawyer, but a bombastic advocate on the college lecture platform, a glib promoter on the talk show circuit, a producer with Hollywood contacts, and an author who had achieved the magic best-seller, a kind of all-purpose promotional agency calling itself grandly the Citizen's Commission of Inquiry, which would "investigate" the righteousness of your cause, ferret out your enemies, and proclaim the findings before the appropriate dramatic forum, whether in the courts or in Congress, with Hollywood or Madison Avenue. You might even get Dick Gregory to raise money for your cause and fashion a few one-liners in his performances. (In the aftermath of Jonestown, Gregory proclaimed the proof of a CIA conspiracy to be the "fact" that all the bodies were face down.)

By August 1978, Jim Jones had become dissatisfied with Charles Garry as the Temple attorney, and Mark Lane may have smelled this from afar. After pursuing the Stoen case and investigating a number of the Temple's wild delusions, after being the medium and the mouthpiece for many of the Temple charges and theories, seemingly without qualm or complaint for a year, Garry abruptly began to be described in Jonestown rallies as an "old fool" who had told all his courtroom secrets in his book, *Streetfighter in the Courtroom*, including how to rig a jury, and who was probably senile. Erratic and humiliating commands to Garry were sent from Jonestown with the apparent intent to disgust him and force his withdrawal.

The situation was ripe for the Lane-Freed treatment. With a strategy that had worked with James Earl Ray, Donald Freed made the first visit to Jonestown in late August on an apparent cultural mission. He evinced an interest in doing a book about the People's Temple, based on the sentimental stories of Jonestown residents, a kind of oral history of how these people had endured "the witch hunts and hysteria of the 1950s, the big assassinations of the 1960s, Vietnam, and Watergate," this era of history as Freed told a Jonestown audience, "when the bullet not the ballot determined our history, and America became the name of a nervous disease." But Freed also went to Jonestown proclaiming the "intense interest" of a Hollywood producer, Paul Jarrico, to do a feature-length film on the Jonestown wonder. Jarrico was a figure of some note in the Hollywood Left, for he had been a target of McCarthy attack in the fifties after his union-sponsored film, *Salt of the Earth*, about Mexicans in a Southwestern mining town appeared in 1953. Since the mid-fifties, Jarrico had lived in artistic exile in Paris, and only in recent years has spent more time again in Hollywood, as his McCarthyite blacklisting turned into a badge of honor. Freed had talked with Jarrico about Jones, but Jarrico had certainly given no authorization to represent intense interest to Jim Jones. Still, the film fantasy quickly became a topic of conversation between Freed and Jones when Freed arrived in Jonestown. On August 22, Jones drafted a letter to Jarrico announcing the Reverend's willingness to cooperate in making a feature-length theatrical film on Jonestown and conveying his understanding that Jarrico was then "negotiating with a major star to play the role of myself." The fact that the letter misspelled Jarrico's name was a measure of the seriousness of all this.

Jonestown, of course, had been scrupulously prepared for the visit of Donald Freed, but the preparation was for something he was not, something more important sounding, and Freed lent himself to the fraud breezily once he arrived. Jones touted Freed as the maker of the successful and compelling movie *Parallax View*, or, if not the maker, the author of the book upon which the movie was made. Neither was true. *Parallax View* was produced by Alan Pakula, whose company had never heard of Donald Freed, and the novel inspiring the film was written by Loren Singer. Still, before Freed's visit, *Parallax View* was screened a number of times in Jonestown, with Jones providing a taped commentary alongside the sound track. The movie was so deep and so complicated, Jones told his toadies, that even he, with his IQ of 173, did not pick up all the hidden themes in the film the first time. Jonestown was instructed to tell Freed how much they liked "his" film.

But much more important, much more ominous, than simply one more Jonestown fraud, *Parallax View* became a centerpiece in Jones's propaganda about "the way it is in the USA." The film was the best of the conspiracy genre, starting and ending with official coroners' inquests finding *no* conspiracy in the killing of two U.S. senators and laying out the professional conspiracy that worked, twice, in between. If one lived in Jonestown, two images from the film endured: the spectre of the hidden conspiracy, and the actual killings of the two senators. If Jonestown was now living a Hollywood script, it would have to settle on Leo Ryan for a member of the lower house two months later. Just before the first senator was shot in the back at the outset of the movie, he said to an Independence Day audience, as Congressman Ryan might have, "Independence Day is very meaningful to me. Sometimes I've been called too independent for my own good."

Like so much in this story, the certification of *Parallax View* as correct entertainment for Jonestown was rich in irony. At one point in the film a test, the parallax test, was administered to the hero, its purpose being to surface the anger, frustration, and repression that make a real killer. It was a test that Jim Jones should have taken himself. Some of the questions were these:

- Knowing important people makes me feel good because it makes me feel important.
- My friends always end up double-crossing me.
- I want people to remember me when I'm gone.
- I like to win when I play games.
- There is something not right about my mind.
- Someone is out to get me.
- I would like to be an actor.
- I see things around me that other people do not see.
- Sometimes a little thing will run through my mind for days and days.
- I am never embarrassed.
- I am at my best in large groups.
- I am often frightened when I wake up in the middle of the night.
- The person whom I most admired as a child was a woman.
- I don't like to see women smoke in public.

Once the hero of the movie, Warren Beatty, passed this test by the "division of human engineering" of the Parallax Corporation, a Parallax agent said to the hero, "You know, Richard, in working for the Parallax Corporation, I've found that people who've had real trouble in their lives, the ones with so-called antisocial tendencies, I can give them a sense of their own worth. It's very rewarding, believe me. You're invaluable, Richard, because in a risk situation, I believe you'll go right down the line."

If Freed wished to use Jones, Jones got the best of the deal. For in a speech to Jonestown and in a Temple interview for Guyanese radio, Freed excelled admirably. He perfumed Jonestown with windy, ponderous superlatives, calling it a new heaven and a new earth, an "exemplar of what Norman Mailer calls the renascence locked in the unconscious of the dumb" (a dubious compliment), a sophisticated experiment in dialectic materialism, a saga expressing "the collective past of suffering," which would have an "exponential" impact on the world. Given the "amazing plasticity" of the residents, no place on earth offered such "a microcosm of what we loosely call human nature," but it was a gamble in human nature too, for to neutralize what Arthur Koestler called "the poison gene" in humanity, which had led to constant war and slavery in history, in Jonestown "love was the catalyst for change in people's life," and anger, expressed without guilt, was liberating.

In the jungle, removed from any reality but the sylvan walls, this pretentious and dangerous claptrap dripped with false profundity, and it served Jones's purpose beautifully. Freed's "eloquence" was overwhelming, Jones told the audience, as if to say it was all right if they had not understood the "famous author." It was dangerous because this was outside validation, not only of the historical but the literary beauty of Jonestown, and how were they now to know any different? And Freed had obviously been to enough black rallies to understand the dialectic between the orator and his audience. He gave them what they wanted, talked about the "invisible government" in America, centered in Washington, where he had just been. The journey from Washington to Jonestown was from the city of lies to the city of truth. If Freed, with his credentials, saw this as the new heaven, who were they to dispute him? For the radio, the author was asked what he had in progress. Enthusiastically, he responded with four things: the Martin Luther King investigation, a book about the war against the Black Panthers, a "popular history of the CIA," and a new approach to Shakespeare's *Macbeth*. As Jones represented it the night after Freed left, Freed had expressed "interest" in coming to live in Jonestown, to establish a great university there, or at least a world conference center where socialists around the globe could discuss the shape of the future. If such a scholar and linguist, with all his successes, wanted to leave the USA, which had now become like the movie *Z*, who were they to have qualms?

On September 5, in San Francisco, Freed joined his cohort Mark Lane for a three-hour meeting with a representative of Charles Garry, and, of all people, the Inspector Clouseau of the Jonestown case, the "private investigator" Joseph Mazor. On the surface, its purpose was to discuss the movie deal. But the meeting's level of cynicism rose so high, it spilled over into farce. Freed began the meeting by representing his producers' interest in a "real life story in a real foreign country with a real large group of people and a colorful idea," but while the filmmakers would naturally employ a normal amount of dramatization ("normal but not pathological") and poetic license, they hoped to enlist Joseph Mazor in the project for his wealth of knowledge. The proposition was simple: Mazor would tell them all he knew about the People's Temple, and, in return, would assume the role of himself in the movie, as an investigator hero. "Investigative journalists and private investigators are becoming a new kind of hero, because the public wants to know," Freed said strokingly.

Mazor was suitably bashful. The closest he had ever been to acting had been the career of his father, he said, whose biggest role had been as the music teacher in *The Benny Goodman Story*, but Mazor could look at a movie role as he looked at any job. He had served in the past as Jim Jones's arch foil, leader of phantom commandos, friend of Timothy Stoen, and Nazi and Interpol villain for over a year. Now, working together with Jones in a Hollywood dramatization would be a pleasant change, just another job, indeed a glamorous one.

As the creative artist in the crowd, Freed kept the discussion to the story line. The motivations of Timothy Stoen interested them all, theatrically speaking. "The moment of his turnabout is the dramatic flashpoint," Freed remarked. But Mazor cautioned that the story was still developing, and he parceled out a few stories of Temple frauds and atrocities, as well as coy references to his fantasized commando raid. The Kaituma River was very swift, he said, and which of them would know any different about the anaconda-like stream? Did they know that he had involved Idi Amin in the case?

"[Amin] was close to the president of Guyana," Mazor brazened.

"Is that right?" Lane said.

"So I made an attempt to get Idi Amin to intercede with the president of Guyana," Mazor said.

"Did you go to Uganda to talk to him?" Lane asked.

"No."

"That was a good decision. That was wise," Lane retorted.

"I asked Idi Amin to intercede with the president of Guyana in order to get this mess squared away. He says he called him."

"Idi Amin said he called the president of Guyana?"

"Whether he did or not, I do not know," Mazor confessed.

"You appealed to one of the leading humanitarians of the world on behalf of the children!" Lane remarked.

"Yes, everybody laughed at me when I did it, but I said what the hell have we got to lose but a few hundred dollars in phone bills and travel expenses," Mazor said.

Not to be outdone, Freed spun stories of how forthcoming Jonestown residents had been in relating the indignities like incest in their past lives, as part of their oral histories. They had also told him openly of the spankings that had gone on in the Temple. Their stories were positively Dostoevskian, Freed proclaimed, not realizing that with his literary incendiarism and conspiratorial games, *he* was now making a far better Dostoevski character than any of them.

"I want to assure you, there is no attempt to whitewash," the scholar exclaimed.

"The story line at this point is in a great deal of confusion," Lane interjected as understatement.

"Except the Elmer Gantry story," said Freed.

"Who is the hero, Don?" Lane asked.

"Well, it's an American popular story. I think Jones is going to be shown as a very charismatic and contradictory figure in an Elmer Gantry sense. There's going to be some healing and there's Communism and healing and capitalism and so forth and so on."

"Are you saying healing or phony healing?" Mazor asked.

"The audience can draw their own conclusion when all is said and done," Freed replied. "Whether it's the Father Divine [or] Elmer Gantry approach . . . doesn't hurt the film, because people like to see even a Dillinger. They like to see *The Sting*." So long as the high purpose of Jones was presented, who cared about his methods? "Stoen appears to be crazy. . . ."

"I have a friend who's crazier than a bedbug," Mazor offered helpfully.

"They can be played upon," Freed replied.

"I see a lot of confusion around Jones," Lane said, "but I don't think that's a big problem. . . . But I see a straighter line for Stoen, especially if it's not his child. . . . Stoen is the most interesting character in the whole thing, don't you think?"

"I see Jones as a kind of crackpot down the line," Mazor said. "But I never had any real gripe with [him] other than the fact that he got a lot of little kids down there that I want accounted for. . . . At times I have an ax to grind with everybody in the whole case."

"*Worms*," Freed remarked, uncharacteristically judgmental for once. "How about that for the working title of the film?"

But would *Worms* sell? The real money was in a theatrical production, Freed instructed, but if they decided to tilt toward a documentary, the cash could mount up with television rights and worldwide distribution.

In the week that followed, things moved quickly. Unwitting of Mark Lane's efforts to supplant him, attorney Charles Garry traveled to Jonestown with a briefcase full of legal problems. On the agenda was the astonishing consequence of the movie meeting: that Joseph Mazor would also travel to Jonestown (if Jim Jones would pay for the trip). As Jim Jones packaged it to his following, whose heads by now must have been dizzy with all the perplexing intrigue, Joseph Mazor had "stepped out of the high ranks of the conspiracy" because he hated Timothy Stoen. (The source of Mazor's hate was not explained in Jonestown, but for others, Mazor, the ex-convict, would criticize Stoen for practicing law in a fashion for which he could be disbarred.) Mazor was suddenly a "former conspirator turned informer" who was ready to convey the innermost secrets of the Concerned Relatives. But Jonestown should beware, for Mazor could be a double agent. Residents would know Mazor upon his arrival by the "brisk handshake" with which Jones would identify him (an uncustomary gesture for Jones), whereas he would greet Charles Garry and the "great author" Mark Lane (when he would come a week later) with a big hug. Jones laid out a number of tests he would employ to judge Mazor's sincerity. From the informer, they would hope to learn how to identify the CIA agents in their midst, who Timothy Stoen's case officer in the CIA was, how John Victor Stoen figured in the conspiracy, what further assassination attempts or mercenary actions were planned, what Interpol was up to.

Charles Garry arrived in Jonestown before Mazor, and after a day or two there announced that the experience had "rejuvenated" him. The night before Mazor's arrival Garry joined in the charade. In a speech to the assemblage, Garry urged the community to be courteous to the informer, for they hoped to discover information that would "help us destroy the enemy where the enemy should be destroyed." At last, they might get an answer to the key question: "why a beautiful group of human beings like yourselves have been haunted, pushed around, and maligned for no other reason than to be able to get together collectively and do things most of us thought were impossible." Jonestown had become a monument to the double entendre. They were "pioneers in the Golden Rule," Garry said, then mixing his literary references, giving an example of the biblical question, "Am I my brother's keeper?"

Between Charles Garry and Mark Lane and Donald Freed and Joseph Mazor, the situation had reduced to a competition to see which of them could ingratiate themselves the best with Jim Jones. Ejaculatory statements about the People's Temple were the coinage of the dominion. Mazor arrived the consummate conspirator/informer/buffoon. To hear him tell it, he carried a revolver and a microrecorder in his boot; he promptly told Jones to his face that the Bishop was a thief and an "asshole"; he wrote two diaries, one for Temple security, one for himself, the latter presumably written in lemon juice that could later be ironed into script. All along, he would relate later, he knew there was no movie prospect, because he had called the producer, Paul Jarrico. In the language of the jailhouse, with which Mazor was so familiar, the movie deal was a Mark Lane "scam." But since Jones did not know that and desperately wanted the movie to glorify himself,

Mazor had made himself indispensable to the phantom movie, partly as personal protection, which he bolstered with a claim that he was traveling under diplomatic portfolio.

But to a witness, Mazor's deportment in Jonestown was somewhat different. This account had the private investigator spinning fantastic, elaborate, detailed descriptions of the mercenary attack that he had led in September 1977, including the confession that *he* had fired the shots at Jim Jones. In his no-nonsense voice, he conveyed inside-sounding information on Timothy Stoen's CIA connection. To one who heard it, Jim Jones was literally drooling at Mazor's narration, for of course it corroborated even the wildest allegations of the Bishop to his audience. Mazor even went so far as to criticize the Jonestown security system, suggesting that Jones should wear a bulletproof vest, arm his troops, and fence the place. It was all in a day's work.

The last of the curious mythmakers arrived on September 16. To support his claim that Mark Lane was a great author, Jones more than doubled Lane's literary output to eleven books and conferred upon him an honorary degree, calling him "Dr. Mark Lane." Since Lane had once been elected very early in his career to the New York State Legislature (before he gained his national reputation as a "scavenger" and "chief ghoul of American assassination"), Lane now became a former congressman. To the congregation that night, Dr. Lane established his bona fides by reciting his stock college lecture on the conspiracy that killed Martin Luther King, Jr., and after forty minutes of that he got to the point. Coming to Jonestown was like spinning in a time capsule. First you enter Guyana and you are back in the nineteenth century, feeling the mood of British imperialism and colonial backwardness. "Then [in Jonestown] you don't just come up to the twentieth century. You're in the future all of a sudden. . . . Either this is the future or there won't be any."

"That's so true. That's so true," Bishop Jones interjected sentimentally, and applause rippled through the congregation.

"This is the way it used to be in the United States, before it was the United States, 40,000 years ago," Lane continued. "An old chief at Wounded Knee told me: The first 40,000 years, it was fine. It's the last 500 years that have been pretty bad."

"That's true," Jones pitched in.

"People living together in a communal way, living with respect for one another, in harmony with nature, no polluting, no destroying. Back in the United States you can't drink the water, you can't breathe the air, and this is reflective not just of the poisons in the air and water but the poisons in the political system as well."

Poison seemed to be on everyone's mind.

Jonestown had been a rare experience and an absolute inspiration, he told them, but it was time to be self-serving. He would criticize them for only one thing: they had failed to get the word back to the American people that an experiment in the future existed and had succeeded. People in the United States knew in the abstract that there had to be *something* better.

"And it is *here!*"

Jones thanked him lovingly. "We felt so alone, so desperately alone. No one in journalism would give us a fair shake. It's so helpful to have someone with this background tell what's happening in Fortress America, because my voice gets monotonous. To hear from this distinguished man the nightmare we're under. We are living under a dangerous cloud, and we must do something before it's too late." Once again the double entendre.

The following day, Jones and Lane struck a deal. For about $6000 a month Lane's "team" would devote three months of full-time work. Suits would be filed; investigators employed; Lane and Freed would speak at dinners and rallies. Freed would serve as the undercover agent, his cover being that of an author researching a book, and a "Jonestown Support Committee" would be formed. Lane promised to talk to Dick Gregory about raising money for it.

On his departure from Guyana, Lane delivered his first salvo. To a Georgetown press conference, he announced the findings of his weeks-long "investigation." All the charges against Jim Jones, he was now able to state "conclusively," were false. "Without question there has been a massive conspiracy to destroy the People's Temple and a massive conspiracy to destroy the Reverend Jim Jones." From the "full confession" of a "key witness," as Mazor was now to be called, they had uncovered the two-year-old conspiracy of the CIA, FBI, and other U.S. organizations. Within ninety days, the People's Temple, this "model community," would file a legal action involving millions of dollars against the conspiring agencies of the U.S. government.

"The People's Temple is a powerful force for change within the United States," Lane proclaimed, "and the establishment of a cooperative community of Jonestown is the utmost embarrassment to the very worst elements within the United States government."

Since this is a story which operates largely on the psychological level, the only real consequence of Lane's posturing related to the deteriorating mind of Jim Jones. The U.S. Embassy in Georgetown was irritated by Lane's statements, to be sure, and a cable was sent to Washington about them. But there had not been a consular visit to Jonestown for over four months. Richard McCoy had completed his tour in Guyana and was back in the United States. His replacement had scrubbed a scheduled August visit because it was raining. But five days after Lane's press conference Jones wrote to, of all people,

President Jimmy Carter. The four-page single-spaced letter, marked URGENT-URGENT-URGENT, revealed Jones's dangerous demise. It was a rambling, disjointed tract, which even told his story of John Victor Stoen's paternity, as if a married man who had lusted in his heart after women would understand another who had consummated the lust. Jimmy Carter should sympathize with the Reverend, after the indignities suffered by the President's friend Bert Lance, Jones suggested. Even at this late date, Jones held onto the gesture of preacherly behavior. The People's Temple had always spoken well of the United States, he wrote the President, and while they espoused "Christian communal socialism," they did not mean for this to be a bad reflection on the government of the United States, but only "upon the racists who spit upon people like my wife who adopted [with me] a black child." Jones signed the letter, "In His Service, Jim Jones."

Meanwhile, back in the United States, Lane prepared his proposal for a counteroffensive against the massive conspiracy. On the legal front, it contained nothing new. In effect, it proposed the same conventional use of the Freedom of Information Act which attorney Charles Garry had been trying for over a year, without turning up the first indication of any conspiracy. Still, the words of the Lane proposal tooted bravado. An "intensive intelligence operation" would be needed to support their forthcoming multimillion-dollar lawsuit. On the public relations side, besides Lane's own public appearances, his team would place stories in the journals of the Left about "the miracle of Jonestown" (Lane had already talked with the editor of the Gray Panther magazine) and try to interest perceived friends like Geraldo Rivera at ABC News. The matter would be brought to the attention of Andrew Young, and Dick Gregory had already promised to make a Jonestown visit. The sole fresh idea in all of this was the suggestion that the People's Temple open an "embassy" in Washington, D.C., to press its lobbying efforts, and the embassy could be located in a building near the U.S. Supreme Court which Lane owned and which would soon be vacant. Among his many talents, Lane was also a diligent realtor.

In early October, Lane did his number in San Francisco. He repeated what he had told the press in Guyana, but he now confirmed the attack on Jonestown by *twenty* men armed with *rocket launchers* and small arms. Referring to Joseph Mazor only as the leader of the attack and an employee of Interpol, Lane described the commando plans to knock out Jonestown's generating plant and sweep in under the ensuing darkness to rescue the children. But when the mercenaries found no barbed wire or minefields, they contented themselves with sniping at the community for six days. While this must have amused the readers of the *San Francisco Examiner*, the Reverend Jim Jones in Guyana could feel that the counteroffensive was under way.

A month later, when Congressman Leo Ryan finally decided to make his trip to Guyana, he was instructed to deal with the Temple's attorney . . . Mark Lane. Lane's displacement of Garry was virtually complete.

[4]

The year 1978 began well for Leo Ryan. For several years, environmental groups, particularly the Greenpeace organization, had protested the gruesome annual bludgeoning of harp seal pups on the Canadian ice cap, and in 1977, to the considerable irritation of the Canadian government, the U.S. Congress passed a resolution asking the Canadians to reassess their policy of permitting the slaughter. It was an emotional issue to which Leo Ryan was inevitably drawn, for seals and whales were at least as important as people in his district, and since he was chairman of an environmental subcommittee in Congress, his mandate was clear. The fact that the U.S. government had no authority whatever in Canada (Ryan might have gone to Alaska), that no congressional action of any substance was possible, that whatever lobbying for a halt to the kill could best be done from Washington with the plethora of facts already available did not deter Ryan. He would go to see for himself and take with him whatever newsmen were interested.

The trip to the ice cap off the east coast of Labrador was vintage Ryan. Any dramatist knows that when two men or groups with opposing passions clash, theater is possible, and here was an exotic situation well suited to the visual display of television news, where the Canadian officials were certain to be ruffled by an American interloper, and where in the brief treatment of television Ryan could only emerge as a courageous and colorful hero, protesting personally an inhumane atrocity. So in March 1978 he went and he saw, and he was told by a Canadian official dressed as a sealer to go back to the United States and mind his own business; and when he came back to his boardinghouse in Newfoundland and the cameras were turned on, he looked ashen, as he said:

"After what I have seen, I do not want to hear the reasons. I do not want to argue the pros and cons with you anymore. I just want to say, Enough! Enough! Just quit!"

At the time of this first national success of Ryan's theatrical politics, the People's Temple as an issue had been slowly percolating in his mind for a year. His approach to constituent service eschewed public meetings in the district, in favor of personal visits to voters' homes, and in March 1977 he had visited the San Bruno home of Sam Houston, an acquaintance of the Congressman's going back to teaching days, when Houston's son, Bob, had been Ryan's student. And Bob was the focus of an emotional visit in the spring of 1977, for he had joined the People's Temple and was working two jobs to support his family of two daughters and to turn over as much as $2000 a month to the Temple. Six months earlier, Bob Houston had decided to leave the Temple. On the night he announced his decision, he was found mangled beside the railroad tracks in the rail yard where he worked nights. The police declared the death an accident, but Sam Houston was sure his son had been murdered. His two granddaughters, in their early teens, were in Jonestown, receiving their father's social security checks and presumably adding to the support of the commune, since Bob Houston had consigned the customary power of attorney to the Temple.

To Ryan, Houston laid out his facts and fears about Jim Jones, and the human dimension touched the Congressman, for his own nephew had been drawn into scientology and religious cults had been a topic of considerable family discussion. Toward the end of the meeting Ryan and Houston embraced.

"Whatever I can do to get your granddaughters back and make sure they are safe, I will do, no matter what the cost," Ryan promised. He further invited Houston to let other families with Temple problems contact him. Soon enough Ryan began to hear from more and more families, first in his district and then outside. The congressional delegation within San Francisco was very much subject to Jones's political influence, since the Reverend still held his position as the chairman of the Housing Authority. The Congressman from San Francisco, Philip Burton, had provided Jones with one of his most exuberant endorsements (used as part of the People's Temple's promotional material):

> The Reverend Jim Jones has taken to heart the biblical injunction, "faith without works is dead." He has translated his commitment to action. He has worked to alert others to the injustices which exist in our society and he has worked tirelessly with those who seek to correct these injustices.

So Congressman Ryan was both close enough and far enough away to be an effective challenger, without causing himself undue political harm.

During the summer of 1977, Ryan began to keep a record of the mushrooming contacts, and toward the end of the year he initiated his first inquiries to the executive branch. On December 8, 1977, he wrote to the Secretary of State, asking for measures to return Jim Jones to the United States to face the California court order granting custody of John Victor Stoen to Grace Stoen. Perhaps Jones's passport might be investigated, Ryan suggested. Three weeks later, the State Department replied that there was nothing it could do about Jones, since the Stoen matter was in the Guyana courts and since Grace Stoen had signed over the custody of her child to this "religious group."

As the flow of families to Ryan increased during the spring, Ryan's staff noticed a curious pattern developing. Each time Ryan would write the State Department in behalf of a distressed relative, his congressional office would be swamped with injured correspondence from the People's Temple in San Francisco and Guyana. How did the Temple get their official correspondence, and so quickly? the staff wondered.

In this connection, Congressman Ryan made a critical declaration. He received a letter from the San Francisco office of the Temple, suggesting that someone posing as Congressman Ryan was writing to government agencies in support of Timothy Stoen. Didn't the Congressman know what a seedy character Stoen was? Ominously, the letter concluded:

I want to forewarn you of this misuse of your name, which I feel sure you would in no way condone.

Ryan replied forcefully:

Please be advised that Tim Stoen does have my support in the effort to return his son from Guyana. In addition, a longtime friend of mine, Sam Houston, has told me his granddaughters are being held in Guyana.

I am most concerned about the conflicting reports about access to your church in Guyana. Please let me know if I may visit your camp in Guyana as a part of my official oversight plans for this year.

Whatever protestations of impartiality Ryan might make to the Temple from here on were undermined by this letter. He now became the congressman plotting in the class enemy's war room.

In April 1978, the Accusation of Human Rights violations against Jones landed in Ryan's office, and while the same document dove deep into a State Department file cabinet, as an embarrassment never to be pulled again, it became the catalyst for Ryan's personal involvement. The reference in the accusation not only to Carter's human rights policy but to the Universal Declaration of Human Rights adopted by the United Nations in 1948 caught Ryan's special attention. By the summer of 1978, he had concluded that something had to be done, but he was still operating as the congressional club member, trying to get the State Department to do its job. Not satisfied with the State Department exonerations of the Temple, Ryan requested State to send a special investigative team to Guyana. By this time, Ryan's staff had learned that the department was relying solely on the work of Richard

McCoy, and that in Washington McCoy's reports were simply being "rubber-stamped" by the department. This, put together with the speed with which the Temple protested Ryan's meddling, heightened the staff's suspicions of Richard McCoy.

Besides the central human rights focus and the enduring Stoen case, the Temple matter grew more complicated legally, as it widened to embrace possible social security, tax exemption, and customs violations. Ryan concluded that he would have to build a legal record of his own, given the unsatisfactory responses from the requisite agencies. In the summer of 1978, he hired a young lawyer part-time to conduct interviews with Concerned Relatives and to advise on the ever-expanding legal problems. Bit by bit, the Ryan staff became infected with the same paranoia which the Temple spread to all who touched it, believer or apostate, investigator or investigated. Ryan's new employee was the son of his administrative aide, and by the late summer, as the son would traipse off on interviews with Concerned Relatives, the father would follow at a shadow man's safe distance to be sure that there was no setup. Spies seemed to hover everywhere in the story, including the grayest recesses of the government bureaucracy.

In mid-September, Congressman Ryan had his first meeting with a State Department official on Jonestown. He got more of the same timid caution, an echo of the constant refrain that this was a matter between private citizens, a religious group protected by the First Amendment, a small South American country in which the United States preferred the posture of nonintervention. Getting the same old stuff, the Congressman began planning for a trip, bolstered by frequent meetings with Concerned Relatives, whose personal dilemma touched him. But, unlike the mission to the pristine icy wilderness of Labrador, the mission to the fetid Guyana jungle did not exhilarate him. While the planning went forward, Ryan kept the back door open to cancel. Without success, he tried to interest every member of the California congressional delegation, then every member of the House Foreign Affairs Committee, in joining him. One committee member finally agreed to go: Congressman Edward Derwinski of Illinois, who had been a consistent and passionate advocate of human rights for the enslaved citizens of Latvia, Lithuania, and Estonia, and therefore could philosophically appreciate the issues Ryan was raising. But as the difficulties and possible dangers of the trip became clear, not to mention Ryan's reputation as an accomplished performer before the cameras, Derwinski canceled out, pleading a scheduling conflict.

Fittingly close to Halloween, for this had become a political Halloween story, Ryan made his final decision to go, after meeting with Concerned Relatives in California. The date was October 25, 1978. To his staff, he announced his decision grim-faced, for this time, apart from the fact that the trip was good politics and good constituent service and might even make national headlines for him again, he was not looking forward to it. By now he had a distinct sense of possible danger. The Deborah Blakey affidavit, with its report of weapons, security guards, and mass suicide drills, had been brought to his attention. His staff interviews with apostates were hair-curling. And he was receiving intelligence from a freelance journalist named Gordon Lindsay who had drafted an astonishing article about Temple bestialities for the *National Enquirer*. But then, the *National Enquirer* was not exactly a journal of record, and Ryan considered Lindsay's story sensational fare for the checkout counter at the supermarket, not something you would want to base a congressional investigation upon. The Ryan staff passed on to the Department of State these various reports of danger, but at no time did the department confirm a basis for concern. While the State Department sought consistently to discourage the Ryan trip, it did so solely on the complaint that it would cause diplomatic problems. In short, as plans for the trip became firm, Leo Ryan was unsure where the truth lay. If there were danger, his code of politics imprisoned him: you could not do your job if you were afraid.

The dates for the trip were set for November 14–20. Ryan had to be back in Washington on November 21 for a hearing on saving whales. On November 7, he was reelected to Congress with 61 percent of the vote.

To this point the need for some outside force to penetrate Jones's empire was indisputable. The issues were important. The established diplomatic and investigative agencies were ossified. Perhaps only a skillful politician, ready, as Ryan often described his role, "to kick down doors," was up to the job. That had been required to make the trip to the polar ice cap. The technique would now get its tropical test. But if the need for a congressional visit was clear, the manner of its formation was crucial, although Leo Ryan could not have known that. His politician's instinct not only to fulfill his mission but to milk it for every ounce of promotional value now took over and it doomed him.

The freelance journalist, Gordon Lindsay, soon caught wind of Ryan's planned trip and called to inquire if he might not be part of the congressional delegation, given the help he had rendered Ryan's staff. That, of course, was impossible, the Ryan aide replied. Lindsay did not know at that time that Jones had authorized a reported payment of $7500 to Mark Lane to acquire the unpublished article. It is not clear whom Lane paid for the article, but he did get it, and when Jones saw the piece, Lindsay became the only journalist to receive the status of class enemy. The article confirmed that it had been Lindsay who had circled over Jonestown in a light plane at treetop level, sending the residents scurrying for cover and causing one of Jones's seniors to have a heart attack. Still, Lindsay was eager to join the Ryan mission in some capacity, and the *National Enquirer* had refused to pay his way. So Lindsay contacted Don Harris of NBC News, who at the time was at work on an NBC special on American cults. In a matter of a day, NBC national news declared its desire to go along, and Ryan responded:

"If they want to go along, that might be a good way to break it and build up public opinion in this country." To the People's Temple, he continued to profess impartiality (a protestation the Temple could not have believed, given his earlier declaration of support for Timothy Stoen), but in his mind Ryan was beginning to believe there was more truth than fiction to the wild allegations.

In Guyana, meanwhile, the Temple's first response to Ryan's announced visit was hostile. In Jonestown and in Georgetown, Temple apostles were describing Ryan as a member of the John Birch Society and a supporter of the right-wing military dictatorship in Chile. Into this curious mix, Lawrence Mann, the Guyanese Ambassador to the United States and escort for Temple courtesan Paula Adams, introduced himself, performing more as the Temple's ambassador than Guyana's. On November 4, Mann met with American Ambassador John Burke, and they discussed the Temple's declaration to the American Embassy not to receive Congressman Ryan in Jonestown. Mann professed to regret the Temple's decision as bad public relations, but to accept the rationale that Ryan was rudely trying to force his way into a private domain and should have better manners. The Temple was convinced, Mann told Burke, that, in the language of Burke's later diplomatic cable, "the codel [congressional delegation] was hostile, would be arriving with well-developed prejudices against PT and merely wanted an on-the-spot visit to enable codel to return to US and reiterate prejudiced view of People's Temple community with more authority than before. PT officials had apparently cited to Mann visit by NBC camera team as proof positive of codel's bad faith."

Within an hour of the conversation between the two ambassadors, Sharon Amos called the American Embassy to say that the Temple had *not* closed Jonestown's front entrance to Ryan, but rather wished to set three conditions for his visit: (1) that the congressional delegation be balanced, later clarified to mean a member of the congressional black caucus come with Ryan; (2) that no media accompany Ryan to Jonestown; (3) that Mark Lane be present for Ryan's visit.

Several days later, Lane wrote to Congressman Ryan, conveying the willingness of the Temple to receive the Congressman under certain circumstances, but saying that he (Lane) was preoccupied with his show before the House Assassinations Committee with his famous client, James Earl Ray. Lane complained of consistent oppression of the Temple by the U.S. government. Already two countries hostile to the

United States (which he left unnamed) had offered asylum to the Temple communards, and "if religious persecution continues and if it is furthered through a witch hunt conducted by any branch of the U.S. government," they might just accept. If they did, it could result in profound embarrassment to the American government.

Lane's letter infuriated Ryan, and the Congressman's reply reflected his fury. He disclaimed any desire to oppress or persecute the Temple. His purpose was simply to talk with members whose parents had expressed concern. While he had heard many negative comments, he confessed, he wished to give the other side a full hearing. But the references to a witch hunt "disappointed" him, and the ones to an exodus to yet another country adverse to the United States puzzled him.

"Your vague reference to 'the creation of the most embarrassing situation to the American government' does not impress me at all. If the comment is intended as a threat, I believe it reveals more than may have been intended," Ryan wrote, implying Jonestown had something to hide. He was going to Guyana on the dates announced, and Lane could be there or not, as he chose. As kicking down doors went, Lane's was flimsy.

On November 9, Ryan met with the NBC team. There was no doubt that both the Congressman and the newsmen appreciated the potential danger of their assignment, and each side reassured the other that they were tough enough and fearless enough for the mission. Ryan spoke of his Folsom Prison escapade and Harris of his Vietnam experience. The others on the NBC crew had between them ample combat duty that included not only Vietnam but 1960's race riots and the Middle East. Indeed, Harris had chosen his crew precisely for size and battle readiness. His producer was a former paratrooper. Even the question of whether they should bear arms was discussed. But Ryan had a transcript of Lane's Georgetown press conference, with its allegations of CIA attempts to infiltrate and destroy the Temple, and so he feared that weapons, if they were discovered in his delegation, could be provocative, even used as an excuse for violence. If gunfire broke out, the Temple could claim the codel fired first.

The following day, with the boss still in California, Ryan aides met in Washington with Deborah Blakey and Grace and Timothy Stoen. As the three apostates retold their stories and expressed their fears, their listeners' attitude was at first skeptical, for the three had once been enthusiastic practitioners of the very Jonesian tactics they now described in detail as dangerous and evil. But for several aides who were now assigned to the trip, this was the first face-to-face hearing of the charges against Jones. While the staff made allowances for the passion of apostasy, apprehension grew. Ryan's legislative aide, Jackie

Speier, began to have premonitions of her own death and updated her will. Yet she was making the trip at her own expense and had been affected by Ryan's philosophy of denying fear to do a job. In California, Ryan's administrative aide, Joe Holsinger, tried for the last time to talk Ryan out of the mission, but a year before Holsinger himself had run before the bulls of Pamplona and so his authority as the voice of caution was weak. Balancing the apprehension, however, was the fact that at no point, especially in briefings with Richard McCoy at the State Department, considered the real Temple cognoscente, was concern for the safety of the congressional delegation ever expressed. If the Department of State or the CIA saw any danger in the mission, surely, felt the staff, it would be conveyed. Moreover, numerous outside visitors—including diplomats, politicians, and Guyanese officials—had already been to Jonestown, without the least difficulty.

Word of Ryan's trip was spreading rapidly. Once NBC was committed, the *San Francisco Chronicle* and *Examiner* assigned correspondents. Soon *The Washington Post* joined. Suddenly the press party numbered nine, which for a congressional junket was very large. Apart from the pleasure that Ryan got from this press excitement in his trip, he began to feel that the press provided a measure of protection. The press, in turn, felt that the Congressman's presence protected them. In fact, the symbiosis spelled the reverse. Had either group gone without the other, they might have survived. Soon Concerned Relatives were calling, for here was an opportunity to have, for once, a forceful spokesman for uncovering the truth at the bottom of the horror. Fourteen relatives, including Grace and Timothy Stoen, announced their intention to make the trip.

To the Temple, Ryan lamely maintained that neither the press nor the Concerned Relatives were part of his official delegation, but it was a futile effort at hairsplitting. From Jonestown, the assault force looked formidable and, for once, it was real. A flamboyant congressman who had officially sided with Timothy Stoen; a contingent of their most effective class enemies; a national television crew advised by the class enemy, Gordon Lindsay; the two major dailies of San Francisco, where the last of the Temple's friends and supporters were; and a reporter from Washington who could potentially galvanize the interest of the federal government in yet more investigation and interference. The reputation and, in effect, the very existence of the Temple poised on the outcome of the visit.

On the weekend before the delegation departed, Don Harris began interviewing on camera the principals on both sides of the dispute. To the Temple supporters he delivered the assurance that he was not out to do an exposé.

"I have absolutely no idea at this point what the story will look like, favorable or critical to the Temple. . . . By and large, your biggest safe factor is that we really don't care how the story turns out."

Perhaps he did not care, but he did know what his story was, as his producer Robert Flick later testified. It was a story of enslavement by a fanatic. Whether he could prove it on film was another matter. Then, in the cast of ethics and professionalism, he delivered what the Temple could only see as a threat.

"If we have to file in a hurry, give us the name of somebody in Georgetown or here," he said, "because there will be time for only one phone call, that's all. To say, we are filing, the story will be negative . . . or we are filing and you don't have anything to sweat. That's all I can do for you. That's all I'm supposed to do for you. That is all ethically we can promise anybody."

In Jim Jones's construction of the world, this was it. This was the moment. There would never be another like it. His existence, the existence of his life's work, his bid for history came down to one phone call.

From Georgetown he ordered a 100-pound drum of potassium cyanide. It arrived on the *Cudjoe* several days before the press and congressional and class enemy phalanx arrived in Guyana.

T W E L V E

Apocalypse

[1]

IF ONE WERE to imagine what a successful Ryan mission might
have been, it would be this: that the Congressman would
skillfully use his power as an official representative of the U.S.
government to gain entry to Jonestown, that he would manipulate the
press in his party toward that end. Once in Jonestown, he would
interview those on his list and perhaps discover that some did indeed
want to leave the encampment; that he would penetrate the elaborate
front of Jim Jones and establish him as a fraud and a master of slaves. In
doing so, he would emerge as the hero of a seven-minute story on
NBC's "Today Show." Past the airing of his heroic mission on
television, the outlines of the success are indistinct. Ryan would be
obliged to make a report to his congressional committee, but the
grumbling behind his back would surely be loud. So there was a bizarre
American cult in the South American jungle. So its leader was mad and
had tried to prevent the escape of apostates. So a committee member
had pierced the fraud and brought out a few dissidents with him. So
what? What business of Congress's was it?

Yet, politics must intersect with entertainment. The grumbling in
the cloakroom would not be heard across the continent. Ryan's
constituency would love it. Their congressman was becoming nation-
ally famous. By theatrical standards, from the press interest in the trip,
success was already assured—whether the Congressman got into
Jonestown or not, whether the trajectory of his comet ever targeted the
eye of Jim Jones's orbit or not. For here was a mission beyond the gray
business of the hearing room and the constituent letter. Here was a
politician engaged in his world and his age, grappling personally with a
profound symptom of the spiritual dearth of the 1970s.

Indeed, Congressman Ryan boarded a plane for Guyana not expecting ever to see Jonestown. He would use every trick, every device he

had learned to break down the gate of Jonestown. He would put pressure on the American Embassy to put pressure on the Guyanese government to put pressure on Jim Jones to gain access. But in his mind he knew he would be impeded somewhere, perhaps all along the way. When it happened, the final plan was to board a plane with the press and a few distraught relatives, fly to Port Kaituma, approach the locked gate of Jonestown, and, preferably with a sullen, gun-toting guard in the background, hold a press conference. This would prove to an American television audience that Jonestown was not what Jim Jones said it was. The only problem with this fallback strategy was that his steamy press conference probably would never make the air, for it would not be much of a news story. A locked gate would have clarified little in this sea of conjecture. Yet, this minor spectacle seemed the likeliest outcome. Ryan had already experienced the icy diplomatic embrace of the Privacy Act and the First Amendment of the Constitution. As for the Guyanese government, Leo Ryan went to Guyana with a report from several sources that Jim Jones had paid a personal retainer of $1 million to the Prime Minister of Guyana, Forbes Burnham.

For Jim Jones, the dimensions of success were less worldly. He had reached the critical juncture where he could register his lethal blow against capitalism and fascism in one final glorious moment. Given the state of his health, this was surely his last chance. This Congressman had played into this grandiose obsession in ways that only Father Jones could know. His flock was finally in the right frame of mind to join him. Their mix of fear and love, fatigue and conviction, had taken months to brew. There had never been an opportunity so good as this. Yet, sick as he was, he retained enough command of the situation to control his appointment with history moment by moment, for he seemed to appreciate how close to the ridiculous his grand scheme was.

On November 14, Congressman Ryan departed from New York for Guyana on a note of apprehension. It had occurred to several of his aides how easy it would be for the Temple to sabotage his airplane. It was as if the vibrations from Jonestown had been felt in New York: the episode from *Parallax View*, perhaps, that showed the sabotaging of a jetliner, or even Jones's statement to the packed Pavilion that the Congressman's plane might just fall from the sky. Before Flight 227 boarded, a Ryan aide discussed with a Pan American official what would be involved in a bomb search and was informed that the bags would all be brought alongside the aircraft, each passenger claiming his own piece and putting it on the conveyor belt for the hold of the plane. Any unclaimed bag would then be searched. The procedure was devised with the assumption that no saboteur would willingly go down with the plane—an assumption which later was proved inaccurate where the People's Temple was concerned. But it seemed a great deal of trouble, this search, and after several discussions with Ryan, the party decided not to request the bomb alert.

As the Ryan party readied for departure, Sharon Amos was issuing a press release in Georgetown, announcing that the Concerned Relatives had now enlisted a right-wing congressman, a supporter of the Pinochet regime, in their cause, and that while Ryan was ostensibly coming to "investigate" charges against the Temple, the trip was really "a contrived media event, staged to manufacture adverse publicity for the Jonestown community, hopefully by provoking some sort of incident." In a nice twist of the same language used against the Temple, the press release also put Ryan "on official notice that [the Jonestown residents] will be requesting Guyana police protection in the event that attempts are made to enter the Jonestown community against their will." Regrettably, no such official request was ever made to the Guyanese police, not by the Temple, nor by Ryan. The Embassy had specifically informed Ryan that it could not provide any security for his trip.

On the morning of Wednesday, November 15, Ryan met with Ambassador John Burke and was given a little good news. The Temple had tentatively agreed to receive Ryan and one aide alone in Jonestown on Friday, no press, no Concerned Relatives—but the details would have to be worked out. The Ambassador was anxious to remove himself from the middle of these negotiations, and Ryan wanted that as well. Burke and Ryan were Irishmen of a very different sort. Their stubbornness took different shapes. Burke was the controlled, overcautious stickler for the rules; Ryan the stormy iconoclast. They did not hit it off. Upon the Congressman's arrival, the Ambassador staged a proper briefing, which included slides of Jonestown. The most Ryan could say later about the show was that the cleared land and solid construction of the place had impressed him.

Nor was Ryan particularly warmed by the Temple's limited invitation. For a start, it stripped him of the personal protection he felt the press afforded. It gave nothing to the relatives with him. Where was the political theater in it? Besides, the original plan had called for a trip to Jonestown on the following day, Thursday, and a plane had already been chartered. But Wednesday dragged on with a lunch at the Embassy and a meeting with the Guyanese Foreign Minister, most of which was absorbed with talk of American sugar quotas. By late afternoon there had been no word from the Temple. Ryan began to smell a stall. He gathered with the relatives for a status conference, allowing the cameras to film it. He promised to try direct communication with Jonestown that evening, for the situation was now for Jones and him to resolve. He praised the relatives for their patience, which was far more than he would have been able to muster were he in their shoes. "I have no relatives there. No financial commitment. No emotional commitment. I'm simply here in response to questions which have been asked. My job is to separate out the emotional tension between Jim Jones and you, and sit down and talk with him. In the interest of fairness, his point of view needs to be represented before I make up my mind as a member of Congress." But he was being sucked inexorably into this poignant human dilemma, losing sight of his official reason for being there. At another point in the meeting he defined his purpose differently.

"I intend to keep pushing as long as I'm here," he said. "There are 900 Americans living in a remote place. Relatives who want to see their kids, and that's why we're here. The more there is resistance to that request, the more reason there is to question the claims that [the Temple] has made. We all come from a society where families are important. There are families badly split, and we should be able to effect a change in that."

If Ryan were able to travel to Jonestown the next day, he hoped to persuade Jones to permit the relatives to visit on Friday. But as the sun dipped toward the horizon on Wednesday, only a few preliminary calls between Sharon Amos and a Ryan staff man had taken place. So, after dinner with Burke, Ryan took the matter on himself, catching a taxi to the Temple headquarters at Lamaha Gardens.

"Hi, I'm Leo Ryan, the bad guy. Does anyone want to talk?" he said cheerily as he strode into their living room. Out of thirty stunned communards, Sharon Amos was one of the few who would talk. All other conversation in the room ceased awkwardly. But Ryan mustered his charm, and the initiative went well, at least by Ryan's account. At one point he told Amos he wanted to visit Jonestown, but not just get the "two-dollar tour." He really wanted to talk to people.

When Ryan returned to his hotel later, he bubbled about his minor triumph, and the following morning Sharon Amos conveyed to a Ryan aide her pleasure with the meeting as well. Perhaps one of the Concerned Relatives and a few correspondents could accompany the Congressman on his Friday trip after all. But later Thursday morning, Ryan blundered. He convened the press, invited several Guyanese reporters, and got carried away in describing his coup of the night before. He had seen no signs of religious life in the Temple headquarters, only plaques of various humanitarian awards for Jim Jones. If this was not a religious organization, why was it tax-exempt? "There is a posturing of religious belief, but I'm not sure it exists," he said. Would they get into Jonestown or not? the press wanted to know.

"If [they] refuse me entry, then this is a prison. There are social security laws involved here, finance and tax laws, as well as passport regulations, and I intend to pursue that through every area of the U.S. government."

His menacing tone went further. Referring to his emotional touch-stone of Folsom Prison, he made note of the Red Cross Convention on the Treatment of Prisoners, and its provisions requiring face-to-face contact. This tough talk, of course, got back immediately to Sharon Amos, and she called a Ryan aide to express her shock and disappointment. The Congressman questioned their faith, had mentioned Jonestown in the same breath with Folsom Prison and the Red Cross Convention on prisoners. His objectivity was now in doubt, and his trip to Jonestown the following day was now "up in the air." It would have to be ironed out when Temple attorney Mark Lane arrived in Guyana, after midnight. When Ryan was informed that Lane was coming after all, he was amused.

"I knew he wasn't going to pass it up," he said.

Shortly afterward, Ryan also learned that Charles Garry would be coming with Mark Lane that night. Now the play would have comic subplots.

"We're going to have an interesting team to work with now," he chortled. Garry, Lane, and he, at least, played on the same magnetic field.

Later on Thursday afternoon, the American press requested another meeting with Ryan. With Don Harris elected as their spokesman, they wanted to air their concern about the uncertainty of the entire affair. The reporters had already agreed to dispense with journalistic competitiveness. Toward the end of the session the producer for the NBC team, Bob Flick, surfaced the growing, unspoken apprehension. What if something went wrong? At first, Ryan dismissed the problem. Nothing would go wrong. But what if it did? Flick persisted. This was an official U.S. inquiry, Ryan replied, and if there were trouble, help would be forthcoming. He left the distinct impression of the U.S. Marines on a rescue mission.

On Friday morning, Ryan greeted Mark Lane and Charles Garry on a hotel patio, and inevitably several reporters gravitated to the clutch with pencils sharpened. Belligerently, Charles Garry objected.

"I didn't know this was going to be a media circus," he growled, a veteran of many such entertainments himself. "We can't have a meeting if we are going to have the press here." Replying in kind, Ryan refused to order the press away, whereupon Garry and Lane stomped out with showy pique, only to hold their own press conference in the hotel lobby. The two rings of the circus thus defined, the official U.S. inquiry seemed headed for an ignominious collapse. But the characters relented and agreed to meet in private upstairs. In a hotel room, the civility of the negotiations improved only slightly. Ryan admitted to a fixed opinion about Jonestown, but added his mind was open to change.

"I don't care what *your* position is," he said gruffly. "We're going to go whether you want to go or not. There will be two seats for you. The plane will leave at two o'clock, with or without you."

It was slightly before noon. Ryan seemed to be off for his dry press conference at the closed gate to the commune, but what he did not know was that a Temple truck had been parked in the middle of the Port Kaituma airstrip, defying *any* plane to land.

Lane and Garry repaired to Lamaha Gardens to talk by radio to Jones. Earlier in the morning Garry had threatened to leave on the 1:00 p.m. plane for New York, and had called Lane and Sharon Amos "assholes," so ruffled was he by his fall from grace. Now, Garry was at least speaking civilly to his competition. The lawyers agreed to urge Jones to allow Ryan and the press into Jonestown.

But when Jones came on the radio, he sounded as if he were dead. That, at least, was Garry's impression. Lane put forward the attorneys' recommendation. Jones would have nothing of it. He ranted about his righteousness, about the perfidy of traitors, etc., etc. But there was little now that tirades could accomplish. The Congressman was on his way. He was coming with a planeload of press and Concerned Relatives, a Guyanese government official, and the second in command at the U.S. Embassy. With the matter unresolved, Lane and Garry hustled to the airport to make the 2:00 p.m. departure. Negotiations could continue in Port Kaituma. If Jones kept his truck on the airstrip, he stood to embarrass himself profoundly, not only to the American public and the American Congress, but to his Guyanese hosts as well. Ryan had won the first round.

A half hour into the flight, the plane suspended, as it were, on the seam of civilization, Jones tried for the last time to turn Ryan back. The pilot of the plane received a message from Port Kaituma saying that the light dwindled rapidly and it was unsafe to land. Perhaps Jones still had some small reservation in his mind that he was doing the right thing. But the pilot was spunky. He would make a go of it, after he passed over the airstrip to judge its condition himself.

On the airstrip, a Temple dump truck and tractor awaited the party. The plane touched down at 3:40 p.m. Temple escorts ushered Ryan, the American diplomat Richard Dwyer, and the Temple attorneys onto the truck with the word that they would proceed to Jonestown, while the press and relatives remained behind at the airstrip—under guard by two Guyanese policemen.

Nearly an hour later, Marceline Jones met this first contingent as it arrived in Jonestown. People came and went amiably within the community, making no particular fuss over the arrival, exhibiting no hostility. In the Pavilion, the band practiced. Marceline conducted what Ryan coined the first "two-dollar tour," past the child care center and the facility for the disabled and the mentally retarded, the other manifestations of their good works. In time, Bishop Jones appeared. The diplomat, Richard Dwyer, was struck by this apparition. In May, Jones had been fat and relaxed. Now he was considerably thinner, his demeanor tense, his pallor gray. His first words were about his poor health and his high fevers. He was defensive and self-pitying from the start. He did not want his people harassed. As the Congressman could see, people came and went as they pleased. Ryan said he was there to see which of the allegations were fact and which fiction, and got right to the point of the newsmen back at the airstrip. Garry and Lane pitched in again with their recommendation.

"OK, let 'em all in, what the hell," Jones said with a wave of the hand.

What about Gordon Lindsay? someone piped up.

"All except him," Jones replied.

As acolytes rushed off to pass the word that the newsmen could come, Ryan expressed his desire to begin interviewing. In a corner of the Pavilion, near sewing machines, where women were making the cute Jonestown dolls, Ryan set up shop. Marceline scurried away to organize a display table for Jonestown handicrafts.

As time dragged on at the airstrip, newsmen sweated under the hot afternoon sun, and one of the policemen grew increasingly relaxed with several reporters. From time to time, once or twice a month, he related, small planes landed to pick up injured Americans from Jonestown. The local people were always told that the injuries were sustained in machete or machinery accidents, but explanations were suspicious.

"When you go there, keep your eyes open," the policeman told the reporter. "We really hate these people. Reverend Jim Jones should have died long ago."

At 6:00 p.m. the tractor returned to the airstrip to collect the newsmen, all except class enemy Gordon Lindsay. An hour and a half later, after inching through deep mud on the Jonestown road, the press joined the Congressman in the early dark of the forest.

For the time being, the Front consumed the Reality. The buildings impressed. The residents were friendly and rational, seemingly well-fed. Coffee was passed around, then hot pork sandwiches and greens and edo roots. Jones presided over the feast, wearing a red polo shirt and only lightly tinted glasses, relaxed and conversational at first. A comfortable Marceline Jones was the consummate hostess. Soon enough, the show began. Deanna Wilkinson and the Jonestown Express roared into the Guyanese national anthem with feeling, followed with "America the Beautiful" (using the traditional words this time), and continued with their customarily superb rock and blues numbers. The visitors were frantically trying to match their preconceptions with what they were seeing. Residents "looked programmed," some observers thought—whatever that was. At one point, in a whisper, Congressman Ryan remarked on how the older members were clapping trance-like to the soul music, as if this amounted to profound revelation. But he had discovered nothing so far to substantiate the allegations of abuse, and much that belied such charges. As the entertainment proceeded, individuals on his list were brought to Ryan to interview. When the politician sensed his moment, he assumed the microphone.

"Questions have been raised about your operation here," he began. "I'm here to find out. I can tell you right now from the few conversations I've had so far . . . there are some people here who believe this is the best thing that's happened to them in their whole life. . . ."

Riotous applause overwhelmed him for more than three minutes. When it finally subsided, Ryan wished they were all from San Mateo.

"It's too bad you can't vote for me," he cracked.

"We can . . . by absentee ballot," Jones responded.

Ryan took the comment at face value. "My work is important to me, and I know it's important to you as well. Thank you for hosting us here tonight. We really appreciate it. I don't want to spoil your good time here tonight with political speeches." If he only knew. . . .

Close to ten o'clock the Congressman and the diplomat Dwyer went to the radio shack to make contact with Georgetown. The ice between the visitors and the believers was melting everywhere. An ebullient Ryan told his staff man in Georgetown that a great show had been put on for them that night, and, of course, he was right about that. In Lamaha Gardens, Temple members began introducing themselves voluntarily to the Ryan representative and conversing freely. Sharon Amos was particularly happy at the way things were going.

In the Pavilion, Jones was holding forth for reporters, as the music continued more quietly. His conversation was disjointed, moving without link from one passion to the next. All his contradictions were on display. He admitted his Marxism and insisted that his was a religious movement. He insisted that John Victor Stoen was his son, bringing the boy forth to bare his teeth, comparing them to his own, and then reacted adversely to the suggestion that he had had an "affair" with Grace Stoen. He described his experiment as a community of sharing, but balked at the label "socialist." "Call me a socialist," he said huffily. "I've been called worse." Since no one had ever challenged his illogic before, he faltered and looked hurt at his obvious inconsistencies. He began to look increasingly ridiculous and seemed to realize it. He hated power, violence, and money, he said with emotion. Did people have normal sex lives in the community? His sexton, Harriet Tropp, sitting next to him, mercifully answered in his place.

"People do fuck in Jonestown," she declared emphatically, citing the thirty-three babies born in the camp as proof.

Through this vertiginous roller-coaster ride, his death mask flashed quickly, but unmistakenly. More than once he declared he wished he had never been born, how much pain and guilt the Stoen affair had caused him, how he was ready to surrender to his enemies. "They can have me," he moaned, as if he were fish bait again. Under the hot television lights, as sweat beads appeared on his forehead and upper lip, he spoke of his 103-degree fever that day. As his interrogation proceeded, he visibly wilted.

Close to eleven o'clock, the entertainment ceased, and the audience drifted out into the night air. To the side, watching Jones wind down like a whirligig, Richard Dwyer stood alone in the shadows. A slender white man approached the diplomat warily, his face etched with terror. He must leave, must leave at once, that night, the man whispered, for he could not remain in the community much longer. Dwyer could not help him, not just yet. It had been decided that the newsmen would return to Port Kaituma, and Ryan and Dwyer would overnight in Jonestown. This Dwyer explained, and after taking the man's name, one Vernon Gosney, he insisted that Gosney seek him out in the morning. The terrified apostate drifted into the night once again, only to find Don Harris, who was waiting for his crew to pack up their gear. To Harris, Gosney passed a note, scrawled with a magic marker, crying for help to escape both for himself and a Monica Bagby. Harris slipped the note into his boot.

With this slight fissure in the facade, Dwyer realized that the situation had altered dangerously, and he went to find Congressman Ryan. As a start, bringing in more Concerned Relatives the very next day was a terrible idea, Dwyer whispered to Ryan. "We've got to get out of the travel business," he said, and Ryan agreed. The newsmen, too, realized the significance of the note, and the danger of it. This was the story they had come for, but, on the other hand, they could not become involved personally in an evacuation operation, not with a desperately ill and volatile leader like Jones. Don Harris particularly knew the perils of that, having covered the fall of Saigon from the roof of the American Embassy. But how could the professional and the humanitarian impulses be separated? This was a story of human tragedy, human enslavement. How could it be reported from afar? This was not personal journalism they were doing, not yet at least. Like Ryan, the newsmen were being sucked into the unfolding horror, becoming an inevitable part of the events to come. By Jonestown lights, their standard, direct questioning of the Father was surrogate disloyalty, anarchic behavior. The implications of their questions amounted to blasphemy. Unwittingly, they were targeting themselves.

An hour later, the reporters were dumped off in Port Kaituma. Characteristically, they got a bottle of good rum and sat down in a joint called Weekend Disco to drink for several hours and tell war stories. In time, a local policeman drifted into the establishment and turned out to be open, even quite anxious, to talk about Jonestown. In due course, he took three reporters back to the police outpost, there mentioning that at least one automatic rifle had been registered to the Jonestown arsenal—against strict government policy. When the three returned to the Weekend Disco, they shared the information. For Don Harris, contemplating his scheduled interview with Jones in the morning, there were now two flashpoints: the defector's note and the automatic rifle.

In Jonestown, meanwhile, Charles Garry was locked in conversation with Jones. Foremost in Garry's mind was the question of his continued representation of the Temple, given the challenge from Lane. As the time proceeded into the small hours, he got the reassurances from Jones that satisfied him. But there was other business, chiefly a letter from Jones's onetime mistress, and close aide, the one Jones had always held up as the most brilliant of his followers, the longtime chief of his Department of Diversions, Terri Buford. Buford had left Jonestown a month before on the mission of working with Mark Lane on the grand counteroffensive against the conspiracy. But in the letter which Charles Garry brought, Buford declared her independence. On her own, she proposed to become a double agent, infiltrating the Concerned Relatives group and occasionally sending vital intelligence to Jones. To establish the high purpose behind her move, she enclosed statements incriminating herself in various illegalities, including one which told of smuggling a million dollars out of the United States. "So you have complete control," she wrote. Further, she had organized most of the Temple's illegalities, so he had the perfect defense for her departure.

But the letter was largely smoke to obscure her withdrawal. Wherever her loyalties were now to lie, the main point came at the beginning.

"I don't know how much longer you are going to live. I heard you on the phone patch the other night and you could hardly get the words out . . . and some of this may be cop-out-itis: not wanting to watch you die."

In discussing the letter with Garry, Jones felt it was authentic, that he had lost another of his most trusted aides, this one spinning out of his orbit into space beyond his pull. A year before, Buford had written another letter, this one as a loyalist. "If we do make a last stand, it will not be as an act of giving up, but rather as a demonstration in the hopes that some people will wake up and give those people who wish to live in equality a chance to do so. It will have to be as a last resort, we will have to have tried everything short of it. . . ."

Now in the wee hours of November 18, she was contributing to Jones's conviction that the last stand had arrived. His whole "structure" was being dismantled: by Congressman Ryan, by the press, by the relatives, but, most of all, by his own people who deserted him now in his sickness and his evil.

[2]

Leo Ryan was up at dawn on November 18, breakfasting on pancakes and syrup with bacon, all cooked over charcoal. In the school tent adjacent to the Pavilion, children giggled at "Willy Wonka and the Chocolate Factory" on a television set. Jones had assured the reporters that a truck would fetch them around 8:00 a.m., but it did not show up in Port Kaituma until after 10:00 a.m. Ryan spent the morning in his interviews in the corner of the Pavilion without harvesting a single dissident. The reporters arrived close to 11:00. Marceline Jones plugged them immediately into her second two-dollar tour. But the reporters were an obstreperous lot and soon deflected in their own directions. Harris conducted several soft interviews with residents, including an emotional talk with Maria Katsaris and her brother Anthony, who had come with the relatives group. The interview faded out with sister and brother in tears, holding hands, but neither changing the mind of the other. Harris's mind was on his promised contretemps with Jones, and he wanted it to take place at the end of the visit. He said to Richard Dwyer that the night before he had learned things in Port Kaituma which he knew would be unsettling to Jones, so he wanted his "hard-hitting interview" to come at the last.

It began near 1:00 p.m. Much of the substance had already been covered in bits and pieces, but this was the interview that mattered. They talked of spankings and the paternity of John Victor, of conspiracy and assassination attempts. Media smear had now substituted for assassination, Jones charged. Harris was relentless. Fifteen minutes or so into the interview, he raised the matter of the automatic weapon.

•   "This is rubbish. I'm defeated. I might as well die," Jones said in sudden dejection, his voice rising. He began to sweat profusely, licking his lips again from the Nembutal in his system. "The guns have never been used to intimidate people."

Harris unsheathed the note given to him the night before, with the names of Monica Bagby and Vern Gosney clearly printed. That marked them as the first to be shot three hours later. Lies, games, perversions: his explanations had lost their credibility. Reports of fresh defectors were passed to him in whispers. Jones was dissolving before the very eye of his beholders.

"Every time they go, they lie," he wailed. "The more that leave, the less responsibility we have. What I thought was keeping them here was the fear of the ghetto and alienation. I must have failed somewhere. I want to hug them before they go. . . ."

Edith Parks, a granite-faced little white-haired lady in her sixties, was first to get Father's ghostly embrace. Her defection took place on national television, for as the cameras whirred at a distance out of earshot, Jones spoke in hushed tones to her, desperately trying to change her mind. The little lady in shorts sat eyes fixed forward, jaw set, not speaking, her hands held firmly in her lap. Soon enough, her whole family had voted to go as a unit, a *blood unit*, defying all his efforts to make blood insignificant. Then came another family, the Bogues, who were having arguments among themselves, arguments of people with identity for a change, but somehow arriving at a rocky consensus to leave. Earlier, Jones had succeeded in splitting the Bogue family, giving the father, Jim, a black companion, and the mother, Edith, a man named Harold Cordell. But Cordell had seen the shipment of cyanide off-loading the *Cudjoe* only days before and saw the execution of Jones's vision coming. In this first group of public defectors, knowledge of the recent shipment of cyanide was the key to their defection. All the talk was ending. The moment of the apocalypse had arrived, and they meant to take their last chance to escape it. They wanted to live.

This clutch of public traitors was white, but a group of black fugitives was also on its way out—but secretly. With street cunning, nine blacks slipped out of the camp early that morning, while Jones and his security force were preoccupied with the commotion of the visit. This group, too, contained blood units, with the exception of its leader, Robert Paul, who had left his wife, Ruletta Paul, nine years his junior, and his three children behind in Jonestown.

To the news of the first defections, Jones crawled deeper into his personal hellhole. Charles Garry stood beside him as the catastrophe hit, and the attorney was transfixed at the sight of Jones's shuddering.

"Jim, what's the matter with you?" Garry asked. "Let them leave. So what? Wish them well and ask them back when they feel like it."

"Oh no," Jones replied, vacant-eyed. "These traitors! All is lost!"

Now there were thirteen who wanted to go. Tension swept through the camp. Defectors were afraid to get their belongings, so Leo Ryan accompanied them back to their cottages, absorbing the hateful looks, comforting the refugees as insults were hurled at them. Residents stood at the doors of their barracks or at a safe distance from the rushings back and forth in the Pavilion, glancing furtively at one another, and back at Ryan. Dwyer could feel it. It was time to get the journalists out of there, and fast. Violence still did not cross his mind. It was just time to go home—right then. Still another family approached him, the Simonses, the father, Al, and his three children. That made seventeen. The Ryan plane would hold only nineteen. Dwyer rushed off to call Georgetown and order another plane to come. The press would have to be bumped. "What's wrong?" Sharon Amos's mystified voice crackled from Georgetown. "Are they bringing sick people?" But Al Simons's wife, Bonnie, did not want to leave. Husband and wife argued. Husband picked up the children's things and started for the waiting truck. Dwyer hustled the defectors and the press toward the truck. A desperate scream knifed out of the air.

"No, no, no," the woman's voice shrieked. It was Bonnie Simons reaching out to her children.

"Don't worry, we're going to take care of everything," John Jones, the Reverend's adopted black son, said to her.

Dwyer and Ryan huddled. If neither of them stayed, there would be retaliation against Al Simons. Dwyer agreed to accompany the party to the airport; Ryan would stay to arbitrate the new custody battle, spending another night. Dwyer hurried back to the loaded truck, through the thick mud. It had begun to rain heavily.

Ryan stood near the Pavilion, talking with Lane, Garry, and Jones. Suddenly, from behind, an arm was around Ryan's neck, a knife point indenting the skin of his throat.

"I'm gonna kill you. This is what you're gonna get," the voice from behind shouted.

For a split second, Ryan thought it was horseplay. The knife felt like a ball-point pen. He collapsed limply backward, batting the knife away as he fell, realizing this was no joke. Lane had time to grab the wrist of the assailant, holding the knife away from Ryan's neck. Garry got the attacker in a head hold. They tumbled to the ground, the knife slashing the assailant and splattering blood on Ryan's shirt. As others jumped into the pile, trying to pin down the attacker, trying to wrest the knife away from him, Jones stood at the side, dazed, acting as if nothing were happening.

But soon he was animated. Screams from the attack reached the truck with the newsmen, and it emptied, Dwyer leading the race back to the Pavilion, the newsmen on his heels. Jones rushed out to stop the charge. A quick negotiation took place. Along with Dwyer, one photographer, Greg Robinson, was allowed to proceed. It marked him for later.

Jones's face was pallid, stupid with fear. "I wish someone had shot me," he said.

"This is a serious occurrence," Ryan said, collecting himself, brave, downplaying the horror. "I've seen good things in Jonestown. This doesn't mean everything's over." If Jones would immediately call in the Guyanese police and have the assailant arrested, Ryan would place weight on that. The Congressman still insisted he would stay to arbitrate the Simons problem.

Dwyer took him aside. "I want your ass out of here . . . and now," the diplomat said, pulling rank. "You could become the focal point of a more terrible incident." Ryan relented, as Dwyer promised to return to Jonestown to handle the Simons matter after the Congressman was airborne.

They moved to the truck. At a distance, slowly licking his parched lips, Jones stood in conversation with several security members, among them one Joseph Wilson, a beefy brute with neatly corn-rowed hair, a New Jersey ex-convict whom Jones had plucked from prison before his time was up. At the last moment, a new defector, draped in a poncho, had joined the contingent. Minutes before, this last passenger, named Larry Layton, had embraced Jim Jones.

"You will be proud of me," were Layton's last words to Father.

The rain poured down ferociously. Ryan climbed into the cab of the truck, along with the NBC cameraman, intent on more mood shots. Spinning its wheels in the mud, the truck slid helplessly into a ditch and had to be extracted by a bulldozer. Finally they were under way. At the brow of the hill overlooking Jonestown, the cameraman demanded that the truck stop again for more mood pictures. One of the Parks family, Dale Parks, was near hysteria at the delay. To the outsiders, he kept whispering that Larry Layton was not a genuine defector, that he was there to cause trouble, that he probably had a gun. The truck should hurry, for the Temple guards were sure to be after them. The NBC producer, the ex-paratrooper, Bob Flick, made his way toward the back of the truck bed where Layton hung on in silence. Flick was a head taller than the insignificant Layton. If Layton tried something, Flick was ready to throw him off the truck.

The eight-mile trip through rain and mud took nearly an hour and a half. As the truck arrived at the airstrip, the rain ceased and the sun emerged. But the planes had not yet arrived. His besplattered shirt open to his solar plexus, a bedraggled Ryan sat down in the tin shack on the side of the dirt runway, waiting for the television crew to set up its cameras, so he could convey via film the details of his brush with death. Richard Dwyer rushed off to the local constabulary to report the attack on Ryan. When he got to the police hut in Port Kaituma he found the constable drunk and the police radio out of order. In the sky, the planes appeared, first the small Cessna, then the nineteen-seat Otter.

With the planes on the ground, Ryan began his interview.

"Where do we go now?" Harris asked toward the end.

"A report will be filed," Ryan said. "I've asked that the man be arrested as soon as possible, because the reputation of the People's Temple as a place of law and order is at stake."

Harris thanked him for his time.

"Can I just add, there are a lot of good people who are there on a positive and supportive and idealistic basis, trying to do something that is different and important to them."

On this generous note, Ryan turned to the details of boarding the flight. Richard Dwyer arrived back at the airstrip now with the policeman, bearing a shotgun. Dale Parks frantically kept insisting that Layton was a plant, that he should be searched. The matter was debated. Minutes passed. With his shin-length poncho still on, Layton slipped onto the small plane, stowing a revolver under the seat. The planes were parked thirty feet apart. A Ryan aide stood between the two planes, deciding who should board which plane. Finally it was decided that everyone would be searched. Layton was called out of the Cessna and directed to board the Otter. He objected fiercely. Congressman Ryan had promised him he could go out on the *first* plane. Ryan conciliated. What difference did it make? Layton was searched and then allowed to reboard the Cessna. Soon he was joined by Dale Parks and his ten-year-old sister Tracy, by Vernon Gosney and Monica Bagby, the original defectors. The pilot started the motor.

At the door of the Otter, the other refugees were searched and boarded. The newsmen waited their turn. Three hundred yards down the airstrip, the Temple dump truck reemerged from the Port Kaituma road, followed by a tractor pulling a flatbed trailer. Nearly abreast of the Cessna the dump truck stopped. Three men emerged, striding toward Ryan. The tractor trailer crossed the runway and halted between the two planes.

Inside the Cessna, Larry Layton was screaming. "Hurry up and take off! There's going to be trouble!"

The Cessna began to taxi. The three Temple angels shoved a few local bystanders to the side. One snatched the shotgun from the policeman and pushed him back as well. A fistfight is about to break out, one of the reporters thought.

Men rose from the flatbed trailer and began firing rifles. Ryan was hit first, his body dropped, wrapping around the tire of the plane. Dwyer was hit in the rump. The fusillade was intense. Inside the Otter a bullet tore off the top of a fugitive's skull. Inside the Cessna, Larry Layton shot Vern Gosney in the chest, Monica Bagby in the back. Dale Parks rose to restrain the angel. Layton shoved the weapon into Parks's chest and pulled the trigger. The gun misfired, but Parks fell back in his seat. Layton turned again to Gosney and Bagby, shooting them both a second time. Parks recovered and wrestled Layton to the floor. Outside, people were running to the bush for their lives. Bodies were strewn around the plane, some dead, some feigning death. There was a brief cease-fire. Several who lay still, waiting for their coup de grace, heard footsteps as the angels trod among their victims. Three more shotgun rounds thudded point-blank into the chief enemies, making sure. The last blast slammed into the face of Leo Ryan.

[3]

As the trucks left Jonestown, missionaries moiled about their camp aimlessly. There was no more hysteria. The tension of the place ebbed away as the combustion noises of the trucks on the road faded. Marceline Jones was soon on the loudspeaker, soothingly urging everyone to return to their cottages and apartments. Everything was fine. They would later discuss the events of the day. Time passed languorously as the clouds passed and the sun shone once again. Charles Garry was feeling positively mellow. Apart from the attack on Ryan, the weekend was, on balance, a success. Only fourteen had left—fourteen out of 920 was not bad. The community was intact. Most satisfying of all, he had received assurances from Jones that there would be no more interference from Mark Lane. His personal satisfaction blinded him to the cosmic disaster stirring about him.

Almost halfheartedly, he advised Jones to report the knife attack on Ryan to Port Kaituma by radio and have them come to arrest the assailant. The man's name was Don Sly, Jones told Garry. His wife was a leader in the Concerned Relatives group. Like Larry Layton, Sly had this special need to prove himself to the leader. Even at this late hour, Garry was still sunk in his naiveté.

When the truck disappeared from sight, Garry turned to Jones. Up until the Ryan attack, Garry felt his side had won the public relations battle. So a few rotten apples had left, so what? But the knife attack was different.

"This [knife attack] was the act of an agent provocateur, Jim," Garry declared, still frightened by the vacant look in Jones's eyes. "No one but an agent provocateur would do that."

"No, the people are just angry," Jones replied. Garry looked around him. He had seen no one angry. Anger, like love, had ceased to be a possibility in Jonestown. Only counterfeit emotions remained. And with counterfeit emotion no spontaneous action is possible. The script had been written in advance by Jones. There was some room for changes and deletions, depending upon the creativity of the actors, but the basic plot would stand.

Jones had planned the knife attack, and now he could say their situation was hopeless.

———————◄ ►———————

Garry invited Lane to go for a walk. As they strolled, Lane spoke of things—apparently new and startling to Garry—of unhappiness, of madness, of danger in Jonestown. In time, as they walked several hundred feet from the Pavilion, they were approached by two Jones apostles, one the head of security.

"Charles, what do you think of the future of this organization?" the security chief asked.

Garry's instinctual caution now asserted itself. "The future is great," he replied, "but there should be more democracy—more freedoms than apparently people have."

On the loudspeaker the call to gather in the Pavilion resounded. All around Lane and Garry residents poured from their cottages. Their mood was festive. It was Saturday, a holiday, a day for TV and games. Jovial jibes at the lawyers hung in the air. You guys can go. We want to stay. The bleating of lambs to slaughter. Garry and Lane joined the flow.

The Bishop sat on a bench, in despair. Next to him sat his chronicler, Harriet Tropp.

Lane tried to be upbeat. "This can be the best day in the history of Jonestown," he said cheerily. "The positive aspects of Jonestown have been seen and filmed. The Congressman told me that he'll write an objective report and that there will be no hearings."

"You're crazy! You're crazy!" Tropp shrieked at him.

"All is lost," Jones moaned. A squad had followed the Congressman with every gun in the place, he said, a squad of eight led by Wilson, the ex-convict, two former heroin addicts, a hunter, a karate expert among them. His "red brigade."

"I didn't know you had any guns here," Garry said. Jones ignored him. Maria Katsaris appeared, pulling Jones away from the outsiders. He was back quickly.

"You and Mark will have to leave," he addressed them. "Your lives are not safe. People are angry at you, too." Anger now became the code for violent attack.

As the mythmakers rose to leave, Jones spotted a crumpled cigarette packet on the ground, the trash of newsmen. He rose to retrieve it, crumpling it further and dropping it in a receptacle. The place must be a model when we leave it, he had said often.

Lane and Garry were escorted to the guesthouse. From there they watched men go to a small building, contiguous, and emerge with guns and a large ammunition box. Soon Don Sly appeared, taking a seat on the steps of the guesthouse.

"Don, what happened to you?" Garry inquired, still in the fog of his idealism. "Did you flip your lid this afternoon?"

"In all deference to you, Mr. Garry, I'd rather not discuss it," the angel quipped. His eye was on the comings and goings of the psychopomps. "When do you want me up there?" he kept calling out to them anxiously.

"This does not look good," Lane whispered. They had to get out, but how? They would surely be seen. Perhaps it was too late. At the fence around the guesthouse, two men with rifles had now replaced Sly. In the distance, Jones's voice floated across the clearing. The centurions had the blush of ecstasy. The lethal blow against fascism and racism was about to be delivered.

"Aren't there any alternatives?" Lane asked.

"No," they chirped in unison.

"Well, Charles and I will write your story," Lane said with a touch of brilliance, the cunning of a survivor.

"Fine," said the pair. One of them gave Garry the salute of the San Quentin Six, then they embraced, Jonestown style.

———⊷ ⊶———

Jones assumed his pedestal, adjusting the scepter microphone. For the last time, this Prince of Omega, the Caesar Godhead, left his secular station and invested himself in the Office.

"I've tried to give you a good life," the Master began. "In spite of all that I've tried, a handful of our people, with their lies, have made our life impossible. There's no way to detach ourselves from what's happened today."

Those who left had committed the "betrayal of the century." Those who remained sat on a powder keg. They could not simply wait for the catastrophe to overwhelm them. That was not what they had in mind for their babies. He invoked Jesus, restoring Christianity for a fleeting moment.

"It was said by the greatest of prophets from time immemorial: No man takes my life from me. I lay down my life. . . . If we can't live in peace, then let's die in peace."

As they applauded, he warmed to the theme of betrayal. The synthesizer music began. The soft tones of a spiritual singer washed over them. He repeated the words of an idolater: if this experiment had worked for but one day, it had been worthwhile. It was time to touch them all. All his languages, all his tricks, all his voices must go on display. This was his sermon in the swamp. He was calling in all his debts, and the tape of history was rolling.

"What's going to happen here in a matter of minutes is that one of our people on that plane is going to shoot the pilot—I know that. I didn't plan it," he lied, "but I know it's going to happen. They're gonna shoot that pilot and down comes that plane in the jungle. And we had better not have any of our children left when it's over, because they'll parachute in here on us," parachute in as if they were the avenging angels of a wrathful Sky God. The suggestion brought the first scream of hysteria.

"So my opinion is that you be kind to children, and be kind to seniors and take the potion like they used to take it in ancient Greece, and step over quietly, because we are not committing suicide. It's a revolutionary act. We can't go back, and they won't leave us alone. They're now going back to tell more lies, which means more congressmen. And there's no way, no way, we can survive."

His opinion, his decree thus announced, he called for discussion. Was there dissent? Never, never dispute the Father in a white night; it was a law burned into their minds. If there was dissent, it would be planned. His foil searched for her courage. As she did, he talked on, building his case. If the children were left, they would be butchered. If they went on a hunger strike, they would be striking against their Guyanese friends. It was too late for them to get their enemies—that would have to be left to the angels. Finally, the foil asked about Russia. The debate raged, Jones's deception on the Soviet covenant made clear, but it was too late for Russia, and he grew bored with the subject.

"I look at all the babies and I think they deserve to live," the foil, Christine Miller, said.

"I agree, but much more, they deserve peace."

"We all came here for peace," she said.

"Have they had it?" he retorted, besting her. They, not her.

"No."

"I tried to give it to you. I've laid my life down practically. I practically died every day to give you peace." His self-piety, his sacrifice again. Could they rise, or descend, to his level? "And you still don't have peace. You look better than I've seen you in a long while, but still it's not the kind of peace that I wanted to give you. A person's a fool to continue to say that you're winning when you're losing."

To light candles, to curse the darkness: before, this was how they posed their dilemma. Now the twain were joined. Before, he had scoffed at the Epistles of Paul: "Servants, obey all things in your masters, according to the flesh, not with eye service as men pleasers, but in singleness of heart, fearing God. . . . Masters, give unto your servants that which is just and equal, knowing that ye also have a master in heaven." Now in his vainglory, he evoked Paul.

"Paul said there is a man born out of this season. I've been born out of this season just like all you are, and the best testimony we can make is to leave this goddamn world."

The servants cheered, the raptures of slaves. The master ordered the potion. The crystals from 500-gram plastic bottles sprinkled into the purple solution of flavored drink. The syringes were scattered on the wooden picnic tables by the fistfuls, needles attached to some, making them weapons. Dr. Schacht marshaled his nursing corps. Ruletta Paul, twenty-four years of age, wife of Robert Paul, leader of the fugitive band that had slipped into the jungle that morning, stepped forward with her child in her arms. For her special guilt, atonement was to serve as first example. The child opened its mouth. The doctor squirted the liquid far back toward the uvula. "Children," Paul had told the Colossians, "obey your parents in all things, for this is well pleasing unto the Lord."

For Dr. Schacht, the problem was purely scientific: how to concoct a mixture that would kill quickly, painlessly, almost pleasantly. As the Bishop told them more than a year before, this had been worked out carefully by a Father who was deeply loving, a people who were truly caring. Dr. Schacht had poured in the appropriate measure of liquid Valium. Had he measured wrong?

"Oh, God, we're dying. It's starting to hurt," someone cried.

"Great God, who said that?" Jones asked in irritation, then relented. "Come on up and speak, honey." He harked back to their enemies. They were responsible for this.

"We win. We win when we go down. Tim Stoen don't have nobody else to hate. He'll destroy himself." So that was their victory. They must all die, so that Timothy Stoen would be deprived of an object for his hatred. For this inane absurdity, it took the Prophet's clairvoyance. Christine Miller was going too far. The foil was becoming sincere. She punctured his ridiculousness, and the centurions began to heckle her. "You're afraid to die." "You're no fucking good, God dammit." "You're only standing here because of him." She absorbed the abuse, as she watched the babies and small children being carried out into the field. Jones made a show of protesting her dissent, as he directed the communion.

"Hold it. Everybody hold it. Not much longer. Lay down your burdens. I'm going to lay my burden down by the riverside. . . . When they start parachuting out of the air, they will shoot some of the innocent babies. Can you let them take your babies?"

The congregation responded as it had been taught. Did no one pinch himself? Did someone not, at least, exchange a quizzical glance with his neighbor? Jann Gurvich? Christine Miller reached for her last argument, her final challenge.

"You mean you want to see John die?"

For a year and a half he had entwined their blood with his: *they* must face death to prevent *his* child from being snatched away. How important was his blood tie now? What was the shape of his selfishness?

"What?" he said, startled, buying a second to think.

"You mean you want to see John, the little one, die?"

"John? John? Do you think I'd put John's life above others? He's no different to me than any of these children here. He's just one of my children. I don't put one above another. I can't separate myself from your actions or his actions. If you'd done something wrong, I'd stand for you. If they wanted to come and get you, they'd have to take me."

Christine receded into the mass. He complimented her. She was honest, and she had stayed with him, not running away with the betrayers. Her life was precious to him, as precious as John Victor Stoen's. Now, he could get on with it. Now, he saw that this was the will of the sovereign being. The Sky God was reinstalled. Had they noticed that only white people had betrayed them? Even he was deceived at the end. As the children came for their potion, he blessed them. Peace. Peace. Peace. Peace. Peace. The peace of God which passeth all understanding.

"I've tried so very, very hard from the time we were here," he groaned. "Together it's just easy. It's easy. Yes, my love."

"At one time I felt just like Christine," a woman said, "but after today I don't feel anything, because the people that left here were white, and I know that it really hurt my heart."

"It broke your heart, didn't it?" he said, selectively sentimental.

His adopted son came to him, whispering the news from the airstrip. He announced it frantically: "It's all over, all over. What a legacy! What a legacy!" Ryan was dead. Many of the traitors were dead. The red brigade had showed them justice. Theirs had been an act of provocation. His voice rose with urgency. The process was too slow. Children's screams filled the arena.

"No, no, please, no," a boy's scream pierced the pandemonium.

He issued orders. "Please get some medication. There's no convulsions with it. . . ."

There *were* convulsions. There was vomiting. The potion took four minutes to work. He wanted it to work faster. The Guyanese soldiers were coming. Quicker. Keep moving. Faster. It was an administrative problem. A nurse tried to help.

"The people that are standing there in the aisles will have to move," her flat usher's voice announced. "Everybody get behind the table and back this way, okay? There's nothing to worry about. Everybody keep calm and try to keep your children calm. They're not crying from pain. It's just a little bitter tasting. We have lots of little children here and we will serve them."

He called for Annie McGowan, so the business of transferring the

Temple fortune to the Russians could be conducted amid the growing carnage. As he did, the head of security stepped forward to testify on his past experience of therapy to the dying, of how he had experienced the reincarnation of others, of how pleasurable getting a new body was, new and free of the nagging deficiencies of this one. He might have been describing an orgasm; perhaps this was Jones's orgasm of the grave, reaching its climax in the process of reincarnation.

"You'll never feel so good, family. I tell you, you'll never feel so good as how that feels."

It was the cue for other last testimonies to Father.

"Folks, this is nothing to cry about," a celebrant rejoiced. "We should be happy about this. We should cry when we come into this world. But when we leave it, we leave it peacefully. I was just thinking about Jim Jones. He has suffered and suffered and suffered. I'm looking at so many people crying. I wish you could not cry . . . but just thank Father."

There were still communicants who clapped. More gratitudes were delivered, but the Bishop was getting short-tempered.

"Please, for God's sake, let's get on with it. We have lived as other people have lived and loved. We have had as much of this world as you're gonna get. Let's just be done with it. Let's be done with the agony of it."

But the agony of it persisted, the organ strains and the Valium doing little to dampen the pain. These things take time. It would take three hours to finish the job. By "serving" the little children first, Jones's managerial talent surfaced again: having murdered their children, how strong could the parents' will to live be? He fortified their guilt for this crime against nature with a metaphysical argument: they could not separate themselves from the crimes of their archangels.

"You can't separate yourself from your brother and sister. No way I'm going to do it. I refuse. I don't know who killed the Congressman, but as far as I'm concerned, *I* killed him. You understand what I'm saying. *I* killed him." They understood: they had killed him too.

The Bishop preached on, repeating his exhortations, shifting blame to his enemies, harping on the worthlessness of this life, and embracing death as a friend, while Mother Marceline circulated among the crowd, hugging them, telling them she would see them in the next life. They should lay down their lives by the riverside. It was the River Styx now. Several times, the devil implied he might survive his hell.

"Do you think you can endure long enough in a safe place to write about the goodness that has been done?" someone shouted over the din. Think of the literature Albert Speer produced from Spandau.

"I don't know how in the world I will ever write about us," he replied mournfully. "It's just too late."

Later, he wailed, "They can take me and do anything they want, whatever they want to do with me. But I want to see you go. I don't want to see you go through this hell anymore. No more, no more, no more. . . ."

The reverberation of his voice was overwhelmed by the screams of children.

Pandemonium was hell's capital, and no amount of his brilliant, loathsome oratory or his organ player's dirge or his monster-doctor's Valium could keep the place from consorting with chaos. On the perimeter, the centurions trained their rifles and crossbows. Some waded into the herd to help inject the obstreperous. At his children's antics, Father grew angry.

"Stop these hysterics," he scolded. "This is not the way for socialistic Communists to die." He was right about that, at least. "We must die with some dignity. We had no choice. Now we have some choice."

He meant the choice of the group, not the choice of the individual, but the two were dangerously moving into opposition.

"You think they are going to allow this to be done, allow us to get by with this?" . . . This crime against humanity he seemed to mean. "You must be insane." The growing weakness of his noble arguments occurred to him. His accent shifted to their crime, their responsibility, his naked power.

"Mother, mother, mother, please mother, please mother, please, please, please, please. Don't do this, don't do this. Lay down your life with your child, but don't do this." Be mannerly in your slaughter.

"We are doing this for *you?*" a woman shouted at him. Was it a final, bleating rebuke?

He ignored it. "Free at last. Peace. Keep your emotions down. Keep your emotions down, children. It will not hurt if you will be quiet," as if hurting, like the slight bitter taste of the potion, was the point.

As youthful screams melded with music, he tried history.

"It's never been done before, you say? It's been done by every tribe in history, every tribe facing annihilation. All the Indians of the Amazon are doing it right now. They refuse to bring any babies into the world. They kill every child. They don't want to live in this kind of world. . . . The Eskimos? They take death in their stride." His final identification was with the aborigines of the world.

But they would not be dignified, not his notion of it, anyway.

"Quit telling them they are dying!" he demanded, as if lying to the children was more dignified. "If you adults would stop some of this nonsense! ADULTS! ADULTS! ADULTS! I call on you to stop this nonsense. I call on you to quit exciting your children when all they are doing is going to quiet rest. I call on you to stop this now, if you have any respect at all. Are we black, proud, and socialists?"

"YES," came the diminished response.

". . . or what are we? Now stop this nonsense now.

"All over, and it's good." This cadence suggested the Bible again. *And God saw everything he had made, and behold, it was very good.* "No sorrow that it's all over," he sighed. "Hurry. Hurry, my children. Hurry. Let's not fall into the hands of our enemy. Hurry, my children. Hurry."

The children were gone. The old and the infirm were next. From somewhere came still more to try to please him with flatteries. For once, he needed no further gratification.

"Where's the vat, the vat, the vat? Where's the vat? The vat with the green potion." He brushed them aside, matter-of-factly mistaking the color of the stuff. "Bring it here so the adults can begin. If you fail to follow my advice, you will be sorry. *You will be sorry.*"

In the radio room, Maria Katsaris directed the final details. Three aides, all white, were called and given their mission to carry the letters and the cash to Feodor Timofeyev. Later, all security bearing arms, some twenty-five people, were summoned. There was to be no mayhem among the guards at the end. Meanwhile, Katsaris messaged to Georgetown in code what was happening. Angels were to be dispatched to Georgetown hotels to murder the remaining enemies there, particularly Timothy Stoen. Then they were to kill themselves. How was it to be done? the question returned. They had no firearms in Georgetown, no potion. Slowly, in Morse code, the letters came back: K-N-I-F-E.

Then Katsaris gave her last order to the radio operator.

"Now tell Georgetown that we're having a power failure," she ordered. This transmitted, she held out her hand. The operator yanked a critical part from the transmitter and handed it to her. She walked off to her private ceremony in the West House, dying in Jim Jones's bed.

———————————◄ ►———————————

At Timehri Airport, the small plane had landed, and the two pilots were immediately helicoptered to Prime Minister Forbes Burnham's residence for debriefing. Burnham had already conveyed the news to Ambassador Burke by telephone, and Burke in turn had sent a flash message to Washington. In time, the report came from Richard Dwyer in Port Kaituma that four were dead, including Congressman Ryan and Don Harris, five severely wounded. As the evening wore on, the White House called a Ryan aide in California with the news.

"How do you know?" the aide asked.

"Because we've got a CIA report from the scene," the White House replied.

At Lamaha Gardens, meanwhile, unaware still of what was happening, Sharon Amos was softening. She invited her ex-husband, one of the Concerned Relatives, to dine with her and their daughter at the Temple house. It was a friendly, cheerful reunion. The husband spent much of his time in cordial debate with his twenty-one-year-old daughter, airing out their differences, but by the end of the meal blood had overcome training, and their bond was reestablished. After seven o'clock, the husband rose to leave. He embraced his daughter, a rather hefty girl, especially as she stood next to the four-foot-eleven frame of her mother. And then he embraced Sharon Amos.

Not long after, Amos assumed her post in the radio room. With the news from Jonestown, she contacted San Francisco, instructing the Geary Street apostles to move high up on the band for an emergency dispatch. Frantically, San Francisco searched for a connection, without success. But in due course the telephone rang.

From a great distance, Amos's voice crackled urgently.

"Do what you can to even the score."

The code had been in force for a long time. It meant the last stand had come, and the avenging angels were to go forth against the iniquitous. But they were not dispatched. In Georgetown, Jones's son Stephan and several others did go to the hotel where Timothy Stoen waited for news, but the young Jones's only thrust was verbal. "Why did *you* cause all these deaths?" he said lamely. No knife was drawn, not there, not in San Francisco—not yet, anyway.

Hysterically, at the Temple House, Sharon Amos screamed the news to the seventy-five or so communards, urging that their ritual of the knife begin. It had been decreed from Jonestown. Her mates looked at her dully. She was not Jim Jones. This was not Jonestown. They never liked her much anyway. Outside the cars of another reality puttered by. In disgust, she climbed the stairs to the second-floor bathroom, summoning first her son aged ten, her daughter aged eleven, then her hefty daughter Lianne aged twenty-one, and, finally, Charles Beikman, the forty-three-year-old idiot ex-Marine. Lianne brought the butcher knife. First, Amos slit her young daughter's throat, then her son's. Then she had Beikman hold her twenty-one-year-old daughter, and that was the end of Lianne. Finally, she started on herself, and the loutish Beikman finished the job.

———————————————

When the troops approached Jonestown more than a day later, spread out in battle formation, inching into the camp in full combat attire, expecting the mad charge of fanatics, they found a few signs of resistance. The old man lying in the ditch, pretending to be dead. The injection marks in the skin of eighty-three out of one hundred bodies were randomly examined (was it forcible injection?). The occasional contorted limbs of a victim looked arranged for protection against attack. And resistance took different forms: the overt and covert defections, Stanley Clayton's escape, the escape of the security man who told the police the improbable story that he bolted when a nurse asked him to fetch a stethoscope—what good was a stethoscope at a moment like that?—the brazen arrival of the three lieutenants into Port Kaituma, asking to be arrested.

But the overwhelming preponderance of the evidence pointed to acquiescence, to complicity.

And they found Pastor Jones. His body lay, face up, on the steps of his manifold pedestal, his red, dime-store shirt falling open on either side, exposing his soft belly, his head upon a pillow, his eyes locked open skyward. The bullet had entered behind the left ear and departed from the right temple. Its path was consistent with suicide by a left-handed person, but Jim Jones was right-handed. A .38-caliber pistol was found thirty yards from his body. In his stomach was a lethal dose of the barbiturate pentobarbital, which had not had time to circulate through his system. So at his last moment he had needed a fistful of pills to steel himself to meet his Maker.

His hand lay limp on the fold of his belly, his middle finger bent to the center of his palm in a gesture of teaching, his passion waned away at last.

Nirvana.

Epilogue

THE CLOUDS, the infernal heat, the occasional shower dropping its burden suddenly and capriciously, reporters talk endlessly of bodies, making the inevitable Vietnam comparisons. At tables in the greasy airport restaurant, they gossip lightly of bureau chiefs and White House press operations. The Guyanese are using survivors to identify the dead, one says. Were they given any choice, I wonder? Flies cover the plastic amber airport seats in battalions. I move outdoors into the humid breeze amid the brilliant, heavy-petaled passionflowers redolent with overbearing, succulent allure. Across the airfield, an American military transport is parked, waiting. I am not in a conversational mood. I have never felt this combination of dread, nausea, incipient madness.

At last, our plane is ready. The passengers, forty-odd newsmen and a photographer, two magazine writers, and I trundle onto the aircraft. For some reason, I am relieved that the plane is of a different kind, larger than the one that took the Congressman in. Once in the air, we turn back sharply and are soon over the vast, buff Demerara River. Islands in the middle of the expansive life force are dollop-shaped, as if they were pancake batter poured on a slanted pan, half formed, in wait of being seared on the other side. As we climb, tiny wisps of mist hang close to the green expanse below—steam, I deduce, rising from the vast, fecund jungle floor. So green is the forest now that I cannot discern the undulating terrain from the flat. Only when a black stream slithers through the unrelieved verdancy do I perceive contour, change, interest, hope. The occasional trouly roof of an Indian hut dots a coil of these reptilian waters, like a barnacle.

Without warning, we pass from shimmering white sunlight into a thundercloud. Streams of water move horizontally across the plane window. Outside, a small rainbow encases the Rolls-Royce patch on the plane window and gives me reassurance, a touch with Western civilization and technology. In time, we descend, buffeting, and finally break through the grayness into a low mountainous region. Ahead, the houses of Matthews Ridge protrude from the saddle of the scraped mineral hilltop. Beyond, the dirt airstrip appears, delineated by misshapen oil drums, dangerously close, it appears from my angle, to a tree-covered precipice on the far side. The wings of the plane dip up and down, as if the bush pilot is having trouble drawing his bead. Close on to the palisade, we bank sharply over an open swamp, the huge bones of greenwood trees rise, their tentacle root structure exposed above the water, reminding me of South Carolina cypress without generous Spanish moss. Closer the trees come, their tops like vast broccoli spears, speckled occasionally with brilliant purple blossoms. I close my eyes, a holdover from one bad landing ten years before, and at length feel the rattle of the wheels meeting the pebbly oil-soaked dirt strip, holding firmly despite the suggestion of loose screws. The cabin bursts into applause. As we taxi back from the end, I notice two black soldiers, completely naked, standing in the still water of the swamp, watching our arrival with mild attentiveness, making no effort to cover their copious organs—one holding a fish in one hand and a stick in the other.

The December heat pushes against me as I emerge onto the plane steps. Some twenty-five yards away, a Guyanese helicopter stands ready. Its American make and Vietnamese contours are disguised by its garish coat of green and red, the country's colors, and the angular "golden arrow" of Guyana's flag painted on the chopper's snout, symbolizing "the forward thrust into the future of a young and independent nation." Its rotors start up immediately, their percussion blades whipping the buoyant heaviness, but failing to roil the air around me. My urgency is the least, and I recede to the back of the crowd, as the national reporters fight one another to make it onto the first ride. Many have brought large, empty shoulder bags to stuff whatever documents they can make off with. It is every man for himself, one tells me. This is a competitive situation. Competitive? In my insensibility, I do not understand.

I drift to the slant-roofed, flesh-colored shack which serves as the Matthews Ridge terminal. On a knoll above, a billet presides over the airstrip and next to a flagpole with a faded, ragged-edged flag; soldiers in fatigues languish, smoking and watching these American reporters take swipes at one another with long-lensed cameras at the helicopter's doors. By the shack, two teenage soldiers, the younger one aged fifteen, lean on a battered Land Rover with their Cuban-made rifles beside them. Over the wooden door of the shack, a sign in script reads:

MATTHEWS RIDGE AIRPORT
All outgoing passengers *must* take a malaria
blood test, anti-malaria tablets, and collect
a card before going on the aircraft.

The itch of primitive disease is everywhere.

On the side of the airstrip, a clutch of local officials gathers around the Regional Minister, a large beefy man wearing a round-brimmed palm-frond hat which sets off his deep purple-black, bumpy complexion and his snaggly teeth. As I approach him, he appears to engage suddenly in pressing business with an aide, but I am persistent. It is hard, in that group, not to notice me. He is guarded, rarely looking me in the eye, in the familiar fashion of a downtrodden servant in the Old South, as he disclaims knowledge of the situation. Perhaps he is not used to lying. He was posted here only a month before, he says, an appointment based on the consistency of his "virulent" socialism with that of Bishop Jones. He answers questions perfunctorily, his sleepy eyes panning the curious scene, passing off his executive officer as the man with real knowledge. I ought to talk to him, but of course he is not there just now. The conversation drifts away into safe waters: the friendly quality of the word *forest* against the unfriendliness of *jungle*.

The garish helicopter brushes back and forth over the sharp ridgeline every twenty minutes or so, depleting the waiting crowd. To pass the time, I chat with a young, scar-faced man, a malaria extermination officer who had taken the train from Port Kaituma that morning to be at the airport in case an unexpected plane dropped in on the way to Georgetown. Several days before, he had traveled to Jonestown with friends, just to satisfy his curiosity, he says. I think of the reports of looting, and the Amerindian stopped as he carried a refrigerator out on his back, the spoils. His friend had met Jones before, he declares proudly, had seen the inside of Jones's cabin even. On the wall, so his friend had reported, there was a picture of Jones and his father, in an American Indian headdress, a chief's headdress, just like the ones in the movies. And when Jones would take off his sunglasses, his friend had said, you would look into his black eyes and feel a tremble of fear.

Finally, it is down to the provincial reporters: Dayton, Ohio; Modesto and San Jose, California; and me. There is no more delaying this, as the chopper appears once again above the ashen, dust-swept ridge. We lift and turn. The nose dips and we climb, shaking, as if this contraption were an airworthy washing machine in a spin cycle. The ridge recedes, and we are cast again onto the sea of green serge. We sweat in silence. After a time, between the helmets of the two pilots, a scrape in the forest appears on the horizon, and soon enough we are banking sharply over shiny tin roofs and an orderly collection of cheery, pastel-colored cottages, descending abruptly into the repellent monument.

The others leap from the helicopter, running, hunched, under the blades twirling twelve feet above, as if this were combat. I am in no rush to make for the heart of this debacle. My first impulse is admiration. Such a large area cleared. To my right, the forty or more small, brightly painted cottages are well laid-out, solid structures. Perhaps they had been badly overcrowded, but what true millennial pioneers could expect creature comforts in their sacrifice of faith, and, besides, 40,000 board feet of lumber lay on the dock in Georgetown, earmarked for housing in Jonestown, waiting to be picked up.

Banana trees dot the pathway to my left, leading away from the cottages to the larger structures on the brow of a far knoll. The flow is that way. A soldier in fatigues falls in behind me, a Cuban submachine gun the size of a fiddle tucked under his arm. I shuffle after the others. The path dips, bridging a small stream, and there, in the grassy crevasse, a cheap suitcase lies open, its wet contents scattered about, as if tossed away in haste as having no value. The first of the six board and batten dormitories bears the identification "Jane Pittman Gardens." The vision of that old, heroic black woman struggling up the courthouse walkway in the Deep South of the 1950s to take a defiant drink of water at the whites-only fountain crosses my mind, and I shudder. I pass through a bower, decoratively covered with flowering vines, notice a hummingbird at work, and note the attractive arrangement of red-leaved crotons, flamboyant yellow and red pepper plants, with their beautiful red and yellow flowers that turn to bitter fruit; papaya and plantain saplings sprucing up the structure. In front of the building there is a hole stuffed with old suitcases, clothing, C-ration cans. The next dormitory appropriates Harriet Tubman, the conductor of the Underground Railroad before the Civil War. It is boarded up now. As I tarry with my escort, a tiny howler monkey appears in the eaves of the building, baring its teeth and emitting a grotesque, laughing screech. The soldier laughs back and then pulls a bandana over his nose. On past the Sojourner Truth apartment (Sojourner Truth, that illiterate evangelist for emancipation and women's rights), to Cuffy Memorial Baby Nursery (Cuffy, the Nat Turner of Guyana). Nailed to the wooden side of the nursery are rudimentary cutouts of a frog, a monkey, a white and a black baby, and I think of their brochure: "Every day at Jonestown the laughter of children rings through the air. Our children are our greatest treasure" . . . and of my own daughter, my only child, safe at home in North Carolina, then eleven months old, as I notice by the building a baby's nurser, an old can of Similac, an overturned potty, and a crumpled discarded wrapper for a sterile syringe.

Past the pole with its loudspeakers, I walk along Cuffy Way to the Main Pavilion, surrounded now with the muddy furrows of a deep plow. I pull my collar across my nose, noting the putrid carcass of a dog, lying there like a metaphor. Underneath the shiny tin roof of the open-air structure, tables and benches are piled one upon another. On the stage at the far end cymbals and the amplifiers of the band are heaped, ready for the trash bin. On the far side, the display board with the map of the United States and Guyana and of Russia remain intact. Toward the rafters, the exhortations, religious to the last, remain, with different meanings now.

All that believed were together, and had all things in common.

Acts 2:44

Where the Spirit of God is, there is liberty.

2 Cor. 3:17

And finally, his aquamarine, wooden throne, with armrests, and white mussed pillow, raised on a white pedestal. Above it, the creamy block letters on the dark background proclaim and threaten:

THOSE WHO DO NOT
REMEMBER THE PAST
ARE CONDEMNED
TO REPEAT IT

The epigram, stolen from George Santayana, then abused and distorted and in the end sullied, took on its real meaning when the devil's throne was surrounded with his dead idolaters. Santayana wrote those lines in his *Life of Reason,* as he was describing not history but three stages of life. Progress, he wrote, comes in manhood and rests on the ability to change, to adapt, to retain past experience and learn from it. When past experience is not retained, infancy is perpetual—the condition of children, savages, and barbarians. In old age, wrote Santayana, memory again is lost, the person rigid, and thought degenerates into instinctive reaction, "like a bird's chirp." In that passage, the philosopher was addressing the problem of flux or constancy of human nature, not the cumulative, recorded story of man. But in a totally different essay on history, he saw its worth in its application to the moral values, pertinent to the political and emotional life of the present.

When Jones created his wonder and his abomination, and then extinguished it in contempt, the Santayana epigram became relevant only to the atrocities of the past, not to some epic mission with which he clothed his seedy personal ambition. His heroes had been Patrice Lumumba, Stephen Biko, Salvador Allende, Paul Robeson, and Victor Jara, especially Victor Jara. The Chilean poet had been of modest origin, and as Allende had taken power, Jara's songs, so uplifting to the poor people of the state, had become the staple of the regime. On the day of the junta's coup, Jara had been herded into a stadium with six thousand others, and after a week there, he was recognized. The fascist soldier and the poet had exchanged sharp words, and the soldier took his rifle and smashed Jara's knuckles on both his hands. And then he presented the poet with a guitar. Now play, he said. Now sing. And somehow, the poet played, and the six thousand people in the stadium heard him sing and so enraged the soldier that he shot Jara dead many times before the throng. Victor Jara especially was Jim Jones's hero. Jehovah Jara, he had called him at the last moment. I'm joining you, Jehovah Jara. But if there was such a separation in another world—into clutches of revolutionaries or poets or peons, Jones was really joining others: like the midget in the corner of the caricature, he was joining Hitler, Nero, and smaller figures like John Wilkes Booth who had committed crimes chiefly to join the history books.

If his following had been intent on the life of reason, or even truly on the life of useful rebellion, they would have cast him away long before in his base falseness. He had reduced them all in the jungle, whether through fear or inclination or cowardice, to chirping harmoniously like birds, or buzzing with their insect-like will, and yet, most had no place else to go. Perhaps in doing so, he proved that such subjugation was possible in the modern age and was not merely the magnificent argument of a great writer like Dostoevski. Perhaps his laboratory proved again how thin the veil over man's bestiality still is. Perhaps that unspeakable accomplishment has value as a warning to civilized man.

Santayana probably would have been amused at the use of his epigram turned epitaph. For in the same passage he wrote: "It is remarkable how inane and unimaginative Utopias have generally been. This may help console those who think the natural conditions of life are not the conditions that a good life can be lived in. The possibility of essential progress is bound up with the tragic possibility that progress and human life may one day end together. . . . Mortality has its compensations: one is that all evils are transitory, another that better times may come."*

To Jones, there was no context for any biblical or philosophical

---

*From George Santayana, *The Life of Reason*, © 1953 by Daniel M. Cory (New York: Scribner), p. 85.

thought other than his own aggrandizement. Like so many other sayings, he picked the Santayana quotation up as if it were a bauble, in the rough of intellectual thought. It was as if the world's wisdom was reducible to a book of quotations, from which one could select gems and arrange a resplendent mosaic of his own magnificence. That his arrangement of so many ironic and contradictory thoughts attracted so many in modern America lends tragedy to them as victims, and invidiousness to him.

Without any larger rootedness, many can play his game. For in so many different situations and in so many different voices—exultant and melancholy, brilliant and imbecilic, prophetic and absurd, terrified and triumphant, self-pitying and insincere—I can hear this master of technique say:

"You don't cast pearls before swine."

I remember little more from that trip to Jonestown on November 27, 1978. The SMILE sign in the brick factory, perhaps. The soldier breaking down a door of a cottage for me and the Russian language tapes inside. And the journey back to Georgetown.

From Timehri Airport, we pressed into the rickety bus provided by the Information Ministry. It was dark by that time. I tried to close my eyes, but could not. Halfway into Georgetown, we passed through a small roadside settlement where the stilted houses and the tiny, onion-shaped mosque with its minarets pressed close onto the high-way. The bus slowed, where a throng of people had gathered. As the bus inched past the crowd, a photographer in front of me shouted out for the driver to stop. The passion of the demand compelled the driver to obey instantly and he eased the bus to the side. The photographer tore out and ran back down the road. After ten minutes or so he returned. Yes, it had been an accident, he announced, but the victim was only bruised. All his life signs were strong, and we could proceed. Later, I learned that the photographer was a physician from San Francisco who did his photojournalism on the side to break the routine of the emergency room. This had been his second trip to Jonestown. The first had been six days earlier, when the bodies were strewn about in the open air.